SELLING OUT

SELLING OUT

The Gay and Lesbian Movement Goes to Market

Alexandra Chasin

palgrave

First published 2000 by
PALGRAVE™
175 Fifth Avenue, New York, N.Y. 10010 and
Houndsmills, Basingstoke, Hampshire RG21 6XS.
Companies and representatives throughout the world.

PALGRAVE is the new global publishing imprint of St. Martin's Press
LLC Scholarly and Reference Division and Palgrave Publishers Ltd
(formerly Macmillan Press Ltd).

ISBN 0–312–21449–9 hardback
ISBN 0–312–23926–2 paperback

Library of Congress Cataloging-in-Publication Data
Chasin, Alexandra
Selling out : the gay and lesbian movement goes to market /
Alexandra Chasin
   p. cm.
  Includes bibliographical references and index.
   ISBN 0–312–21449–9 (hardback) ISBN 0–312–23926–2
(paperback)
   1. Gay consumers—United States. 2. Lesbian consumers—United
States. 3. Gay liberation movement—United States. I. Title.
HF5415.33.U6C48   2000
306.3'3 08664' 09073   99–43339
                                       CIP

A catalogue record for this book is available from the British Library.

Design by Letra Libre, Inc.

10 9 8 7 6 5 4 3 2

Printed in the United States of America.

For Nan

CONTENTS

PERMISSIONS

ACKNOWLEDGMENTS

As a big believer in the wonders of collective action, I must give big thanks to the wonderful collection of people who realized this book project with me.

I am very grateful to the individuals and institutions who have had the foresight and the dedication first to preserve and then to make available gay and lesbian historical materials. I appreciate the assistance of Billy Glover at the Homosexual Information Center; Russell Kracke and Liz Mordarski at the Gerber/Hart Library; Yolanda Retter at the Lesbian Legacy Collection, One Institute; Desiree Yael Vester at the Lesbian Herstory Archives; and Jeanne Cordova.

I also appreciate the time and thoughtfulness of the people with whom I corresponded or conducted interviews. They are: Chuck Collins, co-Founder and co-Director of United for a Fair Economy; Julie Dorf, Founding Director of the International Gay and Lesbian Human Rights Commission; Michele Frost of the Trans-National Company; Susan Horowitz, publisher of *Between the Lines;* Karen Pratt and Elaine Noble; Todd Putnam of the Institute for Corporate Responsibility; Sean Strub of Strubco; Javid Syed of the Asian and Pacific Islander Coalition on HIV/AIDS, Inc.; Carla Wallace, a founder of the Fairness Campaign and a member of the board of the National Gay and Lesbian Task Force.

For my ongoing education in the matters at hand, I am indebted to the following: the entire board and staff at IGLHRC (past and present), whose brilliance, integrity, and effectiveness sustain my hopes for progressive queer politics; partner-in-crime Katherine Franke for her insightful reading; colleagues Laura Tanner, Christopher Wilson, and Juliana Chang, whose stamina sustains my hopes for a vital and just academy; Cathy Cohen, Joshua Gamson, and Jessica Neuwirth for the conversations; and my students in "Identity, Consumption, and Citizenship" at Yale, whose responses to a syllabus crammed with material from this book challenged me to articulate my purposes more clearly.

I might acknowledge debts of gratitude to institutions grudgingly, were it not for the Bunting Institute of Radcliffe College; it was a pleasure to work in the collaborative ethos nurtured there, and to work with the stupefyingly extensive resources, from those embodied in the staff of the Bunting to those bound in Harvard's many libraries. My experience there set this project afloat, buoyed up by the encouraging reception of early versions of this work by all of my "sister fellows." Of these, Barbara Smith, Farah Jasmine Griffin, Jeanie Taylor, and then-director Florence Ladd especially communicated their convictions that this work was worth pursuing. Barbara has continued to support the project with well-timed missives of information. The Bunting also brought me Jane Kamensky, to whom I am deeply grateful, whose painstaking editorial work and continual moral support amounted to midwifery, even as she was bringing her own human baby into the world.

Grants from the Radcliffe Research Partnership Program and the Boston College Undergraduate Research Assistantship Program sponsored a great deal of the support work necessary to complete a task of this magnitude. How lucky I was that such work was carried out by Johanna Brodsky, Nikki DeBlosi, Sarah Gordon, Ana Lara, and Kathryn Schwartzstein, all of whose work has benefited the project materially, and whose feisty spirits have assured its author, beyond doubt, that there is a formidable next wave of feminism and humor just breaking.

I have also been assisted throughout, and consistently astounded, by the multiply and ferociously talented Kerri Gawreluk. Her contributions to this project—in the form of her creativity, her unsurpassed research skills, her intellectual acuity, her friendship, and her endurance—are incalculable. Nobody has shared with me a commitment to this book like Kerri has.

I am grateful to Miranda Joseph for a long-term, mutual, loving, and personal-is-political tutorial in capitalism, gay identity, and life in general; to the true-blue Mary Jean Corbett for the wit and wisdom she has shared with me for so long; to Elizabeth Graver for her professions of faith in my writing, and her exacting eye; to Judith Butler for all her support and for sorely needed perspective. Along with them, Douglas Bellow, Shay Brawn, Ed Cohen, Jodi Delibertis, Bob Chibka and Marj DeVault, Anne Fleche and Jane Ashley, Nan Herron, Roz Jacobs and Laurie Weisman, Deb Kennedy, David Lein, Debra Minkoff, Kathryn Rensenbrink, and Jill Schneiderman fill out a life in which friendship helps me work and helps me stop working.

I want to thank my whole family, and especially my father, Richard Chasin, who took such an active interest in this project. I am also extremely grateful to Malaga Baldi, my agent, for her quick and determined response to the ideas here and for her deadpan delivery of news. She and Karen Wolny, my editor at Palgrave, invested in the work at its most sketchy and gave it the chance to develop. Massive editorial intervention has been generously, excellently, and invaluably tendered by the inimitable Nina Manasan Greenberg. Ann Lehman Katz has also had a profound, if mysterious, influence on the process of writing this book.

To my friend Ira Livingston, who meets me at the most primitive and most exalted places, and who deconstructs the boundary between them in the constant exchange of phone calls, metonyms, and literal miles traveled, my unending thanks. Ira, for doing things with words with me, for a sense of the meaning of "unconditional," thanks again. Finally, thanks to Nan Buzard, for California orange juice, for the fruits of lessons in negotiation, for her hardworking brain and heart, and for making me so happy I could write a book.

LIST OF ILLUSTRATIONS

FIGURES

PREFACE

When I first conceived of this project, it had a very different shape than the one eventually taken by the book in front of you now. I began with the observation that the twentieth century in the United States saw the rise of social movements based in identity. While this trend certainly had its origins in the nineteenth century—in the women's movement and the abolition movement, in particular—it was in the twentieth century that identity itself became a primary basis for social groups organizing for political and civil rights. Further, I observed that in the twentieth century advertising and marketing developed in such a way that market growth began to depend on, and to produce, social identity as a basis for buying and consuming goods and services. What, I wondered, was the connection between identity-based political and social movements in the twentieth century and the niche marketing that sought to capitalize on identity-based communities?

It seemed to me that a number of social groups had gone through a similar process: As they formed into political movements organized around identity, those social groups focused on expanding their rights and on promoting their visibility as good citizens worthy of acceptance into mainstream U.S. culture. The women's movement, the civil rights movement, and the gay and lesbian movement have each struggled for enfranchisement. Each of these movements experienced critical junctures at which it suddenly made significant progress, moments at which it won legislative or judicial battles, or moments in which it suddenly began to enjoy dramatically increased social recognition. And at these moments of enfranchisement, I noticed, movement constituencies became target markets.

For example, when women were granted the constitutional right to vote, in 1920, advertisers began to address women as consumers in an unprecedented way. Likewise, the civil rights movement won the passage of the Civil Rights Act and the Voting Rights Act within two years of the first time an African American was pictured in an ad in a general circulation publication in 1963.[1] After the Civil Rights Act was passed in 1964 and the Voting Rights Act in 1965, African Americans began to be targeted by national advertisers who had previously addressed whites in the quest for a mass market. Similarly, in the 1980s and 1990s, gay men and lesbians entered public discourse in the United States in new ways. At the very moments that AIDS activism—as well as debates about gays in the military, gay marriage, and antidiscrimination legislation—hit the newspapers, the television talk shows, the streets, and the courts, gay men and lesbians suddenly appeared as the ultimate niche market. Why would there be such a pattern? Why would social groups that had worked so long for enfranchisement become ripe for niche marketing in their moments of apparent success? How are citizenship and consumption related to each other? And the most troubling question of all: What impact has such marketing had on the movements in question?

In a fellowship proposal, I articulated a project in which I would look at the historical relation between consumer behavior and political rights. I would look at what had happened to the women's movement in the 1920s, following enfranchisement and during the advertising blitz aimed at women.[2] I would investigate how the beginning of true market incorporation of African Americans in the 1960s and 70s had affected the civil rights movement. And I would explain the impact of niche marketing to gay men and lesbians on the sexual liberation movement. As is now obvious to me, that was an ill-conceived project. There were too many variables. Gender, race, and sexual orientation are very different kinds of identity. The 1920s, 60s, 70s, 80s, and 90s are very different historical periods. There was no proper basis for comparative claims. So I reoriented.

I decided to write about just one case, and the case I knew most about was the lesbian and gay movement and market of the 1990s. As a longtime activist in the movement, as someone directly subject to target marketing to gays, as a board member of a gay and lesbian human rights organization, and as a scholar of sexuality, I felt better prepared to undertake the study of this case than any other. However, in working on this particular case, I often thought about the connections with other movements and niche markets. I continue to believe that there is a general trend that bears studying. Indeed, I suspect that the lessons of the lesbian and gay community may be applicable to other cases.

The short answer to my questions is that the capitalist market makes possible, but also constrains, social movements whose central objective is the expansion of individual political rights. Over the course of the twentieth century, as a function of the rise of consumer culture, political rights have been increasingly recast as economic liberties.[3] This means that social movements focused on winning rights are increasingly drawn into market-based tactics and objectives. In this way, the market promotes assimilation into a homogeneous national culture, encouraging identity difference only to the extent that it serves as a basis for niche marketing. The long answer—an explanation of the reasons that the market eventually undermines the radical potential of identity-based movements for social change—unfolds in the following pages. These pages point beyond identity politics, beyond nationalist conceptions of liberation, at the same time that the very existence of this book proves that identity politics and identity-based production and consumption have changed social institutions in dramatic, and sometimes progressive, ways. My work is not a condemnation of identity politics, any more than it is a denial of the fact that legal rights are necessary tools for freedom and equality. This work does, however, make the argument that rights, while necessary, are insufficient—and that identity politics is, in turn, inadequate—to the task of building a movement for social justice, where social justice is understood to provide all people with *access* to the full range of social institutions, over and above the equal *right* to them.

This is a book about a movement, a manifold, growing, self-contradictory entity, an entity so fundamentally plural that calling it a movement at all risks minimizing the internal differences within it. Nevertheless, I do call it a movement, partly in order to distinguish concerted movement activity from the vast amount of social activity that takes place *without* the intention to effect social change. Under the rubric of "movement," many folks have tried to implement their visions for a better society, and I mean to honor such work. But I also use the word in the singular in order to refer to dominant strains of the movement, which I must do in order to describe and analyze those strains. This description and analysis are preoccupied with the way that dynamics of domination and subordination work in both the gay and lesbian movement and the gay and lesbian niche market. For the same reason, I use the term "gay and lesbian" to describe the movement, without the addition of more inclusive terms, like transgender, bisexual, two-spirited, queer, or questioning. Those terms refer to identities that are marginalized when they are not ignored outright in the "gay and lesbian movement." My decision not to use those words is meant to reflect the marginalization at work in the movement. The absence of those words in these pages therefore fails to reflect my personal opinion that transgender, bisexual, two-spirited, queer, and/or questioning people may indeed suffer oppression that has everything to do with heterosexism and sexism, that people with those identities ought to be fully incorporated into any movement that truly concerns itself with sexual liberation, and that their relative lack of representation in any movement for social justice casts doubt on the legitimacy of that movement.

For many observers and participants, the existence of a thriving gay and lesbian movement and a thriving gay and lesbian market is a sign of progress, if not success. Much has been written about the gay and lesbian market, especially in the gay press and in the advertising trade press, almost all of it celebratory. Commentators cavil about the economic clout of the gay and lesbian community and the importance of being recognized and represented in the marketplace. Advertising targeted to the gay and lesbian community appears purely optimistic about the political rewards of consumption. I offer here another point of view: a socialist, antiracist, feminist perspective on the thriving movement and market, according to which everything is not so rosy, according to which "pink dollars" are an occasion for very serious reflection.

From this point of view, we have not "arrived." We have not trounced the forces of homophobia, have vanquished neither the religious right nor the Republican Congress, have not disarmed discriminating bosses and landlords, stayed the fists, guns, or speech of people everywhere whose hatred for gay men and lesbians expresses itself in conscious or unconscious violence. We are not yet safe, not yet equal, not yet free, not yet even acceptable. This critique exposes the "dirty laundry," the internal conflicts of the many strains of an infinitely diverse population that is called variously a community or a movement, but that is only inaccurately described by any singular noun. I believe that the cultural, political, and social health of that population depends on airing those conflicts. But of course, it will be necessary to do more than air them in order to work together across lines of race, gender, class, and political opinion.

I am not interested in vilifying individuals, or even groups. I *am* interested in identifying, describing, and understanding institutional mechanisms and systems of practice, for the purpose of changing them for the better. Do their effects include harm to some people and advantage for others, *as a rule?* Yes. Do I mobilize my own political opinion (which is both idiosyncratic and consistent with an identifiable camp of political opinion) in evaluating the meaning of harm and advantage? Yes. Does that mean that I think any generalization, based though it is in systematic analysis of entrenched practice and entrenched norms, could accurately describe every member of any given social group? No, of course not. If it is true that women, as a group, make 75 cents to each dollar made by men, as a group, does it follow that there is any single true claim that can be made about all men, or each man? No. Or all women, or each woman? No. If I assert that white people regularly and systematically enjoy a range of advantages based on the social meanings of white skin, does that mean I think that any two white people have ever experienced that privilege, or inhabited other aspects of their whiteness, in the same way? No. The point is that if this book criticizes anything, it is not people. It is ideas—the ones I think harmful—and the practices that militate toward their institutionalization.

A few other disclaimers are in order here. First, this is not a book about gay and lesbian politics in relation to mainstream politics. While the subject matter is closely related, mainstream politics is a distinct topic, and one that has been written about already.[4] Neither is this a book about gay and lesbian culture and style. Again, this topic is closely related to my present concerns, but I have tried to maintain a distinct focus on manifestations of the gay and lesbian niche market in its economic and political aspects, leaving aside the ways in which they are also, of course, manifestations of cultural expression, taste, subjectivity, and lifestyle. This too has been written about.[5] *Selling Out* is about the specific nexus of movement politics based in gay and lesbian identity and market activity based in gay and lesbian identity.[6] Finally, there are missing chapters or phenomena that would hold great lessons for a study of the interaction between the movement and the niche market but are not included in this book (for reasons of length), such as the gay travel, pornography, and book publishing industries.

This project bears all the hazards of an interdisciplinary undertaking. While I am well situated to bring together, for synthetic analysis, materials from different fields, I am not an expert in some of these fields. My primary sources involve archived documents and a few interviews, yet this is neither a work of history nor one of journalism. A story unfolds here across the twentieth-century United States, but it is not intended to be comprehensive, nor does it offer the balanced presentation of all points of view; it is intended to point to thematic continuities between gay and lesbian experience and the experience of other identity groups, and to offer a partial account of the ways in which identity is a source of belonging in a national community and of the ramifications of mobilizing identity as an instrument of politics and commerce. Other sources include academic and nonacademic books, but perhaps my most important source is direct observation of the movement and community of which I have been a member for over twenty years. And yet this is not a properly ethnographic text from the point of view of a participant-observer, especially since it delivers no conclusion about the subjective experience of other members of the group. I make sociological claims, and yet this analysis is far from quantitative. If it is closer to qualitative sociology, it is perhaps too invested with an avowed political program to qualify as any kind of social science. Owing a great deal to my training as a student of literature, of "discourse analysis," and of Cultural Studies, this is an interdisciplinary project with a political purpose. Whether it is fuzzy economics, American Studies, queer manifesto, or otherwise, this book is offered in the spirit of open inquiry and exchange.

INTRODUCTION

Sexuality serves as an especially dense transfer point for relations of immanent power precisely because it crystallizes around the distraction of a natural individual personal mystery all the material economic and political strands which tie the individual to both state and market, and it is through such material distractions that capitalism clearly demonstrates yet again its ability to confuse us.[1]

—David T. Evans, *Sexual Citizenship*

Gays are the epitome of capitalism.[2]

—Steven Shifflett, former President of Houston's Gay Political Caucus

THE DOMESTIC PARTNERSHIP
OF THEORY AND HISTORY

There are many ways to tell the story of the emergence of modern gay and lesbian identity, of gay and lesbian community and culture, of the gay and lesbian movement in the United States. Some tell it as a story of morality, in which same-sex sexual behavior is designated as immoral (in every period from the biblical past to the family-centered modern era) and is then sometimes, and in some places, redesignated as acceptable, especially in view of increasingly persuasive and public demonstrations of the moral rectitude of people who happen to engage in same-sex sexual behavior. Others review the history of law, in which changes in legal codes have simultaneously named and criminalized those acts of dubious morality and certain social "dis-ease," followed by or intertwined with, legal reform.

Still others write about medical pathology and psychiatric categories, of diagnoses and treatments, followed by or intertwined with the progressive enlightenment of medical and psychiatric codes and institutions. Many would relate a tale of social development—the vicissitudes of mainstream tolerance for a minority behavior, and sexual behavior at that. For some, the history of gay and lesbian community turns on the growth of ghettoes in coastal urban centers, where gay and lesbian community made possible the development of gay and lesbian community institutions, from those producing gay and lesbian culture to those serving the needs of people ignored in the larger society. Then again, some versions of the story focus on brave, even unwitting, individuals who paved the way for freedom of sexuality and freedom of cultural expression, or on individuals without hope until they came together in collective action. In turn, collective action is understood to have enabled the development of a political movement that fights for civil rights, a movement that in the late twentieth century continuously and successfully added to its basic righteousness visibility, numbers of people, and, not least, money. Gay and lesbian life in the United States, of course, unfolded through all of these processes and more, including the backlashes against and within them. Gay and lesbian identity, community, and movement also unfold through economic processes. The relationship between gay and lesbian commercial life and the organization of a political and social movement based in gay and lesbian identity forms the subject of my book.

While religious, moral, legal, and medical systems have profoundly influenced the gay and lesbian movement—and while that movement has worked hard to purge those systems of their historical homophobia—economic systems have also affected the course of the movement. It is impossible to isolate wholly economic influences from other forces, but it is equally impossible to understand the history of gay and lesbian political life in this country without considering the ways that identity and identity politics function in the marketplace. The way that gay men and lesbians in the United States come to understand themselves as "gay," and as "American," has everything to do with understandings of the relationship between citizenship and consumption. In turn, citizenship and consumption are only intelligible in relation to ideas about nation, sexuality, market, race, class, gender, and the public and private spheres. This book attempts to look at all these terms in relation to each other, and over time. This analysis of the relationship between the gay and lesbian niche market of the late-twentieth-century United States and the contemporary gay and lesbian social and political movement reaches back over the whole century, but the book focuses on the period from the late 1960s to the turn of the century, and most closely on the 1990s.

At the broadest level, the relationship between the gay and lesbian market and the gay and lesbian movement has its roots in the co-emergence of the modern Western liberal democratic nation state and modern (and postmodern) forms of capital. In other words, the political and economic context in which the gay and lesbian movement arose shaped that movement. Of course, capitalism and liberal democracy are more than historically contemporaneous; ideas and practices link them indissolubly. Revisiting the earliest links between capitalism and liberal democracy makes it clear that gay identity and gay identity politics are equally functions of a liberal discourse of individual rights, on the one hand, and a capitalist economic arrangement, on the other.[3] Political claims based in gay and lesbian identity—claims to privacy, to choice, to free expression, to individual rights—clearly came to be heard more frequently in the United States in the latter half of the twentieth century through state institutions. But political claims have been made in the market arena as well, by and for a range of identity groups. Gay and lesbian liberation struggles have pervaded many social arenas—this project focuses on the causes and effects of waging those struggles in the marketplace.

LIBERALISM AND CAPITALISM

Why is personal liberty intertwined with economic freedoms? The answer has a long history. John Locke was one of the earliest theorists of the relationship between individual political rights and the marketplace, and he remains one of the most influential: "the ostensibly Lockean political vocabulary of law, right, liberty, equality, and property remains at the heart of contemporary political discussion."[4] And even if those words have very different meanings now than they did in the seventeenth century, nevertheless, "that vocabulary itself has been solidified, regularized, and institutionalized over the past three hundred years in ways that extend its historical horizon from the English constitutional crises of the seventeenth century to the political struggles and controversies of the present."[5]

Certainly that vocabulary resounds in the modern gay and lesbian political movement, signifying the movement's central concerns for almost fifty years in the United States. What is less obvious, but equally important, is that the same vocabulary has become increasingly prevalent in the niche market in and around which gay and lesbian identity has been elaborated; the rest of this book attends to the ways in which the liberalism of the movement is reflected in marketing to and by gay men and lesbians. But what, in particular, does Locke contribute to an understanding of the contemporary arena of gay and lesbian political and commercial life? Precisely, he formulates the indissolubility of citizenship and property, of political and commercial being:

> Though the earth, and all inferior creatures, be common to all men, yet every man has a *property* in his own *person:* this no body has any right to but himself. The *labour* of his body, and the *work* of his hands, we may say, are properly his. Whatsoever then he removes out of the state that nature hath provided, and left it in, he hath mixed his *labour* with, and joined to it something that is his own, and thereby makes it his *property*.[6]

For Locke, then, the first and most basic unit of social life in the state is the individual, the "man." This theoretical individual bears rights granted by natural law and protected by civil law, and the very first right of that individual is the right of possession. Through labor, the body and its products are the first rightful possessions. And entailed in the right to property in the body is the right to exchange property in the marketplace. So, for liberalism, freedom is freedom of choice, originally the freedom to choose to trade one's labor for a wage. Beyond the most fundamental right to property in one's body is the right to exchange the labor exercised by that body. For Locke, "a man's energy and skill are his own, yet are regarded not as integral parts of his personality, but as possessions, the use and disposal of which he is free to hand over to others for a price."[7] In the twentieth century, identity would become both a personal feature and a thing to be negotiated through market transactions.

Meanwhile, back in the eighteenth century (and less concerned than Locke with establishing a philosophical grounding for rights), political economist Adam Smith describes market mechanisms in *Wealth of Nations*. Positing first the distinctly human "propensity to truck, barter, and exchange one thing for another," and taking as given that the legal exchange must involve possessions, Smith takes Locke to market.[8] As with Locke's, Smith's writings maintained a deep influence on the way that capitalism was understood for centuries to follow. Labor, for Smith, is an act that generates value; the subsequent act of commodity exchange sets values—the monetary values of labor and commodities—in relation to each other. In the process of exchange, value is negotiated and agreed upon, and equivalencies are made material in the form of money.[9] Because social negotiations of value form the basis of virtually all social meaning, commodity exchange both entails and produces social meaning in societies in which wage labor acts as the basis for valuation. These features of a market society form the core conditions in which identity can come to function as a unit of exchange, a unit of social meaning, a basis for public political practice as well as private acts of consumption.

At the theoretical level, the right to possess oneself and other things, the right and the freedom to exchange one's labor for wages and one's wages for goods, are rights and freedoms equally available to all. Any "man" would be free to act in the marketplace to procure Locke's "satisfactions." All men are free, in terms perhaps more familiar to Americans, to pursue happiness. That is, they are free to purchase it with the value they have generated by selling the labor that they possess by natural right, if they possess nothing else.[10] Liberal theory thus posits that "each person is the proprietor of his or her own capacities and is free to employ them in the search for a means of satisfaction, which become possessions—thus freedom is possession."[11] However, liberalism not only allows for financial inequality to develop in the market, it also imagines a government whose job is to protect its individual subjects unequally. At the same time, the innovations proposed by Locke and other Enlightenment thinkers included the radical idea that the power of government over citizens should be limited. This is crucial.

First, some people inherit wealth while others do not. So individuals do not enter the market equally endowed, even if they were then equally waged. Second, individuals have different capacities, from which it follows that different people's labor is valued differently. Third, capacities are not the sole determinants of wages; prejudice and discrimination—a long tradition of them—make the labor of women and people of color less valuable in this country than the labor of men and white people, respectively. From the vantage point of the late twentieth century, Patricia Williams sums up these factors with the simple historical observation that "Certain races are worth more in the marketplace."[12] Adam Smith was quite aware that liberal market theory allowed for the perpetuation of economic inequality and was untroubled by it. Wealth, for Smith, was a thing possessed—property, as Locke would have it. And "Wealth, as Mr. Hobbes says, is power."[13] From a perspective more concerned with social equality, serious problems result from the power differences inherent in market capitalism, difficulties as basic as agreeing on the meaning of social justice. Theoretically and in practice, there is a tension between the liberal value of individual freedom and the structural inequalities that are also protected by the state.

This tension between individual freedoms and a state that protects unequal accumulation leads to a paradox for rights movements. Movements appeal to the state to extend greater rights to more individuals and social groups, but the state to which they appeal is one designed to leave significant regulatory power to the market. Meanwhile, market operations do not in and of themselves increase or diminish rights. Market operations do, however, tend to consolidate and even amplify existing economic inequalities. Thus, expanded rights tend to enhance the economic privilege of those who are already economically privileged. This tendency has been demonstrated for African Americans and for women. For gay men and lesbians, it means that gay men and lesbians with money are better served both by state intervention and regular market practice than gay men and lesbians without money.

THE LIBERAL STATE AND THE MARKET

In the liberal state, people are "equally" free to pursue happiness by purchasing commodities with the wealth they have generated and/or inherited. Theoretically, then, this market regulates itself through the rational actions of self-possessing and self-interested individuals. What is the role of the state in this model? Such a state protects the rights of those individuals, rights to life, liberty, self-ownership, and property ownership, which is to say, happiness. Here is the problem. Because different individuals have varying amounts of wealth, the state's treatment of each person differs. This is because, as Smith observed, the acquisition of property simultaneously implies social inequalities, resentments, and fear of crimes actual and emotional.[14] For example, in Smith's influential model, the poor necessarily hate the rich, so much that the rich have reason to fear the poor. Moreover, the rich deserve to have the civil government protect them and, by extension, their God-given right to happiness via property ownership. One critical function of liberal democratic government, then, is to defend wealthy people against poor people.[15]

Doesn't this situation compromise the state's ability to protect all individuals equally? Yes. Smith is clear on this: "Civil government supposes a certain subordination"—the subordination of poor to rich.[16] So from its inception the liberal state was designed to accomplish two distinct objectives simultaneously: to protect the free agent from an interfering government, and to protect property holders from non-holders. Thus, class antagonism joins structural inequality among the legacies of liberal democracy, and liberal democracy cooperates with capitalism in building systems that tend to enhance the power of individuals who already have some, while disadvantaging those who do not. Governmental and market systems share these tendencies. So do political movements focused primarily on expanding the rights of a single identity group.

It is crucial to note that the qualifications for voting, which historically linked property and citizenship quite literally, have changed dramatically over time. At the time of the European Enlightenment, in which Locke and Smith were writing, individuals with the right to approve of or change their government composed far less than half of the population. Natural law, to Locke, made only Protestant, white, male, able-bodied, free, propertied adults "equal" and hence brought them into community with each other. In this way, property requirements for political participation converged with the requirements for citizenship, or membership in a national community. But the restrictions on enfranchisement have long been debated. The movement for universal white manhood suffrage was hard at work throughout the eighteenth century and half of the nineteenth century in the American colonies and then in the United States, trying to eliminate property requirements for voting. Largely successful by the 1860s, this movement was of course succeeded by movements for suffrage for nonwhite, nonmale citizens. The Fifteenth and Nineteenth amendments legalized suffrage for women and people of color.[17] However, although both the composition of the citizenry and the legal texts defining it have changed considerably since Locke's time, the natural rights framework given by Locke still underlies legal and economic practice in the United States. Proposed expansions to the category of the "individual" enlarge the community within which people would be theoretically equal, but such expansions have usually preserved, and even enhanced, the link between rights and property, and the market as the field in which the distribution of social power is largely negotiated.

It is plain to see that there are extreme limits to the equalizing possibilities of the law, especially in light of its entanglements with the market. For example, from a system of slavery—within which an African worker or worker of African descent was legally prohibited from selling her/his labor in order to generate her/his own compensation at all—to a system (as longstanding now as that of slavery) of compensation—in which those of African descent are systematically paid unequally for the same work as white workers—nonwhite racial identity has been worth less in the marketplace. The existence of laws prohibiting racial discrimination in the marketplace—besides being a frighteningly recent and increasingly threatened phenomenon—does not prevent such discrimination from happening, and it is not, in fact, designed to prevent it from happening. Such laws potentially punish those who discriminate and potentially compensate those who have suffered discrimination, and they thereby offer, theoretically, a disincentive to discriminate. But law does not prevent violation of law, and countless lawsuits attest to an ongoing racial inequality in the many stalls of the contemporary marketplace. The law and the market, then, cannot be the only tools utilized in the fight for social justice.

Over the course of the twentieth century, in particular, "in the first world economies of the global chain, citizenship has increasingly focused on the rights of citizens as consumers."[18] The preservation and enhancement of rights as property rights have grave implications for rights movements. Referring to contemporary politics in the United States, Patricia Williams notes that in the 1990s debates on social issues were consistently relocated to the marketplace, with a conservatizing effect:

> The debate about equality has shifted to one of free speech; legal discussions involving housing, employment, and schooling have shifted from the domain of civil rights to that of the market and thus have become "ungovernable," mere consumption preference. It serves us well, I think, to observe the ironies as well as the consistencies, the currents of desired investment and unintended disenfranchisement that flow on and on and on beneath the surface of our finest aspirations.[19]

Here, Williams argues that the slippage between politics and the market conspire to feature consumption as the chosen, the ideologically elect, act of choice. I am intent on exploring the unintended disenfranchisement that is an effect of conceiving of political rights as market-based rights. Seen in this light, the extent of a person's enfranchisement determines his or her ability to express consumption preferences. Furthermore, "these degrees of non-citizenship incite the further fragmentation of communities with sectionalised access and activity to and in specialised markets," through the mechanisms of what Williams calls "laissez-faire exclusion," which has the same effects as discrimination.[20] The gay and lesbian community and the gay and lesbian market, in their shifting positions of legitimacy and power, are implicated in this phenomenon.

CAPITALISM, SUBJECTIVITY, AND GAY IDENTITY

Of course, capitalism is not a simple machine that has operated uniformly and evenly for hundreds of years. In fact, changes within systems of production and consumption have not only enabled liberal rights movements, they have also enabled the development of a range of forms of social identity. In the United States, the relationship between economic life and personal life has changed as modes of production and consumption have changed. Yet throughout the era of possessive individualism, "the relations of exchange among individuals with respect to their possessions are the basic form of social relations."[21] How have relations of exchange mutated, and what are some of the attendant mutations in social relations in the United States over the course of its life span? How are gay and lesbian identities related to economic shifts? More specifically, what does the gay and lesbian niche market have to do with the history of capitalism?

Because identity-based production, distribution, and consumption are functions of consumer culture, and because consumer culture is a relatively recent development within the growth of capitalism, the answers begin in the distant past. Among European settlements in the colonial period, and even through the early-middle nineteenth century in the United States, economic arrangements centered around the household. As a rule, both production and consumption took place in the home, on a small scale. The scale of production was a function of the size of the household—meaning family plus servants and/or slaves—as available labor was largely limited to members of the household. Consumption meant the immediate use of tools and (mostly perishable) goods. Those objects and goods were grown, sewn, and hewn by their consumers, or by local artisans or skilled laborers. Over the course of the nineteenth century, as industrial modes of production became more developed and more prevalent, production increasingly took place outside of the home. Wage-earning individuals ventured out of the house for work and brought back cash with which to buy goods and services. A sexual division of labor, which had already split up chores along gender lines inside the home, tended to send men into industrial production jobs and leave women in charge of childrearing and unpaid domestic work. Of course, there have always been women who worked outside of the home, but statistically and ideologically, the rule was that women remained in the private sphere. As both jobs and goods became available outside of the home, the development of a free-labor market enabled great numbers of individual wage-earners to survive outside of the family.

In his pathbreaking work, "Capitalism and Gay Identity," historian John D'Emilio draws the link between this economic development and modern sexual identity in the United States.[22] While there have always been same-sex sexual practices, it was not until individuals could subsist outside of heterosexual families that gay identity arose. By identity, I mean a kind of self-understanding, a description of an entire persona named for, or understood through, the practice of homosexuality.[23] Furthermore, as industrial capitalism encouraged the growth of cities and as more and more individuals left rural areas for those cities, it became possible for homosexuals to seek out other people who were organizing their social identities on the same basis. Thus, gay social life also began to emerge. By this reasoning, it seems that capitalism, in the United States, made possible both gay identity and the beginning of what we might call gay community by the early twentieth century.

D'Emilio further observes that as the family's productive function waned, the family began to perform a new kind of cultural work. Because commodity production still required the reproduction of the labor force, there continued to be an economic need for the family, as the dominant institution within which sexual reproduction takes place. But as the private household ceased to operate as the main site of production, something less expressly economic had to justify the social need for the family: "Reflecting the separation of personal life from production, a new idea has emerged on a mass scale: that of human relationships, and human beings, as ends in themselves."[24] This perspective suggests that the development of personal identity has taken place

within a more general expansion of the importance of internal, subjective, and affective experience. Perhaps, then, the increased viability of
gay social identity reflects an increased range of choices among identities, along with the rise of the very concept of identity over the course
of the twentieth century. If family was still required for the reproduction
of "human beings," and if the family was still active as a central unit of
consumption, it seems logical that the increasing emphasis on identity
would be matched by the growth of possibilities for establishing identity through consumption.

Examples of recorded histories of the convergence of gay social life
and commercial activity go back at least as far as the nineteenth century.
Again, while it seems quite likely that people who engaged in same-sex
behavior also convened socially in commercial establishments before
this time period, I am, like D'Emilio (and Michel Foucault), distinguishing between sexual practices and their authors, on the one hand,
and people who understood and enacted their social beings as bearers of
homosexual *identity,* as members of that "species," on the other.[25] Describing leisure time spent in bars, restaurants, and theaters, and noting
landlord-tenant relations in which gay men participated, historian
George Chauncey's work on the development of gay male culture in
New York from 1890 through World War II demonstrates the inextrica-
bility of the formation of a social identity from commercial life.[26]

CONSUMER CULTURE

Most theorists agree that the twentieth century brought a shift from a
production-based economic life to a consumption-based economic life
in the United Sates. Of course, production and consumption are closely
linked—you can't have one without the other.[27] If consumption makes
commodity production meaningful, and if people increasingly commodify themselves as their first social act (by selling their labor for
wages), one imagines that consumption also mediates the production of
social identities. This function of consumption came into its own in the
twentieth century, in which the domestic sphere shifted to become a
center of consumption rather than production, and in which the ideol-

ogy of personal life—and of "subjectivity"—began to replace production as the glue of that sphere. As liberal democracy and the capitalist market presumed subjective individuals with the free choice of selling themselves, they also implied that the same individuals had choices about consumption.

In a consumer culture, subjectivity is negotiated in the marketplace; in the twentieth century, subjectivity was more and more often articulated as identity, and therefore identity too was negotiated in the marketplace. The market, like the court and the legislature (and all of these are arenas within which identity claims are meaningful), depends on the ideology of free choice. Advertising, whatever else it conveys, always attempts to assure consumers that they are capable of choice in a market that presents a truly competition-inspired variety of goods. At stake in advertising are the choices of the liberal consumer-citizen—choices in the ballot box and at the market, choices of regulatory regime and "lifestyle."

Interestingly enough, the emergence of gay identity toward the beginning of the twentieth century was roughly contemporary with the development of pictorial advertising. Advertising itself was not a new phenomenon, but around the turn of the century both the nature and the scale of advertising changed. The first experiences of mass culture on the part of U.S. consumers were related to newspapers and magazines, which began to be "mass" distributed in the 1890s—at the same moment that "advertising began to provide more than half the revenue for newspapers, and that ads for national brands took a prominent place alongside classifieds and ads for local merchants and department stores."[28] The role of the press in the transformation from local to national markets repeated itself in the growth of a national gay market. Mass culture, and the advertising that subsidized it, also had an ideological function: "The ideal of, and popular demand for, democracy in a large nation required mass culture."[29] The ideology of democracy, of the subjective experience of choice and participation, was born again and again in mass-cultural instruments (such as magazines) themselves borne on national markets. Thus, mass culture and the consumption of it have been linked with the prospect of freedom and equality. One scholar locates the origins of this linkage in the 1920s, but he argues that it had currency for the duration of the twentieth century: "From the period of the 1920s, commercial culture has increasingly provided an idiom within which desires for social change and fantasies of liberation might be articulated and contained."[30]

While techniques of advertising changed over the course of the twentieth century, many operating assumptions have persisted, as have some of the social functions advertising performs. Advertising exercises an ideological function through its content, through the pictures and stories with which it sells consumerism generally as well as specific commodities. In particular, advertising, like all forms of ideology, "hails . . . individuals as subjects."[31] In the very act of addressing themselves to people, a variety of social institutions with ideological projects—school, church, and the media, among them—actually shape people's identities. Through this process of hailing, institutions call into being, or constitute, "subjects" of ideology, people who recognize themselves in the way they are addressed. Thus, such institutions call into being an individual who appears to enjoy "a free subjectivity," an individual, that is, who appears to be "a centre of initiatives, author of and responsible for its actions."[32] This theory calls into question the idea that social actors make free choices in an open field of possibility. It suggests, instead, that the individual is never fully outside of ideology. Furthermore, this theory is helpful for an analysis of the gay and lesbian niche market because it keeps alive the question of how much choice consumers really have, at the same time that it recognizes advertising's power to hail (and thus bring into being) people with gay or lesbian identity: "By addressing gays and lesbians as consumers . . . marketers and advertisers constitute them in important ways (i.e., render them identifiable and intelligible), particularly in a capitalistic society."[33] However, it remains to consider the exact character of that constitution.

In addition to addressing individual consumers, advertising may also hail consumers as members of identifiable social groups. With reference to advertising in the early twentieth century, one historian observes, "Advertisements also contributed to the shaping of a 'community of discourse,' an integrative common language shared by an otherwise diverse audience."[34] Just as advertising in the early twentieth century hailed immigrants as members of ethnic groups, offering them a route to Americanization, so did advertising in the late twentieth century have the power to bring a gay community into public being. Simultaneously, it subjected gay men and lesbians to the idea that emancipation could be achieved through the market, particularly in the mode of assimilation, especially through consumption. In other words, "Marketing to gays and lesbians serves to legitimize them in the U.S. as individuals and as members of a subculture."[35] It remains to be seen whether the promise of enfranchisement through consumption is a matter more of subjection or of legitimation, and whether it extends equally to all members of the group.

LIBERALISM, RIGHTS, AND GAY IDENTITY

If gay identity and community arose over the course of the twentieth century in and around a marketplace in which wage-earners strike out on their own and build their identities through their consumption practices, the gay and lesbian movement arose no less in a regime of possessive individualism. Arising in and against a network of medical, legal, and cultural oppression of homosexuals, the gay and lesbian movement has consistently focused on expanding individual rights. Of course, the character, tactics, and aims of the movement have changed over time, but the drive for the full range of the benefits and privileges of citizenship has always been present, if not dominant, within the movement since the 1950s. Arising too in an age and place of liberalism, the movement held at a premium the right of individuals to possess a (homo)sexuality. Whether conceived as an identity feature or a behavior, (homo)sexuality is always conceptually located in the body. Because the body is private property, as long as it properly contains its sexuality within a domestic sphere, what is at stake, according to liberal logic, is the right to privacy. Of course, the right to privacy (and to homosexuality) must be won in the public sphere—in the courts and the legislature, in the media, in "public" opinion. The meanings of "public" and "private" appear to be crucial for resistance movements, in light of the fact that "All struggles against oppression in the modern world begin by redefining what had previously been considered private, non-public,

and non-political issues as matters of public concern, as issues of justice, as sites of power."[36] Homosexuality has long been regulated
through public mechanisms, from church law to secular law to medical
practice, but since homosexuality became a matter of social identity, its
definition as private has been at the heart of the movement.[37] Andrew
Sullivan's proposed solution to the "political" problem of homosexuality, for example, upholds liberalism's public-private distinction.[38]

Attempting to classify identity as a private matter is a fundamentally liberal project. Liberalism seeks to insulate public—or political—
matters from private matters, which are designated as nonpolitical.[39]
And it is the state, that most expressly public of fixtures, that fixes that
insulation. At the same time, however, the market defines the private
sphere as the place where social identity is established. As publicly produced commodities get sucked into the private sphere to be consumed,
personal products—namely identities—spill out of the private into the
public. As group identities emerge from the aggregation of individual
identities, "the groups contesting for space within the many-sided public enter the arena on the basis of their identities, identities that are
under pressure from the powerful reshaping forces of postmodern capitalism. One reaction to this penetration of capitalism . . . is protest
movements concerned with personal and collective identities, questions
of culture and personality."[40] In other words, capitalism contributes to
the formation of individual identity, which in turn contributes to the formation of identity-based social movements. For the most part, identity-
based protest movements focus on the rights of the individual, the
expansion of which reforms the capitalist market as a site of representation and enfranchisement. Just as civil rights struggles, particularly
those based in identity, are incipient in liberal democratic theory, civil
rights figured as market rights are incipient in relations of capital.

Like gay and lesbian niche market activity, and like social identity
more generally, gay and lesbian identity has been lauded as an instrument of both personal betterment and progressive social transformation.
Jeffrey Weeks is a preeminent theorist of gay identity for whom "Identity . . . is a necessary way of weaving our way through a hazard-strewn
world and a complex web of social relations. Without it, it seems, the
possibilities of sexual choice are not increased but diminished."[41]

Speaking for many who think of identity as politically and psycho-socially useful, Weeks's assertion of necessity masks the fact that "identity" is a tool particularly well suited both to the reinforcement of an ideology of choice and to the quest for enfranchisement. In fact, identity is only one of many possible compasses with which to navigate the social world; as a political tool, it is particularly powerful in the fight for liberal rights. I do not believe that mobilizing identity ends in a proliferation of "possibilities of sexual choice," nor that identity is a necessary basis for configuring strategies for political or social freedom. Weeks forgets the very lessons of Foucault that he means to invoke. As Foucault would have it, subjects are no more and no less free now than ever; they are merely subjected to different ideas and practices.

However, designating individual political rights as the most important political objective, as the gay and lesbian movement increasingly did in the late twentieth century, shores up the system of individual and "possessive" rights granted by God and protected by the state. Hence the uncanny appropriateness of Weeks's historical observation of the emergence of individuality for gay men and lesbians in the 1950s: "For the 'sexual minorities' coming to a new sense of their separateness and individuality during the same period—male homosexuals and lesbians particularly—the finding of 'identity' was like discovering a map to explore a new country."[42] In the United States, that new country *was* the United States. In other words, the exploration of the possibilities of gay or lesbian identification coincides with the exploration of the nation. As the following chapters will demonstrate, ideas about gay and lesbian identity in the United States are deeply interwoven with ideas about American identity. At every turn, the idea of nation, U.S. citizenship, and their attendant values will pervade discussions of identity politics and identity-based consumption. It will be shown that "nationalism" is one of the vehicles for transporting the goods of assimilation between the movement and the market.

Weeks characterizes the United States as a place "where class loyalties are less fixed, politics more coalition-minded, 'minority' politics (especially the struggles of blacks) better established, and social loyalties more fluid," than in Europe, "where gay movements . . . have largely been subordinated to more traditional progressive politics."[43] It is only in the United States, he asserts, that "sexuality has become a potent political issue."[44] While the comparison with Europe (perhaps paradoxically, given Weeks's national and geographical location in England) rehearses American exceptionalism, it also significantly ignores gay movements in the rest of the world.[45] Holding aside my reservation about his comparative assessment, I must take issue with his statement that women and men "have mobilized around their sense of sexual identity . . . because it was in their sexuality that they felt most powerfully invalidated."[46]

There is a great deal of evidence from women of color, lesbians and gay men of color, and nonidentified queers around the world that they do not feel that they have been most powerfully invalidated "in their sexuality."[47] Writers such as Barbara Smith, Gloria Anzaldúa, Cherríe Moraga, and many other lesbians of color testify that sexuality is not the primary basis of their "difference" or oppression. Indeed, as Moraga would say, "The danger lies in ranking oppressions."[48] When he contends that "sexuality" is the prime stigmatized difference of the homosexual, Weeks posits a presumptively white gay male citizen. Interestingly, this citizen's profile resembles that of the presumptive consumer in the gay and lesbian niche market, the very market that promises to redress inequality and invalidation: " . . . market segmentation strategies may be seen to operate as democratizing mechanisms, in the sense that they include people who are not typically included in more narrow conceptualizations of the U.S. market. Indeed, there is a profound sense of social validation and legitimation that is experienced by individual gays and lesbians and gay/lesbian communities as the result of increased accommodation as a market in capitalist society."[49] If validation were all that gay men and lesbians missed, then enfranchisement might mean equality and market accommodation might mean freedom. If all gay men and lesbians were white and middle class, and if lesbians were men, property rights might be what they most needed.

In other words, liberals imagine that rights are what gay men and lesbians lack and what we need. If industrial and postindustrial capitalism have enabled us to imagine locating component parts of our identities where we are unfree and unequal, if those economic arrangements have enabled us to build a movement dedicated to rectifying those conditions, they have also encouraged us to imagine our oppression *partially* and to design our liberation accordingly. We may be working to enfranchise the gay or lesbian part of ourselves, but if we separate out, even provisionally, that part from other parts, such as our race or class, we will necessarily neglect to work for the freedom and equality of those other parts. And as gay men and lesbians are differently raced, gendered, classed, aged, abled, and even "sexualized," so gay liberation, were it to come, would still leave many gay men and lesbians unfree and unequal.

WHO, OR WHAT, IS LEFT OUT

On a very practical level, not everyone has equal opportunity to exercise her/his rights. In recognition of the gap between theoretical and practical equality, theorist Mary Poovey usefully addresses the consequences of an exclusive focus on individual rights as a political objective. The occasion for Poovey's argument is the abortion debate, in which the language of "choice" has a distinct meaning, but one that is indeed related to the concept of consumer choice discussed above. She writes:

> the argument for abstract rights will always simultaneously mask and assume a set of social conditions that actually defines those rights and delimits who has access to them. Once exercised, "rights" and "choice" cannot remain abstract, and the concrete situation in which they are embedded limits what these concepts mean and who will be able to exercise them. It is because of the situatedness of practice, not incidentally, that the differences of race and class always return to haunt the abortion issue once an abortion statute has been implemented, for in practice and in everyday situations, race and class are determinants that often make more difference than sex.[50]

This logic may be imported from the abortion debate to the gay and lesbian movement; it resonates with the claims of people who feel that their sexuality is not the only and not the primary feature of identity on the basis of which their rights have been limited.

Clearly, Poovey's critique of the radical limits of abstract rights challenges the theory that identity-based market operations can expand access to rights for a whole social group, since individual socioeconomic status varies within all social groups. Sexuality (like any other identity feature) is only one aspect of any individual's necessarily composite identity, so identity-based market strategies for gay and lesbian rights may ignore differences among gay men and lesbians, such as those of gender and race. Meanwhile, assumptions about gender difference are at work in the gay and lesbian niche market: "Lesbians' relative invisibility in lesbian/gay consumer profiles may also reflect the legacy of anti-market sentiment among some lesbian-feminists, i.e., their equation of capitalism with patriarchy and resulting reluctance and/or resistance to market participation."[51] Yet, I would add that gender does not determine levels of anticapitalist, or even antipatriarchal, sentiment. Such nonidentity features as political opinion clearly play a role.

Thus there is a problem with formulating a target market on the basis of gay and lesbian identity. One such formulation holds that "homosexual males and lesbians constituted a definable market segment only so long as *specific activities, interests, and opinions dealt with their sexuality.*"[52] But lumping "homosexual males" and "lesbians" together, which is done in the service of identifying a target market, completely erases the gender difference *between* gay men and lesbians.[53] Simultaneously, a gay and lesbian consumer group is asked to feature its sexuality as the basis of its consumption. Of course, the answer to the question of whether—and if so, where—to locate difference, is not easy and differs according to context and political goal.

The problems inherent in claims of difference have beset liberation movements throughout U.S. history. Civil rights movements have had to argue, on the one hand, that nonwhite people are "naturally endowed" with the same intelligence and capacity, and therefore the same rights as white people. On the other hand, affirmative action and other remedial strategies need to call on the very material differences that history has produced, categorically, for nonwhite people. Feminists have explicitly been divided over "whether to press for a world in which sex becomes irrelevant, or to argue for a future in which sexual difference no longer acts as a basis for making us unequal."[54] Self-avowed feminists argued for special protections for women workers in the days of active labor reform, while other self-avowed feminists argued for no special protections. The same tension provides a challenge to the development of sexual harassment law today. Another problem is that the erasure of difference produces the image of a universal individual, who is always imagined as white and male. Liberalism imagines a free agent who is, in fact, dominant, rather than universal: "Obviously the liberal hero was male. Less obviously liberalism relied on gender differences to preserve the purity of its ideal type."[55] Here again, the dogged contradiction returns. The very differences erased are crucial to the formation of the image of the universal individual upon which mass marketing depends, and to the typification upon which target marketing depends.[56] It is well worth asking whether the process by which the gay and lesbian market and movement attain national proportions is not the same process by which gay men and lesbians come to have exactly what other citizens have, no more and no less.

As I said, there are gay men and lesbians for whom sexuality is not the primary source of their difference from the universal ideal; the insistence on the primacy of sexuality ignores other identity features, such as race and/or gender and/or religion, and thus generates an assimilationist politics that reduces diversity to a superficial value, a matter of choice in the food court. Incorporation of diverse identities on these grounds has the same effects as the reworking of the word "integration," according to Williams, who shows that "'Integration' itself has been transformed in meaning, now used glowingly by former segregationists like Jesse Helms and Strom Thurmond—and rejected by many former civil rights activists—as having come to mean a form of assimilation that demands self-erasure rather than engagement of black contributions and experience."[57] To the extent that a roster of diverse identities includes gay men and lesbians, they also face the possibility of assimilation. And for gay men and lesbians, as for African Americans, "integration" can mean the erasure of all but the most superficial manifestations of social difference.

Liberal political movements tend to seek, first and foremost, if not exclusively, legislative and/or judicial reform, or rights. Often, but not always, this involves the extension of already-existing rights to disenfranchised groups. For example, women and African Americans have had to have extended to them—at different times—the right to vote, a right already enjoyed by adult white male citizens. In this light, the right to gay and lesbian marriage is a liberal objective because it involves the extension of a right. (Technically, in fact, marriage is a privilege, more than a "right," but many gays are fighting for the right to the privilege.) To be fair, many liberal agendas seek cultural change in addition to expanded rights, but frequently the kind of change sought has an assimilationist cast to it, meaning, for example, that it would open mainstream social forms to gays, rather than fundamentally change the structures that have historically excluded gays. Examples are marriage, religion, media, athletics, even masculinity and femininity. So marriage, again, is not just a right, but a social form that, if extended to gays, would tend to de-emphasize, rather than preserve, distinctions between gay and straight culture. I call the emphasis on similarity between gay and straight rights and culture, particularly when gay culture changes to look more like straight culture, a kind of assimilation, and again, I call this a liberal cultural politic. A liberal cultural politic does admit difference, but it often prefers to contain difference, or to see it manifested relatively superficially, emphasizing, for example, that we are all human (meaning similar) under (the varieties of color of) our skin.

When I use the word "progressive," by contrast, I mean to refer to an agenda that is much broader than the one of winning political rights, and broader even than the kind of social change that would enable disenfranchised groups to engage in mainstream social forms. I consider a value on access to be the defining difference between progressive and liberal agendas. Rights are all too theoretical to all too many people. Without a lawyer to argue them on one's behalf, without an education that effectively makes one aware of them, without the health care that makes it possible to enjoy them, rights alone may be cold comfort. A progressive agenda, therefore, must concern itself not only with discriminatory laws and social inclusion, it must attend to the sources and effects of economic injustice across the entire populace. Whereas an issue such as gay marriage, or gays in the military, is the very picture of a liberal-reform, equality-seeking, rights-based, single-issue movement goal, a progressive platform is informed by multi-issue and multi-constituency concern for access. Liberal initiatives quite often rely on, or answer to, identity-based interest groups, where coalition is the by-word of the progressive movement.

SELLING OUT: THE GAY AND LESBIAN MOVEMENT GOES TO MARKET

The 1990s have seen the rise of the production, distribution, and consumption of commodities aimed at a gay and lesbian market. In the same decade, gay and lesbian issues entered the public arena in unprecedented ways; gays in the military, gay marriage, and gay adoption were debated in courts, in legislatures, and in the media. A social movement whose origin many date to the Stonewall Rebellion is largely responsible for formulating these issues. What, then, is the relation between the recent growth of gay and lesbian market activity, on the one hand, and a continuing political and social movement, on the other? In the last three decades of the twentieth century, in which the market became dramatically hypersegmented, hyperspecialized, and globalized, gay men and lesbians in the United States saw the emergence of a liberation movement with our name on it and the growth of gay and lesbian institutions of all kinds. It has been demonstrated that a sense of community is established through participation in institutions, so that gay community, in particular, or the belief in it, would be established through participation in gay institutions.[58] For decades that participation took such forms as attending house parties, drag balls, bathhouses, or bars, buying physique magazines, and/or reading certain literature such as *The Well of Loneliness* or *Death in Venice*. More recently, opportunities for participation have proliferated and have become more and more public; they now include attending gay-themed and/or gay-authored Broadway productions and movies, joining any number of support groups, working in or utilizing any of thousands of service organizations, logging on to queer email groups, and attending demonstrations in Washington. Note that all of these acts constitute or imply some form of consumption; each one is imbricated in consumer culture.

All of this market activity naturally multiplies opportunities for identity-based consumption for gay men and lesbians. Of course, people engaged in same-sex sexual behavior have consumed commodities for as long as there have been commodities; what is new is the constitution and consolidation of a social identity in the marketplace. Advertising is one of the central agents of that constitution and consolidation. Indeed, gay and lesbian identity and community were effectively consolidated through the market; in the 1990s, market mechanisms became perhaps the most accessible and the most effective means of individual identity formation and of entrance into identity-group affiliation for many gay people. When consolidated this way, group identity can form the basis of a political movement for rights equal to those of other citizens; capitalism has, as it has had for centuries in the West, liberal and liberalizing effects. In other words, capitalism enables a political struggle for rights. More specifically, group-based activity in the marketplace is dependent on, and essential to, political organizing for legal rights and protections based in identity. That's what identity politics is. The same economic forces, however, or maybe capitalists in particular, tend to favor the displacement of that struggle back onto the market; this displacement accelerated in the 1980s as "the commodities on sale became the entire machinery of citizenship."[59] The corollary effect is that consumption becomes a form of political participation, perhaps supplanting other, more direct, models of participation. What are the consequences of defining an individual act of private consumption as a mode of political participation? In this book, I argue that identity-based marketing and consumption are intimately related to identity politics, and that, working together, they are inimical to progressive political change.

Chapter 1 looks at the explosion of discourse around the gay and lesbian niche market. Of course, self-avowed gay men and lesbians have been active workers and consumers for a long time, and even as early as the 1970s the media began to formulate the idea of a gay niche market. But in the 1990s, that idea became more elaborately formulated, and in a variety of venues. Along with noting the sheer proliferation of claims about gay and lesbian purchasing power, consumption habits, brand loyalty, and other market behaviors, this chapter analyzes the assumptions about gay and lesbian identity, as well as the marketplace, that are embedded in those claims. Most important, the assumption that politics can be practiced in the marketplace pervades discussions of the gay and lesbian niche market. In order to see how this assumption reshaped the gay and lesbian movement, Chapter 1 lays the groundwork for examining how the movement and the market interact. Each succeeding chapter takes up a particular form of interaction between market activity and movement activity.

Chapter 2 takes up the history of the lesbian and gay press in the United States, which has indeed served a crucial role in expanding the movement. But the gay and lesbian press has done more than disseminate movement information; it has also conveyed values through its editorial contents. At the same time, the gay and lesbian press has grown to national proportions; glossy national gay and lesbian magazines came into their own in the 1990s. Chapter 2 suggests that in the course of its growth, the gay and lesbian press has shared certain features with the movement. In particular, forgotten or hidden parts of the history of the press obscure the race and gender dynamics that brought the press to its "national" status, thus mirroring dynamics at work in the movement. In addition to serving a national constituency, the white- and male-dominated gay press has contributed to the formation of a gay "nation," which means that this nation is more representative of certain interests in the community and less representative of others. This set of observations about the similarly unrepresentative press and movement—both of which nevertheless make explicit and implicit claims to represent the entire community—naturally raises the question of what the relationship is between gay and lesbian "nationality" and nationality in the United States.

In the history of the gay and lesbian press, as in the history of the mainstream press, advertising has had a key role. Chapter 3 takes up the question of how advertising to the gay and lesbian niche market has contributed to the idea of a gay nation and how that nation relates to the United States. Referring to the way that advertising has historically worked to assimilate immigrants into U.S. culture, this chapter examines the ways in which advertising to gay men and lesbians carries messages about assimilation. In short, this body of advertising frequently promises that consumption is a route to political enfranchisement as well as social acceptance; such a promise conflates consumption and citizenship in theory, while ignoring the fact that economic status determines what kind of access individuals have to the marketplace and the political arena.

Gay men and lesbians, like other social groups—whether identity-based or interest-based—have enacted the idea that consumption is a form of political participation by boycotting various products and services. With this form of market activity, as with the growth of both the press and advertising, the formation of a gay nation resonates with the formation of the United States. The colonial boycotts of British imports indicate that boycotts contribute to building national identity, and in this way they resonate with the boycott of Anita Bryant and Florida orange juice in 1977. Chapter 4 focuses on boycotts—the theory of economic democracy behind them—and on the gay and lesbian response to Anita Bryant as a pivotal moment at which the movement began to function on a national scale. Consideration of a more recent "economic campaign" against a Miller Beer distributor in Louisville exposes tensions between large national organizations and smaller local and grassroots organizing efforts in the late 1990s, a period when those national gay organizations clearly dominated the landscape of the movement in terms of resources and visibility.

Chapter 5 gives sustained attention to these tensions. It begins with the commonsense observation that because a social movement requires money in order to function at all, the movement itself is a site where politics and economics interact. How, then, does money affect the structure, the personnel, the tactics, and the objectives of the movement? This chapter explains a number of mechanisms for funding gay and lesbian nonprofit activity—the activity of advocacy organizations, in particular. This chapter argues that most of these mechanisms, in one way or another, promote a liberal political agenda; a white, male, middle-class leadership; and the growth of large national organizations. By contrast, the same mechanisms effectively diminish the resources available for smaller, local, grassroots, and/or politically off-center organizations. From corporate donations to individual donorship to "partnering" to foundation giving, the many ways in which the movement funds itself have a mainstreaming effect on the movement as a whole. Pride marches serve as a case in point and the so-called Millennium March provides an exemplary occasion for tracking the relationship between the movement and the market.

The concluding chapter offers a critique of identity politics as reinforcing the quest for individual rights and failing to address the systemic disadvantages faced by gay men and lesbians who are not economically privileged. Ultimately, then, I argue that gay identity politics, in collaboration with gay identity-based consumption, tends to underrepresent women, people of color, poor people, sick people, and very young and very old people. The movement, as configured around gay and lesbian identity and single-issue politics, fails to serve all our interests. Thus the book ends with a plea for rethinking identity as the basis for political organizing. Rather than arguing for the elimination of identity politics altogether, since it has, after all, effected significant social change, the book instead argues for political alliance, for a multi-issue, multiconstituency coalition focused on economic justice.

1

CAVEAT EMPTOR, OR BUYER BEWARE!

Even though the history of the gay and lesbian emancipation movement has been a fight for equal protection, the fair application of laws, public visibility, and the general public's acceptance of their moral legitimacy, as a group gay people are developing more than a political identity. They are in fact manifesting an economic and commercial identity as well as a cultural, philanthropic, and spiritual one.

—Grant Lukenbill, *Untold Millions*[1]

THE GAY AND LESBIAN NICHE MARKET OF THE 1990S

The 1990s was a banner decade for gay men and lesbians. Representation of gay men and lesbians on television, in newspapers and magazines, in courts and in legislatures, in the workplace, and in pride marches and other public forums, increased dramatically. In mainstream media, as well as in gay and lesbian media, gay men and lesbians appeared in greater numbers of public images, and in more elaborate images. Of all the representations circulating in the 1990s, perhaps none was more striking than the image of gay men and lesbians as the latest, the ultimate, the yet-untapped niche market. Descriptions of this market and its "explosion" proliferated; they were descriptions of an imagined body of consumers with gay and lesbian dollars ready to be spent in the pursuit of gay and lesbian lifestyles. As a Strubco ad proclaimed, "The

Gay & Lesbian Market Is Exploding!" (See Figure 1.1.) What kind of pictures did those descriptions paint of the gay or lesbian consumer, of the gay and lesbian community, of money itself? Who offered those descriptions, in what venues, and for what purposes? What were the unintended effects of describing "A Market That's Educated, Affluent, and Homosexual"?[2] Rather than providing another set of claims about this supposed niche market—rather than assessing the consuming habits of, the spending power of, or the quantity of dollars circulating among, gay men and lesbians—I will offer a qualitative analysis of the descriptions themselves, and of the effects of *their* circulation.

In the 1990s, economists, consultants, journalists, and advertisers began to debate at full throttle whether there really was a gay and lesbian niche. Prior to the 1990s, a small trickle of articles touting a gay market had appeared in the mainstream press, and they did indeed prefigure some of the major themes that would recur in the torrent of coverage in the nineties. Perhaps the earliest of these appeared in the *New York Times* in 1976, in a story about the efforts of the gay press to attract mainstream advertisers. Gay publisher Donald Embinder was quoted explaining that homophobia on the part of most advertisers inhibited investment in the gay and lesbian community, but simultaneously claiming that such advertisers could nonetheless be persuaded of the profit to be made in that community. A nearly lone voice in the wilderness at that point, Embinder inaugurated a claim that would become quite common in the 1990s; he said that bringing mainstream advertising dollars into the gay and lesbian economy would promote "the business of liberation."[3]

Another early story heralding a gay and lesbian market was printed in the *L.A. Times* in 1977; "S.F. Gays Carry Heavy Clout in Politics, Finance" claimed, "Unencumbered with the costs of raising families, homosexuals acquire property on a mass scale."[4] This early claim matches the later designation of gay couples as "DINKS"—consumers with Double Income and No Kids. The article also described gays as active consumers, quoting the editor of the gay newspaper *Bay Area Reporter* as saying that "'Gays and Orientals are buying up everything that isn't nailed down.'"[5] Implicit in these articles is the assumption that people shop on the basis of their identities, or on the basis of their inclusion in

The Gay & Lesbian Market Is Exploding!

Have you ever tried cardpack advertising?
Have you ever rented gay and lesbian lists?

If not, maybe now is the time. The gay market is growing exponentially. Hundreds of marketers are flocking to appealing demographics, sky-high response rates and cost-effective marketing methods.

STRUBCO's Community Cardpack and Sapphile mail three times per year to 150,000 households. Soon we will be introducing new regional decks in several cities across the country. Advertising rates begin at less than $1,000. Cardpack advertising is easy, incredibly inexpensive, and creates a measurable response.

STRUBCO's National Community Masterfile now totals over 500,000 names, virtually all gay men and lesbians. Rent as few as 3,000 names, just in your area, to test direct mail for your business. Rental rates begin at $75 per thousand names for a one-time use.

For further information, return this card or call directly to:

CARDPACK INFORMATION
   Charles Conard (212)242-1900
   Marge Barton   (212)666-6992

LIST RENTALS
   Charles Ching (212)242-1900
   Alec Bentley   (212)242-1900

Thanks very much. We will look forward to hearing from you.

Figure 1.1 "The Gay & Lesbian Market Is Exploding!"

an identifiable social group. Also implicit here is an equation between ethnic or racial identity on the one hand, and sexual orientation on the other, the two groups equally implicated in the tendency toward identity-based consumption. Finally, this article also displays the irrationality that characterizes a good deal of the discussion. Such irrationality took many forms in the 1990s; in this 1977 article, John Schmidt, a wealthy insurance broker and head of a gay businessmen's association, averred a groundless "'belief that gay businessmen are more successful than straights.'"[6] Note, too, that "gays" here refers to gay men, signaling the spectral place of lesbians, or women, in almost every discussion of a "gay" market.

Also in 1977, a gay market was invoked in San Francisco's *Bay Area Reporter.* An editorial by Paul Lorch announced that "Gays are literate, affluent, and 'au courant.'"[7] Calling gays the "last untapped minority market," Lorch asserted that consumers in this niche market "spend what they have or earn on the NOW," rather than saving for the future as their straight counterparts presumably did.[8] Using language and assumptions that would pervade the discussion of the gay market in the 1990s, Lorch also wrote, "Increasingly, Gay dollars are the target of anybody with anything to huckster. In conjunction with the ready cash of the Gay market is the loyalty of the Gay consumer to the Gay businessman."[9] Indeed, gay entrepreneurs, followed by more mainstream producers, did go on to identify and target a gay market in the 1990s, often on the assumption (or advice of gay marketing consultants) that, relative to straight consumers, gay consumers were unusually loyal both to gay concerns and to brand names. However, while such claims abounded in the 1990s, there has never been any statistical evidence for special loyalty on the part of gay and lesbian consumers.

Another example of pre-1990s discussion of the incipient niche market, *Newsweek*'s 1979 article "Where the Boys Are" describes gay resorts on the east and west coasts. In this article, which expressly names men as its subject, women do indeed make an appearance. Citing real estate values as a function of the development of such largely male-dominated resorts as Provincetown, Key West, Russian River, and The Pines, the article does, however, quote the owner of a women's bar.[10] Pam Genevrino, then-owner of Provincetown's Pied Piper, states that "Gays and straights are all here for the same reasons: to make a buck, improve our community, and enjoy life."[11] In so saying, Genevrino articulates the most common assumption running through all commentary on the gay niche market: patronage of gay-owned businesses, circulation of gay dollars, profit by gay entrepreneurs is tantamount to improvement in the quality of life for gay men and lesbians. In other words, the consumption of gay goods and services has the same effect that the social movement is trying to achieve through political means. Few people ever asked what it means to think of dollars, commodities, or services as having an identity; few ever questioned the assumption that identity-based subeconomies benefit all members of the identity group in question. Only in the 1990s did a critical opposition arise questioning the effects of using economic means to achieve political goals.

This small spate of news about the gay and lesbian market that came out in print in the late 1970s was short lived.[12] The 1980s brought, along with the Reagan-Bush administrations and AIDS, a nearly total silence on the topic. Following an article in the *New York Times Magazine* entitled "Tapping the Homosexual Market" in 1982, there was little, if any, mainstream coverage of a gay market; even in the gay media there was relatively little written on it.[13] In 1987, *American Demographics* (a mainstream advertising trade magazine) ventured into territory it would go on to feature prominently in the 1990s. In the first small attempt to push open a door shut by homophobia and sealed by AIDS-phobia, the magazine reported that "AIDS patients are a tiny fraction of America's gay population. Most gays are healthy, and many are affluent."[14] These "facts" were evidenced, according to the magazine's "Business Reports," by the experience of Neil Feinstein, who had been, to great success, operating nightclubs in Denver, Tampa, New York City, and Washington, D.C.[15] Clearly AIDS and the conservative administrations that refused to discuss it openly had had a dampening effect on the discussion of a gay market, so that there was a gap of several years between the late 1970s and the late 1980s in that discussion. In 1989, *American Demographics* would once again refer to a gay niche market, noting about the gay neighborhood in Houston, Texas, that "Marketers have not yet found Montrose."[16] But they would soon find Montrose and every other enclave of the newly targetable gay market. Within three years, *Marketing News* would proclaim that "Mainstream Marketers Decide the Time Is Right to Target Gays."[17]

Between 1991 and 1993, *American Demographics* was joined by the *Wall Street Journal,* the *New York Times, Advertising Age,* and other mainstream publications in featuring news of a gay niche market.[18] In 1993, *Advertising Age* could issue a "Special Report: Marketing to Gays and Lesbians," and in 1995, *American Demographics* could announce that the gay niche market was "Out of the Closet."[19] In 1994, The Center for Lesbian and Gay Studies at the City University of New York sponsored a conference called "Homo Economics" on "Market and Community in Lesbian and Gay Life." By 1995 Grant Lukenbill had published his book-length plea to mainstream marketers: *Untold Millions: Positioning Your Business for the Gay and Lesbian Consumer Revolution.* In 1996, the *Journal of Homosexuality* published a special issue, later released as a book called *Gays, Lesbians, and Consumer Behavior: Theory, Practice, and Research Issues in Marketing.*[20] Lesbian and gay business expos began cropping up in cities around the country; the first annual expo in New York City was produced in 1994. These expos were intended to publicize both gay and lesbian businesses and mainstream producers who targeted the gay market. They often had disappointing public attendance, but they were a clear indicator of the belief in the existence and growth potential of a gay and lesbian market. A number of newsletters put out by gay and lesbian professional associations echoed the hype, such as the headline of the online newsletter of the Gay and Lesbian Travel Industry that heralded the "Market of the Decade." Professional gay associations such as the National Lesbian and Gay Journalists Association, and business associations such as the Greater Boston Business Council proliferated, while gay and lesbian employee groups organized in workplaces.[21] Thus, throughout the 1990s, there was an explosion of discourse about the gay market published in the mainstream news media, the gay media, the advertising trade press, and scholarly journals.[22]

One gay market research firm, QuotientResearch, began publishing a monthly "Newsletter of Marketing to Gay Men & Lesbians" in December 1994 (see Figure 1.2). *Quotient* reported regularly on "Sponsorship

Figure 1.2 "Gay $ Gay Power . . . Tap It with *Quotient*"

Opportunities," on ad agencies "serving" gay audiences, on new advertisers in national gay magazines and gay media more generally, and on lesbian and gay business expos and conferences, and it featured such special stories as the macho "So, Just How Big Is the Gay Market, Really?"[23] Also established in 1994 was "America's gay business letter," *Victory!* A bimonthly newsletter dedicated to acknowledging "the success of gay and lesbian business entrepreneurs throughout the world, as a means to motivate and inspire tomorrow's business leaders," *Victory*'s regular columns included an index of gay-friendly stocks, advice on "Power Investing," and Per Larson's "Empowerment," which offered counsel on financial strategies.[24] These two publications take for granted a bullish gay market, but more than that, they associate "gay money" with political power for gay men and lesbians. These publications—along with *Clout! Business Report*—were not long-lived, but their existence speaks, once again, to a phenomenal burst of activity and discourse centered around the idea of a gay and lesbian market in the 1990s.[25]

This discourse exploded as a result of many factors, but perhaps the most significant was the market research conducted and distributed by a handful of gay marketing firms. Of these, Simmons Market Research Bureau and a small firm called Overlooked Opinions probably had the most widespread, as well as the most notoriously destructive, effects. Simmons' earlier surveys had less dramatic impact; then, in 1991, Overlooked Opinions announced that gay men had an average annual income of $42,889, while lesbians earned, on the average, $36,072.[26] These figures exceed average income figures for men and women in general, largely because they are based on a nonrandom sample; Overlooked Opinions' sample comes from periodical readers, as well as lists compiled at events and bookstores. In the mid-1990s, Overlooked Opinions reported that gay household annual incomes averaged $55,000 a year. Again, these numbers are inflated relative to the general population. They further claimed that gay men and lesbians earned $514 billion annually. As exposed in an important analytical piece in *Dollars and Sense,* these figures portray gay economic status very inaccurately, based as they are on a disproportionately white, affluent, male, and educated sample.[27] The exposé helped discredit Overlooked Opinions' survey, but not before the figure had been seized on by right-wing groups opposing antidiscrimination legislation—like proponents of Colorado's Amendment 2—arguing that such an affluent social group didn't need "special protections."[28] While some commentators on the gay market have subsequently dissociated themselves from this "research," many gay media entrepreneurs exploited Overlooked Opinions' figures in their appeals for corporate advertising.[29]

Another firm, Rivendell, also produced a great deal of market research with the purpose of winning advertising for gay papers, but it was a bit more careful to confine itself to claims about the readership of gay male publications rather than the whole gay community. Nevertheless, their ads can seem to represent all gay people as male, highly educated, and affluent, with consumption patterns that include unusually frequent travel, liquor and music purchases, and the like (see Figure 1.3). By contrast, a 1994 study produced by the Yankelovich firm produced figures for annual income that were significantly lower than Overlooked Opinions' figures, reflecting an average annual income for gay men of $21,500 ($1,000 *less* than men in the overall population) and $13,000 for lesbians (negligibly greater than women in the overall population).[30] Slowly, some marketers became more careful to qualify their claims about the gay market, relying more and more on the

GayMarketMuscle

Almost twice as likely to own a vacation home*

8 times more likely to own a computer notebook*

11.7 times more likely to be in a professional work position*

5 times more likely to engage in regular exercise at a private club*

5 times more likely to have taken 15 or more domestic flights in the last 12 months*

5.9 times more likely to own a home theater system*

Twice as likely to own individual stocks and 1 1/2 times as likely to be invested in mutual funds.

Than the Average American, according to the 1997 Simmons Market Research

Flex Your Ad Dollars

According to the Simmons Market Research Bureau's 1997 study, our 753,000 Gay and Lesbian readers earn an annual average income of $47,000: a 35 billion dollar market. Advertising in mainstream media is not enough to reach this loyal consumer group. Simmons discovered that 93.7% of our readers are likely to purchase a product or service advertised in our publications. For greater impact, target this dream market directly by advertising in the National Gay Newspaper Guild.

National Gay Newspaper Guild

Bay Area Reporter
Bay Windows
Dallas Voice
Frontiers
Gay & Lesbian Times
Houston Voice
New York Blade
Philadelphia Gay News
Southern Voice
Washington Blade
The Weekly News
Windy City Times

Rivendell Marketing Company • P.O. Box 518 • Westfield, NJ 07091-0518 • 908-232-2021 • Fax: 908-232-0521

Figure 1.3 "Gay Market Muscle"

Figure 1.4 "Target the Gay and Lesbian Market"

Yankelovich data, except when referring narrowly to readers of gay magazines, and then usually attaching asterisks or fine print that acknowledged Overlooked Opinions as the source. Facts were extremely hard to come by in this arena. Hype was not.

THE DREAM MARKET (see Figure 1.4)

The dissemination of bogus statistics about gay and lesbian (but mostly gay male) income and expenditure was swift and far and wide. Even after those statistics had been discredited, they were still quoted. And wherever they appeared, they were linked to claims about personal identity, political status, and the desires of the gay community as a whole. *American Demographics* printed a typical formulation in 1995: "The gay and lesbian market is an untapped gold mine. Because gays are highly educated and usually have no dependents, they have high levels of disposable income. And because these consumers are disenfranchised from mainstream society, they are open to overtures from marketers."[31] Leaving aside for a moment the demographic inaccuracies, note that disenfranchisement is thought here to make gays particularly vulnerable to target marketing. Exclusion from mainstream culture is cast in political terms, but the solution for it is offered in the market. Characteristically, consumer culture offers redress for the disenfranchisement of those who have traditionally been cast as "other" on the basis of their identities. Arising together with consumer culture early in the twentieth century, "The social perception was one in which people ameliorated the negative condition of social objectification through consumption—material objectification."[32] In other words, marketing asked people to view their own entrance into the marketplace as a corrective for past social alienation. This technique of redress, by definition, works as a program of acculturation and assimilation for consumers of various identities. Specifically, for gay men and lesbians, this would mean that gay identity-based consumption would ameliorate homophobia. With respect to the gay and lesbian niche, "The gay business class. . . . uses an open rhetoric of liberation and self-expression through commercial strength and consumer power. It offers a version of gay freedom which is based on the visibility and power of gay markets. . . . The positive, thrusting confidence of gay marketeers appears to make a refreshing change from the familiar reiteration of suffering, persecution and passive victimhood."[33] Through target marketing to gay men and lesbians, then, producers and advertisers could theoretically serve a dual purpose: generating sales and soothing the wounds of homophobia. Ultimately, however, even if gay men and lesbians were welcomed into the larger polity through consumption, the change would be a superficial one, for it would leave intact the channels of profit. Thus at least one feature of early consumer culture persisted in the 1990s: "The mass-produced goods of the marketplace were conceived of as providing an ideology of 'change' neutralized to the extent that it would be unable to effect significant alteration in the relationship between individuals and the corporate structure."[34]

Meanwhile, descriptions of the gay and lesbian market as a "gold mine" took up, and further spread, misrepresentations of the demographics of the gay and lesbian population. In 1992, *American Demographics* quoted the results of the Overlooked Opinions survey as fact: "Businesses have overlooked the fact that gay people often have more discretionary income. . . . They also travel more often simply because they have no children. Twenty percent of gay men go to a fitness club at least ten times a month, and 17 percent of gay women read a book every day."[35] No statistical analysis is necessary to recognize inaccuracy here: many gay men and lesbians do have children. And even among a sample of disproportionately better educated "gay women," it is very difficult to believe that 17 percent read at the rate of a book a day. The $514 billion figure was also bandied about at least as late as 1997.[36] If the results of the Overlooked Opinions survey supposedly revealed, however dubiously, that all gay men and lesbians combined earned that amount of money annually, an ad for the magazine *Victory!* mobilized the same figure in a different way: "In 1992 our community pumped $514 billion into the nation's economy." "Pumped in" is not a very specific phrase, but it is more likely to be interpreted as a statement about expenditure than as one of earnings. "Knowledge is power," claimed *Victory!* in the same ad, but of course, misinformation is of particular value. My point is that even though representations of the economic position of gay men and lesbians were shaped by political and market interests, rather than by the reality of that position, those representations could not avoid carrying ideological messages.[37]

IT'S NOT ABOUT POLITICS, IT'S ABOUT MONEY

A recurring claim in rhetorical constructions of a gay market attempted to eliminate the taint of politics from that market. Especially, but not exclusively, advertisers and marketers stressed the profit motive in their appeals to mainstream corporations and denied any connection between business practices and political tactics. For example, a senior vice president of marketing and communications for CBS in New York, George F. Schweitzer, asserted that "Buying ad space is not a political statement . . . it's an advertising strategy."[38] Likewise, gay marketer David Mulryan made a plug for the gay market by telling *Marketing News,* "Take away the politics and it's good sound marketing."[39] At its most basic, the claim that business and politics are distinct entities reflects a belief that the market is amoral. More particularly, it can reflect the hope that corporations would not let the image of militant oppositional gay and lesbian politics deflect dollars from gay entrepreneurial enterprises like list selling, marketing, and publishing.

A less cynical interpretation held that the visibility of gay men and lesbians in mainstream advertising, on the one hand, and mainstream ads in gay and lesbian media, on the other, signals or generates tolerance by, and inclusion in, mainstream culture. But that is an equation with a political basis, and thus is incompatible with a distinction between politics and business. It was not uncommon to find contradictory claims: the gay and lesbian niche market is not a matter of politics, *and* it's a matter of good politics, as in Grant Lukenbill's statement of the case. On the same page he writes, "American business does not have to become a forum where gay and lesbian political battles are fought," *and* "They will recognize that their profits are no longer immune from the issues surrounding gay and lesbian freedoms—both in the courtrooms and the marketplace."[40] Lukenbill's contradiction is apparently reconciled in his bottom line: "The business leaders who are taking a stand and establishing or reaffirming their commitment to gay and lesbian emancipation are taking a stand for their own economic prosperity as well."[41] With his equation between profit and progressive political outcome, Lukenbill echoes the many voices that celebrate the possibilities for cooperation between the gay and lesbian niche market and the gay and lesbian movement.

IT'S ABOUT MONEY *AND* POLITICS

Plenty of people argued that gay and lesbian commerce *was* political. From this perspective, if the historical economic disregard for gay men and lesbians was governed by homophobia, then the new acknowledgment of a gay market demonstrated a new attitude, and the *Wall Street Journal* was right when it announced that "Overcoming a Deep-Rooted Reluctance, More Firms Advertise to Gay Community."[42] Again, opportunities for identity-based consumption for gay men and lesbians seemed, to many, to signal an invitation into mainstream culture, the turning of the tides of homophobia to enfranchisement. This interpretation of target marketing to gays allows that the market has moral agency. It also allows for the argument that homophobia is bad for business. Thus, profitable and ethical business practices would equally suggest targeting the gay market. As gay nightclub owner Neil Feinstein put it, "Prejudice hurts, but it also decreases competition."[43]

Furthering this logic, financially and morally sound business practices would themselves constitute political action. Targeting the gay market would advance the cause of political enfranchisement, as in the preamble to Gay Biz's "Pride Directory Online": "The businesses you see listed in these pages have done more than step forward for our rights, they have paid to be a part of this professionally run directory and solicit your business. The more successful these like-minded business people are, the more rapidly our right to choose same-sex partners will be secured."[44] There is no explanation of how the businesses have, in the past, stepped forward for gay and lesbian rights; there is, indeed, no logical connection between their stepping forward and their presence in the directory. The only logical connection is between paying to be part of the directory and showing up in the directory. Why is making that payment doing "more than" fighting for rights and how have the listed businesses done the latter? We don't know. The implication, not logically derivable here, is that by the very act of paying to be included in the directory, the businesses listed have advanced the political struggle for gay and lesbian rights. The directory promises that any business that has paid to be listed is "like-minded" with the reader of the directory, a promise that makes unwarranted assumptions about the businesses (presumably on the basis of their payment) and about the reader as well. Finally, the directory indicates that the future success of these businesses will forward the political cause for rights. Rights, like the right to list in this directory and the right to "choose" partners, are figured here as the automatic result of identity-based production and consumption. Business practice and political action are one; there is no mention of—perhaps no need of—political action outside of the commercial sphere.

By the same token, in discussions of the gay market (in the gay and straight media) in the 1990s, political activism had two ends: securing rights and generating consumer demand. The year 1993 was a key year for gay marketers, and for the conflation of political and economic tactics, not least because of the March on Washington. In an article entitled "Businesses Offering Products for Gays Are Thriving: Rise in Activism and Public Acceptance of Lifestyles Increases Demand," the *Wall Street Journal* reported that "With the gay rights march in Washington this weekend, the market is brisker than ever right now."[45] Cindy Cesnalis of the catalogue company Shocking Gray commented on the popularity of gay pride flags and pink-triangle and lambda jewelry, saying that "devices that stamp 'Queer $' on currency, and imitation military pins with gay-rights insignia are all on the rise . . . we're constantly re-ordering pride flags."[46] In buying merchandise designed to display "gay American" identity, in patronizing gay-owned businesses, in exercising options in the market, consumers joined forces with political activists.

In terms of realizing one's social or political vision, socially responsible shopping is sometimes effective and almost always more successful than shopping without one's values in mind. I am not saying it is wrong or retrogressive to take consumption seriously as a tool for registering preferences in a field of limited choice. I am saying that I think it is worth speculating on the effects of reducing politics to symbolic and economic phenomena. One scholar theorizes that "Representative groups of homosexuals and lesbians . . . may publicly organize to attain further housing, insurance, medical, parenting, marital rights, etc., but they do so whilst the gay community's majority spends significant proportions of their income in pursuit of distinguishable gay and lesbian lifestyles in segregated specifically gay social and sexual territories."[47] In other words, private identity-based consumption might to some extent come to seem like an adequate substitute for public activism, among consumers who otherwise support progressive social change.

IT *IS* ABOUT POLITICS—*BAD* POLITICS

As should be clear by now, most of the media reports of gay wealth in the 1990s, like the claims for the viability of a gay niche market, were celebratory. They celebrated the idea that gay entrepreneurs and mainstream corporations alike could make money while making the gay community as a whole more politically powerful. What's not to celebrate?

The fact is that while a very few gay people might make money from this market, there is no reason to think that their financial profit amounts to either economic or political betterment for the whole identity group. Indeed, the optimistic claims and reports were not just misleading or inaccurate, they were also embedded in the logic of identity politics; they assumed or insisted that all gay people share political purposes. In a small independent 'zine, an alternative voice decried the commodification of queer things and queer people represented by the merchandise displayed by Rainbow Pride. The writer in *Rude Girl* emphasized both the falsity of, and the investment in, the *appearance* of unity.

> Not surprisingly, Rainbow Pride abounds in the new and wretched incarnations. A Pride jacket, pride soap (with optional "Lufa" sponge), pride T-shirts, flags, shorts, windsocks, headbands, hats, camera straps, towels, bathrobes ($139.95! Hubris!), suncatchers, necklaces, and a lamp which prizmatically projects a rainbow onto the wall. If the gay community ever held hopes of any real unifying symbolism or reverence with this Rainbow Flag, I believe they have blown it.[48]

As the exclamation points above suggest, the cost of enfranchisement, the property requirement, prices some consumers out of citizenship. In this manner, gay-identity marketers, in their assumption of group unity on the basis of sexuality, cover over class differences in the gay and lesbian community. From the oppositional point of view expressed in *Rude Girl,* the political aims symbolized by the Rainbow Flag are undermined by class difference and/or the indifference of marketers to those aims. On the one hand, a gay community with symbols of its own status as a nation (flags, military pins with gay rights insignia, currency) presents the appearance of unity. On the other hand, that appearance is conveyed in commodity form, so that its ownership is not equally available to poorer gay men and lesbians. As *Rude Girl* points out, enfranchisement in the commodified gay nation comes to look like enfranchisement in the United States: "for the queer shopper with even more disposable income at his disposal they [Rainbow Pride] offer what must truly be the centerpiece of the catalogue and indeed the centerpiece of the entire Gay Civil Rights movement: A Limited Edition

Franklin Mint Stonewall Commemorative Plate!"[49] This "centerpiece" is a Franklin Mint plate commemorating the symbolic birth of the gay rights movement. This item collapses gay and American identity into an object that stands for money, and it seems to imply a unity of gays and Americans. The unity implicit here, then, not only covers internal differences within either grouping, it also stands for pure assimilation: gay identity *is* American identity. In this way, the plate, itself a commodity that refers to money, offers full citizenship, or enfranchisement, to the consumer.

SAMENESS AND DIFFERENCE

Claims about the American identity of gay men and lesbians abound in the literature on the gay and lesbian market. It is as though the "explosion" of the market confronted gay men and lesbians all over again with a question that the social movement had already been dealing with for years: Are gay men and lesbians the same as or different from other Americans? And do we want to be the same as other Americans? Looking at the gay market in 1996, *New York Times* advertising columnist Stuart Elliott thought gays were "ambivalent about whether they want to stand out or fit in."[50] But some researchers would make bolder claims about gay men and lesbians, reporting that "lesbians and gay men are surprisingly settled and want to be portrayed as 'no different than anybody else.'"[51] The language and the logic are those of assimilation.

In 1987, in a description of the extent to which mainstream culture in the United States had absorbed gay style and gay iconography, critic Frank Rich wrote of the "homosexualization of straight culture" as "the most dramatic cultural assimilation of our time."[52] In the intervening decade, kitsch and direct-action politics (markers of distinctive "gay"ness) gave way to style magazines and the prioritization of struggles for same-sex marriage and inclusion in the military (markers of American identity). Ten years later, writing in *New York* magazine, Daniel Mendelsohn argued that that process had become inverted; by 1997, he saw the "heterosexualization of gay culture" as the most dramatic cultural assimilation of our time.[53] Mendelsohn further felt that commodification was closing the distance between straight and gay identities, to the extent that either identity was "basically a set of product choices."[54]

For gay men and lesbians in the United States, assimilation is not simply a process of absorption into straight culture, but also absorption into American identity, what I have been calling enfranchisement. Thus, the gay and lesbian niche marketers frequently portrayed gay men and lesbians as a social group with an assimilation drive, a social group whose consumption practices showed its members to be just like other Americans. In the formulation of marketers, national, even patriotic, sentiment united gay and lesbian Americans with straight Americans. For example, Lukenbill asserted that "It would be genuinely hard to find a more deeply passionate group of people more staunchly dedicated to the values of democracy and free enterprise than those within the gay and lesbian community in America today."[55] Lukenbill's goal is to neutralize the stigma of gay men and lesbians as countercultural and politically oppositional, and he achieves it by describing gay and lesbian passion as safely unsexual; gay and lesbian passion is not for sex, after all, but for all things related to American identity. Of course, under the sign of American national identity, democracy and free enterprise fit together, synonymously.

Participating in the transformation of gay men and lesbians into Americans, gay marketers Kahan and Mulryan compared gay and lesbian assimilation to the assimilation of ethnic immigrants into the American cultural mainstream:

> Just as second- and third-generation immigrants leave their neighborhoods to forge lives in mainstream America, research shows a shift of gay and lesbian households to suburbs like Royal Oak, Michigan, outside of Detroit, and the District of Columbia suburb of Takoma Park, Maryland. . . . [G]ay men and lesbian women are moving out of traditional gay "ghettos," as increasing tolerance, if not actual approval makes it easier for them to achieve the same American dream house that nongays prize.[56]

Nothing less than the American dream is at stake in the claim that gay men and lesbians share the aspirations of other Americans. In order to win advertising and enter into citizenship, gay men and lesbians had to persuade mainstream advertisers that they pursue happiness in the market, just as other Americans do. An article that sought to establish the viability of a gay and lesbian niche in a historically gay neighborhood in Houston, Texas, noted that as Montrose became more economically vital, it became less like a ghetto and, simultaneously, less distinctly gay: "Montrose is a much tamer place than it was a decade ago: bars now are more like social clubs, with less drinking and cruising, and the two bath houses are used primarily for physical fitness. There has been a significant drop in drug use among gays, and there is a new emphasis on healthy living and safe sex. Health-food stores are thriving, as are tanning and hairdressing salons. Gays are dressing less flamboyantly."[57]

Gay men in Montrose were choosing to dress in conformity with current straight fashion, according to this article, and they were also reported to have become more active in sports, as though the booming gay economy there was restoring masculinity to men, and as though commodification might remove the threat of gender instability from homosexuality. Perhaps most unthreateningly of all, homosexuality (in this rhetorical neighborhood) no longer posed a threat to the American family. Gay men were into sports, while lesbians all over the country were acting in greater accordance with the expectations of traditional femininity: "The market is also increasing as homosexual Americans, especially lesbian women, openly develop families, conceive or adopt children, and build quasi-traditional households as they stake their claim to legitimacy on the American scene."[58] Crucially, legitimacy is claimed through reproduction of "quasi-traditional" social forms, which is to say, sexual reproduction. Behind claims that in "gay and lesbian America, family is not dead" lie assumptions about the way that identity—here, both "gay" and "American"—is established in the market.[59] If gender and sexuality could offer gay men and lesbians a point of identification with the mass of Americans, instead of a point of difference from them, the market could facilitate this opportunity for assimilation. What is at stake in these equations is "the extraordinary American system of making and representing but also what amounts to the systematic making of Americans: the notion of 'The American' as an artifact and product, something mass-produced and reproduced."[60]

By presenting gay men and lesbians as Americans, Grant Lukenbill sought to assure potential advertisers that "Americans of homosexual orientation feel all the same emotions about life, God, and country as Americans of heterosexual orientation."[61]

Indeed, Lukenbill describes the history of the gay and lesbian movement in fairly monolithic terms, so that its heightened profile in the 1990s will not undermine the appeal to mainstream corporations to advertise to a gay and lesbian market. In rather confusing language, Lukenbill equates the foundations of capitalism with the foundations of the movement: "it is the very same elements crucial to the survival of free enterprise that also make up the self-evidently held truths, morals, and building blocks of the contemporary equal rights movement among gay and lesbian Americans."[62] Certainly, the movement's civil rights orientation goes back as far as its origins. But Lukenbill revises sexual liberation and rejection of gender roles out of the history of the movement. Lukenbill's representation of the movement is correct but incomplete. What he leaves out of his equation—inequalities that limit access to the fruits of free enterprise—are the same problems under-addressed in a gay and lesbian movement that focuses preponderantly on the expansion of individual rights and legitimation by mainstream culture.

In general, identity-based consumption shares with identity politics the tendency to foreground one identity feature while relegating other identity features to the background. Politics and consumption based in gay and lesbian identity make sexual identity salient, often ignoring the fact that gender, race, and class determine the ability to choose freely in the market. With respect to gender, marketers had to acknowledge that women, as a group, are in a different economic position from men, as a group.[63] Of course, women were quite frequently ignored, and the "gay" in gay market quite often exclusively referred to men, simply because men were more likely to spend more money. Those few marketers truly interested in reaching lesbians were advised to use distinct marketing techniques. For example, a session entitled "Fags are from Fire Island, Dykes are from Maine" at a 1997 gay and lesbian business expo drew attention to gender difference, but this was an exception.[64]

Racial identity was also ignored when the market played on sexual identification. Although racial difference, like gender difference, plays a determining role in the availability of market choices, race was not an explicit theme in many discussions of the gay market in the 1990s. But serious charges had been leveled against the gay market in the 1980s, if the definition of market includes such things as employment opportunity. A resource guide for gay and lesbian people of color reported that "there is not, to the best of our knowledge, a single Gay/Lesbian community in the United States where people of color are employed to any significant degree—certainly not in numbers approaching their portion of the population."[65] The author, Michael Smith, reported that he had heard people of color call the gay and lesbian community a "satellite" of the white community, in which "jobs are almost never advertised; they are simply passed among White people."[66] Besides Smith's, numerous charges of racism in the lesbian and lesbian-feminist communities were published in the 1980s by lesbians of color.[67] While the "Old Boy network" to which Smith referred shifted in subsequent years in such a way as to open employment opportunities to more people of color—and while the sheer number of such positions increased greatly—there was still an acknowledged "glass ceiling" for people of color in gay and lesbian organizations in the late 1990s.[68]

In 1983, Smith also charged gay and lesbian commercial ventures with racist discrimination, writing "Today in almost every Gay/Lesbian community in the United States there are public places where people of color routinely face discrimination when trying to enter."[69] Detailing a number of techniques for denying people of color admission into gay bars, Smith's resource guide advised gay men and lesbians of color of the ways in which white bar owners attempted to circumvent legal prohibitions against discrimination, which included "going private."[70] Individual rights and a free market might liberate privileged gay men and lesbians, but racial and gender difference and oppression could stand directly in the way of the equal enjoyment of rights and equal access to market pleasures. As Nicola Field writes, "This is the quandary of gay romanticism and the contradiction of seeking social change without changing the class system. You are special; you are the same. . . . You need to form a self-reliant community; you want to be incorporated into the mainstream. You need to separate, you need to integrate. . . . You want massive social change but you don't want to tamper with the class system. You want gay liberation but you don't want to look at the causes of gay oppression."[71]

THE COLOR OF MONEY

Another set of assumptions deeply embedded in discussions of a gay and lesbian niche market has to do with the idea that identity adheres to money. Each mention of "gay dollars," "dyke dollars," or "pink dollars" expresses a belief that money can manifest gay identity.[72] This belief has a long history, and it is not confined to gay identity; identity has been thought to adhere to money before, to transform it into black dollars, Jewish dollars, white dollars. In each of these cases, the idea was that the possessor of money communicates his or her identity to money, so that a dyke dollar would begin life as a dollar possessed by a dyke. More important, that identity then circulates with the money, so that dyke dollars would be dollars spent by a dyke and they would maintain dyke identity after leaving her possession. The idea that identity circulates along with the money spent by a person of a given identity is perfectly demonstrated by the rubber stamp "QUEER $$$," which is designed to be stamped onto bills. The reproducible sign dramatizes the belief that identity attaches to money.

This superstition entails several expectations for gay men and lesbians in particular. For one thing, it presumes that gay and lesbian visibility would be increased by the circulation of visibly queer money. Presumably, nonqueer people seeing and touching the bills would know that a queer person stamped those bills and would therefore have to acknowledge that queer people exist. That same nonqueer money-handler would know that a queer person had *touched* those bills; therefore, the queer and the nonqueer money-handler would have theoretically touched through the medium of the money. These confrontations between the queer and the nonqueer are only imaginable if identity adheres to money.

At various points of circulation—the moments of transaction that precede and follow the relatively static phase of possession—identity could attach to money. Theoretically, money comes into one's possession as some form of income, then it is possessed, and then it is spent. Theoretically, any or all of these phases could render money gay or lesbian, and any gay or lesbian consumer transacting with a gay or lesbian vendor is exchanging gay or lesbian money. But in every claim that a consumer is helping the gay and lesbian community by making purchases from a gay or lesbian vendor, the identity of money is shown to be unstable. The assumption behind such claims is that the existence of gay or lesbian money is good—good for the whole community—and further, that the more gay or lesbian money and expenditures there are, the better for the community. On a practical level, claims that a consumer's purchase will benefit the community are often supported by the promise of material benefit: the vendor will make financial contributions to the community. But the problem with identity money here is exactly the same problem that attends identity politics. The consumer's idea of community—and benefit to it—might not be the same as the vendor's idea of benefit to the community.

Identity politics tends to preserve and promote the myth that identity adheres to money. Like other appeals for identity-based consumption, "Buy Black" campaigns have rhetorically associated African American identity with money, founded as they are on the belief that African Americans as a group will benefit from patronization of businesses owned by people of African American identity. Within the assumed circuit, an African American consumer exchanges his or her dollars for goods or services of an African American producer, or even distributor, and in so doing the consumer affixes an identity to the money transacted. Although a transaction should normally neutralize the social meaning of money, reducing it to an abstract quantity, this identity-based transaction turns dollars into black dollars. The idea is that the producer or distributor will recycle these identity-etched dollars back into "the community," thus improving conditions for everyone. This cluster of assumptions has appeared behind a range of political platforms, from those of Jack Kemp to Jesse Jackson to the claim that African Americans remain stuck in the underclass because, and to the extent that, black dollars circulate less than other identity dollars.[73] Indeed, subscription to this myth may have helped swell the ranks of the African American middle class, but it has not effected a structural change in the forces that reproduce and aggravate economic inequality, the same forces that systematically disadvantage African Americans in the market.

By the same token, it is unclear why more gay and lesbian dollars exchanged with more gay and lesbian vendors is better for the whole community—even if all of its members agreed on what "better" means—when it is clearly gay and lesbian entrepreneurs who get richer.[74] While more gay and lesbian dollars spent may translate into some proportion of sorely needed contributions to gay or lesbian nonprofit organizations, a much greater proportion usually goes to the vendor's income. The popular, if unconscious, belief in a gay nation also contributes to the widespread belief that increased circulation of gay dollars guarantees a better life for all gay men and lesbians. Along with the idea of a nation goes both the fantasy of a separate economy and the fantasy of a nation as a place within which capital is bounded.[75] However, capital does not stay inside the boundaries of identity-based communities.[76] Neither does it stay inside of national boundaries. Like mercury to mercury, capital tends to go to capitalists, wherever they are, sloughing off the traces of any identity it might temporarily appeared to have borne. This feature of money is mystified by campaigns to buy black or gay; even the injunction to buy American goods is hard to obey, as multinationals and free-trade policies unite materials and labor from multiple nations in a single commodity. You can rubber stamp your bills but you never do see that money again.

Exchanges of capital, far from preserving and communicating identity, actually launder the social meanings out of money. Money, by definition, is an abstraction of social value. It functions as a standard equivalent, bringing values of very different kinds of goods and services into meaningful relation to each other. Does one really know anything about one's money other than how much of it one has, how great are one's income, debts, expenditures, and expectations?

In the opening moments of the 1990s, in a *Newsweek* article predicting "The Future of Gay America," historian Martin Duberman spoke of the social and cultural condition of gay men and lesbians: "You have to minimize your differentness from the mainstream in order to win acceptance. But in fact the whole value of the subculture is in its difference."[77] Without intending to refer to it, Duberman perfectly characterized the central paradox presented by the gay and lesbian niche market. While gay men and lesbians debated the cultural, political, and economic value of claiming distinct gay or lesbian identity as against assimilation into straight American identity, the marketers invested in the gay and lesbian niche discovered that sameness and difference amount to the same thing: profit. Thomas Frank analyzes the cultural shift that transformed rebellion, dissent, diversity, and constant change into slogans and commodities in the 1990s, and that also transformed those same values into principles of business. Advanced capitalism accelerated the process by which initially countercultural forms were appropriated until counterculture itself became the prime commodity. For example, women consumers have been targeted through appeals to their femininity as well as appeals to their liberation from the strictures of femininity, but this scenario reduces women's liberation to a market function and thus defuses its political import. In the same way, when gay men and lesbians were targeted as consumers, difference in sexual orientation became not only marketable, but also less different. This is how gay and lesbian "counterculture" became "capitalist orthodoxy, its hunger for transgression upon transgression now perfectly suited to an economic-cultural regime that runs of ever-faster cyclings of the new."[78] Identity politics and identity-based consumption hinge on both sameness (imagined within an identity group, as in "unity") and difference (from the majority culture, though "the new," however deviant originally, itself comes to define majority culture more and more quickly). Because market culture increasingly reduces the distance between sameness and difference, identity politics increasingly serves capital. Identity politics has been a powerful and productive tool for changing culture and law throughout the twentieth century, but its co-optation and commodification will ultimately undermine its transformative possibilities.

"I'M GOING TO DISNEYLAND!"

The recurring themes and issues in all the talk about the gay and lesbian niche market in the 1990s were dramatized in a television show watched by an estimated 43 million viewers. The *Ellen* "Coming-Out Episode," broadcast on April 30, 1997, set its heroine's coming-out in economic metaphors and expressions, as well as locating it, literally, in a market. This historic sitcom broached new territory on prime-time TV by having the protagonist come out as a lesbian; not incidentally, it did so by reproducing a number of the assumptions about identity, sexuality, and consumption that had circulated in the discourse of the gay and lesbian niche market throughout the decade.

The show opens with Ellen's date with an old male friend, at the end of which Ellen rebuffs his romantic overtures and leaves his hotel room. Within minutes of being "read" as a lesbian by his female colleague, however, Ellen rushes back to her date's room, desperate to prove her heterosexuality. As she reenters his room, she pursues him physically and verbally. "Show me the money" are her words, which simultaneously constitute a plea for a disclosure of body parts and of sexuality, and (especially) for a confirmation of her heterosexuality. But the deal is never consummated; Ellen's heterosexuality is left unconfirmed, and no "money" is shown or exchanged. Ellen is left to negotiate her sexuality on her own.

Later that night, at the very moment of coming to gay consciousness, Ellen dreams of making a trip to the grocery store. The store is the precise site of Ellen's psychic reassessment of her sexual identity. In the dream, all the values at the store are sexual ones, the monetary values of the commodities reassessed in terms of lesbian identity. "How much are those melons?" asks one woman of fruit another holds in front of her chest. In the figure of the melons, the lesbian body is merged with the commodity; the joke is, they really *are* melons and thus revise the usually denigrating reference to women's breasts. A moment later, the express check-out counter opens to consumers with "10 lesbians or less." In this distortion of familiar check-out terms, a direct correspondence is made between lesbian and commodity. And the conflation continues. As her groceries are rung up, Ellen mishears the total she must pay, thinking she owes "A lesbian twenty-nine," as though she must tender lesbians to the cashier. Not only does money have identity in this dreamscape, commodities too have identity, taken on through possession by a gay owner, so that Ellen's automobile becomes "your gay car."

After her dream-assisted sexual awakening, in fact, on her next outing, Ellen and her friends patronize a lesbian coffeehouse. In each of these moments, sexual identity is a function of market activity.

At one point, the show refers outside of itself, to its host network and sponsor. After Ellen comes out in therapy, her therapist asks, "What are you going to do now?" Ellen's response is automatic: "I'm going to Disneyland!" The irony is that Ellen is already in Disneyland. For one, she emerges into gay consciousness and identity through commodity consumption in a world in which Disney stands as the premiere symbol of commodification. Yet on another, more literal, level, Ellen—the character, if not the actor—owes her very life to her broadcast by ABC, which is owned by Disney. For the coming-out episode, *Ellen* was mostly sponsored by ads for Disney movies. Clearly, Disney stepped in to subsidize the show following a great deal of controversy about its sponsorship in the preceding weeks. The right-wing American Family Association had launched a campaign urging people to lobby Disney not to air the show and scheduled sponsors not to buy time during it. In opposition, gay men, lesbians, and their allies had organized support for Disney in its decision to broadcast. Chrysler pulled its ad and opened a phone line for viewers to register their opinion about its withdrawal. (General Motors and Johnson & Johnson were also on the original roster of advertisers.) For days and weeks afterward, viewers debated whether the Volkswagen spot that ran during the show, in which two young men drive around in a car, picking up and then later discarding a chair, was "gay vague"—meaning open to a gay interpretation—or not. In other words, the stakes seemed to be very high as Ellen's lesbianism was represented on television—visibility versus corporate censorship. Yet on the gay-friendly side, while many called the relevant corporations and encouraged their friends to do so as well, some dissented; one individual registered his observation of the great differences "both in scale and in social significance, between the injustices borne by disenfranchised people and the injustices borne by the star of a sitcom who works for a multi-national, blue-chip, Dow Jones conglomerate who would sell queer Pocahontas dolls in the furthest reaches of the globe if it could secure profit margins tomorrow."[79] Wondering if this was what gay and lesbian politics had come to, this observer recapitulated the claims and counterclaims about the gay and lesbian niche market that ran through the 1990s.

The connections between that market and the gay and lesbian political movement are embodied in one particular character on *Ellen*. Susan, the object of Ellen's affection, has been in a same-sex relationship for nine years and stands as the authentic lesbian in this episode. Playing on the stereotype of gays as recruiting straights, Susan jokes that Ellen's denial of her lesbianism will have to be reported as the failure of Susan's recruitment effort. "I'll have to call headquarters and tell them I lost you," quips Susan. Here, Susan implies that she is aligned with some political movement offstage, perhaps the movement represented in the commercial break—Human Rights Campaign sponsored an ad about employment discrimination that aired during Ellen's coming-out episode. In any case, Susan's membership in the gay movement is implicit, but her prize from headquarters, when she does finally make the recruit, is quite material—it is a toaster oven. At the broadest level, everyone is invested in Ellen's sexuality—even her friends attempt to cash in on it by betting on it. Ellen's entrance into gay identity is thus measured by the commerce that enables it. The representation of Ellen's sexuality stands at the intersection between a gay and lesbian movement that has prized affirmation along with civil rights, and a community whose very visibility was, in the 1990s, a function of its status as a niche market. The movement implied but not seen on *Ellen* is a large bureaucracy recruiting consumers for the cause, and in this way it is not so different, after all, from so many American institutions. Of this, viewers gay and straight could rest assured.

2

THE GAY AND
LESBIAN PRESS
AND THE "BUSINESS
OF LIBERATION"

Presents the full range of lesbian and gay life.

—Ad for *OUT* magazine quoted from *USA Today*

A PARTIAL HISTORY OF THE
GAY AND LESBIAN PRESS

Perhaps more than any other institution, the gay and lesbian press has been a key site of intersection between the gay and lesbian political movement and the lesbian and gay niche market. The history of that press recapitulates the history of both the movement and the market, but more important, the gay and lesbian press embodies the complex relationship *between* the movement and the market. Hence, in the history and structure of the gay press, the relationship between the movement and the market comes to life. At least as early as the 1950s, gay leaders, recognizing that "effective internal communication is essential for an organization to articulate its ideology, develop a political consciousness among its members, increase its size, and sustain itself, . . . established that producing publications would be a central element in their strategy for social change."[1] From the news-letters of early "homophile" organizations, a thriving gay and lesbian press evolved.[2] This press has acted as an organ of information distribution for the movement and for marketers large and small. Moreover, the gay and lesbian press has played a pivotal role in making gay men and lesbians think of themselves as gay, and as members of a gay community. Most important for my analysis, the press has acted as the prime mechanism by which the community, the movement that represents it, and the corresponding niche market have attained national proportions.

The gay and lesbian press began to emerge in the late 1940s and 1950s, onto a cultural and legal landscape in which the Comstock Laws still loomed large. Established in 1863, these laws prohibited distribution of information about contraception and abortion, as well as sexually oriented materials; they held sway for almost a century, significantly controlling printed materials related to homosexuality. In 1957, Allen Ginsberg's *Howl*, first censored on grounds of obscenity, defeated those charges in the Supreme Court. A year later, a publication of one of the homophile organizations, *ONE*, ultimately defeated obscenity charges after a four-year-long legal battle in the Supreme Court.[3] Both of these decisions helped to roll back the state's legal jurisdiction over the distribution of printed materials that were sexually explicit, and in particular, had homosexual content. Although it would be most obvious to begin a history of the gay and lesbian press with the appearance of gay and lesbian publications, I think it is very important to begin this history before their appearance with the observation that censorship accounted for the almost complete lack of printed material generated *by* gay men and lesbians until the 1950s.[4]

As one mechanism of control relaxed, however, another began to exercise over the gay press the influence it was already exercising over mainstream media. That is, the market began slowly to replace the state as the arbiter of what kinds of homosexual content could be distributed through what channels. In the same year that *ONE* took the U.S. Postal Service to court on appeal, the first known advertisement aimed at gay men appeared in its pages. The very issue—October 1954—that had provoked obscenity charges from the Postal Service for its editorial content also contained an ad for intimate apparel for men.[5] Displaying festive intimate apparel—available with or without rhinestones—this ad did not explicitly address its readers as gay, but it appeared in one of the few homophile publications of the time. There was already a market for physique magazines and for pornography, but with the Win-Mor ad, a gay market was hailed through a political/cultural outlet. Since then, the market has expanded, meaning that the numbers of consumers willing and able to consume on the basis of their social identity as homosexuals has grown, and also that the targeting of gay men and lesbians by producers of every stripe has dramatically increased. Again, while these quantities increased over the course of four decades, their growth in the 1990s was remarkable. At the most basic level, the fact that the market shapes the gay and lesbian press simply reflects the fact that publishing and distributing require money. Immediately, therefore, my analysis confirms the commonsense observation that people with money have made the decisions that have determined the course of the gay and lesbian press. But I go beyond this observation in discussing the way that the course of the gay and lesbian press has, in turn, paralleled the course of the movement.

Because economic factors play such a large role in determining the emergence of the gay and lesbian press, and because that press has had such an intimate relationship with the movement, the same economic factors have significantly affected the emergence of the movement. When the press has enlarged the audience for the movement, it has concurrently swelled the ranks of its activists; in other words, the growth of a consumer market and the increase in potential activists are simultaneous. Other market-based institutions have affected the movement, but the press has been central to its development. The press grew slowly and fitfully, but by the 1990s the gay and lesbian press in the United States had arguably achieved a national scope. This chapter briefly chronicles the gay and lesbian press over the years, in order to bring to light certain hidden or forgotten traces of the divisive effects of economic pressure on that press. I argue that as the gay and lesbian press became "national," it reproduced those effects on an ever-larger scale. Ultimately, the problem is that the divisions—of class, race, and gender—that have influenced the development of the press have also pervaded the movement, partially on account of the close relationship between the press and the movement.

ONE PRESS?

On the one hand, the gay and lesbian press helped create a sense of gay identity and community for its readers; on the other hand, its operation from the 1950s onward suggests that gay and lesbian publications were themselves created by individuals who had a sense of both gay identity and community. This was a circular process that would continue as the publications proliferated and their audiences grew in size. A preeminent historian of the gay and lesbian press, Rodger Streitmatter, points to the function of the press as unifying gay men and lesbians. Over the course of decades, as distribution has grown in numbers, the reach of the press has spread geographically, and gay and lesbian periodicals "have linked the drag queens and 'dykes on bikes' at the head of the gay pride parades with the lonely and frightened individuals still deeply hidden in the closet. The publications have connected lesbians with gay men, as well as those of us who grew up in tiny towns such as Princeville, Illinois, with those from the gay meccas."[6] Certainly, the gay and lesbian press has promoted connection and community formation, but as Streitmatter also notes, the gay and lesbian press has not equally linked all gay men and lesbians in unified readership.[7]

There is no simple formula available: in addition to promoting community, the gay and lesbian press has promoted divisions. For example, race is, with shockingly few exceptions, not addressed as a theme in issue after issue of periodical after periodical of the white-run gay press. I would speculate that this absence is an effect of the personnel of the gay press. Among producers of gay-themed publications, white people have dominated; perhaps their identity explains the tendency to neglect race as a primary marker of difference among gay men and lesbians. Perhaps white producers of the gay and lesbian press have intentionally avoided airing differences or "dirty laundry" within the community. In any case, white writers and publishers appear able to ignore race—racial identity, the effects of racism, and racial difference—

more easily than people of color can. Thus white control of the gay and lesbian press is illustrated in the featured contents of the press, which in turn contributes to racial division in the readership. The gay and lesbian press thereby reproduces an ideology of white dominance. Exceptions have been found in expressly leftist and progressive journals, which were, and are, relatively few and dubiously viable, particularly in the 1980s and 1990s. Moreover, the 1990s have seen a rise in race niches within the gay press, so that there are now publications produced by, and targeted to, African American gay men and lesbians, Latino/a gay men and lesbians, and Asian gay men and lesbians.[8]

The position of women in the gay press is more complicated. Given a bit more lip service than people of color, women have not, in fact, worked in significant numbers on the staffs of most gay periodicals, have not been the main subjects of reportage, editorializing, or advertising, and have not read male-run periodicals in nearly the same numbers as men. The *Advocate,* for example, which will clearly have to stand as the organ of record (because of its longevity and its circulation), has consistently failed to achieve gender parity in its readership.[9] The numbers have never even been close; for most of its run, the readership of the *Advocate* has been at least 90 percent male.[10] Again, certain periodicals must be excepted; for example, *Gay Community News* has consistently placed women in significant staff positions, has reported on women's issues, and has reached many women.[11] But by and large, women—with drastically fewer resources at their command than men—have turned to a nearly autonomous, and expressly feminist network of periodical publishing created, sustained, and read by women. While the majority of women's publications have been printed by white women, these enterprises have, more often than men's, tried to engage with issues of race. Though invitations to women of color to write, guest edit, and read hardly demonstrates equal access to these publications, the publications themselves present a greater racial diversity in their contents than do most gay men's publications, by and large. Expressly feminist and lesbian-feminist print media have been, as far as it is possible to tell, almost completely unread by men.[12]

In the pages that follow, I reproduce a very brief history of the lesbian and gay press in the United States in order to uncover hidden and forgotten parts of that history, as well as to provide a context for analyzing the implications of the commercialization and national scope of the gay and lesbian press.[13] A partial but inclusive history and an analysis of the specific ways in which the press has interacted with the movement can shed light on the current configuration and politics of the movement. This is not, however, an exhaustive history of the gay and lesbian press; in particular, I focus on exclusions from the dominant male press rather than providing an alternative account of the lesbian press or of publications by and for gay and lesbian people of color. While this strategy may risk replicating the exclusions I mean to critique, the critique itself requires a focus on the racial and gender politics of the gay male press. Furthermore, I believe it is the white-dominated gay male press that has effectively constructed images of a national gay community, and it is that press that is most intimately related to correspondingly dominant strains in the political movement.

The Continuing History of the Gay and Lesbian Press

According to Rodger Streitmatter, the first gay publication was a lesbian magazine of sorts. "Lisa Ben," a Los Angeles secretary who took as her pseudonym an anagram of "lesbian," hand typed, hand copied, and distributed to her friends a collection of stories and letters. Launched in 1947, *Vice Versa* clearly reached beyond Lisa Ben's circle of immediate friends; she asked people to pass it on to other "gay gals," and they seem to have done so. Ben's initial goal was to enhance her own social life, in particular to give her (and others) a way to meet people without going to the bars. For some time afterward, the lesbian and gay press would set itself against bar culture, asserting the moral superiority of the press over that culture. Whereas the former involves reading and writing and maintains the privacy of its patrons, bars involve bodies physically (and also appear more overtly sexual), while they sacrifice the privacy of patrons. This moral hierarchy not only speaks of a certain classed value of mental over physical activity, it also downplays the value of social and collective action. This attitude was hardly explicit in *Vice Versa,* but it was definitely central to the philosophy of *ONE,* the *Mattachine Review,* and the *Ladder*—the three periodicals that followed *Vice Versa* into print. These publications are credited with really opening the era of the gay and lesbian press, by virtue of their affiliation with homophile organizations.

First published in 1953 and 1955 respectively, the *Mattachine Review* and *ONE* are the two publications often deemed the first step in the emergence of a gay press.[14] Both were newsletters tied to homophile organizations, the Mattachine Society in San Francisco and ONE, Inc. in Los Angeles. From a contemporary point of view, those publications, like the organizations that produced them, were relatively accommodationist. The *Mattachine Review* in particular seemed to accept the characterization of homosexuals as sick and deviant, but it pleaded for acceptance nonetheless. Both publications mobilized experts—usually psychiatrists and social workers—to comment on how gays could be cured, how it was possible for homosexuals to hold steady jobs and perform well if they controlled at least some of their urges, and importantly, how homosexuals should be entitled to civil rights in spite of their affliction. These periodicals enjoined readers to observe convention and live "decently," in the hopes of proving that homosexuals could be productive members of society, individuals worthy of such rights. By the standards of the time, however, *ONE* may have been the more politically engaged, articulating the position that homosexuals were fully citizens and denouncing mistreatment of gays as a violation of citizens' rights. Critics have characterized the "pre-Stonewall" press coming out of those organizations as "apologetic," accommodationist, and assimilationist.[15] Hal Call, editor of the *Mattachine Review,* confirmed this assessment of early editorial strategy, saying, "To get along we had to go along. We had to stay in step with existing mores of society. We had to because we didn't have the strength of tissue paper to defend ourselves."[16] In other words, neither the Mattachine Society nor ONE was in a position to fight for a press that could safely flout existing mores. Their newsletters were funded almost entirely by the personal subsidy of editors, supplemented sometimes by the contributions of friends and members. In the 1950s, advertising was not a significant source of funding for the gay press; this left editorial control in the hands of the men who produced these publications.

In the 1950s, the Daughters of Bilitis, a homophile organization of and for women, introduced the *Ladder,* edited by Phyllis Lyon and Del Martin. The *Ladder* started out with an accommodationist approach like its brother publications, providing an outlet for women readers while initially advising them not to dress or act masculine or go to bars. Given a lesbian culture in which butch/femme roles were prevalent, this stance could very well have alienated potential readers. It is unclear whether the *Ladder*'s early philosophy says more about the internalized homophobia of its producers at the time, or whether it represented a kind of realpolitik, recognizing that only invisible lesbians were safe lesbians. In any case, while such publications betrayed various fears and a certain class bias, they reported on the activities of their respective organizations and, over time, on news of relevance to gay and lesbian people, whenever they could. (The *Ladder* changed its political stance over time and under the management of different editors.) At this point, of course, the financial limitations of these operations made it impossible for them to get news first hand, or even to check their sources.[17] However, these early publications offered a perspective different from the mainstream newspapers, whose coverage of gays was both slight and evinced a strong heterosexist bias.

In the 1950s, mainstream newspapers reported on homosexuals purged from the military and from the federal government, and on raids of bars, sometimes naming the people arrested. Portrayed as threats to everything from decency to children to national security, homosexuals (mostly male, mostly white) had been represented numerous times in the mainstream print media (the invisibility of gay people of color and lesbians was even more total in the mainstream press than it would become in the gay press). By the early 1960s, the mainstream press had noticed the gay press as a manifestation of an increasingly organized gay subculture.

In late 1963, a *New York Times* article entitled "Growth of Overt Homosexuality Provokes Wide Concern" reported, incidentally, on the state of the gay press.[18] With an aspect of mild horror, the *Times* claimed, "The homosexual has a range of gay periodicals that is a kind of distorted mirror image of the straight publishing world. Thus, from the Mattachine Society and other serious homophile organizations, the homosexual can get publications offering intellectual discussion of his problem."[19] That the homosexual was a "he," that he had a problem, and that his social relation to heterosexuality was one of "distortion" were unremarkable assumptions. What was news, to straight readers and to the majority of gay readers of the *Times,* was that "he" was beginning to produce and consume a specialized press. The article went on to describe "a wide range of magazines and papers designed to appeal to inverted sexual tastes" at the newsstand. But rather than elaborating on the publications of the homophile organizations, the *Times* pointed to "the so-called body-building publications presenting, under the guise of physical culture, photos of scantily clad, heavily-muscled men, and others peddling outright homosexual pornography in text and illustration."[20] Gay men in the mainstream news media were thus reduced to their sexuality, which was itself clearly designated as pathological. Notably, however, gay men in 1963 appeared to be building a cultural infrastructure, which was incipiently commercial; simultaneously, they displayed signs of social and political organizing.

Alongside and consistent with other burgeoning social movements and their publications—from civil rights to women's liberation to antiwar—the gay press adopted a more militant, confrontational attitude than it had previously had. According to some historians, this new attitude arose in the mid-1960s, while others locate the new "sexual liberationist" rejection of accommodationism as part of the "post-Stonewall" moment.[21] Publications such as *Vector, The Homosexual Citizen,* and *Drum*—which began publishing in the mid- to late 1960s—asserted that "Gay is good" and encouraged readers to fight for gay rights. Clark P. Polak, editor of *Drum,* lambasted those who sought tolerance as "Aunt Marys who have exchanged whatever vigorous defense of homosexual rights there may be for a hyper-conformist we-must-impress-the-straights-that-we-are-as-butch-as-they-are stance. It is a sell-out."[22]

Inevitably, a press renegotiating its position on assimilation would necessarily renegotiate its position on citizenship as well, and in the press of the 1960s, the first rumblings of an intention to fight for enfranchisement are audible. Whereas earlier publications had gone so far as to say that gays deserved the same rights as other citizens if they acted in conformity with heterosexual norms, *The Homosexual Citizen,* in its title alone, articulated an unconditional claim to full citizenship. One of its editors, Lilli Vincenz (ironically, an immigrant from Germany), commented on the title in the January 1966 issue: "These words must seem irreconcilable to the prejudiced. All we can say is that these people will be surprised—for patriotism and responsible participation in our American democracy are certainly not monopolized by white Anglo-Saxon Protestant heterosexuals."[23] Of course, as confrontational as it may have seemed at the time, this claim for rights is equally a claim for the patriotism, the Americanism, of gay men and lesbians.

In the 1960s, the gay press contributed to the formation of gay community by reporting on the events of the movement, but also by constructing an audience. Readers of gay publications recognized not only reportage of interest to themselves as gay people, but in-group language and references to in-group behaviors. Sociologically speaking, the construction of a subcultural group—and more important, of a group consciousness—depends on the generation of common symbols, vocabulary, and mores distinct from those of the majority culture. For example, younger members of the gay press moved away from the judgments of their predecessors and forged links between the gay bar culture and the readership of gay publications, frequently by utilizing slang related to gay bar activity and gay sex. If using slang in reporting even partially blurred the generic divide between the personal ads and the featured contents, this may have been one of the moves that helped open the door to advertising more broadly.

Gay subcultural vocabulary was one of the "symptoms" of the "Growth of Overt Homosexuality" reported in the 1963 *New York Times* article quoted above. The very emergence of the word "gay" as a self-designation by homosexuals seemed to reveal the existence of a linguistic code that was part and parcel of the construction of a gay community: "'Is he gay?' a homosexual might ask another of a mutual acquaintance. They would speak of a 'gay bar' or a 'gay party' and probably derive secret amusement from innocent employment of the word in its original meaning by 'straight'—that is, heterosexual—speakers."[24] The mainstream press, then, in its discovery of a gay press, simultaneously discovered the link between the gay press and an elaborate subcultural infrastructure based in gay identity. On the one hand, gay language, gay identity, and gay community in the 1960s were a function of growing gay commercial enterprises, such as the press and the bars. On the other hand, these commercial institutions and their patrons established their identities by claiming sameness with *and* difference from majority culture in the United States. Inevitably, the growth of an identity-based movement and market required a renegotiation of "American" identity.

Two years after the *New York Times* article on the gay press and gay lingo, a relatively early example of sympathetic sociological research sought to explain the phenomenon of subcultural code construction among gays. Interestingly, the explanation of gay identity begins with the example of dominant code construction, and with a reference to national identity: "United States is a symbolic universe. A person is born 'an American' and learns to differentiate himself or herself from other peoples, learning also the 'superiority' of Americanism. The world of Americanism is supported by various symbols, such as the flag and the national anthem."[25] For gay people in the United States, the first symbolic system in which they are trained is one of national belonging. U.S. national belonging depends on differentiation from non-Americans and a belief in the moral goodness of being American; the distinctive moral value of national identity is expressed symbolically, as by the flag and anthem. Language, of course, serves as another symbolic tool in the construction of national identity.[26] Likewise, belonging to the gay subculture (as it began to be elaborated *and* as gay and straight presses began to cover it in the 1960s), depended on differentiation through symbolic means, differentiation from the straight majority by language, both on the streets and in the press. (By the end of the 1970s, there was even a gay flag—the rainbow flag was developed in 1978—and there were constant references to popular songs as gay anthems—such as "I Am What I Am" and "I'm Coming Out.") At the same time, articulations of sameness to other Americans remained prevalent in the gay press and in a movement that increasingly conceived of itself as a civil rights movement intent on enfranchisement for gays.

In 1974, the sociologist of gay subculture was already aware of the tension between gay liberation and "de-assimilation" on the one hand,

and assimilation into the national body and "symbolic universe" on the other: "Gay persons in our society are born into this symbolic universe, and for many of them the American-Puritan tradition has been a crucial element in their socialization and identity formation. The transition to a gay community, identity, and world thus necessitates a partial change of the symbolic universe. The change remains partial because . . . gay people remain within the symbolic universe of the United States as a whole."[27] To the extent that the gay press began in the 1960s to incorporate the gay idiom, it rendered linguistically the conflict between assimilation and de-assimilation that would play out politically over the course of the next three decades. With prescience, the sociologist reduced that conflict to the following formula: "gay knowledge has two tasks: to teach the differentness of gay as well as its sameness."[28] In this way, the press not only produced a growing body of consumers for itself and a growing body of readers concerned with news of the movement, it also produced a printed embodiment of the political tensions within that movement.

The readership of the gay press grew in size, although it didn't grow very quickly; by 1965, combined readership for gay publications in the United States was probably about 7,000. At the same time, the press began to reach toward the bodies going to bars. Now often distributed free in bars, the gay press enacted a rapprochement with the bars. *Vector* would "acknowledge that the bars played a central role in the lives of many urban homosexuals and constituted the one site where large numbers of otherwise scattered, invisible gay men gathered. . . . *Vector* embraced the culture and celebrated its ability to equalize persons of diverse social strata. Indeed the magazine rightly identified gay bars as central to the growth of the movement."[29] Even as gay publications began to cross into bars, most bar goers did not find gay publications there; therefore bars retained a community-building function that print could not hope to match. According to one memory of the summer of 1972, "gay bars were not simply for cruising, but . . . they were community centers, public meeting places, town squares, clotheslines people could hang over to gossip, and bulletin boards. There were no bar rags then or local gay papers. The bar was where you found your information."[30] At the same time, following the establishment of the Oscar

Wilde Memorial Bookshop in New York in 1969, and with other gay bookstores and women's bookstores cropping up around the country, gay and lesbian publications could be bought by means other than subscription. Thus bookstores also served to distribute the new publications; like bars, bookstores served to distribute various other kinds of information as well.[31]

Like the gay press, gay bars have had contradictory effects, contributing to community formation while reinforcing divisions within the gay and lesbian community. While bars have been sites where collective action became not only thinkable, but necessary, it is very important to remember that gay bars have often discriminated on the basis of gender and race. On the one hand, bars produced collective resistance to repressive state actions, so that the Stonewall Rebellion of 1969 was an innovation on a well-rehearsed system of response to police raids. On the other hand, all gay bars in the 1960s were not equally accessible to all gay men and lesbians. Therefore, when the gay press embraced gay bar culture, it embraced a culture largely populated by white men, and a culture in which gender and race prejudice and discrimination often took place. For example, in 1977, eight people, represented by the National Lawyers Guild, won a judgment of sexual and racial discrimination against the Grand Central Bar & Restaurant in Washington, D.C., which had excluded women, blacks, and whites accompanying blacks. The *Lesbian Connection* reported that the decision was "the culmination of nearly 5 years of legal and political work by various gay groups and individuals against discriminatory practices in a number of Washington, D.C., gay bars."[32] There were also bars that served primarily gay and lesbian people of color, which points to a racially segregated bar culture among gay men and lesbians. Again, such segregation has been at work in the political movement as well, so that the larger movement organizations tend to be white dominated, while distinct organizations have, from the 1960s onward, been established by and served the interests of gay and lesbian people of color.

In the late 1960s and early 1970s, the kind of radical activism that turned the raid at the Stonewall Inn into a spontaneous and sustained street uprising was also expressed in various print forms. Much of the printed material that called people to meetings or enumerated radical political programs was ephemeral. Posted on street lamps or wheat-pasted onto billboards, a great deal of news and opinion was not formally published. However, there were several short-lived publications that voiced the now-legendary confrontational rage against bourgeois, mainstream society. Using many of the same techniques as contemporaneous social movements, radical gay men and lesbians expressed some of the strongest anti-assimilationist views in the history of the movement. These techniques included a proliferation of press outlets.

By 1975, there was already enough gay press activity to justify reviews of the state of that press. In a review in *Margins,* Louie Crew noted that while there was little to show on the national front, he could speak glowingly of the few papers and journals that did exist, praising the straightforward function of the press to help construct the reading audience as movement participants: "The Gay press is a vehicle for building and affirming the very Gay community that this society has actively tried to suppress and thwart."[33] This vehicle most often took the form of the bulletin: "Sizeable space is devoted . . . to Gay civil rights activities, meetings of various Gay professional organizations, events in the nonGay institutions that could have effects on Gay people as Gay people."[34] Citing the press as a "primary source of information," Crew also described the press as affirming diversity under the unifying sign of homosexuality. Placing a premium on inclusivity, Crew opined, "The Gay press functions to unite many of the Gays who read it; and the rich catholicity of the Gay press affirms the diversity of class, of education, of wealth, and of intelligence in the Gay community. . . . No matter how high or low, rich or poor, bright or stupid . . . in this society a queer is still a queer."[35] At that point, the *Advocate* and the *Gay News,* both papers with a decidedly male orientation, were the only papers Crew could point to with "national" significance—and the *Gay News* was published in England! Notice also that Crew's definition of diversity does not explicitly include racial or gender diversity.

In the 1970s, the gay press reflected "the shift of the gay movement toward a more mainstream, civil rights perspective," and by the middle of that decade, there was a thriving local gay press; many large cities—including Los Angeles, San Francisco, Chicago, Boston, Washington, Philadelphia, and Cleveland—had their own gay paper.[36] While the early gay papers were not conceived as strictly local in content, their extremely limited circulations make claims to a national standing dubious. The difference is that aspiring national publications attempt to cover news or offer commentary from all over the country (although they tend to offer largely urban, even coastal urban, material), while local papers tend to offer, and draw on, resources based in the urban center in which the paper is located as well as the surrounding state or region. What is important here is that the national publications address—and thus help constitute—a national readership, while the local papers address local and regional residents. Historically, however, local papers have grown much more steadily than attempts at national publications. Local gay publications have always been much better able than national ones to give accurate information about when and where events would take place, they have been better able to offer local coverage, and they have enjoyed a steadier stream of local advertisers. Mostly, advertisers in this local press are gay businesses. The local gay press, then, no less than the national press, simultaneously addresses a readership and a market. But the national press, by definition, has a special role in defining the gay readership as a national body, as well as a national niche market.

By the late 1970s, the range of voices had diminished, and while radical activism was still featured in the gay press, the central focus shifted toward the legislative and judicial arenas, and away from the bars and the streets. Perhaps the best example of this is the reporting on the organizing in response to Anita Bryant's homophobic crusade in 1977. The whole affair followed from the passage of an antidiscrimination ordinance in Miami, and gay media coverage focused heavily on the fundraising and organizing methods of a few prominent leaders, the visits to Miami of certain celebrities, and the popular vote that revoked the ordinance. By way of popular activism, the gay press was indeed preoccupied with one kind of action more than any other, and that was boycotting. In other words, popular activism was being redefined as market activity. A new professionalism in gay journalism, more money, and changes in technology paralleled the application of professional political methods, as the Anita Bryant case also makes clear. (See Chapter 5 for an in-depth treatment of the debate over boycotting Anita Bryant and Florida orange juice.) The new professionalism was also demonstrated, among other ways, in the formation of the Gay Press Association in 1981; eighty journalists attended its inaugural meeting.

Gay papers demonstrated their growing dependence on and allegiance to advertising as AIDS emerged in the early 1980s. The demonstration was particularly grisly in San Francisco: because so many of the advertisers that sustained leading local gay papers (The *Sentinel* and the *Bay Area Reporter*) were bars and bathhouses, and because the earliest available information about AIDS appeared threatening to such businesses, some papers intentionally misrepresented the few facts they knew about AIDS. They intentionally misled readers about the safety of bathhouses and downplayed the seriousness of AIDS (even joking about its causes), unwilling to risk losing advertisers. When declining patronage forced bathhouses to close, and consequently to cease advertising, both the *Sentinel* and the *Bay Area Reporter* lost several pages from each issue. As George Mendenhall of the *Bay Area Reporter* put it: "We were bleeding. Without the ads for the tubs, we weren't sure we'd survive."[37] (While viatical and pharmaceutical advertisements may be seen as a kind of replacement for bathhouse ads, the latter tended to subsidize local papers whereas the former tend to subsidize national publications.) The *Advocate* was slow to pick up on AIDS, although it had less dependence on local business advertising than San Francisco's papers. Before it finally reported on AIDS in 1983, the *Advocate* had earned the public wrath of Larry Kramer, who would go on to champion an organized and militant response to any and all institutions obstructing the drive for services and the search for a cure.[38] This example is extreme, but it serves well to dramatize the conflict of interest between some of the political functions of a press—namely, community building and movement building—and the profit motive.

While a trend of anticapitalist, antiracist sentiment visible in gay male periodicals of the early 1970s quickly petered out, a less-visible alternative gay male press persisted in at least one periodical, namely *RFD*. In a report on *RFD* in the *Advocate* in 1982, editor Edwin Bridges spoke in a language that was already largely outmoded in urban centers: "We feel that perhaps we're not ready for assimilation because we still don't understand who we are," Bridges explains. "To deny our differences from the straight majority is to deny where we're coming from

and what we're for. Being gay is not a simple issue of sexual preference."[39] Produced by and circulating chiefly among nonurban dwellers,
RFD could still, in the 1980s, attend to "gay consciousness." Offering a
true alternative to the precepts governing the majority of gay male periodicals in the 1980s, *RFD*'s critical stance toward assimilation, its emphasis on differences between gay and straight cultures, and its
assertion that gay identity was not simply a function of sexual behavior
certainly distinguished it from the *Advocate* and other journals of the
period. "Politically, we're non-assimilationist because we want to develop our own ways of speaking, our music, our own unique experiences."[40] Bridges must have understood that he was speaking in a way
that hearkened back to an earlier moment in the gay liberation movement when he stated that the magazine was geared toward "Rediscov-
ering some of the innocence of childhood, some of the sissiness in it, the
nonconformity we have always felt." Again he noted that such difference was "not something we have to hide or forget about."[41]

Meanwhile, in a nearly separate sphere, lesbian feminists were creating new publications, arguably more diverse and more radical than the
larger press network serving gay men. Often run by collective editorial
bodies, lesbian-feminist publications attempted to incorporate nonhierarchical political principles. *The Furies, Lesbian Tide, Dyke,* and *Ama-
zon Quarterly* were just a few of the publications that came out in the
early and mid-1970s. Operating on dramatically fewer funds than their
male counterparts, and with far smaller circulations, these publications
focused more expressly on political ideology—producing it, spreading
it, and discussing it. Many of these publications tried to provide a forum
for conversation; *Lesbian Connection,* for example, consisted entirely
of items submitted by readers. Other lesbian-feminist publications focused on the development of lesbian culture. *Sinister Wisdom* and *Conditions* printed mostly poems, stories, and essays, elaborating in these
genres analyses of sexism, heterosexism, and to some extent, racism.
Azalea: A Magazine by Third World Lesbians, established in 1977, may
have been the first publication by lesbians of color. While the rest of the
lesbian publishing scene was certainly white-dominated, collectives
often included women of color. Nevertheless, the Black Women's Issue
of *Conditions,* which was guest-edited by Lorraine Bethel and Barbara

Smith in 1981, gained immediate and far-reaching recognition; this special issue could hardly have been the event it was if it had not been so exceptional.

Radical voices in lesbian-feminist publications were ultimately only slightly less short-lived than they were in gay male publications. No doubt the onset of the lesbian sex wars contributed to the decline of the lesbian-feminist trend; Samois's s/m anthology *Coming to Power* gained a relatively large readership beginning with its first printing in 1979 and then went into subsequent printings. The Barnard sex conference in 1981, as well as the lesser-known conference organized at the same time by the Lesbian Sex Mafia, changed the nature of the conversation about lesbianism. The pro-sex movement challenged a sexual ideology (often associated with separatism) according to which butch-femme roles, penetration, and s/m were rejected as holdovers from oppressive heterosexual relations. This challenge had a strong impact on the nature of the printed work that would come from lesbians thereafter. As one important example, *On Our Backs,* a magazine that celebrated— and printed—lesbian pornography, started up in 1984 and helped integrate lesbian-feminist and pro-sex lesbian readers. This is not to say that lesbian-feminist periodicals ceased publishing altogether; *Conditions* and *Sinister Wisdom,* among others, continued to provide a cultural outlets from lesbian-feminist perspectives, and newspapers, such as *off our backs,* continued to offer a radical feminist perspective without being expressly "lesbian."

Critiques of racism in the women's movement and among white lesbians compelled a change in the way many lesbians read, wrote, and published. The year 1981 was something of a watershed; in that year, in addition to the Black Women's Issue of *Conditions,* the annual meeting of the National Women's Studies Association, at which Audre Lorde and Adrienne Rich were the keynote speakers, exploded into a conversation about race and racism among women and lesbians. The same year, *This Bridge Called My Back* was published, and shortly thereafter, the Kitchen Table: Women of Color Press was founded, in recognition of the fact that women of color had so few venues for their written work.[42]

While lesbian and feminist publications and organizations were dealing with racism, the gay press confronted the continued spread of

HIV and AIDS. AIDS reporting soon turned serious and AIDS coverage became a constant in the gay press from the early 1980s to the mid-1990s. Because of the enormity of the epidemic, because of the range of responses to it—from the direct action of ACT UP to the massive service sector surrounding AIDS—there was much to report on. The gay press, in part pressured by powerful individuals (notably Larry Kramer), expressed anger and grief, and in this, it showed a seriousness of purpose. In this moment, the correspondence between the press and the political movement resurged; both the press and the movement, on the whole, directed as many resources as possible toward providing accurate information and opportunities for engagement with the crisis. Both the press and the movement sought to publicize information about AIDS in an era of official silence about it. (In the eight years of his presidency, legend has it, Ronald Reagan never spoke about AIDS publicly.) This may have been the last moment at which the gay press sustained attention to political action, specifically by emphasizing information over entertainment. Also in the 1980s, "outing" became both a political tactic and news; Michelangelo Signorile, columnist for the *Advocate* and *Outweek* made a mission of revealing the homosexuality of closeted gays, and also of defending the practice of doing so.[43]

In the 1990s, national gay and lesbian magazines came into their own. In the first two years of the decade, over six new glossies were born, although not all of them survived. Six years later, there were thirteen national gay magazines. Some of these were geared to a "general" gay audience, while others were geared toward subniches, such as *In the Family*, aimed at gay and lesbian parents. In 1997 alone, six new national gay and lesbian magazines were launched; in the same year, the number of local gay and lesbian newspapers dropped from 92 to 87.[44] To say, therefore, that the category of national magazines exploded in the 1990s is not to say that this spelled the immediate demise of the category of local papers. But there may be some connection between the growth rate of the circulation of local newspapers (3.1 percent from 1996 to 1998) and that of national magazines (22 percent for the same period). From 1997 to 1998, the numbers were starker: local papers grew in circulation by 4.3 percent as compared to the 53.6 percent growth for national magazines. In the same year there was "an increase in ad pages in National Magazines, . . . despite the fact that the number of publications in this category more than doubled."[45] In growth of revenue, national magazines outstripped local newspapers by 60 percent from 1996 to 1998, almost 34 percent from 1997 to 1998 alone. National magazines, in other words, experienced robust growth in the 1990s, particularly in contrast to the growth of other gay and lesbian periodical categories.

It is easy to think that the gay press preceded and produced the gay movement, and certainly the two have worked together quite closely. But I would argue that neither clearly preceded the other; they were, to a great extent, interdependent and coemergent. The Society for Human Rights, the very first known homophile organization in the United States, was established in 1924, when there were already social networks that brought homosexual men and women into contact with each other.[46] There was a small gay market already in the 1940s, when historians place the appearance of the first gay or lesbian publication. There were already bars where gay people tended to congregate and there were already small service economies centered around gay life, particularly in the cities where so-called gay ghettoes would grow first and biggest, San Francisco, Los Angeles, New York.[47] Furthermore, there were already mail-order distribution schemes for soft-core porn and other sex products. These concerns—both bars and mail-order businesses—operated under compromised legality, as did the publications designated as the pioneers of the gay press. On the one hand, the press and the movement grew together over the course of decades. On the other hand, such a progressive version of history neglects forgotten chapters, as well as the fact that such growth has produced critical changes in the very nature of the movement and the press.

THE BUSINESS OF LIBERATION

While the early 1990s represented a period of dramatic and sudden proliferation of national glossy magazines for both gay men and lesbians, as well as an expansion of local newspapers, and while this is the period in which the talk of a gay market became centrally featured in the gay press, announcements of a gay market had been trickling into print for a long time. Debates about the relationship between the press and a gay market had appeared, albeit with less fanfare, in the pages of the gay press for decades. From early on, the gay press led a double life—as discussed above, by the 1950s homophile publications explicitly served the unprofitable function of information distribution while quasi-erotic publications continued to thrive financially. In 1961 and 1965, *Citizens News* and *Cruise News & World Report,* respectively were founded by entrepreneur Guy Strait. Conceived from the start as business enterprises rather than activist publications, both were dominated by advertising and self-promoting articles for Strait's mail-order business in male erotica.[48] Also in the 1960s, *Drum,* while manifestly a political organ, became the first gay magazine to turn a profit, which it accomplished through an arrangement with Guild Press. Guild Press was a pornography business that printed *Drum* for free in return for publication of sample pictures in the journal. When *Drum's* editor discovered that Guild was selling *Drum* independently, he called off the arrangement and started his own mail-order business.[49]

Whereas ads for local gay businesses (most prominently bars, bathhouses, and sexual paraphernalia vendors) and personal ads had subsidized gay publications from the late 1960s through the mid-1980s, slowly, as the 1990s approached, the gay men's press began to win more advertising from straight, and increasingly corporate, sponsors. In the process, the gay press more significantly contributed to the consolidation of a gay niche market, changing the relation of the gay community to the United States as a whole and changing, too, the relation of the press and the social movement to the economic and political mainstream of the nation. If "the gay media, particularly the nationally circulated *Advocate,* provided an outlet for the marketing of the emerging gay consumer culture," this indicates that the gay media facilitated the construction of the gay market.[50] At the same time, the growth of the gay and lesbian movement, the increasing numbers of out lesbians and gay men, and other gay and lesbian businesses all contributed to the growth of the gay press. The relationship was reciprocal.

The gay press's transition from exclusive sponsorship by gay businesses to sponsorship by mainstream corporations is perfectly illustrated by the shifting status of sex ads in gay publications. In 1979, the *Advocate* printed an article on the proliferation of the gay press (and its "problems") in which its "infamous" classified ads were described as the *Advocate's* "most distinctive characteristic."[51] Recapping the history of these ads, the reporter, Scott Anderson, recalled that "Sexual contact ads have been a part of gay (and pseudo-gay) publications since the 1950s, when announcements in code language appeared discreetly in body-building and sci-fi magazines."[52] Still featuring sexuality as a definitive difference between gay people and straight people, these ads, according to Anderson, "bring people together at the organizational and social level, especially those who live in remote areas or have specialized sexual repertoires."[53] In this way, the sex ads performed the historically typical function of the gay press, that of unifying gay people across geographical distance, and they did so in the face of repressive social measures that enforced the invisibility of gay people. Anderson also stressed the financial dependence of the gay press on sex ads, an assessment still accurate more than a decade later.

Nevertheless, the financial value of sex ads began to lose out to the value of attracting mainstream corporate advertising. In 1990, the *New York Times* reported that *Outweek* had eliminated its phone-sex ads, "its most lucrative ad category."[54] Those ads had accounted for 35 percent of its revenues, which was not an unusually high percentage for gay male publications. As Joseph DiSabato of Rivendell Marketing Company estimated in the same article, phone-sex ads, together with ads from locals businesses such as gay bars, restaurants, doctors, and travel agents, accounted for "90 percent of the revenues in most gay publications."[55] *Outweek's* motive for purging the sex ads from its pages was to make the magazine "more attractive to skittish national advertisers."[56] Admitting that the move might be financially risky at first, Grant Lukenbill expressed confidence that "we will become the first to attract the Budweisers and the American Expresses."[57] The *Advocate* opted for a related strategy two years later, issuing a sex-ad publication separate from its featured-fare publication. Winning the kind of advertising that Lukenbill had predicted and DiSabato had banked on, the *Advocate's* sex-purged publication went on to grace newsstands, to be represented at gay business expos, and, indeed, to grow in circulation.

The sex ad phenomenon—its early integral relation to the gay press and its subsequent elimination in favor of corporate advertising—only pertained to men's ads in periodicals whose staffs and readerships were predominantly composed of men. One reviewer of the gay press, Willard Spiegelman, points to this phenomenon as the paradigmatic difference between men's publications and those that were partially (or presumably wholly) staffed by women and/or politicos, such as the *Gay Community News:* "*GCN* advertises for a staff writer who must have 'a commitment to feminism and social change'; *The Advocate* indulges readers' dreams, e.g., 'Attn Surfer Type: Hunky ex-Marine Captain wants you to fulfill fantasy with him in his jeep.'"[58] In a harsh and stereotypical representation of female, particularly lesbian—and also "leftist"—attitudes toward sex, Spiegelman contrasts sexual affirmation with political progressiveness. Note that for him, the former is represented by the gay male press, the latter, by publications "like" *GCN* (as though there *were* other publications like *GCN*):

> Many gay women react with self-righteous indignation and puritanical disapproval to the lurid quasi-pornographic photos and special requests in these pages. Indeed if *The Advocate* has made any serious contribution to our understanding of sexual mores, it has been its implicit challenge to the humorless and often grudging seriousness with which leftist journals like Boston's *Gay Community News* (one of the few periodicals to have women in major editorial positions) expect everyone to toe a clear line on sexual matters.[59]

Spiegelman allowed that "feminist militancy" against sexual fantasy and pleasure was perhaps starting to soften as expressions of lesbian involvement in s/m became more common in the early 1980s. However, lesbian opinion no more brought about the demise of sexual content in national gay publications in the 1990s than it had tempered sexual content in the preceding decades. As Spiegelman notes, "Of course, women's feelings about sex notwithstanding, objections have been voiced by mainstream advertisers, causing the break-up of sex and news."[60] That is, the shift was strictly a function of market speculation on the part of those publications, which was part speculation about advertisers and part speculation about readers. To address readers as a consumer market more than as movement participants was a self-conscious decision, at least on the part of the *Advocate.* In the words of its former publisher David Goodstein, "The *Advocate* is for middle-class readers—radicals don't read, they don't have the time."[61] About the same phenomenon, a progressive perspective held that in "portraying the homosexual as a 'good consumer,' the *Advocate* promoted an ethic of 'liberation by accumulation' in which 'social acceptance and mobility could be achieved by buying the correct accessories.'"[62]

The *Advocate* was the first so-called lifestyle magazine, the first national glossy to strike this editorial attitude, the first to garner advertisements from mainstream corporate producers, but the tension between a liberationist ethic and a consumerist ethic was already explicit in the gay press in the 1970s. Referring to philosopher Herbert Marcuse's concept of repressive tolerance, an editorial in the *Bay Area Reporter* in February 1977 questioned the political effect of the commercialization of the gay press. Forecasting the "swallowing" of the gay press by "the middle-brow giants," Paul Lorch theorized that "the establishment, co-ops [*sic*] the revolutionary, the radical programs and projects. It absorbs them into an ample bosom, smothering them, defusing them, defanging them."[63] In strikingly misogynist imagery, Lorch imagined that the stability and absorbency of capitalism would ultimately exhaust the revolutionary "thrust" of the gay press. A month later, Lorch predicted, "The question that will confront us all in the next five years is no longer whether we will achieve our liberation and enjoy our civil rights, but whether we will be able to preserve our identity."[64] Yet he did not see this question arising from the paper's commitment to commercial success; as he revealed in the very same column, "At the *B.A.R.* we are pledged to ever-improving copy, wider coverage, a larger readership. And yes . . . even a profit."[65] Also observing that the emergent gay press was, by its very existence, pressuring the straight press to cover gay news in order to remain competitive, Lorch accurately predicted the process by which gay culture's difference from straight culture would diminish as gay commerce increased.

Claims to the affluence and trend-setting character of gay male consumers, intended to appeal to straight marketers in the straight press and based on an appraisal of the gay press, also go back to the 1970s. In 1976, the *New York Times* printed a story on "Homosexual Magazines in Bids," which reported that Donald Embinder had taken out a full-page ad in *Advertising Age* offering information about the gay market in an attempt to interest marketers.[66] Embinder was the publisher of the soft-core gay magazine *Blueboy,* which had a circulation that had risen in the previous year from 26,000 to 160,000. The *Times* mentioned that a coupon attached to Embinder's ad had brought 488 responses, and also that Embinder considered the fashion, liquor, and hi-fi equipment industries his best prospects; furthermore, Embinder believed that it was the role of the gay press to convince those industries that gays were affluent enough to more than repay the costs of advertising to them.

The *Times* story went on to say that unlike *Blueboy,* the *Advocate* paid "little attention to national advertising because an outside expert examined the market and delivered a negative appraisal."[67] Embinder's initiative was clearly ahead of its time, but it did anticipate the direction the gay press would head in the 1980s and where it would arrive in the 1990s. David Goodstein, editor of the *Advocate* in 1976, claimed then that his publication's circulation had jumped 20 percent in the previous seven months, to 60,000. Perhaps more dramatic was the jump in the magazine's advertising; Goodstein told the *Times,* "A year ago the publication ran about 36 pages per issue. Now it's up to 80 pages and most of its increase has been advertising."[68] Placing those ads were bars, baths, boutiques, and travel agents, i.e., largely local gay advertisers.

Embinder reiterated his convictions three years later in Goodstein's *Advocate.* Scott Anderson's 1979 article on the proliferation of the gay press quoted Embinder and his colleague Don Michaels, editor of the Washington, D.C., *Blade,* on the conflict for straight advertisers considering targeting a gay market: "Some advertisers slam the door in our faces, sure. But others have realized gay people are a big market. Economics over homophobia."[69] Similarly, Anderson speculated that such advertising was the way of the future: "As the gay press taps into mainstream advertising dollars, more and more people will be able to make a decent living in gay journalism and publishing. . . . In turn, these periodicals will serve as examples of successful gay businesses, advancing, in their own way, the business of liberation."[70] Moreover, a successfully commercial gay press would diversify, identifying and serving niches within niches; according to Anderson, "It's not far-fetched that in a few years, we will see titles like *Gaysports, Gay Money* or *Gay GOP.* As the gay press further specializes, the emphasis will shift from news to informational and lifestyle features, with a focus on people."[71] He was certainly right about the shift away from news—of the continuing political movement—in the national gay press; the advocacy function would resurge briefly in the late 1980s to be followed by a definitive turn toward entertainment.

Thus far, the story of advertising is largely the story of the gay male press. The lesbian press has had virtually no access to, and no support from, mainstream advertisers, which no doubt explains the difference in political trends among the gay and lesbian presses in terms of editorial content. Even when gay publications include some lesbian-interest content, the attraction for the corporate producers who advertise there is surely the prospect of the male readership. For example, in recognition of the gender segregation of the gay press as well as the limits of the profitability of lesbian periodicals relative to gay male periodicals, *HX for Him* spun off a sister publication, *HX for Her;* in 1998, 35,000 copies of *for Him* were published, as compared to 12,000 copies of *for Her,* and while *for Him* was distributed nationally, *for Her* distribution remained a local New York phenomenon.[72] (On the one hand, the *HX* family makes a good basis for comparison because it published one guide for men and one guide for women; on the other hand, *for Her* was managed by the same men who managed *for Him,* which is anomolous among publications aimed at lesbians.) In 1999, *HX for Her* stopped publishing altogether. In the late 1990s, a few lesbian magazines, like *Curve,* began to attract more mainstream advertisers, but the figures were nowhere near what they were for more male-oriented magazines.

WHAT, OR WHO, IS LEFT OUT OF THE GAY PRESS

From its inception—whether Lisa Ben or the Mattachine Society is credited for that inception—the gay and lesbian press has been split along lines of gender and race, as I have already argued. I turn now to the lost origins of the splits and to some of their effects. The gay, mostly white male press is dominant by any possible measure—budget, circulation, longevity, advertising, geographical reach, technological sophistication—mainly because most of the available measures come down to money, and gay white men as a group have more money than lesbians of any racial group. As I explained above, it is absurd to speak of the lesbian and gay press as though it were one institution; taking gender into account suggests at least two "gay" presses. To take race into account further fragments that institution; attending to people of color reveals an unevenly enfranchised readership and a press with fewer resources and fewer publications to show than that of white lesbians, on the whole. The obviousness of this observation is belied by the prevalence of the rhetoric of "unity" in the gay press. The fragmentation of the gay press and of the gay community as a whole has been too frequently denied or ignored by a press in which "unity" was the single most commonly invoked value from 1977 to 1990.[73] It is easy now to criticize invocations of unity, but it must be said that gay men and lesbians have had good reason to wish for unity, and to use it as a tool for political leverage. The greater context of homophobia, in general, and the paucity of accurate representation in mainstream media conditioned the kinds of claims made by pioneers of gay and lesbian media. Yet gay men and lesbians have seen inaccurate reflections of themselves in the gay media too.

The gender segregation of the gay and lesbian press is, to some extent, an effect of lesbian-feminist rejection of men, of patriarchal organizations and of the male domination within them, as well as an affirmative choice to work in women-only environments. Yet I believe that gender segregation in the gay press is, to an even greater extent, an effect of the sexism in that institution; sexism certainly accounts for women's relative lack of resources and also for any involuntary exclusion from the structures and contents of the gay press. However, other accounts abound. One writer's dismissive comment, for example, is as inaccurate as it is common: identifying the 1970s as the decade in which the gay press came into its own, he writes, "The gay press reflected the absence of lesbians in the gay political movement of the time."[74] In fact, women were extremely active, both in coeducational political events and activities and in lesbian-oriented political life. If they were less visible in the former, it is because they were often forgotten or side-lined, and frequently they did leave nominally coeducational enterprises when they were so insulted by men that they could not comfortably participate.[75] If women's contributions to lesbian liberation do not count as presence in "the gay political movement of the time," that, too, is an effect of sexism. There is no other way to explain statements that women were absent from gay liberation.

The reason given for women's lack of representation in one of the earliest gay publications indicates an attitude that may have set the stage for future gender segregation in the gay press. As the former editor of the *Mattachine Review,* Hal Call had no interest in "expanding the magazine to include female 'variants.'" Call felt that their exclusion from the *Review* was a natural outcome of the fact that "Lesbians were not under fire the way men were. They didn't have the kinds of problems with the police that gay men had. . . . They [the police] just thought a lesbian was a woman who'd never been fucked good."[76] In other words, the combined effect of sexism and homophobia that informed the way the police thought about and treated women (in Call's unfortunately accurate account) did not count as "fire," for Call. Neglecting the fact that women were indeed harassed and raped by policemen, Call's estimation of lesbian oppression reproduces the very attitude he attributes to the police.

Another common account of their underrepresentation blames women not for being absent, nor for being insufficiently oppressed, but for being feminist. In his 1982 review of gay journalism in *Salmagundi,* Willard Spiegelman explains, in a footnote, why he will not consider women's publications: "Because feminist issues tend to polarize male and female journals, I shall discuss primarily gay male writing in this essay."[77] Here, Spiegelman misrepresents feminist issues as the polarizing force rather than sexism itself, as though it were women's choice that feminist issues were a source of division between gay men and lesbians (or men and women in general), and as though his exclusion of women were an effect rather than a cause of the polarization of men and women, which is to say, of the need for feminism. Women's "invisibility" derives from exactly this kind of exclusion, not from their physical absence from every liberation movement in history; feminism is a response to this and other kinds of discrimination, not a reflection of a *sui generis* desire to polarize.

Aside from a brief period in the early 1970s in which numerous gay men's publications openly attacked capitalism as oppressive to gays, lesbians, and people of color, as well as working-class people, the gay male press has tended not to explore class as an issue. However, even when radical gay male voices critiqued capitalism, they did not often evaluate the class politics of their own growing movement. By contrast—in fact, opposite Louie Crew's review in *Margins*—lesbian activist and writer Karla Jay disparages "either literature or nonfiction without a strong class analysis [as] incomplete and insufficient."[78] Deeply committed to an independent lesbian press, Jay's 1975 review of lesbian publications asserted that "one of the finest achievements of the post-Stonewall . . . Lesbian movement has been the creation of our own independent and vast Lesbian media network in which we present our own experiences."[79] Noting that earlier lesbian publications such as the *Ladder* had found it easier to publish fiction than nonfiction, Jay especially prized the growth of nonfiction genres in the lesbian "media network." Fiction was easier to publish than nonfiction because of the lack of resources for obtaining and checking news stories, but also because it left the author at a safe distance from the published product, thus maintaining her feeling of safety. More important than generic distinctions for Jay was the role of political thought in the development of lesbian culture—a value she attributed to her "leftist feminist background" with the Redstocking collective.[80]

Similarly, in a 1978 review of the lesbian press, Jackie St. Joan lauded the way *The Furies* (out of Washington, D.C.) and *Ain't I a Woman* (out of Iowa City) "expressed the rage of dyke separatism and revealed the depths of the class schism within the feminist movement."[81] For St. Joan, as for Jay, "the arrogance of Marxist politics" was not an unwelcome feature of the lesbian press; it positively defined that press, along with "the subjectivism of the sixties counterculture, . . . the reactions of separatism, the vision of a woman-identified world."[82] *Lesbian Tide, Lesbian Connection,* and *Sinister Wisdom* were some of the journals that informed Jay's opinion that the lesbian print media were fundamentally concerned with the class politics of the movement(s) for gay liberation. By contrast, *Dyke* magazine earned her scorn by failing to meet political standards, forsaking news of the movement for "trite meanderings on such superficial subjects as dyke fashions and interior decorating."[83]

As noted earlier, for many lesbians involved in the lesbian press, political news was greatly valued; however, the perpetual lack of resources that beset so many print enterprises rendered it very difficult to gain access to such news directly. Lack of resources also significantly curtailed production and distribution. *Lesbian Connection* was one of many periodicals that regularly importuned readers for financial contributions. To deal with the high cost of news, *Lesbian Connection* instead offered letters and reports from readers as its main fare. Perhaps this lack of access to news—and solutions such as *Lesbian Connection's*—opened up lesbian periodicals to the charge that they focused too much on opinion and too much on love and relationships. In spite of such complaints, however, women could only infrequently find material about their lives and the conditions in which they worked and lived in gay male periodicals in any period. Listing her criteria for an effective lesbian press, St. Joan explained that she borrowed her standards from the black press. By analogy with the black press, she valued in the lesbian press "quality of production reflective of a seriousness of purpose; I look for a political content reflective of a commitment to overcoming male domination; I look for news reflective of an appreciation of the overall news blackout about lesbians in the male press."[84] Here "quality" refers not to production values, but to effectiveness in dismantling social hierarchies based on race and gender. Yet twenty years later, the lesbian and gay press remained largely segregated, at least at the national level, with different publications serving different gender-based niches within the overall gay and lesbian readership.

Racial segregation has also plagued the gay press, as one letter to *XY* magazine expressed in 1998, noting that *XY* shared this problem with other magazines. The reader was concerned with *XY*'s failure to cover "issues associated with gay minorities—not just blacks, but all races," and urged the magazine to address "diversity" as a theme, and to display "diversity among the models," as well.[85] By 1998, of course, underrepresentation of people of color in the gay press was deeply entrenched. Just as race and racial segregation have been frequently ignored by the gay press, so too have histories of the gay press neglected to treat issues of race and racism. In light of the fact that so many historians have ignored racial segregation when they have written gay history, scholar Tracy Morgan writes,

> the lives of Black gay men were circumscribed by race in the very same arenas through which white gay men came to establish increasingly public lives: Jim Crow military service, housing patterns, and leisure activities. The roots of gay political activism and community building were thus nourished by the same soil in which racial segregation flourished.
>
> [A]s white gay political organizations and neighborhoods were becoming more visible in New York City in the 1960s, Black lesbian, gay, and bisexual Harlemites found that their bars and clubs had either been burned to the ground or were inexplicably closing.[86]

Recovering the body-building magazines of the 1940s and 1950s as "proto-homophile publications," provides a very important corrective to the racist tendency in histories of the gay press.[87] Streitmatter explicitly leaves these magazines out of his otherwise exhaustive account, presumably because "they never identified themselves as targeting gays, although their physique photographs attracted a large gay readership."[88] Neglecting to acknowledge these publications as part of the history of the consumption (if not production) of gay-themed printed matter creates a revisionist history that forgets or otherwise hides the racism that conditioned the earliest manifestations of a more properly "gay" press.

Like more political materials, and like high-art treatments of homosexuality, mid-century physique magazines were subject to repeated obscenity charges. Nevertheless, the genre survived for decades, and was healthy enough to sustain subgenres such as magazines that specialized in "Greek" body-building motifs and all-American publications.[89] The Greek publications showed no African Americans in their photographs, while the all-Americans did display several pictures of African American body builders. Although these magazines were not explicitly aimed at gay readers, they were read by gay men; by the 1950s, they were, in fact, targeted to gay men and consequently were at pains, argues Morgan, to escape the taint of homosexuality. For this reason, white producers of these magazines placed a limited number of African American male bodies in their pages. Because the stereotypical hypermasculinization of black men rendered black homosexuality unthinkable, "The reassertion of a white hetero-masculinity that was neither conformist nor castrated nor queer depended upon an appropriation of the racist fantasy of Black male virility. . . . Thus appropriated, negritude gave to white masculinity an unquestionably heterosexualized toughness . . . that it had previously lacked."[90]

A carefully controlled representation of African American men bought safety for white men who produced and consumed these magazines, cloaking them in "toughness." Certainly "Black men appearing with chains and crates, Latinos framed as in postcards and with tropical props" formed images that effected the subordination of bodies of men of color for white gay readers who "unconsciously" sought to consolidate their racial privilege (motivated by the fear that their sexual identity might jeopardize the privileges of masculinity for them).[91] The appearance of any men of color in these magazines might seem to indicate a value on racial equality, but white men were disproportionately represented. The underrepresentation of black bodies in the photographs of physique publications "can be understood as a conscious or unconscious strategy employed by white publishers to remain connected to the connotations of class and quality generally associated with whiteness."[92] Clearly, the control of representations of black bodies was crucial to the maintenance of a system of class and race privilege for white gay male readers of these publications.

Morgan identifies the brand of masculinity in play in the bodybuilding magazines as "patriotic, strong, and white."[93] If homosexuality was the internal threat, communism was the external threat to the nation; a need to demonstrate patriotism may also have called for the disavowal of the homosexual associations with this magazine genre. The Greek-style magazines, in particular, seemed to promise that the bodies pictured therein could be put to use for national defense, in conscious or unconscious answer to the rejection of gays in the military as weakening national security. The creed of the *Grecian Guild Pictorial* made clear this association between masculinity and U.S. national identity and interest: "I pledge allegiance to my native land, ever willing to serve the cause of my country whenever and wherever she may need me. I seek a sound mind in a sound body that I may be a complete man; I am a Grecian."[94] The conventional feminization of the nation here allows for an implicit assertion of heterosexuality, but the simultaneous allegiance to "my country" and to masculinity naturally fails to cloak the homoerotic slant of the magazine. Rather, this pledge interestingly foreshadows later conflations between national identity and gay identity.[95]

DEEP HORIZONTAL COMRADESHIP

In the pages of the *Grecian Guild Pictorial,* the association between masculinity, whiteness, and middle-class values rhetorically supported U.S. national interests; meanwhile, around the country, gay men read the magazines in which such rhetoric was printed, searching it for evidence that they were not alone. If the men pictured were gay, or even if they were willing to take the risk of being thought gay, if there was enough of a readership to warrant publication of such magazines, or even if publication of these magazines could produce enough of a readership to sustain itself month in and month out, did that not mean that there were others out there somewhere? At the same time as homosexuality had to be disavowed through the visual and rhetorical strategies described above—in fact, in the very act of disavowal—the "nation" was imagined as a basis for common identification among a geographically dispersed homosexual readership.

Simultaneously, homosexual identification might also have provided, in the minds of readers, the prospect of a commonalty, even of camaraderie. The gay and lesbian press has had a particular role in channeling "gay consciousness," or consciousness of gay collectivity, into the idea of a gay nation: "Just as the founding of the first African-American newspaper, *Freedom's Journal* in 1827, has been credited with marking the beginning of a national movement to secure black civil rights, by creating a communication medium that allowed women and men all over the country to converse with each other, *ONE, Mattachine Review,* and the *Ladder* likewise began to build a national gay and lesbian community."[96] In addition to its community-building and movement-building functions, the gay press helped build a specifically national, or rather nationalist, framework for thinking about the community and the movement.

From its origins in physique magazines through its growth as an arm of the gay and lesbian political and social movement to its ascendancy as a profit-seeking enterprise, the gay press attained national proportions in the United States in tandem with the emergence of the idea of gay nationalism. I use "nationalism" metaphorically here; clearly the gay and lesbian movement has never sought, in a serious or sustained way, to create a separate, autonomous state. But "nation" has often been invoked in the movement, and a look at its historical meanings helps explain the relationship of the lesbian and gay movement to other social movements, to the market composed of members of that movement, and to the nation within which the movement seems to seek enfranchisement—that is, the United States.

Even if nationhood had not been so frequently invoked in the context of the lesbian and gay liberation movement, from *Lesbian Nation* to Queer Nation, contemporary scholar Benedict Anderson's work would suggest instructive parallels between that movement and emergent nations.[97] For Anderson, a nation is not a fact of nature, nor is it a structure that persists unchanged through time; rather, it is a historically shifting entity, which, in its modern form, begins as an idea before becoming institutionalized. A nation is an "imagined community . . . *imagined* because the members of even the smallest nation will never know most of their fellow-members, meet them, or even hear of them, yet in the minds of each lives the image of their communion."[98] According to Anderson, the modern idea of the nation arose in the minds of consumers of print media as they imagined themselves as members of a community of anonymous readers with whom they shared the act of reading newspapers. Regularly published and mass-produced newspapers, in particular, endowed readers with absolute confidence that there were other people reading the same papers at the same time, in the same language, and in the same place—a place so big one could not know everyone in it, but a bounded place nonetheless.[99] Here I will suggest that the same thing could be said about gay men and lesbians in the United States—that the rise of a commercial gay press gave gay men and lesbians confidence in the idea that they shared a time, place, and language with other gay men and lesbians in the United States. Again, the nation imagined was, and is, simultaneously based on U.S. citizenship and on membership in a social group based in sexual identity. In other words, the gay nation in question is geographically coextensive with the United States. Lisa Ben, whose *Vice Versa* now stands as a forebear of the commercial gay and lesbian press, consciously promoted such an identification among the imagined community of lesbian readers when she wrote, "Even though my readers may never actually become acquainted with one another, they will find a sort of spiritual communion through this little magazine."[100]

Lisa Ben's production process mirrors that of the early newspapers in the United States: "Printers starting new presses always included a newspaper in their productions, to which they were usually the main, even sole, contributor. Thus the printer-journalist was initially an essentially North American phenomenon."[101] The first newspapers in the colonies "began essentially as appendages of the market. Early gazettes contained—aside from news about the metropole—commercial news."[102] Linking people in the provinces to urban centers, then, has always been a function of the press in the United States. More important, that linkage has been an effect of common interest in commercial news. In fact, the history of colonial newspapers suggests that the (incipiently national) relation of colonists to each other, and to the market, was mediated by newspapers.

If the gay press spoke in the vernacular of gay subculture, as it clearly began to do in the late 1960s, then workers in the gay press, like the colonial printers, "did not carry on their revolutionary activities in a vacuum. They were, after all, producers for the print market, and they were linked, via that silent bazaar, to consuming publics."[103] For the gay press in the late 1960s and 1970s, as for colonial subjects in the late eighteenth and early nineteenth centuries, the consumers of vernacular printed matter were members of the "reading classes," then, as now, "people of some power."[104] In this sense, nationality is more accessible for people with purchasing power. While the press addresses "gays and lesbians" as a unified group, this stance is merely rhetorical. Materially, gay men and lesbians with less social power are "invited into" the nation founded by gay men and lesbians with more social power.[105] Of course, for "literate" classes, organization into a nation is advantageous. Although the idea and rhetoric of the modern nation—actual or metaphorical—draw on the concepts of equality and fraternity discussed in Chapter 1, there is nothing in the idea or the rhetoric that prevents inequality from prevailing in the structure of the nation. Moreover, inequality has historically been structured into the very instruments that call the nation into being: in this case, the gay press. Again, nations of all kinds feature this apparent contradiction; nations are "imagined as a *community,* because, regardless of the actual inequality and exploitation that may prevail in each, the nation is always conceived as a deep horizontal comradeship."[106]

To recapitulate, then, the national U.S. gay community came into being through the imagined comradeship of gay men and lesbians reading an increasingly commercial gay press. In that press, gay men and lesbians read for news of the growth of the movement, they read for news of consumption opportunities that reinforced their belonging in the community, and they read vernacular language that helped delineate the boundaries of the community; the geopolitical space of the gay community in the minds of these readers coincides exactly with the geopolitical space of the United States. The press, its use of the vernacular, its ultimate circulation across the United States, and its address to gay men and lesbians as participants in a liberation movement and a market helped readers to formulate gay nationalism. Because print capitalism generates equations between readers, consumers, and citizens, "the very idea of 'nation' is now nestled firmly in virtually all print-languages; and nationness is virtually inseparable from political consciousness."[107] Accordingly, the development of a gay and lesbian press and the attendant development of a gay and lesbian market went hand in hand with a gay and lesbian political consciousness expressed in the language of nationalism. However, because nationalism implies and even requires unity, it inevitably obscures serious divisions in the (imagined) national body. In fact, nationalism is invested in obscuring all kinds of difference.[108]

The gay nation and the U.S. nation alike were forged in part through print media that recognized and addressed various social classes in different ways. As Walt Whitman (arguably an ancestor of the contemporary gay press) wrote, "the people of the United States are a newspaper-ruled people."[109] Before there was a gay press, and given the occasional, distorted, and hostile representation of homosexuals in the mainstream press, "Undocumented, unaccounted for, homosexuals were in a real way disenfranchised."[110] Asserting the Americanness of newspaper readership, Spiegelman aligns himself with John Quincy Adams in Adams's response to the "perennial American dilemma" between maintaining both quality and a press that is inclusive of diverse voices. Yet, his formula for quality in the gay press applies standards that differ markedly from the standards listed by Karla Jay and Jackie St. Joan. Spiegelman recounts that Adams declined to contribute to a new journal called *Democratic Review*, on the grounds that "'literature was, and its nature must always be, aristocratic; that democracy of numbers and literature were self-contradictory.'"[111] How apt it is that with reference to revolutionary forebears, and to foundational moments in the development of U.S. culture, this paradox should link the language of John Quincy Adams to a review of a gay press on the verge of reaching national proportions.

Just as he set feminism and other leftist politics in opposition to the "best" of the gay press—i.e., sexual content—Spiegelman suggests that the gay press may be opposed to a democratic and inclusive movement for social justice. He writes of the *Advocate*, "The tone has changed, deepened, but the values of the paper are undeniably white, middle-class, and male."[112] Likewise, the readership, when Spiegelman wrote in 1982, was 98 percent male, despite some attempts to address women's issues. In a hopeful critique of the ways in which the gay male press increasingly diverged from serving a broad-based progressive social movement, Harry Britt had written three years earlier, in 1979, "the natural allies of [gay publisher] David Goodstein are those who want a society based on everyone's conformity with affluent white male values. The natural allies of gay people are other minority groups, with whom we can build a free, more just society based on respect for differences between people."[113] The tension between conformity and an imagined progressive alliance was still quite active twenty years later, and it was well dramatized by a panel discussion that took place at the Outwrite Conference in 1998.

THE OUTWRITE CONFERENCE:
THE STATE OF THE NATIONAL QUEER PRESS[114]

The Outwrite Conference is a conference held annually in Boston for gay, lesbian, transgender, and bisexual writers, publishers, and readers. In 1998, Outwrite convened a panel on "The State of the National Queer Press," on which writer and activist Carmen Vazquez (then Director of Public Policy at the Gay and Lesbian Community Center in New York), Jim Baxter (Publisher and Editor of a local gay newspaper in North Carolina, *Front Page*), Gabriel Goldberg (then Editor in Chief of *Instinct* magazine), and Frances Stevens (Publisher and Editor in Chief of *Curve*) were the invited speakers. In a strong statement, Carmen Vazquez asserted that there was nothing "healthy for democracy" in the queer press in the late 1990s. She bemoaned, in particular, the lack of a "community-wide forum," or exactly the kind of function that the press served in the 1970s, especially the lesbian press. The letters sections in *Coming Up* and *GCN* came close to providing that kind of forum, and those publications came closest, in Vazquez's opinion, to enabling dialogue across lines of race, class, and gender. In the 1990s, for the most part, she saw a gay press dictated by "selling advertisements to rich white gay conservative men." As one example, Vazquez pointed out that images of women and people of color were "sordidly absent" from gay papers *LGNY* and the New York *Blade*. Whereas she would have preferred a gay and lesbian press that addressed questions of social difference and inquired into the place of gay and lesbian identity in a wider movement for social change, Vazquez found instead a news editor at *OUT* talking about a "post-Gay world." Ultimately, such a press would inevitably reproduce, rather than analyze, social differences, as demonstrated by an audience member's paraphrase of a Mulryan/Nash advertisement designed to interest marketers in buying space in gay publications: "poor rural gays and lesbians don't read this, but you probably don't want to reach them anyway." Marla Erlien, Editor in Chief of *GCN,* concurred that the commodification of all things gay contributed to the divisions between gay men and lesbians.

Speaking from a similar political perspective, but conceding that financial concerns structured his work, Jim Baxter explained that *Front Page* was not run as a community service, nor as a volunteer organization, but as a business, "partly because it has to, partly because it can." While he hoped that the community service function was nevertheless served by the paper, Baxter located his paper in a competitive context. Another local alternative paper also covered gay issues and events, but Baxter maintained that there was an important political difference between them: the other paper would print the phrase "straight-acting, straight-appearing" in personal ads, which Baxter refused to do. Although he could offer this difference, he felt that a dangerously decreased skepticism of mainstream sources, as well as "some individual voices" and "some local focus," were at risk in the increasingly businesslike operation of *Front Page.*

With respect to the representation of people of color, Robert Ellsworth, then Entertainment Editor at the national glossy *Genre,* seemed sympathetic with Vazquez's concern. "We're trying to help," he said, asserting that the magazine's sparse coverage of the issues, experiences, and cultural work of people of color was "not intentional." "We're not being bigoted . . . I'm actually looking for it . . . trying to find stuff for people of color," Ellsworth insisted. However, his statement lacked all credibility given his claim that "It's very difficult for us to do a profile if there aren't people out there." Of course there are people of color out there. This comment bears a frightening similarity to the claim that women have not been active in the gay liberation movement. If the voices and the work of women and people of color are unheard and unseen in gay media, it is not because they and their work do not exist, but because editors fail to solicit such work or cultivate relationships among different constituencies. Ellsworth was probably being no more deliberately insulting than the editorial policy of *Genre* is deliberately racist. But the effects of both are divisive. Clearly Ellsworth's desire to "help" does not include restructuring the press in such a way that the work of women and people of color might be published.

Ellsworth's former colleague Mark Olmsted, Associate Editor of *Genre,* attributed the magazine's focus on white men's experience and its emphasis on life outside of the political sphere to the demand of the readers. What linked *Genre*'s readers, he claimed, was "their personal lives." "If activist stories sold," he said, *Genre* would print them. But he explicitly dissociated the magazine's treatment of gay identity from the political sphere, and he articulated this dissociation, interestingly enough, as a matter of rights: "Just because we're gay doesn't mean we have a socialist responsibility. . . . Just because we're a member of an oppressed minority doesn't mean we don't have the right to represent our more superficial qualities."

In an interesting twist on the familiar complaint that gay people haven't seen themselves represented in mainstream media, Gabriel Goldberg of *Instinct* magazine expressed his frustration at not seeing himself in gay media; in particular, he didn't see anything "for someone who isn't a political activist." Overtly, he is instead committed to producing material that doesn't say: "This is how you have to be to be a gay person." Echoing the charge that feminists and leftists are humorless, Goldberg asked, "Where is our sense of humor?" This query was directed toward the seriousness of Vazquez's critique, and it was matched in absurdity only by Olmsted's equation between the right to be "superficial" and freedom from the gay "stereotype." With total equanimity, Goldberg observed that niche marketing means that "you have a type of person and each magazine goes to that type of person . . . not everyone is represented" in every publication. But the extreme underrepresentation of people of color in *Instinct* mirrors and therefore reproduces inequality in political representation, over and above dividing the gay and lesbian readership so that Vazquez's hope for dialogue across difference becomes more and more unlikely anywhere in print.

Like Ellsworth, *Curve*'s Frances Stevens seemed willing, in principle, to represent a diverse lesbian population, but she had found that "For every 50 submissions from white women, we get one from a woman of color, so it's hard to print a range of voices." In a contradictory statement, Stevens said both that her magazine depended on advertising and that more advertising meant more flexibility in terms of diverse content. Apparently, it is not the advertising that Stevens finds constraining but the buyers' tastes. In fact, she seemed to argue that increased advertising might enable *Curve* to challenge buyers' tastes: "The cover is what sells the magazine—and so it's hard for us to take a chance and include a lot of diversity on the covers . . . but as we're getting more advertising revenue, we can be more daring, if you want to say, more representative, if you want to say." *Curve* claimed, at that point, a circulation of 68,000—68,000 readers who might not buy a magazine whose cover presented "diversity." It is hard to reconcile Stevens's belief that advertising revenue would enable to the magazine to produce a greater range of voices with her statement that it's hard to print such a range because of the lack of submissions from women of color. Here again is a white magazine editor with the impression that there aren't people of color out there writing and producing enough work. The explanation for white dominance in the gay and lesbian press lies with the identities of the majority of the personnel; the blindness of white privilege to the fact that people of color are indeed working, but without the same access to channels of production and distribution; and to the structure of a press geared toward winning advertising from corporate sponsors. As Mark Olmsted of *Genre* summed up the misunderstanding to which most of the members of this panel seemed subject: "People vote with their . . . money." If gay media producers believe that the market is a democratic arena in which consumers are equally represented, as they are theoretically at the polls, then it is no wonder that an increasingly national gay press failed to address the radical inequalities that split the gay and lesbian population in the United States along lines of race, gender, and class.

THE GAY PRESS PAST AND FUTURE

As Neil Miller summarized the history of the gay and lesbian press, "Beyond its role in creating the new gay consumer culture, the gay media played an important role in disseminating the ideas of the movement of a wider homosexual public."[115] As we have seen, there is no simple cause and effect at work between the gay press, the broader gay niche market, and the gay political movement. They have

been interactive and interdependent from early in the twentieth century. Franklin Kameny, a leading gay activist and pressman in the
1960s, described the interdependency as follows: "It was very much a
continuum. Expressing our outrage in those early publications laid the
psychological groundwork for what was to come. The *Ladder, The
Homosexual Citizen, Drum*—they created the mindset. Everything
builds on everything else. . . . We simply would not have had the riot
at the Stonewall Inn had it not been for the work that was initiated by
the militant gay press of the mid-1960s."[116]

Without gay newspapers, there might have been no Stonewall, but
following Stonewall—as shorthand for a movement that would focus
more and more on winning enfranchisement for individual gay men and
lesbians—commercialization became possible, if not necessary. As
well, the civil rights trend in the movement borrowed, if often unconsciously, the idea of nationalism from the black civil rights movement,
borrowing therefore a model of nationalism according to which the
reestablishment of masculinity is the way to liberation. And the idea of
a gay nation, which underlay a good deal of quite progressive political
organizing, was disseminated by a gay press that itself became a national commercial press. If that press was increasingly dominated by en-
tertainment-oriented content and geared overwhelmingly toward
whites, the gay nation built by it, like all nations, appeared to bring
together a highly diverse and geographically disparate group of people
under a false unity. Hidden parts of the history of the gay and lesbian
press, such as the racial politics of the proto-homophile publications,
show that the gay nation reproduced the inequalities structuring the
United States. The United States is the nation (and the market) within
which the gay nation (or niche) is distinct, and at the same time, the gay
nation slips on the mantle of the United States, ever more so as the
movement that "represents" gay people is increasingly shaped by the
decisions of people with money. The representation of gay and lesbian
people in the gay media is heavily implicated in the way the movement
represents the political interests of gay men and lesbians.

Just as Donald Embinder claimed in the pages of *Advertising Age*
in 1976, the gay market has indeed grown more specialized and more

closely tied to national mainstream corporations. In 1997, it was predicted that such a trend would continue:

> The growth in gay media is going to be in the direction of more spe-
> cialization. We're going to see regional gay and lesbian slick, glossy
> magazine titles, and more diversity in the advertiser base. American
> Express is advertising now and there are all sorts of major advertis-
> ers coming along—like Benetton, Perrier, and Calistoga Water. I
> think we're going to see some media barons buying up a lot of the
> local lesbian and gay papers and achieving some significant scale
> economies in terms of centralizing editorial marketing and business
> operations.[117]

But although occupying the stronghold of a niche may seem like exercising political power, it is power distributed as unequally as the market permits. The kind of specialization that constitutes the healthy
ecology of a niche may seem like diversity, but such diversity actually
cements divisions along lines of identity, reproducing the differences in
social power that already exist. At the same time, the gay press reduced
the distance between gay identity and culture on the one hand, and
straight identity and culture on the other. For example, the April 1999
issue of *OUT* magazine—with its two fashion photo spreads in addition to its fashion column, two beauty columns, fitness column, recipes
for juice cocktails, and dating quiz, among the ads—is virtually indis-
tinct from mainstream or straight-oriented magazines, except for the
gender of the models in pictures of couples and the particular chemical
compounds in the pharmaceutical ads. A column offering "solutions"
to a gay audience that distinguishes between more elusive goals, such
as "a fulfilling love life" or "a more rewarding job" and goals within
reach, like "better skin," indicates that liberation is here understood
quite purely as the liberation of the consumer in a world governed by
the most conventional ideals of gender, race, class, and, quite notably,
age.[118] One full page of the magazine casts a market research questionnaire in terms of fashion: "Maybe Something in . . . Green" asks
readers what kinds of financial services they use, inviting the readership to confirm *OUT*'s speculation that "Our Ouija board tells us that

we're all rich, as a community, in more ways than one . . . just being who we are."[119] Consumption of the April 1999 issue of *OUT* magazine is presented as the equivalent of enfranchisement, an equation illustrated in specific advertisements to the lesbian and gay market and supported by the myth of economic democracy, both of which are taken up in the following chapters.

3

ADVERTISING AND THE PROMISE OF CONSUMPTION

Great events are happening where gay and lesbian consumers make purchasing decisions.

—Grant Lukenbill, *Untold Millions*[1]

I f the idea of a national gay community had formed in the minds of many gay men and lesbians in the United States by the 1990s, this publicly held idea owed its formation to the spread of print capitalism among gay men and lesbians, that is, to the growth of a national commercial gay and lesbian press (traced in the previous chapter). The growth of the gay and lesbian press depends on, as much as it contributes to, the growth of a gay and lesbian niche market, which in turn depends quite heavily on increased advertising to gay men and lesbians. In this chapter, I argue that advertising to gay men and lesbians has played on ideas about national identity in two significant ways. First, such advertising has often appealed to gays on the basis of their identification as Americans. Second, advertising to gay men and lesbians has often promised that full inclusion in the national community of Americans is available through personal consumption. In other words, consumption has been held out as a route to political and social enfranchisement. A brief look back at the origins of mass production and the use of advertising, earlier in the twentieth century, to assimilate immigrants into American mass consumption will show that this kind of appeal has a long history. Just as niche marketing to gay men and lesbians operates on the line between distinctiveness from, and similarity to, dominant American identity, so too does the gay and lesbian political movement. Identity-based marketing and consumption are kissing cousins with identity politics. Each must be understood in relation to the other.

CONSUMING IDENTITY

Early in the twentieth century, mass production techniques developed from technologies that had already made possible large-scale standardized production. Spurred in part by the need for relatively large quantities of textiles, food, and arms during the Civil War, industrialists had succeeded in increasing the production of these and other goods. In order to purvey these goods, industrialists had also invested in improvements in infrastructure; thus oil, steel, iron, and other materials came to be processed or manufactured more efficiently. Meanwhile, late nineteenth-century innovations in photographic technology made possible the rise of pictorial advertising, which came to dominate the advertising industry. Equally and simultaneously, therefore, the manufacture of goods and the manufacture of pictorial advertising began to grow to mass proportions around the turn of the century. In looking at the case of the (paradigmatically American) automobile, the close relationship between the rise of mass production and the rapid growth of pictorial advertising becomes quite clear.

Noting the connection between the growth of advertising and the production and distribution of the automobile in the United States, an early chronicler of advertising commented in 1929 that "if advertising has 'made' the automobile industry, the automobile in turn has 'made' what we know as modern advertising."[2] Once cars began to sell, the automobile industry promoted significant growth in all ancillary industries, such as steel, glass, and suburban real estate development. Crucially, advertising was one of these. While sales of automobiles had begun on a small scale in 1898, and the first few thousand sold without any benefit of advertising, "in the nine years from 1900 to 1909 American production increased from 5,000 cars a year to 127,000 cars a year, and mass was regarded as having truly arrived. Trade-paper and magazine advertising and sensational motor races had done this."[3] But even then, the big boom was still ahead: "from 1910 dates the use of all [advertising] mediums by the automobile, and from that year also dates the greater rate of expansion in sales." In the years from 1910 to 1916, the production of cars and the advertising of cars both increased by approximately 800 percent. In 1914, more than 600,000 cars were manufactured and sold, and in 1924 that number had risen to 4,000,000.[4]

Cars were not only the first products of assembly-line manufacture, they were positively emblematic of mass-production techniques. Henry Ford's adaptation of Frederick Taylor's "principles of scientific management" to the manufacture of automobiles made Ford, his cars, and "Taylorism" famous. This mass production, naturally, required correspondingly mass consumption. In order to be able to afford the development and purchase of new technologies of production, and in order to make them profitable, industrialists needed to "produce" mass consumption, over and above commodities. "It is within such a context," writes social historian Stuart Ewen, "that the advertising industry began to assume modern proportions and that the institution of a mass consumer market began to arise."[5] Modern industrial methods of production also reorganized labor, shortening hours for workers and creating "leisure time" as a fixture of the typical day and the typical week. The regular availability of leisure time could be filled by increased consumption of all kinds, or perhaps increased consumption necessitated shorter work hours for waged workers in order that increased production would have a profitable outlet. Either way, the growth of the advertising industry was overdetermined.

Whereas nineteenth-century advertisements had been informational, almost exclusively composed of words, the rise of photography and then cinematographic technologies enabled a shift to images in the early twentieth century.[6] These technological and economic shifts held great significance for the nation *as* a nation. In an era in which the political, economic, military, and moral authority of the United States began to figure on the global stage, industrial growth was paramount. In

1926, two years after the number of cars manufactured in the United States hit the four-million mark, President Calvin Coolidge addressed the convention of the International Advertising Association in Washington, proclaiming that "Under the stimulation of advertising, the country has gone from the old hand methods of production which were so slow and laborious with high unit costs and low wages to our present great factory system and its mass production with the astonishing results of low unit costs and high wages. The preeminence of America in industry, which has constantly brought about a reduction of costs, has come very largely through the development of advertising."[7] Attributing America's distinction (from other countries) to the changing character of manufacture and the growth of advertising, Coolidge simultaneously cast the working of these industries in terms of national identity.

Given the dramatic shifts in industry that took place between 1900 and 1925—years in which the national wealth quintupled—the following fact is truly astounding: in the same years, magazine advertising growth was even greater than that of the automobile industry.[8] Proponents of advertising credited it with additional virtues; beside promoting production, reducing costs, and increasing wages, advertising was said to encourage education, improve people's sanitation habits, raise their living standards, instill aesthetic values in them, and provide them with necessary and useful information. Similarly, advertising was used to help recast consumption in terms of its significance to national identity, as both a patriotic duty and as a route to Americanization. One observer wrote in 1959 that in the years between the world wars, the consumer was enjoined, by advertisements, to consume constantly: "Otherwise factories would close down from the Atlantic to the Pacific and the golden century would come down in ruins. It was an American's patriotic duty to 'buy till it hurts,' in peace no less than in war." [9]

For historian Roland Marchand, the growth of advertising in the 1920s and 30s reflected and reproduced a collective preoccupation with modernity: the advertising industry embodied a transition to modern modes of production, and advertisements told stories about the relations between modernity on the one hand and the body, work, custom, hygiene, culture, ethnicity, gender, sexuality, and national identity on the other. In the "parables" of private consumption in magazine advertisements of the period, a mass audience was implied, or perhaps imagined, by ad-makers.[10] That audience was middle-class, white, native-born, and largely (but not nearly exclusively) feminine. Brought into being as a coherent group by consuming print commodities and by the advertising that came to subsidize those publications, the audience of commercial magazine readers did indeed fit the description imagined by ad-makers. But that audience also needed to be brought up to speed. Although they constituted the symbolically and demographically dominant "Americans," magazine consumers needed to become acculturated to the relentless onslaught of ever-new manifestations of modernity. Here, too, print capitalism contributed to national consciousness, to the idea of a unified American community. At the time, national mass-magazine circulation and its advertising were the furnace of the "melting pot":

> To national advertising, as well as to editorial matter in our widely read periodicals, has recently been attributed most of the growth of a national homogeneity in our people, a uniformity of ideas which, despite the mixture of races, is found to be greater here than in European countries whose population is made up almost wholly of people of one race and would seem easier to nationalize in all respects. Constant acquisition of ideas from the same sources has caused Americans living three thousand miles apart to be alike in their living habits and thoughts, in their desires and their method of satisfying them.[11]

Initially, then, advertising aimed at producing this kind of mass consumption sought to produce homogeneity. Producers and advertisers were interested in erasing identity differences, particularly between people from different countries of origin. Markedly, in the 1920's, when the advertising industry began consistently to subsidize mass media, "uniformity" depended on the erasure of ethnic differences. Following decades of immigration, the attempt to create a mass market went hand in hand with an attempt to Americanize ethnic minorities. Advertisers have long promised that American identity and the mythical privileges attendant on U.S. citizenship—freedom, rights, justice, opportunity—are available to disenfranchised people if they just consume enough, and in the right ways: "To immigrants, the message of advertising was implicit: only by complete fusion into the melting pot did one gain a place in the idealized American society of the advertising pages."[12] Such fusion would also further the creation of a mass consumer market.

As increasingly standardized products were sold to the growing mass market, their advertising increasingly conveyed standards of American identity. At the same time, the continued growth of the market depended on the incorporation of more, and different, markets. Put another way, competition required producers to transcend local markets and to promote an ideological warrant for consumption by all sorts of Americans. The same dynamics would compel manufacturers to identify niche markets later in the century, but early on this nationalization plan invested in the assimilation of ethnic minorities, and also in the conflation between assimilation and increased consumption. Scholar Stewart Ewen points to the example of Frances Kellor, Director of the American Association of Foreign Language Newspapers, an advertising agency that catered specifically to the immigrant press. Under Kellor's direction, the agency promoted the conflation of "the acceptance of American products with patriotism." It also promoted "the destruction of all cultural distinctions within the nation."[13] Perhaps most succinct is Kellor's affirmation that "National advertising is the great Americanizer."[14] A national press and a national advertising industry, then, were the twin engines of an assimilation drive and of the growth of a mass-consumption society from at least the 1920s.

From the teens through the 1930s, policy-makers and intellectuals questioned whether the foreign-language press contributed to the Americanization of immigrants. Proponents argued that the foreign-language press was an agency of assimilation, that it made immigrants more comfortable, that they would engage more actively in civic participation in a place where they felt comfortable, that literacy (even in one's native tongue) correlated with increased production, and that the foreign-language press thus provided a mechanism of transition into American life.[15] The foreign-language press debate serves as a reminder that specialized commercial presses have been critical in defining relations—long before the gay and lesbian press raised the same issues—between marginal identity groups and the larger social group-ing of "Americans." Eastern and southern Europeans were especially subject to debate regarding the virtues and demerits of retaining native customs—including dress, food, and language—in terms of immi-grants' qualification for participation in the political, economic, and cultural life of the United States. Perhaps the decline of the foreign-language press, as well as that of the English-language ethnic press, by the 1960s indicates that assimilation for those European immigrants was largely achieved. Of course, diminished immigration, World War II, the advent of television, and the hegemonic fiction of cultural unity and conformity of the 1950s also facilitated integration into American political and cultural life.

During the 1920s, when ethnic-press activity peaked, one supporter of that press, William Carlson Smith, conceded that "certain nationalist newspapers" had not favored the Americanization of their readers; yet he felt that the inducement to read would prepare immigrants to partic-ipate intelligently in the affairs of American citizenship. Echoing Kel-lor, Smith asserted that "Even the advertisement of American goods is an Americanizing influence."[16] As a footnote to this assertion, Smith re-ferred to the influence of the mail-order catalogue in an East Frisian community in Illinois. Quoting fellow commentators on the process of Americanization, Smith implicitly imagined a definition of "press" broad enough to include various forms of print-capitalism: "Advertise-ments are found to be significant means of acculturation. . . . One com-mon source of reading for all is the mail order catalogue, of which every household has one or more."[17] It is important to realize that the question of Americanization is a racialized question, applying only to white eth-nic groups and never to people of African descent in the United States. It was not until African Americans were conceived of as a target mar-ket, which was not until the 1960s, that advertising intentionally ad-dressed black people, even as part of the mass market—of which they were, nevertheless, an active part. Gay men and lesbians have also acted as part of the mass market, as both producers and consumers, of course, but not *as* gay men and lesbians. Until the production of the gay and lesbian niche market.

THE RISE OF THE GAY NICHE MARKET

Thus in the early decades of this century, mass production, consumption, and especially advertising came to prevail and to address both mass markets and white immigrant submarkets. Perhaps more precisely, advertising came to address large numbers of people as though they were a single—and American, or at least Americanizable—mass. Meanwhile, the wage-labor system encouraged the growth of cities, and more and more individuals left rural family life for them. Recall D'Emilio's argument in the Introduction that these developments made it possible for homosexuals to seek out other people organizing their social identities on the basis of their sexualities.[18] Of course, suburban life also expanded during this time, but it was in the cities that gay social life began to emerge. By this reasoning, modern modes of production and consumption enabled both gay identity and the beginning of what might be called gay community in the early twentieth century. Gay identity and community, then, are functions of the rise of advanced capitalism and the industrialization of advertising, and they are therefore subject to the promise of Americanization through consumption.

Historically, for the pro-assimilation forces of business and state alike, consumption was an answer to the "problem" of ethnic differences: "interest in mass consumption would equal interest in conformity. Social norms could be managed by and through consumption norms."[19] Immigrants engaged in traditional ethnic practices were often ostracized by the native-born; they were subject to charges of un-Americanism. In effect, "most of the hostilities toward the various ethnic communities could be clearly connected to these people's violation of the norms of consumption. 'I'd like them better if they didn't wear such queer clothes.'"[20] Thus shopping came to bear the promise of conformity, of belonging, of incorporation into dominant social practices and hence into American identity.

There have been, of course, many changes in the way capital circulates between the 1920s and the 1990s, or between Frances Kellor's time and the 1990s, in which gay men and lesbians were aggressively targeted as a viable consumer market. The throughline was pressure on producers to create new classes of consumers, or new niches. So at the same time that producers have needed national markets, they have also needed specialized markets, and it is in this context that "diversity" has become both a social value (however superficially) and an economic imperative. Since 1970, African Americans, women, Southerners, Hispanics, Christian fundamentalists, youth, and the elderly have been among the leading niche markets, and still the drive for market expansion has lead to the invention of new niches. By the 1990s, the contradiction facing gay men and lesbians was that the distinctiveness of our identity served certain economic functions, while it also served as the barrier between us and rights, social acceptance, and access to certain social institutions.

Clearly, the question of whether advertising, among other forms of print capitalism, promotes or retards "nationalism" or assimilation is one that applied in the 1990s to gay men and lesbians much as it applied to so many ethnic European groups from the mid-nineteenth to the mid-twentieth century.[21] This is not to say that gay men and lesbians constitute an ethnic group. The history of the foreign-language press does not prove, or even suggest, that gay and lesbian group formation works the same way ethnic-group formation tends to work.[22] The question here is, does the history of ethnic or racial groups in this country shed light on the situation of gay men and lesbians in the late twentieth century? Certainly there are some significant resonances relating to commercial life. Both gay men and lesbians, as a group, and ethnic groups have been offered the market as a site of assimilation. Or more precisely, the market has enabled both kinds of groups to finesse the choice between "nationalism" and assimilation. That is, the market is the prime mechanism for defusing the conflict between sameness and difference, or between assimilation and de-assimilation.

If an analogy between gay men and lesbians, as a group, and ethnic groups is not theoretically warranted, nonetheless the cases of the immigrant press and the gay press show that there have historically been certain regular effects of specialized commercial presses on particular social groups. For one thing, those groups share a subjection to target marketing. If the foreign-language press served as an agency of assimilation, as its proponents argued, it was successful enough to have rendered itself largely obsolete by 1960. Niche marketing does not ultimately favor seamless identification as "American" on the part of consumers. Such identification might threaten the kind of social diversity that is compatible with a proliferation of niche markets. Therefore, advertising in the gay press encourages both national consciousness and distinct-group consciousness.

With the antecedent of the ethnic press in mind, claims to gay ethnicity take on a particular cast. Because of the ways in which claims to gay identity are negotiated through the market, claims to gay ethnicity tend to serve a marketing program that simultaneously promotes assimilation and identity-based consumption. The 1995 claims of Kahan and Mulryan, two gay marketers, demonstrate the theoretical consequences of seeing gay men and lesbians as a (white) ethnic group:

> It's useful to see the gay and lesbian market as similar to an immigrant market. Like immigrants, homosexuals are birds of a feather. They stick together, support each other, and vote for each other. . . . Like immigrants, they are proud of their distinctiveness but fear being branded as different. In addition, gay men and lesbians exhibit all the characteristics of an immigrant tribe. They have distinctive mores and fashions, language, signs, symbols, gathering places, and enclaves.[23]

Though apparently motivated by a simple desire to convince advertisers that there is a viable gay market to target, this is a complicated passage. Referring to sociological definitions of social groups, Kahan and Mulryan's language recalls early sociological descriptions of the symbolic universe of a subcultural group. But neither the concept of "subculture" nor the recuperation of ethnicity depends on an analogy between gay identity and ethnic identity.[24] Kahan and Mulryan perfectly articulate the way that a range of identities can be manipulated in the market so that difference is not only not threatening, it is not so different from sameness. Such manipulations serve gay people themselves unevenly, offering a set of images that make assimilation through the market attractive, and therefore suggesting that the struggle for enfranchisement need not be a struggle. "Distinctiveness" becomes reduced to style choices, which can be addressed by products; distinctiveness need not lead to political process.[25] Interestingly, gay men and lesbians have shared with ethnic groups high ranking on a list of the most hated groups in the United States.[26] And if distinctiveness is a matter of pride, as Kahan and Mulryan state, such pride can be, and has been, appropriated and commodified. Gay and lesbian "pride," in particular, was throughout the 1970s and 1980s the most common label on demonstrations of gay and lesbian existence, demonstrations that were often oppositional. In the 1990s, "pride" became the name for the corporations that came, increasingly, to run annual gay and lesbian parades; it also became increasingly common as both commodity and pitchword.

DIRECT MAIL MARKETING: CATALOGUE AND CARDPACK

The gay press has been a leading site of interaction between movement and market, and that interaction has sponsored the idea of a gay nation; other forms of print capitalism followed the gay press as it spread out across the United States. After winning the right to distribute through the U.S. mail, and after decades of a nearly exclusive traffic in soft- and hard-core pornography, sex toys, and other sexual content geared to an exclusively male audience, marketers to the gay and lesbian niche market expanded on two print genres in the 1990s—the catalogue and the cardpack. Cardpacks are small packages of advertisements (the size of index cards) for various companies, collated by a marketing company. As two of many mail-order techniques, neither catalogues nor cardpacks are entirely new. Perhaps the most famous catalogue distributor, Sears, Roebuck and Co., published regularly scheduled catalogues offering a broad range of merchandise by 1893.[27] Even cardpacks have their antecedents in the late nineteenth century, when trade cards were distributed through retailers, who gave customers a few at a time as they completed their transactions. Considered the first direct mass-marketing medium, those trade cards sported some of the first picture advertisements and were therefore precursors to pictorial advertising in magazines and newspapers, as well as to the cardpacks of the 1990s.[28]

As these mail-order techniques found their way to the gay and lesbian niche market in the 1990s, the catalogue and the cardpack brought identity-based shopping into the home, echoing, as they dropped through the mail chute, the promise that liberation would derive from sales.[29] Reviewing the "embryonic catalogue boomlet" of the 1990s, one article in the *New York Times* said that "Offerings aimed at gay men and lesbians are developing into a nascent niche in the nation's estimated $54.7 billion catalogue industry."[30] Catalogues and cardpacks are the logical extensions of the general trend toward market segmentation, the process through which advertisers identify niches based on all sorts of identities, affiliations, and affinities. Identification of the gay market as especially affluent and abnormally well educated made sending catalogues and cardpacks to this segment appear profitable. Thus it was logical to send cardpacks into households identifiable as gay.[31]

Catalogues are a central means of privatizing access to printed matter and to consumption opportunities; shopping in the privacy of one's own home differs greatly from shopping in stores. Not only does the store-shopper have to navigate through public places to do his or her shopping, the public shopper also comes into contact with other shoppers. The gay or lesbian store-shopper, in particular, engages in identity-based shopping in places that have traditionally functioned as centers of information as well as sites of financial transaction, such as bars and bookstores. Interestingly, bars and bookstores constituted the community's first information centers, but they also constituted the first public places where identity-based consumption could take place—and such consumption was expressly (as in bars) or incidentally (as in bookstores) interactive, even collective. Furthermore, stores serving a gay and lesbian clientele have usually been located in areas where gay (more than lesbian) business and residence are concentrated.[32] It must also be said that gay or lesbian identity-based shopping, like bar going, has historically carried a physical threat with it; people publicly identifiable as gay or lesbian are at risk of homophobic violence. For these reasons, if gay identity is negotiated in the marketplace, it must be differently composed depending on whether the market is literal and physical or remote.[33]

The privatization of shopping via catalogues does not simply follow public shopping historically, nor do private forms of shopping supersede public forms; they coexist. Shopping through the mail became industrialized later than store shopping, but the U.S. mail-order business was already well over a hundred years old in the 1990s, so in many ways the public and private technologies of mass distribution and consumption have arisen in tandem. However durable the traditions of public and private shopping, the marriage of niche marketing and mail-order techniques is a relatively recent one, and gay people seeking anything other than sex apparatus and paraphernalia have only enjoyed access to identity-based consumption at home since the 1990s.[34]

Catalogues and cardpacks, like other direct mail marketing techniques, depend entirely on lists of viable "prospects," lists that marketers buy from list brokers, other for-profit outfits, and nonprofit organizations. "'The availability of mailing lists is the No. 1 most important thing to having a successful catalogue,' said David Alport, publisher of *Out and About,* a New Haven travel newsletter for gay men and lesbians."[35] The most prominent list brokers sell national lists; Strubco's advertisement for its list not only demonstrates graphically that the nation is the conceptual basis of the lists, it also demonstrates that the nation of gay consumers and the United States are geographically coextensive[36] (see Figure 3.1). If gay national identification and U.S. national identification are compatible, if their compatibility is demonstrated graphically and visually in the commodities described below, then the technologies of mail-order distribution reinforce the interpretation that these two nations are geographically coextensive.[37]

CENSUS: MARKET AS STATE

As the direct mail map indicates, information about consumers—information about their identities, their preferences, and their incomes, in addition to where they live—is the key to mapping out a sales strategy. In order to draw an accurate profile of most market segments, marketers depend on combining census information with direct market research. However, in the case of the gay and lesbian community, there has been no census information available because the federal census has never asked for sexual orientation. Neither have unofficial statistical methods systems generated reliable counts of gay men and lesbians. One problem

Have you tried gay lists?

Strubco is the world leader in marketing of lesbian and gay
lists. In addition to our 500,000 name National Community
Masterfile, we market and manage another 250,000 gay
names. We have access, through our brokerage division, to
virtually any list (gay or non-gay) available on the market.

Strubco also markets package insert programs
(Continental Pharmacy, Shocking Gray catalog and others) and
provides insertion program services with a circulation of more
than 500,000 in the gay market.

Among our exclusive lists are:
Shocking Gray Catalog
Made in Gay America Catalog
Christopher & Castro Catalog
A Different Light Catalog
Creative Time
Community Research Initiative on AIDS
Treatment Action Group
Genre Magazine
New York Native
Christopher Street Magazine
Christopher Street Financial
Donors: Gay, Lesbian and AIDS
Community Consumers
Gay and Lesbian Subscribers
New Festival
Lift the Ban Donors
Physicians Association for AIDS Care
Strubco Enhanced Database

Base rental fees begin at $65 per thousand names, for a
one-time use. Names are available on magnetic tape, disk,
cheshire or pressure-sensitive labels.

Most lists are selectable by gender, state, SCF, zip and
many are selectable by recency or level of response. For free
datacards or further information, contact **Charles Ching** at
212-242-1900, or fax 212-242-1963.

Figure 3.1a "Have you tried gay lists?"

is that the population is self-reporting; given the multiple social disin-
centives to reporting, gay men and lesbians tend to be undercounted in
systems that ask them to designate their sexual orientation.

In order to compensate for non-reporting and non-self-identification, . . .
researchers are developing and refining batteries of behavioral and ge-

The single largest gay and lesbian list in the world is Strubco's famous **National Community Masterfile**. More than 500 not-for-profit and commercial organizations marketing to the gay community have found this list responsive and profitable for their offers.

National Community Masterfile State Counts:

AK	603	ID	546	MT	511	RI	1.871
AL	2.343	IL	16.704	NC	8.054	SC	2.415
AR	1.266	IN	4.912	ND	284	SD	352
AZ	3.699	KS	1.786	NE	1.076	TN	2.878
CA	104.574	KY	2.724	NH	1.962	TX	12.965
CO	5.576	LA	3.729	NJ	12.582	UT	1.179
CT	5.965	MA	19.130	NM	1.743	VA	13.739
DC	10.852	MD	11.875	NV	1.304	VT	1.294
DE	1.102	ME	2.056	NY	61.602	WA	6.754
FL	14.946	MI	8.350	OH	12.140	WI	5.115
GA	7.797	MN	4.960	OK	2.139	WV	1.256
HI	1.812	MO	4.520	OR	6.848	WY	272
		MS	1.039	PA	16.688		

The **National Community Masterfile** is selectable by gender, state, SCF, zip and new movers. For free datacards or further information, contact **Charles Ching** at (212)242-1900. CCP294 or fax (212)242-1963.

Figure 3.1b   "National Community Masterfile State Counts"

ographical indicators to more efficiently and effectively identify gay consumers. For instance, analyses of ticket sales for the gay-themed play *Angels in America* and other gay mailing lists point to gay neighborhoods in the New York area.[38]

Even if this "refined" indicator seems at first to produce only the most obvious fact, and laboriously at that, it still suggests that market research is attempting to reproduce censuslike information. Market research thus invents a demographic category, something like "gay men and lesbians." But the problem of definition besets any attempt to count gay men and lesbians: the group of people who practice same-sex sexual behavior is not the same as the group of people who identify as gay or lesbian. Nor is either of these groups the same as the group of people who see *Angels in America*. There is not an exact correspondence between behavior and the social identity. Meanwhile, among those people who do claim a nonheterosexual social identity, some identify as homosexual, others as gay, or lesbian, or bisexual, still others as dyke, queer, or celibate, to name just a few categories.

Yet, in the face of the impossibility of an accurate statistical count of gay men and lesbians, several kinds of studies have been made. The most famous of these is Kinsey's study of male sexuality, which led him to speculate that one in ten men in the United States was homosexual.[39] Using accepted sexological standards, Kinsey's sample was both random and very large. Other social-scientific academic studies have been conducted in the fifty years since Kinsey's, but none has attained its status. A voter survey study that queried people leaving polling places after the 1992 presidential election was reported in the *New York Times,* but it was neither so random nor so large as Kinsey's study. The survey asked voters to fill out a questionnaire, so the sample was already limited to active and literate voters (a group literally enfranchised), on top of which, it asked for people's self-designations, thus skewing the result incalculably. Comparing this study with a market research study on gay and lesbian income by Overlooked Opinions, a *New York Times* article reported that "The voter survey found that they earned less money than the average voter, while the market research study found that they earned far more than the average American."[40] This discrepancy is just one of the reasons that this article on "Two Pictures of Gay America" had to conclude, of both surveys, that "Neither can claim the accuracy of a census."[41] Clearly, though, in the face of a paucity of credible academic studies, and in the nearly complete absence of official state counts of gay men and lesbians (and attendant demographic information), market research has been eager to step into the void.

However, unlike academic social science research, market research is often proprietary. Designed and used in the interest of profit, "It amounts to a private sociology and psychology of the consumer society."[42] As Strubco's numerical mapping of gay households in the United States indicates, marketers intent on reaching a gay and lesbian niche invest financially and metaphorically in knowledge about who's gay-identified, where, and with what consumption habits. Among producers of gay demographic information, the now defunct Overlooked Opinions has probably been the most influential.[43] Throughout the 1990s, one of the most active gay market research firms was Rivendell Marketing, which, as Overlooked Opinions had done, based its claims in studies of readers of gay publications. Readers, like voters, are an already specialized group, and therefore statistical claims about them do not represent factual claims about the gay community as a whole. Rivendell supplies the National Gay Newspaper Guild with statistics about the readership of gay publications in order to help them win advertising, but Rivendell's ads do not always prominently feature the fact that the claims are being made about readers rather than gay people in general. (See Figure 1.3 in Chapter 1.) While market research often neglects to reveal itself as such, a close look at one example of market research does reveal the investment that gay niche marketers have in the conception of a gay nation among gay consumers.

In 1996, Overlooked Opinions advertised in various gay newspapers and on various internet locations, asking people to call in and participate in a "census." Callers answered questions by pushing their phone buttons, but after ten minutes the survey ended and the call became an advertisement for a gay-owned utilities company called Community Spirit. In the introduction to this survey, an electronic voice announced that Community Spirit was conducting "a census of gay and lesbian North America" in "one of the most important efforts ever . . . to document lesbians, gays, and bisexuals across the U.S. and Canada." Mobilizing the language of "measurable response," Community Spirit played on a kind of gay nationalism, illustrating that gay nationalism is compatible with U.S. nationalism. The inclusion of Canada doesn't disturb this association; on the contrary, while it echoes the familiar late-night TV unit of commercial offers available in the "U.S. and Canada," the survey's extension of the northern U.S. border notably maintains the more racially charged southern border. In characterizing the company as "by our people and for our people," the ad/survey posited a friendly and close, if not identical, relation between the gay community and U.S. national foundations. Draped in the rhetoric of U.S. nationalism and of state bureaucracy, this survey/ad enacts the convergence of market and state, reinforcing the equation between citizens and consumers.

After this introduction, the bulk of the call involved a series of questions that were both demographic—asking for age, race, income, nationality, education, employment, place of residence, sexuality—and consumption oriented—questions about publications read, commodities purchased, value of property owned, cultural events attended. If it was a census at all, it was nevertheless indistinguishable from market research.[44] If it was market research, it is entirely possible that the value of the call for Community Spirit was that it enabled the company to cull the phone numbers of callers and augment mailing lists for sale.[45] So this market research-*cum*-ad-*cum*-census folds the identities of consumers into the identities of citizens in the gay/U.S. nation, quantifying them in language that suggests a corresponding enfolding of state into market. "The people" who count in this census count exclusively as consumers.[46]

LOGO, FLAG, AND MAP

Just as a map symbolizes a specific nation, a logo symbolizes a business; both map and logo graphically represent a body of people, a corporate body. Whereas the former refers to a group constituted through shared national identity, a logo refers to a group constituted through common market activity. However, according to Benedict Anderson, the logo had it origins in the map, making them both instruments of nationalism. Of the "map-as-logo" in the eighteenth and nineteenth centuries, Anderson writes, "In this shape the map entered an infinitely reproducible series, available for transfer to posters, official seals, letterheads, magazine and textbooks covers, tablecloths, and hotel walls. Instantly recognizable, everywhere visible, the logo-map penetrated deep into the popular imagination, forming a powerful emblem for the anti-colonial nationalisms being born."[47] But while the logo ultimately lost its direct reference to nation, increasingly serving as a symbol of business, its mass reproducibility still stands as the feature that links print capitalism to national identity.[48]

Aimed at people presumably unified, or unifiable, by common consumption practices, the logos of national gay businesses implicitly superimpose list after list of gay consumers onto the map of the United States. Some logos make this idea graphic, as in the logo for a company named "Christopher and Castro," in which the street in New York and the street in San Francisco meet, forming the cornerstone for a national gay community of consumers (see Figure 3.2). Signifying the union of the two most famous gay male ghettos in the country, the logo clearly remaps the gay community from coast to coast, addressing itself to an

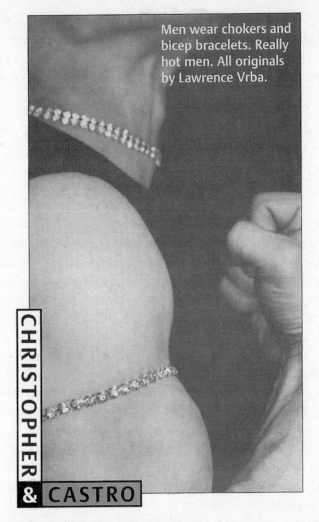

Figure 3.2 "Christopher and Castro"

audience that imagines itself in shared national identity with other gay male consumers in the United States. Ironically, this logo, like the original logo-map, is an emblem for an anticolonial nationalism, in that it unifies the gay nation morally and geographically. At the same time, the logo symbolizes the superimposition of the imagined gay community on the United States, as it suggests that a gay market spans the continent from sea to shining sea. Finally, the ad itself insists on the "real" masculinity of gay men in this newly mapped nation. The Christopher and Castro logo perfectly depicts simultaneous assimilation and de-assimilation.

A ubiquitous cluster of merchandise available to the gay and lesbian niche market illustrates the same union between the gay nation and the United States. The rainbow flag stands as an emblem of gay nationalism, simply because flags are a standard symbol of nationhood. In 1978, James Baker designed the rainbow flag for the San Francisco Pride Parade. By the 1990s, the rainbow flag had been fully commodified. The following objects were all for sale with rainbow imagery, representing just a sampling of available rainbow commodities: aprons, bathrobes, bath salts, beach apparel, beach umbrellas, beam lights (which project a rainbow onto the wall), bumper stickers, candles (short and fat, tall and thin, and for birthday cakes), checks and checkbook covers, clock hands, computer icons, "door markers"/mezuzahs, fridge magnets, gym shorts, liberation rings, license-plate frames, mugs, picture frames, pillows, place mats, pot holders, rain umbrellas, Rainbow Gayme (board game), rainbow-message soap, ribbons, suspenders, soda fountain glasses, tank tops, temporary tattoos, towels, tote bags, vests, wall borders, windbreakers, windsocks, and jewelry of all descriptions, including commitment rings, earrings, pins, and bracelets. Often the catalogues that sell this merchandise make the little joke in their accompanying descriptions, particularly of rainbow clothing, that the buyer would be making a statement . . . a "fashion statement." As usual, the reduction of politics to style implies that consumption can amount to political change.

Also common are commodities that combine the rainbow flag with the U.S. flag. Continuing with the metaphor of nationalism, the gay nation imagined by the national gay press and other advertising media covers exactly the same area as the geopolitical space of the United States. So, while direct mail marketing to gay men and lesbians banks on the nationalized gay market, it is full of pictures that equate the United States and the "gay nation." Item after item in the Shocking Gray catalogue demonstrates visually and rhetorically that gay nationalism and U.S. nationalism are compatible; the spatial overlay—gay nation on United States—is demonstrated graphically in symbols of the movement, but even more so in the commodities for sale in the gay and lesbian niche market.

While this kind of merchandise is widely available for sale in stores from Christopher to Castro streets, from South Beach to Montrose to Silver Lake, the examples that follow come from the Shocking Gray catalogue. In the catalogue, items are presented in photographs, and accompanying captions describe and comment on the commodities pictured. The commodities that illustrate the relationship between the gay nation and the United States include the "Rainbow USA" pin, which superimposes the rainbow colors on the outline of the continental United States. In the Spring 1995 edition of the catalogue, the caption under this pin reads, "Captures it all with simplicity." (See Figure 3.3.) With stunning efficiency, the pin and its caption refer to the capturing of the flag, or the identity between the borders of the United States and the gay nation; the caption further suggests that politics may be played out, with ease, on the playing field of the market.

The Shocking Gray catalogue also proffers a Rainbow USA pin whose caption says, "It's a queer nation after all," as well as a flag that mixes the rainbow pattern (which composes the gay flag) with the stars and stripes that compose the U.S. flag (see Figures 3.4 and 3.5). One such flag (not pictured here) is described as "Gay and totally patriotic," while another flag's description claims that "Gay Pride is just around the corner." (See Figure 3.5.) Then there is a series of merchandise "de-

A Rainbow USA Pin
Captures it all with simplicity.
#50010 $9.95

Figure 3.3 "Rainbow USA Pin"

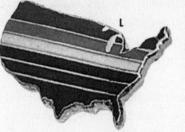

Rainbow USA
pin — it's a
queer nation
after all!
L In beautiful
enameled brass.
¼ x ½".
#50010 $9.95

Figure 3.4 " . . . it's a queer nation after all!"

H Handsome New Glory Flags
For Better Window Dressing
Gay Pride is just around the
corner. Perfect for patios, beach
houses and porches.
3 X 5' #40293 $28.95
2 X 3' #40109 $18.95

Figure 3.5 "Handsome New Glory Flags . . ."

signed to let you express all your patriotism, pride and joy. . . ." (See Figure 3.6.) One jacket in this series sports only elements of the American flag (no rainbow) and has a caption that reads, "For gay and lesbian Americans who stand for freedom." (See Figure 3.6.) The United States imagined here is a country populated by rights-seeking, nation-loving gay and lesbian consumers.

Perhaps the items in the catalogue that mix rainbow flags with stars and stripes ought to be read ironically. I make no claim about the intention behind these objects or their descriptions, nor about their interpretation by actual consumers. Producers and consumers alike may, of course, produce and consume with a healthy sense of camp. If I read them without irony, it is because, regardless of their irony quotient, the nation appears as a central theme in the land of gay retail. My point is not to take such items "straight"; my point is that these items name the

The Colors of Country, Pride and Style

These accessories and clothing items are specially designed to let you express all your patriotism, pride and joy in bold and witty design.

L NEW! Rainbow Cap with Lower Crown
Works with lots of fun outfits. High quality, sturdy and protective. 100% cotton.
#50017 $14.95

M New Glory Stars Rainbow Nylon Vest
Hot look for parades, parties or perhaps the next family reunion? M,L,XL.
#50014 $46.95

N Rainbow Nylon Jacket For Your Spring Wardrobe
This one is perfect. Made of sturdy nylon. Elastic sleeve and waist with mock turtle neck and steel zipper. S,M,L,XL.
Regular #28403 $99.95
Quilted #28404 $109.95

O Old Glory Jacket is a National Sensation of Bold Color
For gay & lesbian Americans who stand for freedom. S,M,L,XL.
Regular #28401 $149.95
Quilted #28402 $159.95

P New Glory Fanny Pack
Flatters from Behind
Water resistant nylon.
#50016 $29.95

Q Stars & Stripes T-Shirt
There has never been a more important time to wave the flag. 100% Cotton. M,L,XL.
#00132 $16.95

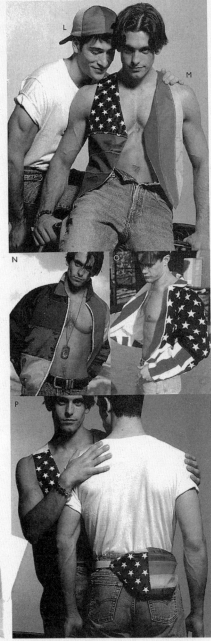

STARS & STRIPES FOREVER

Figure 3.6 "The Colors of Country, Pride and Style" and "Gay and Lesbian Americans"

Figure 3.7 "Stars and stripes gym shorts for all
American boys"

nation and identify it as an idea under active construction. However much it may be in flux, the idea of a gay nation is explicitly and implicitly related both to the commodification of gay and lesbian culture and politics and to the desire for or against assimilation into U.S. culture and politics. Whether quoted with parodic or camp intent, posited as the agent against which to react, or played as a straightforward salute, "nation" is a recurring invocation in the press, as well as in the print-based marketing techniques discussed here, and as such was clearly a matter of active ambivalence and conflict, desire and disavowal, for many gay men and lesbians in the 1990s.

As they are excluded from the liberal idea of nation itself, noncitizens are implicitly and explicitly excluded from this consumption opportunity. This exclusion is reproduced in the description of the only other Shocking Gray item composed entirely of a U.S. flag motif. Shorts adorning a manifestly healthy, young, stereotypically masculine white man are "for all American boys"—meaning simultaneously every American boy, every boy who is all-American, and *not* any boy who isn't American or any American who isn't a boy (or any boy who isn't a real boy) (see Figure 3.7). American and white often overlap implicitly in this advertising world, as in U.S. culture at large. While there are, particularly in the catalogues, some nonwhite models, white people and men are numerically overrepresented. On the one hand, that overrepresentation merely reflects the fact that white people and men have greater purchasing power than people of color and women, respectively. On the other hand, it also reflects, or reinforces, an ideology in which white and American mean the same thing and stand, together, in a relation of domination to people of color and non-Americans.

THE VALUE OF RACE

A 1995 cardpack from Our Tribe Marketing, advertising mostly sex products, manifests a similar racial ideology. In the whole cardpack, there appear to be approximately 100 white models and about 5 models of color.[49] In the only two ads in which I visually identify the models as men of color, the products advertised explicitly thematize race.

One is a video called *Jailhouse Rican,* distributed by a company called the Latin Connection. The other ad pictures a series of videos distributed by Male Instinct: compare the description of *Uncut Hunks 2,* which presents the "European charm of Hans Mueller," with *Latin Fever,* which features "Swarthy Latin types." This latter video promises the "hottest Hispanic humping caught on tape. . . . These hunky honchos can really stuff a burrito. Ay Caramba." The description of another video, *Black Alley: South of the Border,* assures its viewers "The combination of all-male action's best-looking dark-skinned men and Catalina Video's commitment to quality ensure this black and Latin boner-fest will keep you wet and aroused." In addition to stereotyping the models, these descriptions reduce them to either body parts, ethnic/racial categories, or both. Stereotyping, objectification, and reduction are, of course, preeminent techniques of domination. Yet this language is obviously not a necessary effect of the pornographic genre; recall the description of the "European charm" of a white model. There were no videos advertised as presenting "the best-looking white men."

The tendency to collapse American with white is vividly pictured in an ad for videos distributed by Crossing Borders, in which men of color are located on the other side of national borders. In one ad, an apparently Asian man is holding on to a rope, vaguely suggesting bondage or hard physical labor, and resonating with the images in the old physique magazines in which photographs of black and Latin men utilize props such as crates and chains. This ad clearly addresses men whose fantasies feature "exotic" men from other lands, implying that the consumers will be nonexotic men from *this* land. The ad equates all exotic men with each other, thus collapsing untold cultural, racial, and national differences into one package—opposite to, and produced for, the white U.S. citizen, consumer of difference. Ad analyst William O'Barr observes, "When foreigners are treated as a commodity, it is their differences and the exoticism of their lives that are emphasized." These porn ads certainly corroborate O'Barr's observation. By contrast, as was indicated by the premium on Americanizing immigrants earlier in the century, "When foreigners are thought of as a market, advertising emphasizes the similarity of their lives and desires to Americans."[50] The construction of an American consumer of difference has been a continuing project, one tied up with the construction of a mass market. The creation of a mass market involved not only the Americanization of foreigners, but also "the creation of an average, all-American," who was in turn defined in opposition to exotic others.[51]

Similar racial politics were displayed, but strictly within U.S. borders, in mid-1990s Tzabaco catalogues. Billing itself as the Modern General Store, Tzabaco produced catalogues geared toward gay men and lesbians that feature largely items recalling the late 1940s and the 1950s.[52] This may have been an attempt to remind baby-boomer shoppers of early childhood experiences, but it also necessarily hearkened back to a pre–civil rights period. The nostalgia of this catalogue is questionable at best when it appears to display references to Jim Crow race relations with a certain fondness. In an ad for plates, the copy that begins with a reference to service "Pullman style" goes on to say that "This Tzabaco design recalls the days when the great railroads rumbled along southern desert routes to California." (See Figure 3.8.) The phrase "tables set with perfect linens" brings to mind images of African American porters setting those tables and thus notably romanticizes or ignores their labor, as well as the labor of the many Asian workers who built the railroads. And while there may be some shift in meaning between the original appearance of these symbols and commodities and their contemporary recirculation, I am troubled by the way the "Platter, dinner plate and bowls are also crested with an Indian Chief silhouette." Does the camp element of the quotation of the stereotype neutralize its apparent appreciation of symbols of the subordination of people of color? The same question applies to Tzabaco's Lone Ranger and Tonto pocket knife—one in a series of famous pairs that the text describes as "your favorite Western movie idols." Whose favorites? Who is addressed by this catalogue? It reminds me of the joke in which Indians surround Tonto and the Lone Ranger, prompting the Lone Ranger to ask his sidekick, "What are we going to do?" To which Tonto responds, "What do you mean 'we,' white man?"

Serve in Pullman style on our exclusive Superchief Dining Car dishes.

This Tzabaco design recalls the days when the great railroads rumbled along southern desert routes to California. Tables set with perfect linens...and menus featuring prime rib and celery Victor. Today these brand new "old ivory" commercial grade dishes are decorated with forest green bands. Platter, dinner plate and bowls are also crested with an Indian Chief silhouette.

05-063810 **12¹/₂" Oval Platter $82/set of 4**
05-063813 **7 oz. Cup and Saucer $25/set of 4**
05-063811 **10¹/₂" Round Plates $65/set of 4**
05-063812 **5¹/₂" Napper Bowl $48/set of 4**

PRAIRIE FENCE WIRE BASKET.
Sonoma County artist Richard Tatsuo Nagaoka sculpts this rustic simple basket of reclaimed bailing wire. Equally as well suited for holding a baguette as keeping mail on your desk organized. 5"x 20".
05-064200 **Prairie Fence Basket $44**

Figure 3.8 **"Serve in Pullman style on our exclusive Superchief Dining Car dishes"**

These racial politics show up in the gay and lesbian social movement, where the dominance of white people in "many gay groups . . . may cost the movement its very life."[53] Interestingly, cultural critic Jackie Goldsby asserts that the "low level of concern about racism among many lesbians, gay men, and other queers is derived, at least in part, from the tight reins held by gay print media that have restricted the free flow of ideas on the subject of racism in the gay male community, proving once again that ignorance isn't innocent, it's organized."[54] This assertion is only strengthened if advertising is considered along with the featured contents of the gay print media.

THE VALUE OF GENDER

In addition to reproducing relations of domination and subordination with respect to race, the imagery and rhetoric of gays in advertising has also tended to reinforce traditional gender roles. The opening paragraphs of Grant Lukenbill's book *Untold Millions: Positioning Your Business for the Gay and Lesbian Consumer Revolution* sound an alarm to a feminist reader: "The time is nearing when lesbian mothers will promote bleach and fabric softener on national television. Gay male sports figures, sponsored by tennis shoe companies, will soon be emerging as spokespersons for the prevention of violence."[55] If, indeed, women will still be the figures of domestic consumption and unpaid housework, while men will be paid to appear as themselves in the public sphere, then Lukenbill's "revolution" will not apply to gender roles. Many of the most significant gains of feminist organizing have established mechanisms to facilitate and/or to compensate fairly women's increased participation in the paid workforce and in educational institutions, wresting some of the ground of traditionally male-dominated arenas from men. By the same token, some of the greatest theoretical insights of feminism have identified the class interests at work in the relegation of women to the reproductive sphere and the attendant ideological interests in the maintenance of separate gender-behavior codes for men and women. Feminist theory and practice have exposed the socially derived nature of valuing passivity, weakness, superficiality, and emotionality as feminine while valuing strength, activity, seriousness, and rationality as masculine. Feminism has also suggested that there may be liberatory possibilities in deviance from those codes and equations.

Gay liberation, too, enjoyed a moment in which it recognized the validity of feminist theory and drew the connection between the goals of feminist organizing and the goals of gay organizing. In the Introduction to his *Gay American History,* published in 1976, Jonathan Katz wrote that reviewing gay social life "raises questions about the sexual division of labor and power; the manifestations of male domination and female oppression; the nature of 'masculinity' and 'femininity'; and the various effects of sexism on the quality of social life."[56] But if the study of homosexuality once promised to join feminism in raising questions about the nature of masculinity and femininity, its practice in the form of identity-based consumption has failed to deliver. Like the growing number of personal ads in the 1990s that described gay and lesbian people as being and/or as looking for others who were "straight-looking, straight-acting," images in both the gay and straight media seemed to reinforce the desirability of conforming to traditional notions of masculinity and femininity.

Speaking to the appeal of gay men for marketers, Frances Stevens, the publisher of *Deneuve,* a magazine "for lesbians," explained that gay men have often set fashion standards for straight men.[57] (*Deneuve* became *Curve* in January 1996.) Lesbians have been less appealing to marketers, she says, because they have not set trends for straight women, not the "visible" lesbians, anyway, the ones who match the stereotype of wearing "a lumberjack shirt, sandals, and no makeup."[58] According to Stevens, a new era is dawning, one with greater appeal to marketers, one in which "These women are finally deciding that just because they're lesbian, it doesn't mean they have to cut their hair off and buy a flannel shirt."[59] If they won't read *Better Homes and Gardens,* as she says, this means only that they are producing their lesbian identity in the act of consuming lesbian-specific products, like her magazine, but if they see an ad for a certain brand of tampons in the pages of a lesbian magazine, she claims, they'll buy it. This claim, printed as it was in *Advertising Age,* a mainstream corporate trade publication, assures manufacturers and advertisers that lesbians are fundamentally, biologically, and stylistically, female and feminine, and that they will consume in an accordingly gendered way. Lesbian readers may maintain the mark of diversity to the extent that they are susceptible to niche marketing aimed at them, but there is less and less danger that they will forsake traditional gender roles.

Tzabaco, the catalogue company, colludes in the reinforcement of gender roles with the descriptions of its merchandise. The retro style not only hearkens back to pre–civil rights racial relations, it simultaneously conjures up a period famous for conformity along gender lines, a pre-feminist era. Accompanying a photo display of a watch, the copy reads, "Not a limp-wristed watch or one to be hidden in a pocket, this original hangs proudly from your belt loop." Not a limp-wristed watch. Reading this as a metonymic displacement of personal attributes onto a commodity—meaning that a watch doesn't have a wrist but is closely associated with people's wrists because that is where watches are worn—I can only interpret it as a disavowal of effeminate gay men, a disavowal I find not only heart-breaking, but especially despicable in light of the fact that effeminate gay men and drag queens, those gay men who have been unable or unwilling to "pass," have always been on the front lines, as they were at Stonewall, and as they were before that and have been since. In this sentence, effeminacy and closetedness—"hidden in a pocket"—are opposed to hanging proudly. The shadow side of this disavowal is an equally heart-breaking self-hatred, while the opposite of "hiding" is a "pride" that is now associated mainly with identity-based consumption.

The way in which the gender roles have been played out in gay-friendly ads placed by mainstream advertisers is no more heartening. In 1990, Ikea aired a television ad reputed to be the first ever to feature a gay couple. They were white, they were men, and they were shopping at Ikea for a dining-room table. Ikea's advertising agency described the ad as part of a "life-stages campaign," stressing the continuity (read, lack of difference) between gays and straights.[60] As the agency's vice president and group lawyer, Linda Sawyer said, "This spot happens to be about two men, but it is about things everyone can feel."[61] As far as its intended audience, Sawyer went on to say the gay couple is meant to appeal to consumers whom the agency dubbed "wanna-bes."[62] But in addition to provoking the upwardly mobile desires of the audience they were trying to reach, Ikea may have produced a conflation between desire for class enhancement, or increased consuming capacity—wanna-be richer, wanna-be the owners of more furniture—on the one hand, and the willingness and/or ability to imitate other personal features—wanna-be normal American men—on the other. As the *New York Times*'s advertising columnist put it,

> The commercial is noteworthy because the gay couple is presented as very normal. They are not mincing, effeminate, flouncing homosexuals who are going hysterical over the chintz on the draperies. They are two guys. They're a couple, and because they met at a family wedding, you know they are not bitter toward and estranged from their families. This is sort of evoking the stereotype of homosexuals as being knowledgeable about interior decorating but doing it with two very straight-acting straight-appearing guys.[63]

This commentary wavers oddly between appreciating a nonstereotypical and nonhomophobic representation and expressing that appreciation in some of the most derogatory and stereotypical language imaginable. Here is the assurance that gay men are just like other Americans—they are, specifically, like other men, self-made in the image of masculinity. This assurance is lodged in the ad itself as well as in the commentary about it—the desire to assimilate, to erase cultural distinctions, is made manifest through an image of gay men as normal, meaning masculine, but also in their willingness to participate unbitterly in family weddings, or rituals that establish state-sanctioned heterosexual family relationships. Straight-acting and straight-appearing white men who buy tables on TV. Noteworthy indeed.

The advertising in both gay and straight media seems to assure straight and gay audiences alike that gays have opted for the assimilationist strategy and are now in the business of elaborating the gender implications of that strategy. The assertion that gay men and lesbians are just like straight people means not only that the subcultural community is willing and able to Americanize, but that the sexual orientations—gay and lesbian—that once seemed to bear the threat of gender subversion can indeed present themselves as men and women, in the same way that straight people are men and women, masculine and feminine, respectively. In racial terms, too, this advertising assumes a posture that can be described as the political strategy of the movement, whose members, "in their almost uniform whiteness, must look familiar, almost like family, to those who command power in the halls of government and business: they are, after all, largely 'members' of the same race as those in power."[64] The items that top the agenda of some of the largest national organizations do not convincingly highlight feminist struggles any more than they do antiracist struggles; many of those items address either men's needs or women's needs. For example, the repeal of sodomy laws tends to serve men, who have been, overwhelmingly, the victims of the enforcement of those laws, while the current attention to the family, focusing largely on adoption and custody rights, overwhelmingly serves women, in light of the fact that "approximately 95% . . . of queer families are headed by lesbians. The baby boom is being spearheaded by lesbians."[65] I would argue that one of the reasons that gay marriage and gays in the military are such popular objectives is that they co-serve men and women, thus masking or giving temporary relief from the gender segregation that plagues the movement and is graphically demonstrated in contemporary advertising to gay men and lesbians.

Another trend in advertising in gay media helps to estrange gay and lesbian consumers from the radical import of sexual liberationist rhetoric. This trend involves the appropriation of once radical language in advertisements coming from both mainstream and gay producers. From Miller Beer's "Celebrate Pride," to rings sold to commemorate Stonewall that promise that "Your Pride Will Shine Brighter," to the title of Shocking Gray's catalogue, the word "pride" has shifted from the name of local marches and parades that constituted some of the first affirmative moments of collective visibility on the part of gay and lesbian people, to a pitch word (see Figures 3.9, 3.10, and 3.11). On the cover of the catalogue, the word is illustrated by an individual white man enjoying a leisure moment of identity-based consumption, nothing collective (much less coalitional) in sight. As the co-founder of Shocking Gray reveals, "Anything that's pride related sells very well, including luggage, checkbook covers with pink triangles, rainbow flags, etc."[66] The subtitle of Grant Lukenbill's book *Untold Millions: Positioning Your Business for the Gay and Lesbian Consumer Revolution,* is another example of the appropriation of oppositional language. In the telephone survey conducted by Overlooked Opinions (described above), at the point at which the call became an ad, Community Spirit's electronic voice asked callers to "unleash the power" of their money to support gay-owned businesses, theirs in particular. The phrase, "unleash the power" is, of course, borrowed from the UP in ACT UP, AIDS Coalition to Unleash Power, one of the most controversial direct-action groups of the 1980s. "Pride," "power," and "freedom" are clearly the most common words in the names, slogans, and advertisements of companies targeting gay consumers. But for pure self-parody, the best example of the commodification of political language is the nonprofit Human Rights Campaign's merchandise; HRC offers Equality Jacket, Equality Tie, Equality Cufflinks, and more. The *pièce de résistance*, on the penultimate page of one of HRC's catalogues, is the Equality Polo, modeled by a white man, "a new HRC member," reading the stock exchange pages with interest.

While advertising to gays has long appealed to the quest to belong, affirmatively, to the U.S. polity—just as the movement, long before Stonewall, invoked U.S. national creeds and ideals in the same quest—advertising pitched at the gay and lesbian niche market in the 1990s was marked by a striking phenomenon: the repeated incidence of images and rhetoric of U.S. national identity, used by gay and mainstream marketers alike. Throughout the 1970s and 1980s, there were ads in the gay media that played upon patriotism, but they were few and far between. In a trend that accelerated in the 1990s, such advertising pitches—appearing mostly in gay media, but increasingly in mainstream venues as

TEN PERCENT, Pride Issue, May/June 1995

CELEBRATE PRIDE

Miller

Miller Brewing Company Milwaukee, WI

Figure 3.9 **"Celebrate Pride"**

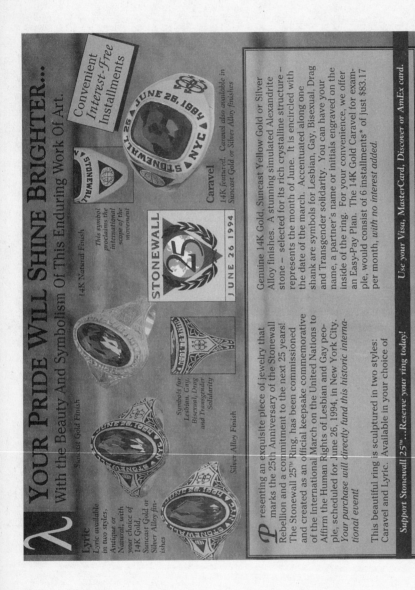

Figure 3.10 "Your Pride Will Shine Brighter"

Figure 3.11 "Pride"

Figure 3.12 "Freedom of Vodka"

well—have forged a visual and rhetorical association between gay and American identity. In particular, the advertising suggests that viewers can obtain U.S. citizenship, or full enfranchisement, through personal consumption of the commodity being advertised.

For example, a SKYY vodka ad that appeared in the national gay glossy magazine *10 Percent* shows a bottle of vodka placed against the background of an American flag, while the caption reads, "Take the Fifth."[67] Appearing in a gay publication and referring to the flag and the Bill of Rights, this ad seems to suggest that the rights of the citizen may be available to the gay consumer. Moreover, it resonates with the "don't ask/don't tell solution" to the "problem" of gays in the military, stressing the "don't tell" part, or the idea that gay identity does not preclude participation in American institutions, but that an outward emphasis on sameness rather than difference makes everything go down smoother. The information in the ad that the vodka is "distilled in America from American grain"—amber waves of it, no doubt—drives home the association between the presumed-to-be-gay reader of *10 Percent* and the description of, and invitation into, a circuit of American production, distribution, and consumption. Here, consumption is the route to belonging in "America," but it is simultaneously the route to assimilation into American institutions that value privacy over coming out and speaking up. If this ad implies that gay consumers might exercise their right not to self-incriminate, then homosexuality is implicitly tainted with criminality. Thus, consumption of a fifth of vodka promises legal status.

For another example of the suggestion that consumption can mean enfranchisement, see the Stolichnaya ad placed in the *Advocate* in 1995 (see Figure 3.12). In it a bottle sits against a background that evokes the flag by means of a star in the upper-left-hand corner and an array of objects that gives a striped effect. On closer examination, these objects turn out to be books, perhaps referring to yet another amendment to the Constitution, the First Amendment, as freedom of speech was the freedom most famously denied to Soviet subjects (who are implied by the brand name Stolichnaya, which is nothing if not Russian). The words "Freedom of Vodka" are stenciled across the design and the bottle in a typeface that seems to be dripping. The stencil typography, together with the drips of what could be paint, recalls the graffiti of student protests of the 1960s; or perhaps it is dripping with blood, implying that the flavored Russian drink had to undergo violent social change to find American-flavored freedom. Following the fall of the Soviet Union, which, news reports informed us, brought freedom to the Russians and other former Soviet subjects in the form of capitalism, this ad makes synonymous American identity, freedom, and capitalism. Its secondary reference to liberation movements of the 1960s, and its placement in the *Advocate,* make gay identity parallel with foreign-ethnic identity and invite both into the liberation of American consuming identity.

In the same year, the *Advocate* ran an ad for Benson & Hedges that pictures the Statue of Liberty and recommends that smokers "Take a few liberties." Its placement in this magazine suggests an address to both gays and smokers—the former should, like the latter, take the liberties held out by the icon of immigrants-made-American. A white man in a uniform and a badge points in an ambiguous way, perhaps toward Ellis Island or more vaguely toward New York (where anything can be done and had and bought). In any case, as an agent of the state, the man is a reminder that the Statue of Liberty stands for U.S. national identity, for the historical composition of the citizenry through immigration. But "she's holding a light" not in order to light the way for poor huddled masses yearning to breathe free, but in order to produce the satisfaction of the consumer yearning to breathe smoke. Such images locate freedom, rights, and liberties in consuming cigarettes, rather than in political participation, or perhaps they conflate the two, equating consumption with political participation.

I read these ads with reference to gay and lesbian themes because of their placement in gay and lesbian media outlets. Most mainstream advertisers do not design ads that can be read as gay regardless of their placement. In other words, they design what are called "gay window" ads or "gay vague" ads, in which the use of in-group language, gesture, and symbol, and the ambiguity of same-sex social groupings or pictures of individuals, are codes for gay or lesbian identity or activity. In this way, they avoid alienating straight consumers while leaving open the possibility of identification with the ads by gay or lesbian viewers.[68] Here again, advertising in effect promotes assimilation and identity difference at the same time; advertisers invest in ads that can be read across identity groups at the very same time that they invest in identity difference as the premise of niche marketing—hence the placement of the ads in gay media.

I don't claim that my interpretations are shared either by the ad-makers or by other viewers of the ad. I am not arguing that advertisements directly provoke or motivate any particular action or set of beliefs. Nor do I believe that advertisements are a straightforward reflection of social values, dominant or otherwise. Most scholars of advertising in the 1980s and 1990s moved beyond the idea that ads provide a transparent window onto values or practices; but clearly ads have *something* to do with social practice. Serving the plain and singular purpose of selling things, ads attempt to forge associations between specific things for sale and the existing belief systems of their prospective buyers. Of course, ads also manipulate, and thus modify, those belief systems, but ads fundamentally depend on provoking associations to beliefs that are normalized (sometimes as aspirations) in the social world in which they appear. Ads must be seen as artifacts produced by the "managerial elite," but particularly as the educated guesses made by that managerial elite about what images and messages will stimulate buying.[69] A very common strategy of ad-makers in this pursuit involves deploying culturally familiar plots, themes, anxieties, and desires, so that ads can be interpreted in relation to those familiar tropes. But that doesn't mean that any particular viewer makes such an interpretation, nor that any consumer thinks or acts predictably in response to advertising. I am not suggesting, for example, that any gay man or lesbian looks at the ads analyzed above and thinks, yes, I can become enfranchised if I smoke or drink that product. My claim is that this body of advertisements—as I analyze it—has clear counterparts in the social movement. I would not worry so much about an ad that dramatizes the idea that assimilation is a cause of liberation and enfranchisement an effect of consumption if I did not see these ideas at work in the movement.

These equations are perhaps nowhere more starkly pictured, in all marketing to gay men and lesbians, than in an ad for the Pride Network. Offering long-distance phone service, the Pride Network was a program of TransNational Communications, which specializes in affinity-based marketing. As part of the program, the Pride Network announced that it would donate some portion of the profits to gay and lesbian nonprofit organizations. In the advertising campaign that promoted this program to gay men and lesbians, actual consumers were photographed. Naturally, each one appeared happy with the phone service. And each one appeared with a caption printed prominently nearby. In one such ad stands a couple—two young, healthy-looking white men, one slightly behind the other with his arms around his boyfriend. Next to their heads, a large caption reads "For Todd and Greg, activism is as simple as a phone call." But activism is not so simple as a phone call. And activism gets increasingly difficult as it seeks to cross lines of race and class, which Todd and Greg appear not to have done. Equating consumption with political participation may flatter readers who would like to think of themselves as supporting the movement for gay rights, and who think that they have made a political contribution by subscribing to the services of this phone company. This ad clearly articulates the idea that acts of consumption constitute political activity. The question is: What are the consequences of this logic? What are the costs of defining an individual act of private consumption as a mode of political participation? The next chapter takes up this question.

Market and movement alike have mobilized symbols of national identity and have capitalized on the tension between assimilation and de-assimilation. While some gay theorists have applauded the appearance of gay people in advertising as a sign of social inclusion, and as an important kind of representation in cultural life, others have noted that the exclusions at work in these representations reproduce traditional U.S. power relations.[70] From one angle, "in a capitalist society, market incorporation is of the utmost importance because it summons a social legitimation approaching that of citizen."[71] But when citizenship becomes an effect of market incorporation, when citizenship in the gay nation converges on citizenship in the United States, only consumer-citizens are truly enfranchised. However, the status of consumer-citizen is not universally available. Given radical inequality in cultural, political, and economic spheres, diversity as a social value—that is, diversity negotiated in the marketplace—tends to pull for assimilation or to eliminate the conflict, the very *difference,* between assimilation and preservation of distinct identity.

4

BOYCOTTS WILL
BE BOYCOTTS

*Unlike Cincinnatus, the bourgeois patriot did not reach immediately
for the sword. He first examined the household budget.*

—T. H. Breen[1]

THE BOYCOTT AS A PROTEST STRATEGY

Just as advertising strategies to the gay and lesbian niche market have included the claim that acts of private consumption constitute political participation, so have certain protest strategies banked on that claim.[2] If acts of purchase could produce desirable social change—such as contributing to the community, allowing consumers to display pride in their personal identities, and positively reinforcing good corporate policy—couldn't the act of withholding purchase force corporations to change their bad policies? Withholding purchase, or boycotting, is a social protest strategy that enjoyed a dramatic resurgence in the 1990s (the same decade in which the gay and lesbian niche market enjoyed explosive growth and visibility).[3] From 1985 to 1993, "the number of ongoing boycotts . . . increased fourfold to nearly 200," according to Todd Putnam, editor of the *National Boycott News*. Noting that the *Wall Street Journal* called 1990 "the year of the boycott," Putnam asserts, in an article entitled, "Boycotts Are Busting Out All Over," that "the 1990s may well be the decade of the boycott."[4] And sure enough, gay men and lesbians used boycotts in the 1990s, as did many movements on both the right and the left. As the particulars of gay and lesbian identity have increasingly been mediated through market exchange, so are they mediated through the purposeful absence of exchange, through boycotting. A look at the theory of boycotting, a brief history of boycotting in the United States, and two selected cases of boycotting will make it clear that when the market becomes the arena of political action, gay and lesbian identity comes to bear a peculiar relation to (U.S.) national identity.

Boycotting goes back a long way in this country, back before the gay and lesbian movement borrowed the strategy from other civil rights movements, back before it was used to supplement labor strikes, back even before the term was coined (which was in 1880 and in Ireland). Indeed, it goes back to the moment of nation formation in the United States. (I will return to this in a moment). In the United States, the boycott has been a strategy used mainly by the left; throughout the nineteenth and early twentieth centuries, boycotts tended to appear as strategies to supplement and amplify labor strikes. At least as early as the early twentieth century, some African Americans boycotted white businesses that would not serve them, and the civil rights movement of the 1950s and 1960s went on to use this strategy in numerous ways, from boycotting products and local businesses, to the famous Montgomery bus boycott that helped bring about the end of segregated seating on public transportation. As these examples show, the struggle for racial equality in the United States has focused on rights of access to the marketplace in the form of lunch counters, public accommodations, and countless other sites of fee-for-service. Classified as a form of "nonviolent direct action"—particularly following the boycott in India led by Mahatma Gandhi, which was articulated as nonviolent resistance to British imperial rule—the boycott, like the sit-in, has been a way to disrupt profitable business practice in the service of social change. In utilizing these strategies, the civil rights movement has dramatized the fact that citizenship is located in the marketplace.

Naturally, then, enfranchisement for African Americans has required economic rights. And other liberal and progressive struggles have likewise fought in the trenches of the market. The fight for women's rights has included the fight for the right to own property, the right to retain wages earned, and rights of inheritance, among other forms of economic rights. Evidently, struggles for economic rights have turned, as though logically, to economic tactics. In an era in which non-violent direct action became quite popular, Cesar Chavez called for the boycott of California grapes; the first such boycott, begun in 1964, was aimed at fruit growers who exploited largely immigrant Mexican and Mexican-American labor. In the 1970s, boycotting served theme-based movements, becoming one of the strategies for the nuclear disarmament movement (which targeted General Electric in particular, then one of the nation's two largest nuclear weapons contractors), for feminists try-ing to stop Nestlé from distributing infant formula in Africa, and for people everywhere fighting apartheid in South Africa. For example, anti-apartheid activists advocated the boycott of certain companies (like Shell Oil) that did business in South Africa, as well as the tourism in-dustry there (notably the entertainment resort Sun City).[5] Divestment, too, is nothing if not a boycott, as a principled refusal to buy or own. In the 1990s, boycotting was used by environmentalists (against compa-nies whose tuna-catching practices hurt dolphins) and by the Christian right (sometimes expressly against companies with gay/lesbian-friendly policies, as with the 1997 boycott of American Airlines by Concerned Women of America, the Family Research Council, and the American Family Association, for the airline's favorable treatment of gay and les-bian employees and customers), and it has remained a strategy to which antiracist activists turn (as just one example, Jesse Jackson organized boycotts against Nike, among other corporations, in the 1990s). The boycott wars surrounding the broadcast of the *Ellen* "Coming-Out Episode" in 1997 offered an example ad absurdum, as the right boy-cotted Disney and threatened other sponsors (namely, Chrysler, General Motors Corporation, and Johnson & Johnson), while sponsors who pulled out as the show's broadcast approached were boycotted by pro-gay forces.[6] Indeed, it is a logical turn to mobilize economic action against economic injustice, but it is a deceptively simple logic. In fact, boycotting strategy is complicated and its effects are ambivalent.

Of course, context and form make all of the above different, perhaps incomparable, cases—if they have anything in common, it is that boy-cotting, in each instance, occupies the intersection between the market and politics. Boycotting is a perfect foil for investigating the differences between economic political action and direct political action from demonstrating to lobbying. Because boycotting has such a long history in this country, because it seems to have picked up steam at exactly the same time that the gay and lesbian niche market exploded, and because it represents a point of intersection between the gay and lesbian movement and the gay and lesbian market, in particular, this study will turn to the question of boycotting in and for the gay and lesbian community.

The first announcement of a boycott organized on behalf of gay men and lesbians was issued by the Glide Methodist Church, the Glide Foundation, and the Glide Trustees in California. According to an article in the *L. A. Advocate,* in November 1967, "All three have just adopted a new policy by which they will refuse to buy goods and services from firms which discriminate against homosexuals."[7] Thus in the first year of its publication the *L.A. Advocate* printed news of the first known instance of a "gaycott." It seems unlikely that this particular boycott mobilized very many people or groups, as it received little further mention in the *L.A. Advocate* or any other publication.

In 1974, "gay leaders" threatened a boycott of Hollywood businesses, in response to LAPD vice squad treatment of gays (gay men, mostly), including entrapment and harassment. Seen by gay community leaders "as a means of applying the only pressure mechanism Gays in Hollywood appear to have," the threat of a boycott was apparently successful in getting the LAPD to issue a new policy and start a project "observing police actions towards gays on the streets, in the bars, and in movie theaters."[8] Already the idea of gay economic power as a political tool was articulated in these instances. But it wasn't until Anita Bryant established Save Our Children in reaction to the passage of a local antidiscrimination ordinance in Dade County, Florida, that the gay community entertained the idea of a national boycott. Before looking at this moment in detail, it is important to understand some of the theory of boycotting.

ECONOMIC DEMOCRACY

Boycotting is the principled refusal to purchase goods or services because of opposition to some feature of their producer(s), the process of their production, or some intrinsic feature of the goods or services themselves. It is a tactic designed to pressure the producer(s) to change policy, process, or product so that it conforms to the principle promoted by the boycotters. As the examples mentioned above indicate, boycotts have been used for a number of different purposes in this country at different times, and by different groups, but at root the boycott is a simple and straightforward strategy, based on relatively few interlocking concepts. All of these concepts cluster around the idea of consumer sovereignty.

Consumer sovereignty rests first of all on the liberal-economic principle that individuals have free choice in the marketplace. When you enter the market, as economists Milton and Rose Friedman have it, "no one forces you to buy. You are free to do so or go elsewhere. . . . You are free to choose."[9] For the Friedmans, individual sovereignty can, and must inevitably, be expressed in the free market, which is to say, as consumer sovereignty. Given a field of radical choice, the concept of consumer sovereignty predicts two principal effects. The first effect is that consumers express their individuality in the market. The second effect, theoretically (and of greater importance here), is that consumers determine what is available in the marketplace, that they determine corporate activity—to put it simply, consumers decide on the product and processes of capital. Demand, that is, dictates supply.[10]

Recent work on ethical purchase behavior explains that "Consumers under capitalism are, according to the ideology, the decision-makers on the allocation of society's resources."[11] Going back as far as the emergence of capitalism, there has been active debate over whether the market is moral or amoral, whether decisions made through consumer purchase behavior tend toward the good, the bad, or the neutral. In classical liberal market theory, if the market is sufficiently competitive, if consumption really takes place in an arena replete with choices among interchangeable products, then consumers will be controlling two things. One is the specific features of commodities—their design and function—and the other is corporate policy and practice—everything from hiring to waste disposal. By this argument, corporations maintain or modify everything, from the material of which a product is made to its availability, according to the tastes of consumers. As a former Chairman of General Motors put it, "This sensitive tailoring of productive resources to the complex and diverse preferences of people, expressed through free markets, is a fundamental though often under-appreciated characteristic of our system. Each consumer, given his free choice, can purchase those products which he feels most suit his own special needs and resources. Unlike the political system, every person can win in an economic 'election.'"[12] According to this theory, freely choosing consumers can express social and political preferences especially effectively in the marketplace.

In addition to tailoring the product specifications to meet consumer demand, corporations are, according to the consumer sovereignty principle, supposed to maintain or modify their policies according to the preferences of consumers. Greater sales seem to constitute a demand for *maintenance* of corporate product or policy, while lesser sales seem to constitute a demand for *modification* of one or the other. Organized boycotts, therefore, articulate, in the negative, the demands of consumers. Often, the organizing agencies are special-interest groups—whether identity based or theme based—articulating a complaint about corporate participation in a particular social problem. Such groups also act as agents of information, revealing corporate practices and policies and enabling informed consumer action. A liberal approach to consumption holds that "Political participation can in this way be increased, with the market at least attempting to 'answer all things.'"[13]

THE DOLLAR-VOTE

The idea that consumption is a form of political participation implies that the marketplace is a ballot box; in other words, the analogy between economic and political arenas creates an equivalence between consumers and voters. Clearly, the rhetorical casting of purchase as "election," together with the idea that market activity can address social issues, suggests just such an analogy. As just one example, the textbook *Lobbying the Corporation: Citizen Challenges to Business Authority* states that "during the boycott of Dow Chemical's Saran Wrap, in protest at Dow's manufacture of napalm, the purchase of Saran Wrap became, in effect, a referendum on the war."[14] The idea of "economic democracy" rests upon this classic statement of the analogy: "With every penny spent the consumers determine the direction of all production processes and the minutest details of the organization of all business activities. . . . The market [is] a democracy in which every penny gives a right to cast a ballot."[15] The left has long held a belief in economic democracy, precisely because it has long recognized the social power of big business as well as the fact that competition among businesses "creates the opportunity to pit one against the other."[16]

The same logic showed up in appeals to the gay and lesbian market in the 1990s, as in Uncommon Clout's appeal to "vote with your dollars." (See Figure 4.1.) Yet the trouble with economic democracy is couched in the statement that "every penny gives a right to cast a ballot." This model conjures a citizen whose franchise depends on meeting property qualifications; every ballot requires the rhetorical penny. Just as investing and divesting require funds, boycotting presumes some amount of discretionary capital, some purchasing power, some money. Disqualified by lack of money, citizens unable to "vote" in the marketplace become thoroughly disenfranchised within this model. Universal suffrage in the economic arena is unthinkable in an economic context characterized by the kind of disparity seen today between the very rich and the very poor in this country.

Which leads to a second problem with the idea of economic democracy. The franchise given by the market is given unequally. Number (read, value) of votes is a function of number of pennies. The analogy between the democratic arena and the market tends toward the following observation: "One's vote in the market, as a consequence of consumer sovereignty, is in proportion to one's wealth. There is a limited franchise."[17] One limit is on equal representation; when greater wealth amounts to greater number of votes, the wealthy have a disproportionate amount of control over the social decisions taken in the market. Another, related, limit is equality of opportunity to participate; people with no money have no votes. While progressive factions in the United States wore down property requirements over the course of almost two hundred years, so that by now virtually all non-incarcerated adult citizens are technically eligible to vote, the graft of the ballot-box onto the market cannot help but have retrogressive meanings. And whereas proponents of

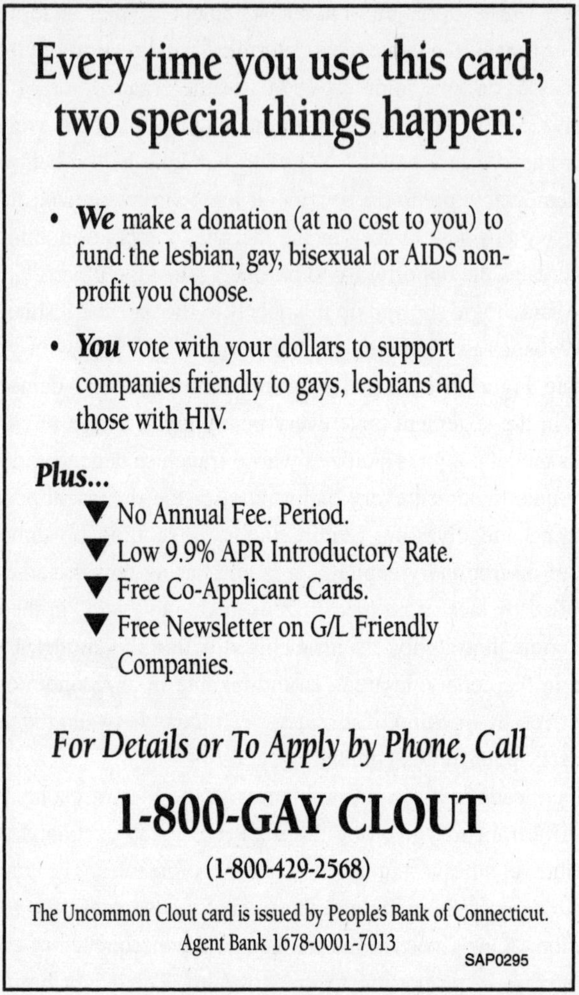

Figure 4.1 "Uncommon Clout . . . You vote with your dollars"

increased civic (and voter) participation consider material impediments to such participation a problem to be solved legally, if not culturally, no solution recommends itself to the problem that consumers are unequally enfranchised in the realm of economic democracy.

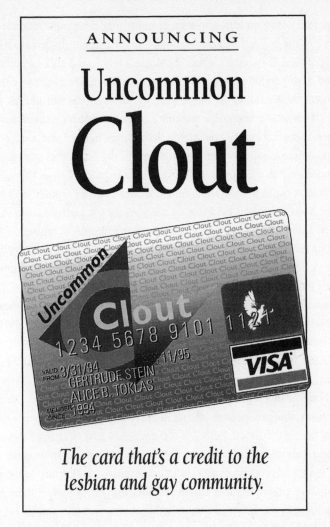

ANNOUNCING

Uncommon Clout

The card that's a credit to the lesbian and gay community.

Another problem intrinsic to a program of economic democracy concerns the question of domain, or the question of what issues the consumer is voting on. When the consumer buys a commodity, is she approving of its color or function? Is she approving of its producer's

corporate policy on hiring women in upper management? Or is she un-
aware of the boycott against the company for its contributions to a certain political think tank? When she doesn't buy, is the lack of purchase
based in principled opposition to a producer's contributions to a certain
political think tank or its hiring policies, or does she not like its new
size? This would become a quagmire of interpretation, except that interpretations are singly predictable. Boycotters believe that a boycott's
purposes are clear and that, given adequate publicity, they account for
reduced sales in the aggregate, if not in each individual case. Very often,
boycotters claim to have had a financial impact on a corporation. I have
never seen published evidence of a corporation's interpretation of reduced sales as a recognition of protest. For example, whenever corporations do admit to reduced sales while a boycott is ongoing, they tend
to give other accounts for the reduced sales. Whenever corporations
admit that boycotts are having an effect, they always say that the effect
is one of "public relations," consistently refuting boycotters' claims that
a boycott's impact has been directly financial, and also refuting the logical inference that bad public relations would hurt sales. Ultimately, it is
probably impossible to measure a boycott's effectiveness in financial
terms; there are numerous cases in which activists and corporations actually agree that a given boycott has had great symbolic value. For corporations, this can mean public relations problems, while activists don't
mind taking the moral victory if a corporation makes changes because
of fears about public relations.[18] (For these reasons, the media surrounding a boycott is of paramount importance. I will return to the role
of media representation at length in a moment.) In any case, there may
be a limit to the kinds of qualities that consumers can single out and
protest through boycotting.

Yet another limit to the success of boycotts lies in the fact that a
consumer must be "in" a certain market for a refusal to buy to be meaningful. The effectiveness of a boycott depends, in part, on who normally buys the boycotted product: "It is important that those likely to
support the boycott are in the market for the boycotted article."[19] Not
buying something the boycotter has never bought and would never buy
may fail to signify clearly the desires of the nonbuyer-turned-boycotter.
For example, irony and futility mark appeals to *New Yorker* readers to

boycott Denny's for its racist practices, or appeals to "family values"–style Republicans to boycott rap music.[20] Once again, this system cannot be counted on to represent, proportionally or otherwise, the political choices of a citizenry. Rather, it points to the ways in which boycotts depend on market niches, if not niche markets. Even when the boycotted article is a mass-market commodity, such as Saran Wrap or canned tuna, boycotters are likely to compose a specialized socioeconomic group, if not a specialized market; this is true because calls to boycott come through particular media outlets, and the media market is elaborately and intensely segmented. In other words, consumers aware of a Saran Wrap boycott or a tuna boycott are a self-selecting group that is constituted on a basis other than desire for Saran Wrap or tuna. These boycotters are more likely to share with each other an antiwar stance or an environmentalist ethic, as well as exposure to quasi-alternative media, than they are to share either with other consumers of Saran Wrap or tuna.

In fact, the empirical evidence indicates that boycotting bears the traces of the theoretical and historical formulation of citizen (meaning voter) as propertied. In other words, boycotters are overwhelmingly the people who count as citizens where citizenship is tied to personal property/capital. A Roper poll conducted in 1989 indicates that the profile of boycotters matches that of socially responsible consumers. People who engage in this style of socially responsible consumption also tend to be employed ("come from two-income families"), if not middle-class, highly educated (most hold college degrees), and "pre-middle-aged adult" ("hail from the big-spending thirty-something crowd").[21]

The demographic study of the socially conscious consumer empirically bears out the logical inference that if every dollar is a vote then those without dollars do not get votes. Presumptively male, he has been found to be a "pre-middle-aged adult of relatively high occupational, economic, and social status. He tends to be more cosmopolitan, less dogmatic, less conservative, less status conscious, less alienated, and less personally competent than the less socially concerned citizen."[22] Consumption, of course, is never an *ex nihilo* social act; it must be preceded by income. This is to say that a class interest unites consumers—and deliberate nonconsumers—as income "earners," defining them against people without income, whether or not they shop according to socially responsible principles. Boycotts, with their emphasis on consumption, may obscure this unity, locating interest in the private arenas where individual consuming takes place; on the other hand, boycotts point usefully to the fact that any act of consumption has social effects.

All of these features of boycotts, like the concept of economic democracy more generally, derive from the principle of consumer sovereignty, concepts and principles oddly embraced by people across a range of political and economic positions. The claim that consumers are sovereign and that they drive the market is a claim made by entrepreneurs, because this claim grounds an argument against government intervention in business. If consumers are controlling business practices, why should government? Liberal economists and political scientists, however, seem to want to argue that the corporation is a public entity, insofar as it has public effects, and thus that its leaders have social and, in effect, political power.[23] They make this claim in order to argue, in turn, for government intervention. If corporations should serve the public good, and if the market does not in fact constrain them to do so, then government should. Furthermore, if corporations set social policy, such effects ought to be controlled in some way by government.

Clearly, both the right and the left use boycotts, yet boycotts may be more consistent, at a theoretical level, with conservative economic and cultural politics than with liberal or progressive political positions, because of the ways in which boycotts reinforce the privatization of citizenship, and by extension the privatization of so many forms of decision making, as shown in such practices as school vouchers (among other privatizing schemes), which are so popular with conservatives. For liberals and progressives, there is more of a contradiction at work; perhaps boycotting, used to aid liberal or progressive social causes, masks the fact that it reinforces the privatization of social decision making.

Within the ideology of free-market economics, personal consumption choices count as citizen participation and purchases figure as elections; perhaps within such an ideology "every person can win this sort of election." But even so, only those with dollar-votes can win. The risk of supplanting civic activity and public process with private individual purchase behavior is a risk that the gay and lesbian community has entertained. A discernible trend in advertising to gay men and lesbians promises the consumer that buying a product represents activism, whether because the company donates some amount of its profits to nonprofits or because subsidizing gay-owned businesses benefits "the community," or because the corporations doing the advertising are "gay-friendly" in policy or practice (in any way from sponsoring events to recognizing gay and lesbian existence in the very act of advertising to it). That is, such advertising uses the logic of free-market economics (unsurprisingly); within this logic, assimilation is the most desirable kind of social change.

According to free-market proponents, leftist "economic democrats," and pro-gay forces working within the market to effect social change, boycotting—like any other purchase behavior—serves as a form of ethical and political action, a form engaged in by consumers. Classical and contemporary liberal market theory agree, furthermore, that consumers, in the aggregate, will, through their spending patterns, demand products and policies that tend toward the moral. In other words, with the right neutral market mechanisms in place, consumers will put the market to work for the common good: "competitive markets and free consumer choice could be relied on to set an economic course which would maximise human welfare."[24] Boycotts form part of the pattern that spells out the common good, a way that rational individual actors train the market toward that good. The boycott is a pro-capitalist strategy because it accepts some very central premises of capitalism— "the argument for ethical purchase behavior becomes an argument for capitalism."[25] It accepts the premise that the market can and should both shape and enact social policy, as well as the assumption that the market will lead toward increasingly moral social policy. Also, as I have said, the concept of the boycott is founded on the premise that the consumer is sovereign, meaning both that he or she acts freely in the market and that his or her freely chosen actions in that market will, together with the free acts of fellow consumers, control the market.

The consumer who may freely choose to boycott as a way of casting a vote for social change is like the citizen whose ballot vote shapes the policy and activity of the state—a theoretical subject that bears certain rights and enjoys certain privileges. Materially speaking, however, this subject bears an identity, and the specific identity features borne by the subject have everything to do with the actual rights and privileges in play in his or her life. Over the course of the twentieth century, as civil rights have converged on economic rights, the marketplace has increasingly constituted the arena within which identity is negotiated; both individual and group identity are developed in relation to exchange practices. Likewise, citizenship has increasingly become a function of exchange practices. Of the many identity features that make up any individual, then, national identity is fundamentally and inevitably worked out in terms of private consumption. American citizenship—its definition, its meanings, the rights and privileges it carries, the identity features with which it combines in any given individual—is very much at stake in acts of consumption, including boycotting.

BOYCOTTING AND THE NATION

Shifting from the theory to the history of boycotting indicates the ways in which the practice has contributed to the definition of the American citizen. The practice of trying to effect change by applying economic pressure to the agents of the status quo goes back to the colonial era in the United States. While the Boston Tea Party is the most legendary example of economic protest in the colonial United States, it was not an isolated incident; rather, it was part of an integrated economic protest against certain aspects of British rule. What is so significant about this cluster of protests is that they contributed to the development of an "American" national identity, and that they did so in ways that have been replayed in the late twentieth century, albeit with a very different appearance.

Specifically directed at undermining the sale of imported British goods in the colonies in the late eighteenth century, a "boycott movement organized to counter British policy allowed scattered colonists to reach out to each other and to reimagine themselves within an independent commercial empire."[26] In his analysis of the colonial nonimportation movement, T. H. Breen argues that this boycott emerged as a response to a political crisis specifically shaped by a dramatic increase in the availability of commodities. "Increasing opportunities to consume triggered intense print controversies about . . . the role of personal choice in a liberal society, and the relevance of traditional status hierarchies in a commercial world that encouraged people to fashion protean public identities."[27] In other words, the boycott served in this period as a mechanism through which the development of a national identity was negotiated in the marketplace, or, more exactly, in dynamic relation with changes in the marketplace. Simultaneously, these developments were a matter of conversation among the colonists, and the conversation addressed political philosophical questions that came out of, and would bear on shifts in, the range of personal identities available to consumer-citizens.

Some of the same conditions facing the white colonists in the late eighteenth century have faced gay men and lesbians in the late twentieth century. In the former period, "Americans living in scattered communities managed to reach out convincingly to distant strangers, to persons not directly known but assumed to share in the development of a new consumer marketplace. . . . They learned about each other through the weekly newspapers that were themselves both a product of and a voice of expanding commerce."[28] In the years of their first couple of boycott attempts (1967 and 1974), gay men and lesbians in the United States also lived in scattered communities, but through gay newspapers they began to be able to connect themselves under an identity banner to other gay men and lesbians. The rapid growth of the gay periodical press in the post-Stonewall years was an essential ingredient of the growth of a gay nationalism; the relation between the history of the gay press and the conception of a gay nation supports the argument that the development of modern nation states depended on the spread of daily mass-circulated newspapers whose readership imagined itself into national unity with other readers.[29] Both the colonists and gay men and lesbians two hundred years later constituted themselves as national groupings through a collective relation to commerce and through aggregate participation in distinguishing their identity both from, and within, a commercial empire.

However, a warning: "To describe this mental process as incipient nationalism would suggest that we are anticipating independence long before the colonists did. The claim is rather that even when Americans most feared political fragmentation, they imagined themselves within a commercial and liberal discourse capable of sustaining self-conscious nationalism."[30] This case must be put even more forcefully for contemporary gay men and lesbians, lest here the homology break down. Gay men and lesbians (as an organized group based in that identity) have never anticipated nor hoped for political independence. The goal among this group is most often one of full enfranchisement within the existing parameters of citizenship: equality, not independence. But those gay men and lesbians who debated, in the pages of local and, increasingly, national, newspapers, whether or not to boycott the Florida Citrus Commission certainly seemed to have "imagined themselves within a commercial and liberal discourse capable of sustaining self-conscious nationalism." Using the fundamentally and historically American and Americanizing strategy of the boycott, the gay and lesbian movement sought to protest first homophobic social policy and then homophobic corporate policy.

SQUEEZING ANITA

On January 18, 1977, prompted by a local gay advocacy organization, the Metro Commission of Dade County approved an ordinance protecting gay men and lesbians from discrimination in housing, employment, and public accommodations.[31] In the following six months, Anita Bryant, entertainer and spokesperson for the Florida Citrus Commission, spearheaded a drive to have the ordinance repealed. Establishing a nonprofit organization called Save the Children, Bryant garnered 60,000 signatures (the requirement was 10,000) and succeeded in getting a referendum on the June 7 ballot of the same year that would put the question to the voters in the county. Countering Anita Bryant brought more fund-raising, more news media, more sophisticated political organizing methods, and more activists in contact with each other than had any previous gay-liberation initiative.

Anita Bryant was not the first person to go into a homophobic frenzy, but the media coverage of Bryant and her mania was unprecedented. Both the content and the frequency of the coverage were of the essence. As with Stonewall eight years earlier, the mainstream news contributed greatly to the possibility of an organized pro-gay response. The Stonewall Rebellion was not the first time police had busted up a bar, nor was it the first time that gays, lesbians, and transvestites fought back. And Stonewall had indeed been covered in the national news media, but reports of Bryant and the opposition to her far exceeded reports of Stonewall. Perhaps Bryant earned this media attention because she was being paid as a spokesperson for the Florida Citrus Commission, perhaps because she was a pop singer, or because she had been Miss Oklahoma. In any case, she was a public figure intent on using her celebrity, however minor, in the service of homophobic political action. But in addition to her intended use of the media, Bryant's publicity helped organize the gay community in at least three distinct, but related, ways. First, the mainstream media coverage motivated people to create, join, and contribute money to organizations that would attempt to counter Bryant politically. Second, reaction to Bryant stimulated the gay press to address itself to a national audience. Third, reaction to Bryant sparked a national gay consciousness; it mobilized concerted action—symbolic and concrete—in which "strangers" could participate and simultaneously forge a "national" identity.

Of all the tactics in operation, and among the various debates about those tactics, none invited more commentary than the question of whether or not to boycott Anita Bryant herself (as a performer) and Florida citrus products (primarily orange juice). While local activists debated whether to represent the issue as one of "human rights" or "sexual liberation" (the human rights approach ultimately predominated) and whether or not to bring in campaigners from out of town (campaigners were, indeed, brought in), people discussed the question of the boycott from coast to coast. (Most prepared orange juice for sale in the United States was at least partly made from Florida oranges.) Thus, it was in response to Anita Bryant that gay men and lesbians first discussed boycotting as a nationwide group protest strategy.

At the historical moment in which the "community" first articulated itself as "national," the community—to the extent that it spoke through the nationally distributed *Gay Community News*—was split. A 1977 commentary in *GCN* explains: "Boston Advocates for Human

Rights says don't boycott. The New York-based Gay Activists Alliance says do boycott. Half the members of your household say don't. Half say do. Your lover says don't. You say do. The issue at hand is one facing any thinking gay person: Whether or not to boycott orange juice and oranges from Florida. The arguments pro and con have been stated and re-stated here and *in publications across the country"32* (emphasis mine). Here, the Boston-based *GCN* referred to the national scope of the debate that had already been raging for months. For example, in San Francisco three months earlier, an editorial offered the mild suggestion that "It might do us well to abstain from drinking Florida citrus products until this affair is resolved."[33] Elsewhere in the same local gay paper, columnist and "Mayor of Castro Street," Harvey Milk made the case more emphatically. In his weekly column in the *Bay Area Reporter,* Milk called on the San Francisco Board of Supervisors, Mayor George Moscone, Cesar Chavez and the unions, gay leaders, and friends of the movement to join gays in boycotting: "There is no reason why EVERY Gay person cannot fight Anita Bryant in the privacy of their own home and bar."[34] Believing in the righteousness as well as the effectiveness of boycotts, Milk reminded readers that "The list of effective economic boycotts is long. Unions and governments use that method."[35] Milk further believed that the gay community should begin to recognize and exercise its capacity to put "economic pressure" to work for political ends. Obviously invoking the Boston Tea Party, Milk pleaded that buying orange juice amounted to "supporting a person who is preaching hatred towards every Gay person," and that if you were "unsure where your orange juice comes from, dump it!"[36] He went so far as to say, "We don't need any mass meetings or rallies. All we need is for everyone to just stop drinking it."[37] This assertion resonates with the logic of consumer sovereignty; there is some political way to conduct your private purchasing that will obviate meetings and rallies. Of course, Harvey Milk was not opposed to political organizing; indeed, he was strongly in favor of it. What I want to emphasize is that at the moment the gay movement went national, its leading spokesperson proposed consumption (in the form of nonconsumption) as a way of participating in the newly national community, even to the point of proposing that this kind of participation might supplant other forms of participation.

PRO AND CON ARGUMENTS

The most forceful argument against boycotting Florida orange juice was issued jointly by the co-chairs of the National Gay Task Force.[38] NGTF's position was either ambiguous or shifting; spokespeople offered conflicting statements of the organization's position at various points. But NGTF seems to have sent out a press release that said that boycotting Anita Bryant amounted to an attempt to deprive her of a livelihood because of views that she expressed when she was not on the job. NGTF's statement was generally understood to accuse boycotters of perpetrating the same kind of discrimination against Bryant's "job rights" that was legal against gay people—discrimination based on the personal life of an employee. This sentiment was echoed by Aryeh Neier, National Executive Director of the American Civil Liberties Union, in the April 21, 1977, edition of the *Sentinel*. Defending NGTF's position as "right in principle and right in tactic," Neier hailed the First Amendment as the principle at stake, the principle of protection for "people whose views, associations, and style of life are unpopular."[39] Implying that this principle was one to which gays as a group must be committed, Neier also argued that boycotting was strategically unsound: "it is essential, tactically, to make sure it is considered unrespectable to deny people employment because they espouse a point of view."[40] In other words, the gay movement could not risk the appearance of hypocrisy.

The same point of view was espoused by columnist George Mendenhall in "How to Deal with a Hate-Monger." Here he praised NGTF, as well as the Alice B. Toklas Democratic Club, for their contention that "employment should not be denied unless the reason for denial is based on a person's inability to perform that task."[41] A similar argument, for Bryant's "job rights" and against the boycott, was articulated in a column called "On the Right Side," which pleaded, "as Americans, and as homosexuals, let us not deny to them the very rights they seek to deny us. Only by guaranteeing them the First Amendment will others see themselves as they are; and more important, will we prove ourselves to be better citizens, and better human beings."[42]

Other arguments against the boycott included that it would be useless since the Florida Citrus Commission had vowed not to dismiss

Bryant, that boycotts were unlikely to be successful generally, and that a boycott would hurt the farm workers who were picking oranges. Some opponents of the boycott argued that it would infringe on consumers' rights to ask them not to buy something, or that it would infringe on corporations' rights.[43] Calling groups that endorsed the boycott "militant rights organizations," poet Rod McKuen sympathized with the leaders of the Miami coalition that simultaneously opposed both Bryant and the boycott.[44] The real danger in Bryant's campaign, McKuen warned was that "Bryant is going to destroy the tax-free advantages churches have by involving them in politics."[45] Rights, then, held a central place in the arguments for and against boycotting, mirroring the fundamental struggle around the Dade County ordinance.

Meanwhile, arguments in favor of the boycott came from far and wide. On the same page of the *Sentinel* as Neier's letter was a copy of one that San Francisco Mayor Moscone had written to the Dade Metro County Commission in support of the antidiscrimination ordinance they had passed (he avoided taking a position on the boycott). The same issue of the *Sentinel* reported that the San Francisco Tavern Guild banned the serving of Florida orange juice in member bars.[46] In fact, an early call had issued from the *Bay Area Reporter*'s front-page headline in February 1977: "GAY MIAMI SQUEEZES ANITA." The related news article reported that "Gay bars around the country have discontinued serving orange juice from Florida."[47] More organizational support came, in the next couple of months, from the Alameda County Democratic Central Committee (who went on record in support of the statewide boycott of Florida citrus declared by the gay movement: "We urge all Democrats. . . . The rights of all are threatened by the Bryant forces' disregard for separation of church and state"[48]); from the People's Temple (a predominantly black church in the East Bay that voted to observe the boycott and to write letters to family in Miami urging the same[49]); and even from a Swedish gay group's international arm.[50] As for denying employment to Anita Bryant, the "American Federation of Television and Radio Artists passed a motion asking its members to deny their services and talents to Bryant. The vote was unanimous."[51] The *Sentinel* reported that "Gay newspapers and organizations around the country have lined up behind a nationwide boycott of Florida orange juice products."

A month after his first proclamations on the subject, Milk once again disparaged opposition to the boycott, complaining that "too many people [were] willing to defend a person's 'rights' to spread hatred."[52] This time, his reference to the Boston Tea Party was explicit: "I urge all to join the boycott. . . . It is a small price to pay for freedom. Two hundred years ago a group dumped some tea into Boston Harbor. A nation won its freedom. It is time for us to dump Florida orange juice. Maybe we will find our freedom coming a lot faster."[53] Here, Milk asks the gay reader to identify with the colonial boycotters who created a national community by debating the virtues and faults of an economic course of action designed to address political problems and to produce distinctly political goals. The "small price" is only the sacrifice of the happiness or satisfaction associated with the commodity and its consumption.

So there certainly was great enthusiasm for the boycott. Calls to action often connected American identity and the rights of the citizen with consumer power. Perhaps the most extreme form of this economic action was proposed by the Gay Guerillas on a flyer dated July 1977:

> The American people should not be forced to support a campaign against human rights every time we want the nourishment of orange juice. . . . We must and can put Tropicana out of business. We are asking that all people of good conscience, especially supporters of President Carter's campaign for human rights, to boycott and/or organize boycott's [sic]of Tropicana and stores that sell it. This boycott [sic] to continue until every American gay person has been guaranteed the right to work, the right to custody of their children and the right to housing of their choice. We ask all those with even greater commitment to join an action we call The TROPICANA RELAY. Take one sharp instrument into a supermarket. (we use a three inch nail.) As you browse, or shop, find the Tropicana section. Puncture as many cans as you can. We suggest five to ten. . . . [W]e can put Tropicana out of business. It's in our hands.[54]

In a less dramatic move, but one with some rhetorical strength, Harvey Milk charged the leaders of NGTF with "Uncle Tomism,"[55] while a *Sentinel* editorial insisted that "every homosexual has a duty to engage in boycotting. . . ."[56] From Milk to the Gay Guerillas, opinions on the boycott were expressed in terms of group identity and group loyalty, particularly with respect to the U.S. polity and the collective body of "homosexuals."

I am not concerned with establishing the accuracy or the morality of any side. Instead, I mean to draw attention to the language in which the debate was cast, highlighting, as it did, everything from First Amendment issues, to the separation of church and state, to consumers' rights, to the terms of revolution and national identity. The terms of the debate demonstrate clearly that personal consumption and political action (particularly identity politics) were closely related in the minds of the debaters. Pro- and anti- alike subscribed to the idea that individual economic choices can, do, and should drive politics. The debate never turned to a consideration of the consequences of reinforcing that relationship.

One editorial drew on an analogy between consumption and political participation by saying that the "American populace boycotts a politician each time it goes to the polls and dumps from office persons with whom it disagrees."[57] It inveighed against opponents of the boycott for their concern with the image of gays as "militant," and it encouraged boycotters not to back down, even if they feared "retaliation." Complaining about the image-minded leaders of the movement, the writer sought to remind them that "the gay movement is a civil rights struggle and not a public relations campaign" and cited the leaders of the Miami campaign as homophobic for deciding to publicize the issue as one of human rights rather than sexual liberation, equating assimilationist politics with the antiboycott position.[58] On the one hand, this logic links "American" political behavior, boycotting, and sexual liberation—an apparently radical equation; on the other hand, in this equation, sexual liberation is recast as national liberation, recalling Milk's comparison between the colonial nonimportation movement and the 1977 boycott.

A letter from Boston proclaimed that "The issue is 1776, inalienable rights, and—for the legalists among us—the Bill of Rights."[59] But following this incantation of patriotic references to individual rights, as well as criticism of the sexism, racism, and even homophobia in the Dade County political arena, this letter goes on to criticize the leadership of the Miami struggle, who had "had a free ride for too long, bleeding bucks out of the community without having to answer for their pro-establishment, pro-capitalist, Goodstein, get-along, go-along line."[60] This comment, too, ends up casting a radical—sexual liberationist, anticapitalist—argument in terms of national identity and the origins of individual rights, which is to say, property rights.

In the pages of *GCN,* Dai Thompson argued for a boycott, writing that "as members of this society, gay people have given far too little thought to our potential power as consumers."[61] Invoking a maturation process that could refer either to national coming of age or movement development (and that also carries sad traces of the theory of homosexuals as underdeveloped heterosexuals), Thompson concurred with Harvey Milk: "money is the real source of power in this country. . . . The gay movement has gone begging for our rights long enough. . . . Instead, [we must] grow up and realize that we live in a capitalistic country where the only way to win equality is to learn to effectively use economic power."[62] This is a plain statement of the logic of boycotting, logic that underlies pro- and antiboycott positions, although here it is clearly intended to promote boycotting.

BOYCOTT NEWS

As the gay nation came into its own in the fight for freedom by economic means, the vehicle for the debate about those means was the increasingly national gay press. While strong arguments for and against boycotting appeared in the gay men's press and in the nationally distributed periodicals aimed at, published by, and written mostly by men, lesbian periodicals also reported on Anita Bryant's activities, albeit with more of a time lag and less of a focus on boycotting.[63] In May 1977, the *Lesbian News* reprinted the gist of NGTF's position without taking a clear stand: "It is important to let the organizations that employ Anita Bryant know that we disapprove of her. However, many Gay organizations—among them the NGTF—have advised against . . . engaging in economic reprisal, i.e., boycotting orange juice, because they feel Gays will lose support by making Bryant a 'holy Christian martyr.'"[64] In effect, the central suggestion to readers of the *Lesbian News* was that they should oppose Bryant by practicing more expressly political forms of politics. A *Lesbian Tide* editorial in the same month—entitled "Stop Bryant Now"—called on lesbians to send money and letters and to join coalitions, omitting any mention of a boycott.[65]

Newspapers are more than a woefully inadequate source of gay opinion in this country. The inadequacy is obvious: many periodical readers—straight or gay—do not write letters to their editors, while many more people do not read periodicals at all. These facts inevitably skew the opinions represented in gay and lesbian periodicals. The readership of gay men's papers and magazines is disproportionately affluent; the readership of lesbian periodicals is disproportionately feminist; and the readerships of both men's and women's papers are disproportionately educated, white, and urban. But even if these periodicals fail to give an accurate sense of the diversity of identities and opinions in the gay population as a whole, they portray one thing very clearly. The differences between the gay men's and the lesbian presses mirrored the gender divide within the movement in the ways I indicated in Chapter 2. In reviewing the coverage of Anita Bryant it is important to remember that periodicals produced by men had more advertising, more readers, more pages, more contributors, and more access to "news," while periodicals produced by women operated on tiny budgets and had few outlets for sales other than subscription. Likewise, men had almost complete control over the organizing in Miami. At some level, this is simply a function of the fact that women as a group had a lot less money than men, but men's virtual control of the Dade County campaign was also a function of sexism—which was visible in the gay press as well as in the movement unfolding in Florida. The gay press also reflects the dominance of men in the movement in its almost exclusive coverage of men—from letters to the editor to reports from Dade County, the only woman who appears is Anita Bryant herself, and as many women commented in "their" periodicals, the representation of Bryant was often sexist.

The newspapers demonstrated the intimacy of the relation between the growing market for the gay press and the movement leadership. Not only did the same money circulate in both arenas—David Goodstein was both the publisher of the *Advocate* and a large contributor to the

Dade County fight—but the nationalization of the press also corresponded with the nationalization of the movement. As the debate extended across the country, so the newspapers extended their coverage across the country. Even relatively local gay and lesbian papers changed their way of reporting news. In San Francisco, the *Sentinel,* for example, introduced a National News section during this period, a section that regularly appeared thereafter on page three of the paper every week. It could also be said that during the boycott, and partly because of it, certain cities—San Francisco, New York, and Los Angeles—came to stand for the gay nation in the same way that gay men's opinions came to stand for gay opinion. In other words, both the gay press and movement are dubiously representative, though they both serve representative functions.

DEFEAT OR VICTORY?

Although the June vote annulled the gay rights ordinance that the Dade County commissioners had passed six months earlier, many people involved in the boycott expressed a sense of triumph. It was impossible not to notice that gay money, gay organizing, the gay press, gay individuals, and straight allies had worked together in new ways. Whether those new ways were good or bad was a matter of yet another debate. In light of the events leading up to it, and with hope for the organizing that would follow, Harvey Milk described the "victory in Miami" in distinctly nationalizing terms: "the entire nation finally opened up and talked about Gay people."[66] He credited Anita Bryant with starting "what so many of us have talked about—a true national movement." Even the protest marches that erupted spontaneously following the vote in Miami showed a spirit of celebration as much as a sense of grief. In San Francisco, in particular, protesters took to the streets; according to one report, protesters bore "A bold red flag proclaiming, 'GAY REVOLUTION' . . . which [made] its way up the flagpole into the windless night. . . . There was total pandemonium."[67]

Two weeks after the defeat of the Dade County ordinance, San Francisco celebrated its annual pride parade. Whereas the pride parade had been, in previous years, "a festive, at times licentious event," the parade committee of 1977 "decided early in their planning to curb public inde-cency and ruled out nudity," planning for a more modest and restrained spirit.[68] Did a sense of defeat cement this decision, or had the decision been made earlier, in a mood of newfound self-consciousness, as people around the country watched the Bryant drama play itself out? The *Bay Area Reporter* accounted for it this way: "The sudden jettison of the Gay rights battle into the national media with Anita Bryant et al. has caused deep concern throughout the Gay community here over the parade—fearing the repercussions of a bad press."[69] In the coverage of the parade, *BAR* published two photos side by side: one photo shows a large crowd, and its caption reads: "A Gay Nation at Civic Center"; the second photo pictures a smaller group of men, some of whom carry a banner and sev-eral placards saying "Save Our Human Rights," while others carry Amer-ican flags.[70] The two nations in question—the gay nation and the United States, were then, and are still, both compatible and conflicting.

If there had been competing values at work in and around Miami during the campaign—sexual liberation versus human rights, pro-boy-cott versus antiboycott, nationalist versus anticapitalist—the evaluation of the campaign and its outcome was also divided. Historian Michael Melgaard lists prominent gay figures who felt that Anita Bryant had per-formed a positive function for the gay community. From Jean O'Leary of NGTF to Bob Basker (of the Dade County Coalition) to Frank Vel (an L.A. activist) to David Goodstein, such leaders credited Bryant with raising national consciousness of gay issues, with giving gays "common cause," as well as a chance to speak publicly. Goodstein observed that Bryant had earned a "Gay Unity Award," having done more "to bring gays together than anything that ever happened before."[71] In a sense, claims of victory implicitly likened the campaign to a boycott to the ex-tent that it was an action whose material ineffectiveness was less signif-icant than its public relations success; in other words, politics conducted in an expressly political mode had less impact than politics conducted as economic and symbolic action.

Others were less prepared to snatch moral or political victory from the jaws of legislative defeat. Writing in the *Sentinel*'s "From the Left" column, Randy Alfred dissented:

"Thank you, Anita, for bringing us together." I'm sick of hearing that line. It is, in short, a crock.

It's not clear that we are "together" in any meaningful way, lasting way. We have an emerging leadership that is suspect, shifty, media-defined, and monopolizing. . . .

If together means one big organization, it may not even be desirable. . . . [W]e should cast a wary eye on any national "umbrella groups."

Thanks for choosing the opponents: a politically inexperienced local gay community dominated by wealthy, white males.

Thanks . . . for thrusting to the fore a group of self-appointed "leaders" who ignore their constituency, over-ride its democratic decision, and have the further audacity to represent themselves . . . as representatives of "the gay community."[72]

Alfred refers here to Ethan Geto, Bob Basker, and Jack Campbell, the men who, backed in part by David Goodstein, raised money from all over the country, lobbied locally, and brought entertainers and politicians in to Miami.[73] According to Alfred (and others), Geto et al. conducted a very centralized and hierarchical organization with its roots in a social club for white men; they ran a "professional" campaign rather than a grassroots, democratically run organization with significant input from members. One indication of the professional nature of the organization is that as much as $450,000 was raised, more than had ever been raised in the gay community for any single public purpose. But its leaders structured the campaign in such a way that women and people of color were largely excluded from decision making within it.[74]

In effect, at the same time that the gay movement became national, it revealed itself as split along several different axes—race, gender, class, and agenda. On the one hand, the diversity of the community and the diversity of the movement were obscured in the way the national gay media represented the new national movement (as naturally, unproblematically) run by rich white men. On the other hand, in the same mechanisms—mostly gay press outlets—in which diversity was obscured, the lack of unity between men and women and between whites and people of color was also demonstrated. Partly through open debate expressed in letters to the editor in both local and national papers and magazines, but also through specialization within the growing market for gay and lesbian publications, gender, race, and class divisions, in addition to philosophical divisions, were expressed. Criticisms of sexism in the Dade County arena and of misogynist caricatures of Anita Bryant appeared in lesbian and women's periodicals—periodicals with very limited distribution, only local advertising, and very little readership among gay men. Substantial criticism of racism in Miami did not appear in the gay press, even though the movement's leaders were not just overwhelmingly white, they were unconcerned with mobilizing in Miami's Cuban community.[75] Criticisms of the sexual and class politics of the Dade County Coalition for Human Rights were not among the featured articles on Anita Bryant, but they could be found in certain columns and in lesbian-feminist journals.

Articulating a national basis for its organization at the same moment in which it revealed its internal diversity and even division, the gay and lesbian political movement made a critical, if unconscious, choice in 1977. The movement, which was first a handful and then thousands of people, chose to represent the community of lesbian and gay people as a cohesive entity, as a body with national unity, rather than as a fractured disunity. This is not the stuff of conspiracy; rather, this was a relatively passive choice to pick up on an already established tradition within a movement full of liberal intentions and liberal tactics, of claims based in founding national documents that referred to individual rights, and that argued for the privileges of full citizenship. In 1977, the movement chose to build its most public strategy on these values. In so doing, it moved significantly toward a deemphasis of the sexual liberationist values that had been the most public face of the movement at least since Stonewall. To supplement this political strategy with a boycott is logically consistent. As a mode of resistance, boycotts may publicly challenge policy, but they rely on individual consumption behavior, and so they reinforce the structures that produce economic and political inequality.

Although there were internal disputes and changes in course along the way, it was effectively the case that a few white men in Miami decided how to fight Anita Bryant; the rest of the community was not a part of this decision. In addition to opting for a liberal rights emphasis, those men chose a "professional" style of politics, a centralized, hierarchical, and undemocratic mode of decision making, one that excluded women and people of color, with a few exceptions. Furthermore, partly as a result of the way it had mobilized contributions from all over the country, the Miami campaign opened the way for the growth of national organizations. Gay and lesbian publications participated in this mobilization by printing solicitations of funds for the campaign, composing for themselves an audience for movement developments that would also constitute an identity-based target market. While local organizations would, in fact, proliferate and grow stronger, the drama in Miami set the stage for a certain kind of conflict between local and national organizing—the kind of conflict played out in and around Louisville in 1995.

Between 1977 and 1995, the gay and lesbian movement grew and changed in myriad ways: advocacy organizations, service organizations, social organizations, cultural projects, and legal organizations emerged, as did many business enterprises and professional associations, and these organizations had a variety of relationships with local and national constituencies. It would be inaccurate to suggest that there was a straight line from the 1970s to the 1990s, or that change was steady, unidirectional, or simple. Such a story would not account, for example, for the direct-action politics of the late 1980s and early 1990s.[76] Also missing would be an account of economic, political, and social changes more generally, changes sometimes described as "globalization." As markets have increasingly become transnational, they have also specialized, and in this context the trend has been toward the elaboration and refinement of niche marketing—even as mass marketing has struggled to persist. Of course, such changes in the economic sphere would correspond with changes in gay and lesbian political organizing, particularly as such organizing had established a tradition of fund-raising and economic tactics. So what happened when niche marketing, identity politics, and a gay movement construed as national but divided internally along lines of race, gender, and class met the boycotting resurgence of the 1990s?

TEA DANCE IN LOUISVILLE

The colonial past, the history of other social movements, and the history of boycotting in the gay and lesbian movement all raise the question of whether, and in what ways, boycotts could enact democratic principles. This question has, indeed, shown up in some contemporary gay boycott coverage. Note, for example, the outrage in *Outweek* over "earnest, hand-wringing editorials questioning whether anyone in the community has the right to launch a boycott, just who is empowered to call one off and who presumes to impose political coherence on gay organizations that choose not to honor boycotts."[77] The conflation of U.S. national identity, gay national identity, and consumption is one of the striking features of the location of social protest in the marketplace. As the *Utne Reader* stated, "The recent flurry of boycotts . . . goes to the heart of what America's all about: buying things."[78]

As boycotts generally proliferated in the 1990s, so did boycotts that centrally involved the gay community. Perhaps the most famous case was the boycott of Colorado and products of Colorado that followed the passage of that state's Amendment 2, which banned local legislation protecting gay men and lesbians from discrimination. This boycott, like the boycott of Coors for a host of unfair and discriminatory employment practices, was a national campaign and was fairly uncontroversial.[79] Regular coverage in the gay press suggested that the boycott was hurting business in Colorado, while equally regular statements from businesses there claimed otherwise. Publicity is the name of the game in boycotts like these—boycotters need to produce publicity about the boycott and businesses need to try to control their images. Other "gaycotts" in the 1990s have included the boycott of Bank of America for its contributions to the Boy Scouts of America, which prohibited homosexuals from becoming scout leaders, and a boycott of Marlboro because of its contributions to the Jesse Helms Museum, presumed to be a tacit source of money for Helms's campaign.

But controversy did surround a particular economic action in Louisville, Kentucky, in 1995; the action, and responses to it from around the country, exposed the fractures within the movement more dramatically than had the orange juice boycott. While conflicts that erupted in the Louisville action were similar to those that had begun to manifest themselves in the 1970s—democratic versus centralized decision making, the distinct and often competing investments of local organizers as against national organizers, the weight of money and power against the value of diverse participation—the Louisville action could only have followed the Dade County vote. Only when the movement could think of itself as national, only when allegiance to a gay "nation" began to eclipse diversity of identity and political opinion, only when national organizations came to believe that funding increasingly depended on opting against the kinds of collective and antihierarchical power structures designed by many grassroots organizations, only then could local and national groups become so squarely opposed on the question of how to "manage" money in the community.

According to Carla Wallace of the Fairness Campaign, the economic action that took place in Louisville came into focus slowly as members of the local gay and progressive communities began to talk with each other about politician Donna Shedd's "stealth approach" to gaining political power.[80] With that power, she planned to work toward the recriminalization of sodomy, the repeal of reproductive rights legislation, and the instatement of a voucher system for area schools.[81] Donna Shedd was the vice president of the Kentucky Eagle Forum and a member of the Republican Party's Kentucky state executive committee, and she was married to David Shedd, the owner of River City Distributing. Aware that River City distributed Miller products, Bartles and Jaymes malt beverages, and Heineken, among other beers, local progressives identified River City Distributing as a key source of support for Donna Shedd and her political activities.

Approached by the *Louisville Courier-Journal* to see if progressive and/or gay groups had called for a boycott against River City Distributing, the Fairness Campaign responded in the negative, but signals of concern about Shedd's potential to rise in state politics kept coming through. In the spring of 1995, the owner of the biggest gay bar in town, the Connection Complex, eagerly called the Fairness office to talk about Donna Shedd and to join with other concerned people and groups. Amid rumors that some nongay neighborhood organizations were not serving Miller Beer because of its distributor's relationship with the antichoice

Donna Shedd, conversations began among a number of bar owners, local pro-choice organizations, the Fairness Campaign, and others. As some Louisville residents cast it, "We're drinking beer that supports her political activity," and in these conversations, they began to envision letting others know about Donna Shedd, her aspirations, and her financial and political connections.[82]

"It was not called a boycott by us—we called it an economic protest, educating the community about where the money went when they bought beer," said Carla Wallace about the education campaign ultimately undertaken by the Coalition for Consumer Justice (CCJ), of which Fairness Campaign was a member.[83] Because River City Distributing accounted for 80 percent of Miller products in the Louisville area, Miller Beer became a focus of the campaign. But the CCJ explicitly stressed the difference between an action educating the public about the distributor's money flow and a boycott against Miller Brewing Company. They were, they asserted, "not attacking Miller Beer nationally, but we had no choice about publicizing who distributes it because of that distributor's financial link to right-wing activities."[84] CCJ did not say that River City Distributing was directly involved in, or making direct financial contributions to, the fanatical right. In his lead statement at a press conference in August 1995, John Scussel, the manager of the Connection Complex, underlined this point. Knowing that the income from River City Distributing made possible Shedd's activity, the Coalition held that they were within their rights to make this information public, so that people could decide for themselves whether to buy Miller products. In an unprecedented show of political commitment, the local gay bars began to cancel their contracts with River City, to carry other beer, to distribute information explaining why, and to provide customers with postcards addressed to Miller protesting its distributor. In its personnel, its focus, and its scope, the action was entirely local, crossing paths with a national entity only in the figure of Miller Beer production, which obviously precedes Miller Beer distribution.

Immediately, the Coalition heard objections to what they were doing; the objections came, overwhelmingly, from outside the local area. For one thing, many people felt that Miller Beer had had an especially good record of support for the gay community, its issues, and its special events. In fact, in a letter condemning the economic education action, leaders of national gay organizations complained that it "unfairly punishes one of our leading corporate champions."[85] Some people were troubled by the idea of punishing a husband because of the activities of his wife; David Shedd, they felt, operated independent of his wife. Some feminists likewise thought it wrong to treat Donna Shedd as though she were not also independent, and they objected to exerting "political pressure on a woman through her husband." Taking exception to Shedd's views, they nonetheless felt it would be wrong to treat her as though she could, or should, be influenced by her husband.

CCJ's disclaimers about a national boycott notwithstanding, Miller reacted swiftly and intensely. "Tom Reed, in the public relations office at Miller, was given the task of making us behave," recounted Carla Wallace. Having formerly been a member of the board of the Gay and Lesbian Victory Fund, Reed approached old colleagues who were national leaders of gay and lesbian organizations; he was looking for partners in suppressing the Louisville action. His consultations resulted in the letter quoted above, which was signed by David Mixner, Sandra Gillis (Executive Director of national Parents and Friends of Lesbians And Gays, or PFLAG), William Waybourn (former Executive Director of the Gay and Lesbian Victory Fund and, by 1995, Managing Director of the Gay and Lesbian Alliance Against Defamation, or GLAAD), David Clarenbach (Executive Director of the Gay and Lesbian Victory Fund), and Mark Barnes (Executive Director of AIDS Action Council). These people technically signed Reed's letter as individuals, rather than in their organizational roles; nevertheless, they did list their affiliations, implying that their signatures carried some unspecified, but definite, relation to the national organizations with which they worked. While Gillis had signed (not in her organizational role), the local PFLAG chapter supported the CCJ and expressed disappointment over Gillis's decision. Reed, among other signers, also approached Human Rights Campaign (HRC) and the National Gay and Lesbian Task Force, the two largest national gay and lesbian political organizations. Sympathetic to Reed but perhaps concerned about taking a stance that would embroil her in controversy, Elizabeth Birch (Executive Director of HRC) told Wallace that she and HRC would stay out of the conflict. But in the course of the lawsuit that followed, subpoenaed correspondence revealed that Birch had indicated to Reed that she would write letters to other people in the national movement urging them to denounce the Louisville effort. According to Wallace, the National Gay and Lesbian Task Force declined to sign the letter out of a belief that they should support local organizing, in principle, whenever possible.

With a number of volunteers, the local coalition persisted in leafletting at events and even went door to door along the business strips. While the response from the national organizations had been harsh, it did not deter the local organizers from pursuing the economic education action. Some people participating in the action seemed indignant that the national leaders had not spoken with them directly and had not "gotten the facts," Wallace remembers. "We felt we were being treated as though we didn't know what we were doing."[86] Participants planned a public press conference, which was covered by Louisville's *Courier-Journal* on August 26, 1995: "The clank of other broken bottles could be heard over the cheers of about 50 advocates of gay rights and women's rights" as they followed John Scussel's gesture of breaking a bottle of Miller Beer.[87]

While the players at national organizations argued that Miller shouldn't control the activities of their employees (i.e., David Shedd), locals persisted in the education effort. At the national level, the argument was reminiscent of the ACLU's argument against the orange juice boycott in 1977: employees should not be punished by employers for their privately held opinions. The public letter signed jointly by leaders of national gay organizations objected to targeting Donna Shedd through David Shedd, and apparently, Shedd herself concurred. She told the *Courier-Journal,* "I am appalled at the insensitivity of a group of men who think that women should be dragged around by their hair when it comes to what political positions they take."[88] Yet local self-avowed feminists remained committed to exposing Shedd's political positions (against women's reproductive rights); they remained committed, as well, to their belief that the income received by David Shedd was jointly owned by David and Donna Shedd, a concept supported by Kentucky law. The coalition held and volunteers continued to contribute.

In January 1996, Miller did fire Shedd, maintaining, however, that the economic protest was not the cause. "In a particular part of town where the campaign's efforts were most intense, there were big sales on Miller Beer, people stocking stores said so," said Wallace. In 1999, David Shedd was selling fences. Wallace pointed out that Shedd became a political pressure point precisely because he was a beer distributor and because of the particular character of the relationship between the gay community and the beer industry. "All you have to do is look at the magazines," she said, to know that the relation is close.[89] In other words, the effectiveness of the economic action depends on whether those likely to support it are in the market for the product in question. This recalls the observation that a boycott must appeal to consumers who are in the market for the boycotted commodity.

The CCJ had decided to use the term "economic action" rather than "boycott" because it wanted to emphasize that the action was a consumer-based educational initiative. They wanted local people to understand the consequences of spending money with River City Distributing, in particular, that in buying a River City product, consumers were providing financial resources for Donna Shedd to spread her ultraconservative ideology. As Eleanor Self of the Fairness Campaign described it, "They were helping to facilitate their own oppression."[90] The Coalition never stated an objective such as the termination of David Shedd by River City. In fact, when David Shedd lost his job and divested his stock in River City, the Coalition "lost access to our primary avenue for educating the community about Donna Shedd."[91] Fortunately, by the time David Shedd was terminated, the Coalition had managed to make its point about responsible consumerism and had publicly exposed Donna Shedd.[92]

What explains the national organizations' antipathy toward the action in Louisville? Why would they be so strongly opposed to an education campaign about right-wing politics and economics? Perhaps it has something to do with the fact that the Victory Fund was getting corporate gifts from Miller, as well as in-kind donations of liquor for fund-raising events. Evidently, PFLAG hoped for the same treatment. Milwaukee-based AIDS organizations were urged by several Milwaukee gay activists belonging to a group that had been heavily funded by Miller not to get involved in the boycott in Louisville, not to question the source of money. Understandably, decades of lack of resources, financial and otherwise, lead activists to want to use any available funds. But by the 1990s, when money was easier to come by for gay and lesbian organizations, and when consumption seemed, in some contexts, to suffice as a political program, the distance had grown between those organizations that depended on corporate funding and those that did not. Because they had more money, more staff, and more friends in business and politics, leaders of the organizations that received the most corporate money were those inclined to imagine the gay community as national rather than local, to affix their John Hancocks to a letter praising Miller Brewing Company, and to imagine themselves leaders of a movement on a representative basis when they didn't ask grassroots organizations what they wanted and needed. In this way, the national organizations of the 1990s shared something with their forebears in Florida twenty years earlier; movement leadership has often become relatively powerful even without serving a truly representative function. Thus local and grassroots efforts can be overridden, and women and people of color tend to be underrepresented, on the national gay and lesbian political scene. Among the national organizations, only the National Gay and Lesbian Task Force denied the request to sign the letter to the CCJ, endorsing the autonomy of local organizers, although it cost them some contributions to do it.

Questions about corporate money stud the landscape for contemporary gay and lesbian activists. Corporations prepared to sponsor nonprofit organizations do have some power over the latter, and nonprofits may have genuinely mixed feelings about accepting such sponsorship.[93] In the middle of the protest in Louisville, CCJ received a call from Community Health Trust (CHT), which is one of the largest AIDS service providers in Louisville. Miller was offering them grants of $5,000 for three years, and the CHT was unsure what to do. CCJ and members of CHT speculated that Miller was trying to buy good will and to undermine the protest; Coalition members met with CHT and indicated that they understood the pressing need for financial support, but that they hoped CHT would make it clear that they did not themselves oppose the economic action. Miller, however, wanted CHT to come out and condemn the protest. Issuing a statement that they were concerned about the protest but did not oppose it, CHT took the money.

THE MORAL OF THE STORY

As much as a boycott represents a particular group interest, a widely held moral belief, or a political ideology, it also represents the consolidation of class interest on the part of earners/consumers. For example, the "Outspoken" column in *Outweek* on August 22, 1990, written amid controversy about whether gays should boycott Marlboro and Miller for their support of Jesse Helms, contends that "the lesbian and gay community has enormous financial power, and we should have similar political clout, but we don't—because we have no history of consumer cohesiveness."[94] It is probably more accurate to say that some gay and lesbian people have financial power, that if they organize in their class that power can be increased, and that any political power associated with a group of gay men and lesbians would tend to correspond with their financial power. But should political power follow from financial power, from their "mettle as a consumer bloc"?[95] Interestingly, this raises a question that was asked in 1977 as well.[96] Perhaps there is no consumer cohesiveness on the part of the lesbian and gay community because there is no one class to which its members belong; thus, lesbian and gay identity interests may be at odds with any given class interest, although middle-class interests tend to dominate inside the movement, just as they do in society at large.

Like the strategy of fighting for rights and like soliciting corporate donations for nonprofits, boycotting, though perhaps necessary, is insufficient. Like target marketing to gays, it is a technique of negotiating for identity and power with capital. And like all negotiations with capital, its effects are ambivalent. Boycotting is a strategy that shores up capitalism, or that capitalism can accommodate or absorb. The logic of boycotting can not be arrested when the picket is over. It is the logic by which purchasing power is equivalent to political power, by which dollars count as votes, by which individuals participate in social decision making, and by which corporations (or markets) figure as government. Boycotting masks the fact that choice—that highest of liberal values—is always invisibly and radically constrained by the options presented, is *not* supremely embodied by individual consumers, and is, above all, exercised by the class of people that benefits most from unrestrained corporate activity. Even if corporations can be made to change policies unfavorable to gay men and lesbians, even if they make contributions, their primary function is still to amass capital in the hands of a few, mostly already rich white men. The other key here is the way in which identity gets negotiated through market behavior so that it becomes just another twist on identity-based consumption—a way of bracketing the comprehensive concerns of people suffering under corporate policies that are unfavorable to them according to some other identity axis. There is, of course, a contradiction inherent in this strategy: "Doesn't this method of change lock out the poor, such as the homeless, from having a voice in change? Yes, just as prison bars prevent political prisoners from engaging in active change. But with every purchase, we can either build more prison bars and create more homeless, or we can invest in economic institutions that support freedom, dignity, and economic empowerment."[97] This is as eloquent a statement as there could be of the moral good of subscribing to economic democracy, yet it makes familiar assumptions that are very important to see, and to question. What are the implications of making social change on behalf of people who cannot participate in the process of change? I'm not saying don't boycott. Do boycott. But remember that the limits of this form of franchise are material as well as theoretical; there are serious limits to what can be "voted" for or against in this way, as well as limits on who can vote this way. These limits attend the construction of citizenship in the market, and they follow from the belief that acts of private consumption can serve as political participation. Such a form of participation may be inevitable, but it narrows the range of possibilities for social change.

5

STRINGS ATTACHED: HOW MONEY MOVES THE MOVEMENT

It takes money, we can conclude, to construct any alternative to the society predicated on the community of money. This is the essential truth that social movements have to confront; otherwise, it confronts and destroys them.

—David Harvey[1]

B ased in gay and lesbian identity, the social movement that seeks rights and social acceptance for gay and lesbian U.S. citizens is constituted largely by nonprofit organizations. A variety of nonprofits fill out the cultural and social scene of, by, and for, gay men and lesbians: service organizations (from hotlines to community centers to AIDS and other health-related service organizations), cultural groups (from theater to film to educational enterprises), and expressly political organizations (from those seeking legislative, electoral, or judicial action to those working in all those areas). Such organizations may have small or large staffs or no staff at all; they may be staffed by a homogeneous or a heterogeneous group of people; they may serve homogeneous or heterogeneous constituencies; they may serve local, national, or international constituencies. These nonprofit organizations also run the gamut of political opinion from left to right. But they all depend on money to function.

Just as the range, size, and viability of gay and lesbian businesses have grown over time, so have the range, size, and viability of gay and lesbian nonprofits. Moreover, the businesses and nonprofits have proliferated and grown in relation to each other. In earlier chapters I drew the connection between the growth of the gay press (an institution that shifted over the last three decades of the twentieth century from non-profit to for-profit) and gay movement growth. Other for-profit concerns, such as bookstores and bars, have played crucial roles in the development of the gay movement. And in the latter years, particularly in the 1990s, nongay businesses have also interacted with the gay movement in various ways. This chapter explores the interaction between for-profit enterprises (as well as various funders) and nonprofit gay and lesbian organizations—particularly *advocacy* organizations—and elucidates some of the ways that such interactions affect the course of the movement.[2]

Money comes to advocacy organizations through a variety of channels and sources.[3] Those channels and sources have regular and systematic effects on the movement: the funding of gay and lesbian advocacy organizations tends to encourage liberal rather than progressive agendas within those organizations; funding favors larger organizations and organizations that are national in scope, while smaller and local organizations find it much more difficult to attract funding; the most common modes of funding for gay nonprofits tend to promote white people and men to leadership positions. Taken together, these effects create a situation in which large organizations dominate "the movement," while that movement increasingly seeks full enfranchisement for gay men and lesbians *as gays*. What gets pushed out of the center of this scene are smaller organizations, organizations that are local in scope, the left- and right-wing fringes of the gay and lesbian community, and the needs of people who are unempowered on the basis of gender, race, class, and other features besides sexual identity. While these trends have been developing for decades, they became more pronounced in the 1990s because the numbers of people and the size of the budgets involved reached a critical mass, because of the sophistication of information systems, and because of the growing gap between rich and poor. The obvious mainstreaming of the gay and lesbian community as a whole during the 1990s also made these trends more visible.

FUND-RAISING

In order to understand these dynamics, it is crucial to begin by understanding the fund-raising techniques engaged by gay and lesbian advocacy organizations. There are many types of fund-raising and many variations on each of these types. The types include (but are not limited to) special events, solicitation of individual donations, fund-raising from members, solicitation of corporate donations (of cash or of goods or services from companies or their foundations), and grantwriting to independent (noncorporate) foundations or government sources. Each of these techniques is designed, by definition, to raise money for organizations so that they may pursue their missions. Pursuing a mission costs money: staff must be compensated, rent and telephone bills and mailing costs must be paid. Raising money, however, is no simple matter. Any tactic for generating funds brings with it certain entailments. While I recognize that fund-raising is a necessary function and that it supports massive and diverse work done by gay and lesbian organizations, I also think it is important to take inventory of the entailments of raising money. The money raised by nonprofits is no different from the money that consumers spend, or advertisers invest, or entrepreneurs earn through profit. It all circulates in the same big bathtub of capital. Without meaning to throw the baby out with the bath water, I undertake to examine the economic mechanisms that connect the consumers, advertisers, and entrepreneurs with the operation of nonprofit agencies.

I will explain these mechanisms in part by showing how they work and in part by giving examples of particular mechanisms with reference to particular cases. The examples are neither randomly chosen nor representative. I have purposely chosen examples that illustrate some of the most difficult dilemmas in fund-raising for gay and lesbian organizations. Take as the first example the "special event," coordinated by a nonprofit organization, and designed to bring in a large enough ticket-buying audience to generate income for that organization. The conventional wisdom in fund-raising holds that special events are often not worth the resources that go into them. They occur rarely in straight fund-raising contexts, relative to their incidence in the gay and lesbian community and movement. The gay and lesbian movement, from the beginning, required unconventional wisdom to guide its fund-raising for several reasons. First, the unpopularity of the cause called for special invitations into the world of the gay and lesbian nonprofit. Second, the fact that the gay and lesbian movement was unknown called for creative ways to publicize the causes associated with it. Third, movement building and community building have been among the most critical needs of the movement. Special events can bring people together in ways that the gay and lesbian community has had few opportunities for, particularly outside of bars and private social networks. While these factors historically made special events more of a staple in gay and lesbian fund-raising than in the mainstream nonprofit world, by the 1990s special events in the gay and lesbian community began to raise concerns about the unintended consequences of the structure of funding for gay and lesbian organizations.

While there are countless examples of excellent events that have promoted community, spread information, and raised money for important purposes, some have caused concerns. Thus, I begin here with the case of a fund-raising event that took place in New York City in the early 1990s. In late 1990, the Lambda Legal Defense and Education Fund and New York's Lesbian & Gay Community Center chose to produce a showing of *Miss Saigon* as a joint fund-raising event. Lambda is the preeminent national legal organization serving gay men and lesbians in the United States, while the Community Center houses meeting space for numerous groups, a library, an information center, and other features. *Miss Saigon* is, according to the activists who tried to persuade Lambda and the Center not to feature it, "the latest in a long line of Western misrepresentations of Asians, perpetuating a damaging fantasy of submissive 'Orientals,' self-erasing women, and asexual, contemptible men."[4]

After learning of Lambda and the Center's intention to produce *Miss Saigon,* Asian Lesbians of the East Coast (ALOEC) and Gay Asian and Pacific Islander Men of New York (GAPIMNY) joined together in the winter of 1991 to convince the organizations to change their plans. Two fairly small and local organizations that had previously worked within single-gender groups, ALOEC and GAPIMNY found that members were willing to work together and, in so doing, "developed an openness toward difference and a flexible negotiating style" that lent vigor and strength to an emerging coalition.[5] The New York Gay and Lesbian Community Center dropped its plans following an "amicable and productive" meeting between coalition members and the Center's board and management, leading the coalition to regard the Center as a "truly New York City–based organization, with stronger ties and commitment to the local gay and lesbian community."[6] Things did not go quite so smoothly with Lambda.

Initially framing its position as a request for the "gay and lesbian community to deal with its institutional racism," the coalition met with Lambda a few times. At the first of those meetings, the coalition's opening statement posed the following question: "What does it mean for Lambda, a civil rights organization that claims to represent all Gay men and Lesbian women, to meet its annual budget with images of us as prostitutes and pimps, 'greasy Chinks' and 'slits'?"[7] Only when its repeated requests met with intransigence on Lambda's part did the coalition determine to stage a protest at the fund-raiser. Interestingly, resistance to Lambda's course of action was internal as well as external. In spite of an eloquent memo submitted by a former temp worker critiquing the "orientalist significance" of the show, a letter signed by seven staff members (all women), and the resignation of their public education coordinator, Mariana Romo-Carmona, Lambda persisted in staging *Miss Saigon.* The coalition was compelled to conclude that with its refusal to respond, Lambda reproduced an "unequal distribution of power and privilege within the gay and lesbian community."[8]

That a national organization focused on advancing and protecting the civil rights of gay men and lesbians could fail to understand the connection between political representation and cultural representation had unfortunate significance. This failure could be interpreted as a signal that Lambda imagined race and gender to be distinct from sexuality both in terms of imagined or active audience, and in terms of the political needs of the gay and lesbian community. Otherwise, the exigencies of fund-raising could have seemed, to Lambda, to excuse or even to require compromising these concerns. One activist offered this analysis:

> As they do in mainstream society, white men hold a disproportionate amount of institutional power in the queer community. Gay white men sit on boards or head up a number of community organizations, and often help determine priorities and programs. In the allocation of resources such as AIDS funding, or the absence of programs that battle breast cancer, people of color have found that their concerns and needs are not automatically given equal shrift.[9]

Thus a broad-based coalition within the gay and lesbian community—including Asian and Pacific Islander Coalition on HIV/AIDS (APICHA) and other gay and lesbian of color groups—having already asked elected officials (especially gay and lesbian ones) to intervene, assembled to protest Lambda's choice by picketing outside of the event theater on the evening of the fundraiser in April 1991. Not incidentally, part of what was at stake in the debate about the show was its representation of U.S. national identity. Apologists for *Miss Saigon* argued that the show was at least critical of the role of the United States in the Vietnam War, but the plot resolution—in which the American former soldier reclaims his Vietnam-born son to raise him in comfort, style, and freedom in the United States—recuperates the very forces that entered Vietnam illegally and with violently destructive effect. These dramatic elements were eerily echoed by the drama that unfolded outside the theater on the night of the fund-raiser/protest. As police moved in on the demonstration and arrested six men, fellow activists felt that the arrests represented "an excessive exercise in intimidation."[10] As the protesters saw it, Lambda, rumored to have called in the police, "drew a line between 'law and order'—Lambda's well-dressed, overwhelmingly white, mainly male donors—and us, mostly yellow and brown skinned, kept at bay by the cops."[11] The correspondence between the drama inside the hall and the one outside the hall also aligned Lambda and the police with each other and with the position of "American" savior (in both the Vietnam War and in the play), while the coalition of protesters would be aligned with the un-American, even anti-American, enemy.

Because this drama took place around a fund-raising event, it clearly pointed to the broader question of how money circulates in and around the gay and lesbian movement. "The incident was just one example of how the mainstream white non-profit queer community just does not get issues of racism, and it is yet another indicator of the chronic lack of representation by women and queers of color," commented Javid Syed of APICHA.[12] At the same time, it was an example of "pan-ethnic organizing against apparent racism and sexism among the large queer groups that were supposed to be representing our constituencies."[13] Among that coalition, the action "created a sense of solidarity—out of it came a lot more trust in each other's work."[14] Nevertheless, that trust was forged in opposition to the political center of the gay and lesbian movement in the United States, and prospects for solidarity between white and nonwhite constituencies within the gay and lesbian community suffered in this incident. On the broader fund-raising landscape, this kind of high-profile event has tremendous symbolic import, but it is not the sole, nor the most financially crucial, kind of fund-raising.

As the ticket prices to the fund-raisers of large national gay and lesbian organizations soared, the prospect for multiracial and cross-class audiences suffered. As the 1990s marched on, the fund-raising dinners and parties of the Human Rights Campaign and GLAAD (Gay and Lesbian Alliance Against Defamation) cost more and more to attend; most such events cost more than $100 per person by the end of the decade. Because of these prices, it seems likely that these events cater to existing donors or bring in more affluent new donors, rather than providing the function of broad outreach or education. For many organizations, this is okay. For an organization trying to maintain and expand programming, fund-raising is, as I have said, simply a necessity—raising funds is its primary objective and expensive dinners fulfill that objective. Many folks in development believe that *other* kinds of events can and should be geared toward outreach and education. I worry about separating out these objectives. I understand that it would be constraining—and probably less financially effective—to reconceive fund-raising so that it met objectives of outreach and education, but I worry that fund-raising events designed with the sole purpose of raising money build community and the sense of movement only among the people who can afford to go. What is generated and perpetuated is a group of people with money and contacts, a group that excludes others on the basis of their class. Many events are simply inaccessible for people without a lot of money. Yet the social aspect of fund-raising events is intimately related to the decision making mechanisms within large national gay organizations, just as the social aspect is a huge part of fund-raising from individual donors.

Individualized fund-raising takes place in private visits, usually between an executive director of a non-profit and one major donor at a time. Sometimes a development director or board member will also be present or will substitute for the executive director. Major individual donors may have a significant effect on a nonprofit's program, especially if such donors constitute the greatest part of a nonprofit organization's annual budget. While some organizations have a greater proportion of corporate, foundation, or membership support, major individual donors are almost always a key segment of annual income for lesbian and gay advocacy organizations. Again, homophobia has contributed to the historical reliance of gay and lesbian organizations on individual donors—foundation dollars and other public sources were largely unavailable to gay and lesbian organizations, with very few exceptions, prior to the 1990s. Another reason that personalized fund-raising is so significant is that visits with major donors take up a good deal of the time of the executive director, if not also the development director. As Julie Dorf, Executive Director of the International Gay and Lesbian Human Rights Commission (IGLHRC), suggests, an executive director could not do her job without paying disproportionate attention to major donors. For an executive director, Dorf says, "It would be dishonest to pretend that you're not going to give more attention to their thoughts and ideas, because of your dependency on them."[15]

Relationships with major donors affect the work of an organization in both more subtle and less subtle ways. The less subtle ways involve donors explicitly attempting to direct or control program work. For example, there were donors who said that they would have given larger gifts if IGLHRC would not count transsexuals among its constituency.[16] Other donors have said that because serving anybody with HIV and AIDS implies serving people who are not gay or lesbian, IGLHRC does

not fit the profile of a single-issue organization, and they prefer to re-
serve their larger gifts for organizations that exclusively serve gay men
and lesbians.[17] Of course, this kind of effect is necessarily structured
into philanthropy. Obviously, there are incalculable numbers of people
who do not give money to any given organization because they are not
compelled by the mission of that organization. Therefore, I am more
concerned here with the subtler effects of relationships with those major
donors who are involved with the operations of the nonprofits to which
they contribute.[18]

At the most superficial level, these relationships, by virtue of staff
time spent on them, are more elaborate than relationships with smaller
donors and with the often relatively large body of people giving at membership level. As Dorf described her relationship with major donors:
"you know more about them and you may even become friends with
them."[19] By contrast, the way a nonprofit gets information about the rest
of its donors and members is limited—information can be gathered
through surveys, or one can pay to have research done, but while useful, these are clearly much cruder ways to figure out who the membership is and what they care about.

Even if they don't directly determine the work done on a daily basis
within a nonprofit, these dynamics have serious implications for the
composition of the leadership of individual organizations and for the
leadership of the movement as a whole (leadership in turn tends to affect choices about what work gets done). Dorf went on to say that most
major donors give money because they "click" with the person doing
the fund-raising, generally the executive director. That is, they believe
in the organization because of its leadership. As a white Jewish lesbian
with over ten years of fund-raising experience, Dorf put it this way: "If
I were a man, if I were older, if I had a Harvard degree, I would have
even more credibility and raise even more money, and if I were obese or
a person of color—anything that would diminish my access—I wouldn't
be as successful."[20] She believes this is true *regardless of the mission* of
the organization. Not all the money is in the hands of white men, as is
sometimes assumed, but it's hard to raise large sums without them.
When an executive director solicits individual donors, she plays up class
similarities with them, a style that may come more "naturally" to those

of middle-class origin. Dorf, for example, often talks about being a homeowner with donors. If the success of leaders depends on sharing the identity of affluent white male donors—or being able to act like them, with respect to social customs and manners—this would certainly favor white and/or male leaders. Perhaps this explains, in part, why there are so few executive directors who are people of color and so few people of color organizations with national status.

Julie Dorf's account is entirely consistent with other accounts, notably Urvashi Vaid's account of fund-raising as the Executive Director of the National Gay and Lesbian Task Force.[21] And the fact that this is a widespread phenomenon is evidenced by a conversation convened by the Task Force Policy Institute Roundtable. At the roundtable, members discussed how to structure a better conversation about race, as well as who should be present. Most of the people in the room were executive directors or co-chairs (in other words, they were senior level policy people), and out of somewhere between 30 and 50 people in the room, three were people of color. On the issue of leadership development, the roundtable entertained the questions of why the leadership was white and why there were no viable national organizations for people of color other than LLEGO (The National Latina/o Lesbian, Gay, Bisexual & Transgender Organization). While there are many people of color among staff in the national gay and lesbian organizations, there was an acknowledged glass ceiling for people of color in those organizations. Present at this discussion, Dorf said, "If we were going to discuss how to change the color of the leadership, we would need to talk about racism in fund-raising. If I were going to replace myself, as an executive director, with a person of color, I would need to find someone who could function well in a white world; that's what it takes to raise significant money from individual donors in the gay and lesbian community." Just as race and gender determine the extent to which gay men and lesbians are represented in the market arena, so do they determine representation in the nonprofit arena. The underrepresentation of women and people of color in the movement is matched—illustrated, as it were—in pictorial advertising targeted to gay men and lesbians and in the gay and lesbian business world. Political representation and media representation are closely linked; in nonprofit and for-profit spaces alike, representation of gay identity often amounts to representation of white people and their class interests, and/or men and their class interests.

FUND-RAISING AND CORPORATE BODIES

Although dependency is a fact of nonprofit life, nonprofits don't like that fact; attempting to prevent dependence on too few large sources, they aim for a diversity of income sources. (An organization that depends on just a few large sources is often financially vulnerable for the obvious reason that the elimination of a single source could devastate the organization.) Hence, over and above the value of their contributions to furthering so much nonprofit work, individual donors also contribute to the diversity of an organization's sources of funding. I do not mean to ignore the benefits provided by generous individuals who contribute large amounts of money. Instead, I want to stress that the structure of funding favors white male leadership or leadership by people who can pass in a white male monied arena. Individual donations are not the only mechanism that produce this effect—far from it. I turn now to other funding mechanisms to show how they too favor not only a certain style of leadership, but also a certain type of organization and a certain politic.

In the 1990s, a few gay and lesbian organizations began to receive donations from national and multinational corporations. During the 1980s, corporations had begun to respond philanthropically to the need for AIDS-related research and services. In the 1990s, some corporations began to make contributions to gay and lesbian advocacy organizations. This represented a real shift in funding trends and significantly affected the budgets of a handful of large national gay and lesbian nonprofits doing expressly political work. Of course, some kinds of political work were more likely to receive such funding than other kinds. A few examples will show how corporate funding tended to support the liberal rights-seeking middle of the movement. My concern is that this form of support had the side effect of "de-resourcing" the right and left wings of the movement; this is what Vaid refers to as "mainstreaming the movement."[22] I believe that the health of the movement—defined as a large number of variously sized well-funded organizations operating across a wide spectrum of political opinion and adequately representing diverse constituencies—declined as the range of viable political positions within it decreased. Of course, corporate donations to nonprofits are extremely complicated in principle, and in practice such donations are made through a wide variety of mechanisms. Again, I use discrete and specific examples in this section in order to raise some questions about the effects, particularly the unintended effects, of some of those mechanisms.

One controversial example of corporate donation was the gift made by Coors to the Gay and Lesbian Alliance Against Defamation in 1998. GLAAD, which frames itself as a media watchdog and therefore, by definition, a watchdog of corporations, received a gift of $110,000 from the beer company. GLAAD's acceptance of the gift aroused the concern of progressives in the lesbian and gay movement for several reasons. First, Coors had a record of funding—through the Adolph Coors Foundation and the Castle Rock Foundation—the Free Congress Foundation, the Heritage Foundation, the Western Journalism Center, and the Promise Keepers, all right-wing enterprises. Second, there had been, for decades, active boycotts of Coors, organized in response to its labor practices (in particular, its famous polygraph test for job candidates, its alleged question to prospective employees about their sexual orientation, and its alleged mistreatment of women and "minority" workers). In the 1990s, in an attempt to open up a lesbian and gay market that had been (however immeasurably and unevenly) exposed to negative publicity about the company, Coors engaged the services of Witeck-Combs Communications, a gay public relations firm. Coors began to advertise to gay men and lesbians and to send representatives to gay and lesbian business expos.

The Coors Boycott Committee formed in order to publicize and denounce the corporation's new marketing strategies, and it accused Witeck-Combs of "vulgar profiteering." For Stuart Timmons of the Coors Boycott Committee, "As a progressive person, I have learned to pay attention to who my historical gay enemies are, and the more you do that, the less shocking it is to see that someone would give a few thousand dollars to gay organizations and millions to bashers like the Free

Congress and the Heritage Foundation."[23] That is to say, Coors' dona-tions to entities that are philosophically opposed looks like a cynical move calculated to pave the way for marketing to consumers of all po-litical stripes. Note too the implication that gay and lesbian consumers can be bought by paltry sums relative to Coors' overall docket. Thus in 1998, the Boycott Committee made an impassioned plea for GLAAD to rethink its acceptance of the contribution from Coors: "We . . . call upon GLAAD to return the Coors money and recover its integrity by adopting serious standards for seeking funding which exclude rank promotion of commercial products and embracing corporations which advance a ho-mophobic agenda."[24] But GLAAD stood by its decision to take the money, which distressed many in the gay and lesbian community. In the words of the Coors Boycott Committee, "GLAAD has been our leading watchdog monitoring 'homo'-hating media and corporations. GLAAD's credibility is a precious thing. It will be shot to hell if it grabs money and prostrates itself to a major bankroller of gay oppression."[25] Without ques-tion, the ability of Coors to manipulate its own image far surpassed the ability of the boycotters to organize against Coors. Coors' public rela-tions victory was demonstrated in its number two overall ranking in a list of "The 100 Best Corporate Citizens" put out by *Business Ethics* in 1996, and its ranking of fourth among the "Ten Best for Gay Men and Lesbians."[26] Coors is the paradigmatic example of the politically trou-bling intersection of movement and market. Its marketing campaign to gay men and lesbians depends on its improved corporate policy, which may in part be a result of indirect movement pressure, but which clearly depends on its desire to market to gay men and lesbians, a desire visible (and taken as a sign of affirmation) even when its policy is not. However, when gay and lesbian consumers buy Coors, they are sponsoring the right-wing institutions to which Coors contributes on a much larger scale than it ever does to gay and lesbian organizations. If the individual con-sumer's dollar spent on Coors is a vote for Coors' social responsibility, Coors casts millions of votes for conservative political action. And for the purposes of *Business Ethics,* contributions to right-wing political or-ganizations mean social responsibility.

Many other corporations also have programs of charitable contri-butions that enable them to speak publicly out of both sides of their mouths. They are often advised to do so by the public relations offices within the corporations or by independent public relations consultants.[27] For example, Philip Morris has been a major contributor to Jesse Helms, a leading voice in the Senate against both gay and lesbian rights and the National Endowment for the Arts.[28] This was at direct odds with its contributions to AIDS research and to "gay causes," like the Gay Men's Health Crisis, and the tens of millions of dollars it gave over the years to artistic programs. Not surprisingly, a boycott of Philip Morris products targeted the corporation's support of Senator Helms. After all, Philip Morris's "support of Senator Helms was undermining the good will that had been created."[29] While the boycott had, according to Philip Morris, "no economic impact," it nevertheless "sensitized us to concerns within the arts community."[30] Thus sensitized, in 1991 Philip Morris pledged to double its contributions to AIDS research that year, while continuing to support Helms. Philip Morris clearly plays to both ends of the political spectrum.

Another controversial issue in the new era of "partnering" between mainstream corporations and gay and lesbian nonprofits relates to the sponsorship of the latter by alcohol companies. Sponsorship is a form of donation in which a business gives money to support a special event, often a benefit. The more sponsorship an organization has for a fundraising event, the greater the amount of money raised that can go to support the work of the nonprofit, rather than covering the cost of producing the special event in the first place. As part of most sponsorship arrangements, the nonprofit that benefits must display the name and logo of the sponsor, as well as acknowledging its sponsorship by any number of means stipulated by the sponsor (I'll detail some of these below). The opportunity for sponsorship by alcohol companies has generated some debate in the gay nonprofit community in light of the fact that alcoholism is, according to some, disproportionately prevalent in the gay and lesbian population. Alcohol companies are not only among the most dogged advertisers to gay men and lesbians, they are also among the most frequent large sponsors of gay and lesbian events.

As just one example, an art installation consisting of 500 pink umbrellas, which was designed as an AIDS memorial to benefit Design Industries Fighting AIDS, that traveled to San Francisco, Boston, Miami,

Dallas, Seattle, Kansas City, and Minneapolis bore the title "Pink Um-brellas: An Absolut Remembrance" in recognition of the event sponsor. Thus every bit of publicity for the event, including its listing in calendars around the country, sported the name of a brand of vodka. Any media coverage of the traveling installation would also represent Absolut. And of course, on every program, at every opening, in each city on the tour, the name Absolut got lead billing. Likewise the "remembrance" became an ad, desacralizing its memorial function. It is not unusual for sponsors to require that organizations hang wall banners at events and print the logo and/or name of the sponsoring company on invitations, programs, and other materials. Of course, it is possible for nonprofits to refuse sponsorship from alcohol companies. However, the cost of such a policy is high; to refuse such sponsorship is to choose not to seek some of the more easily available sponsorship dollars, and in turn to choose *not* to lighten the financial burden of fund-raising. The principled position can be inordinately expensive.

Another way that corporations support nonprofits is through "in-kind" donations. Corporations thereby donate to a nonprofit organization the goods or services that they normally sell. For example, caterers donate catering, printers donate printing, airlines donate plane tickets, and so on. Many companies provide the goods they otherwise sell rather than giving cash. Sponsorship by alcohol companies, for example, often takes the form of alcohol donation, freeing nonprofits from the burden of buying alcohol to serve at events. Of course, this mechanism also returns visibility to the contributing company. In-kind donations are commonly acknowledged in event programs, in annual reports, and by other means. Sometimes the specific forms of acknowledgment are spelled out in contracts between the donor and the nonprofit. So, for example, in the late 1990s, IGLHRC established a contract with American Airlines that is several pages in length. A number of those pages are dedicated to clarifying what American expects in return for the donation of ticket vouchers. Beyond the usual requirements, American asks that IGLHRC staff wear American Airlines lapel pins while traveling. Of greater concern to the organization is the airline's requirement of exclusivity; American stipulates that IGLHRC maintain no partnering arrangements with other airlines. However, the ticket vouchers do indeed reduce IGLHRC's travel budget—a boon to an organization that works with colleagues outside of the United States.

But more to the point here, as Dorf observes, is that corporate sponsorship is "not primarily a philanthropic activity—it's a marketing tool."[31] Appreciating the net benefit for IGLHRC, Dorf speculates that the only other way the organization would be able to get mainstream corporate support would be because "somebody knew somebody." (For instance, IGLHRC gained free access to a conference-call line through PacBell because of the commitment of a former PacBell employee who is "a great guy with a personally philanthropic value system.")[32] Such donations, while useful, are rather randomly available. Or perhaps it is not so random. Perhaps it is another way of demonstrating that broad access is the most important qualification for nonprofit leadership, thus reinforcing the influence of whiteness, affluence, and maleness.

Yet another mechanism for conveying charitable contributions to nonprofits is the affinity credit card, issued by a credit card company that makes contributions in some proportion to expenses charged on the card. With gay and lesbian credit cards, affinity bears a close relation to identity. For instance, although it names lesbians as its primary beneficiaries, the Rainbow Card gives money not just to lesbian causes but also to "women's health care concerns" and to "gay issues" (implying that, as far as identity and/or affinity go, lesbian is not equal to gay).[33] Sometimes, in return for its sponsorship, the bank behind the credit-card company stipulates that it will be entitled to specified uses of the credit-card company's mailing list. There may be a financial downside for the customer, if the interest rate on the card exceeds the lowest rate available on the market. The *Advocate* reports that "there remains a differential between the interest rates charged for gay affinity cards and the best deals available for ordinary credit cards, some of which may charge as little as 7%."[34] If customers saved on the annual fee and on the interest rate and then made an equivalent direct contribution to a nonprofit, theoretically, that nonprofit would receive more money.[35]

It is interesting to note that the appeal of the credit card is the same as the appeal to boycotters. The idea in both cases is that one's political program can be advanced through the market. Thus it is no surprise that the language of boycotting, and the theory of economic democracy behind it, find their way into discussions of gay and lesbian affinity credit cards. The same report in the *Advocate* likens the experience of a customer of the Uncommon Clout credit card to "voting with his wallet."[36] (See Figure 4.1.) Uncommon Clout actually refers to purchases made with its credit card as "buycotting." The Rainbow Card too has a slogan that promotes the idea that personal consumption is an effective mode of political participation; Martina Navratilova stands in civilian garb (or is it gay uniform: blue jeans, white tee shirt, Doc Maartens or knock-offs thereof), arms akimbo, against the bold black-lettered phrase "The power of one." (See Figure 5.1.) The copy goes on to claim that "each of us can make a difference" by using the Rainbow credit card "to purchase an item, travel, or dine out," that is, to use the charge card for private consumption. The difference touted here is for "lesbigay arts, cultural, and civil rights organizations" and for health organizations too. Of course, it is all to the good if such organizations benefit; but apart from the question of which groups do not benefit, there is still a question of the logic that individual acts in the market amount to political participation.

When they speak about the virtues of such mechanisms, marketers invariably add that they enable consumers to contribute money to social and political causes by buying things. Or "without changing their lifestyles."[37] Or "passively."[38] In any case, the 1990s were marked by the extension of privatization and by governmental withdrawal from social programs, so that schools were increasingly subsidized by Coca-Cola, prisons built and run by private industry, and so on. Mechanisms that encourage the support of nonprofits through acts of private consumption help to obscure these changes as well as to mitigate them financially. If consumers can support the social programming that they favor in their capacity as consumers, does that mean that they do not or will not support that programming by other means? At this point, I believe it is impossible to know. And yet, it is difficult not to speculate. Declining voter turn-out could be a result of many factors, and must indeed have multiple causes, but the numerical data on voting do not rule out the possibility that consumers increasingly have turned to consumption as a form of political participation, especially given the increased opportunities for socially based consuming.

The power of one.

$20 off your first **Tzabaco** purchase charged to the Rainbow Card.

"Each of us can make a difference. Every time we use the Rainbow Card we help fund organizations serving the lesbian and gay community."

Martina Navratilova

One Card:

- **Low 6.9% Introductory APR**
- No Annual Fee
- Visa Worldwide Acceptance
- Transfer Any Current Credit Card Balances to Take Advantage of the Low 6.9% APR
- Apply Jointly With Your Domestic Partner for an Increased Credit Limit
- Valuable Subaru Purchase Offer for Cardholders

SUBARU.
Proud Founding Sponsor of the Rainbow Endowment.

One Mission:

- If just 250,000 people get and use the Rainbow Card, $20 million can be earned for the Rainbow Endowment.
- **Already, the Endowment has donated over $100,000** to lesbian and gay health, arts, cultural and civil rights organizations such as:

  AIDS Information Network • Astraea National Lesbian Action Foundation
  Community Research Initiative on AIDS • National Breast Cancer Coalition
  National Center for Lesbian Rights • National Lesbian and Gay Health Association

Get it. Use it. Got it?
www.rainbowcard.com

Call 1-800-99-Rainbow To Apply!

THE ADVOCATE, 1996

Figure 5.1 "Rainbow Card . . . Power of One"

In the growing repertoire of mechanisms for "socially responsible" consumption in the 1990s, partnerships between nonprofit and for-profit agencies found a particularly sophisticated expression in the form of cause-related marketing, a variant of corporate sponsorship. In cause-related marketing, corporations publicize a partnership with a discrete non-profit cause related to a very specific goal. In this way, for example, American Express partnered with the ad hoc Statue of Liberty restoration project. By nature, this market device lends itself to, and relies on, niche marketing. In awareness of the opportunities for niche marketers, Pallotta Teamworks partnered with Avon in support of Breast Cancer Walks. Avon's clientele—women—are particularly likely to be sympathetic to the cause of promoting breast cancer outreach and early detection. This is not an entirely cynical sort of partnership. As with corporate donations, nonprofits doing important work can receive significant support through these mechanisms.

This type of marketing was not new in the 1990s, but its introduction into the gay and lesbian community was dramatic in that decade. Perhaps the most famous arrangement was the partnership between Tanqueray and Pallotta Teamworks—the folks who produced the five annual AIDS rides around the country. For years, those bike rides have raised tens of millions of dollars annually for the AIDS service organizations that have been their beneficiaries.[39] In his attempt to get the enterprise off the ground, Dan Pallotta wrote to hundreds of companies asking for sponsorship before Tanqueray agreed to it. Tanqueray saw that the arrangement would be enormously advantageous to them. For the equivalent of 100,000 advertising dollars, according to Pallotta, Tanqueray got 300 million media impressions, including their logo on every bit of promotional literature for the event, on the fronts and backs of each rider in each ride, and therefore in every bit of news coverage in any visual medium. In this way, Tanqueray also "beat" the ban against the advertising of hard liquor on television in the United States.

Are some causes more viable than others for such a program? And does the rise of these programs undermine the viability of organizations working on less popular causes? Certainly, the eradication of disease is a relatively popular goal. Of course, breast cancer education is relatively difficult to sell, since only women get the disease. And AIDS was even more difficult to sell, which is why Dan Pallotta could not find a sponsor for the rides until 1994, although he had been trying for years. I would argue that the spread of AIDS to nongay communities has contributed to the increased sympathy of the general public and the increased openness of sponsors to AIDS-related events. Even so, by the turn of the century, AIDS was still not entirely disarticulated in the public mind from gay male sexuality, and homophobia still pervaded popular responses to people living with HIV or AIDS. To the extent that AIDS shed the stigma of gay male sexuality, it was not because gay male sexuality was no longer stigmatized. In other words, the massive education campaign around AIDS helped the populace to understand that AIDS was not a "gay disease," but all of that education did little to roll back homophobia.

Yet while government eventually followed corporations and foundations into funding for AIDS, "when you dig deeper, what you see is that there are certain types that are preferred and some that are still shied away from," according to Paul DiDonato, Executive Director of Funders Concerned about AIDS.[40] He goes on to explain that the majority of that funding has gone, and goes still, to research, care, and treatment. Housing has lagged behind, as have AIDS prevention programs. DiDonato says that there is still a lack of understanding of how homelessness and housing issues relate to AIDS.[41] Perhaps where AIDS issues overlap with other stigmatized causes, funding is hardest to find. And among gay-related causes, the smaller, more local, more grassroots organizations, and those working for radical social change, are surely among the least favored by funders. As a result, market-related funding mechanisms—while providing increased visibility for the larger national service-oriented organizations—can contribute to the invisibility and/or the de-resourcing of less mainstream organizations.

There is another way in which corporate donation programs combined with cause-related marketing can help mainstream social movements, especially the lesbian and gay movement. In a refinement of standard forms of corporate giving, the long-distance phone company Working Assets has, by wide agreement, an exemplary program of donations to nonprofit organizations. Giving away one percent of its revenue meant that Working Assets donated more than 10 million dollars between 1986 and 1997.[42] Working Assets makes no pretense to offering competitive rates; its entire appeal to customers lies in its dedication to making significant contributions to selected nonprofits that fall into one of its targeted categories. (In 1997, those categories were: peace, the environment, civil rights, and economic and social justice. In 1998, peace was reformulated as "peace and international freedom," and "education and freedom of expression" was added.) Working Assets' materials are a model of clarity, making it easy for customers to nominate groups that do not appear on their roster, and there are very few restrictions on who can be nominated. For example, whereas some corporate entities favor service organizations over advocacy organizations, Working Assets' recipients include a number of social change organizations, as well as service organizations, in each of the categories.

Also exemplary is the process by which customers participate in choosing how the funds are allocated among the groups that Working Assets has selected in any given year. While that selection process takes place in-house, Working Assets invites customers to "vote" on which groups they would prefer to have receive money. And, particularly noteworthy, the recipients are largely liberal and progressive groups; in this way, Working Assets gives a boost to the left as a whole. Furthermore, Working Assets funds lesbian and gay organizations without gathering them under a categorical heading, in recognition of the fact that gay and lesbian needs cross those categorical boundaries. Yet one of their restrictions does have potentially troubling consequences for the gay and lesbian movement as a whole. They do not fund groups that are "local in scope," reserving their donations for organizations that are "national or international in [their] work."[43] And, given that radical political activity is likelier to inhabit the local and grassroots levels than the national and international levels, is it not possible that Working Assets' contributions have the unintended effect of mainstreaming the movement?

Of course, so long as nonprofits have funding sources, they all face the question of from whom to take money. The decision to receive money from a certain source may be uncomfortable, depending on the mission and analysis of the organization. The decision differs according to the source and so organizations must, and do, distinguish between different sources. Speaking for the Audre Lorde Project (ALP) in New York, Javid Syed said this kind of deliberation is "especially uncomfortable in relation to gifts from multi-nationals; it's not an issue to take in-kind donations from mom & pop enterprises, but when you think of Philip Morris, it's a different concern."[44] At ALP, they try to keep some degree of accountability to political vision. For example, they try to take account of the investments made by their funding sources and thus remain deliberative about those sources. Likewise, they would be cautious about funding from governmental agencies.

"Contributions should enhance our capacity to do good work," Syed commented, "not promote the funder's mission. Yet, wherever an organization takes money, its name and/or its cause(s) can be used to garner legitimacy for the funder."[45] When asked whether corporate funders constrained the direction of program work for nonprofit recipients, Syed said no. He was more concerned with the policies and activities of sponsors and not so fearful that strings might be attached, that is, that program areas would be affected. In this light, ethical problems would arise from being financially connected to a sponsor whose policies or activities are inconsistent with the mission of the nonprofit in question. The program of the nonprofit is not usually in any danger of feeling pressure from funders. This is true in part because funding is so often proposal-driven (meaning that funders are aware of and responding to program plans already made by staff), while corporate donors may remain "laissez-faire" about control. Donors' greater investment is in the use of the name of the nonprofit for credibility and to gain access to the lesbian and gay community. This brings things full circle: corporations want access to the community in order to target it successfully. Julie Dorf explained, "When we approach a corporation, we frame our request in terms of exposure, in as quantified a form as possible, literally citing the number of hits our website gets."[46]

So the quest for legitimacy cuts both ways. Corporate entities may use charitable contributions to boost approval within a social group they are simultaneously targeting as a niche market. At the same time, corporate sponsorship and donations, like corporate advertising, can seem to lend legitimacy to a gay and lesbian nonprofit organization.

According to Julie Dorf, "On the gay and lesbian side, the premium on relationships with corporations is about trying to get money, and also about seeking legitimacy through that kind of endorsement."[47] Corporate support actually attracts gay men and lesbians to nonprofit organizations, inducing them to become rank-and-file members; in this way, too, it compares with advertising, and even with the state (as in Al Gore's presence at a Human Rights Campaign function), in their power to affirm gay and lesbian enterprises: "all the internalized homophobia makes it feel good to have the big corporate names, how excited we are to see Seagram's ads in *OUT* magazine. People seeing those ads believe that too—that there's something good for the movement and that resonates for people, which is all about how pathetic we feel about ourselves."[48] The comparison with the affirmation offered by ads is telling; affirmation through corporate address may have the same limits in the nonprofit arena as it does in the for-profit arena.

If corporations can figure as agents of change—whether they are extracting profits or contributing them to nonprofits—what kind of change can they be said to foster? For one thing, as argued above, corporate giving to non-profits is much more likely to support organizations that are not engaged in controversial advocacy, i.e., anything "political." As Sean Strub puts it, "The more political something is, the more difficult it will be to win sponsorship. Stonewall 25 was perceived as more political than the Gay Games, so they had a more difficult time with corporate sponsors."[49] Compounding the lack of appeal of expressly political organizations is the distinction between service and organizing. Most corporate money is directed at non-controversial services, not organizing. By contrast, progressive foundations tend to deemphasize service organizations; they prefer to fund advocacy groups—even controversial ones—but often avoid those engaged in local grassroots organizing. In an interview about "Fundraising on the Fringe," Ellen Gurzinsky of the Funding Exchange explained that activist "organizations can be battered on all sides by their very nature of wanting to deliver services and be strong advocates for their cause. . . . Initially, it's the services that attract the clients. Then, foundations say they don't fund services. . . . If you're a left-of-center group, you don't see those as different missions in some cases."[50]

Left-of-center groups, like right-of-center groups, may fall out of the equation altogether. Corporate funding for "fringe" organizations is extremely rare. In an interview, David Ford, Vice President and Director of Philanthropy for Chase Manhattan Bank, offered a point of view that is utterly representative of corporate—and noncorporate—funders: "At Chase, we fund a marketplace of ideas," he said. "Chase will support organizations that are to the right or the left on some issues . . . but not extremist ones on either side."[51] And according to a senior lecturer at the University of Washington, School of Social Work, this accounts partially for the small budgets of most fringe organizations. "They have to rely on very unreliable sources of income—bake sales, parties. . . . That's one of the reasons they're such shoestring operations."[52] It is precisely this effect that enforces the mainstreaming of the gay and lesbian movement.

With a very few, very notable exceptions, such as the Astraea Foundation, the Legacy Foundation, the Stonewall Foundation, and the Gill Foundation, even independent foundations do not seek explicitly and affirmatively to fund gay and lesbian causes. Those mentioned are among the very few foundations whose central purpose is to fund gay and lesbian nonprofits. A notable anomaly is the Funding Exchange, which represents a consortium of left-progressive funds whose stated purpose is to give grants to social change organizations; this network has been active since the 1970s and has always been supportive of gay and lesbian work. There is, additionally, a small handful of multi-purpose independent foundations, like the Tides Foundation and the Joyce Mertz-Gilmore Foundation, that do not categorically dismiss such work, but many large liberal foundations did not historically give grants to gay and lesbian groups. This situation began to change in the late 1990s. Rockefeller led the way, and at the very end of the decade Ford and MacArthur began to entertain proposals from gay and lesbian organizations. If more large foundation support were available, that might be a partial solution, but it wouldn't by itself obviate the issue of how donations affect nonprofit organizations internally (say, in terms of leadership) and externally (in terms of social movements more broadly).

In many ways, corporate and foundation sources subscribe to similar assumptions. Most corporations actually make contributions through their affiliated foundations, but while independent foundations have greater freedom than their corporate-affiliated counterparts, they share a preference for supporting safe and centrist organizations. Javid Syed elaborated:

> Among corporate funders, the interest in grass roots is not nearly so great as the interest in national organizing. Foundations, too, show a focus on national organizing, as opposed to both grassroots efforts and international efforts. Therefore, decisions about which leaders and which organizations attain a degree of national presence is determined, in part, by institutions engaged in funding. Thus it falls to people who have access to privilege to support organizations within a national playing field, or to withhold that support.[53]

As I noted above, even Working Assets restricts its funding to national groups, and in addition they decide what defines a "national" group. By some definitions, there are very few authentically national groups with a national base. As Chuck Collins notes, "an organization can have offices in two cities and be on the phone to a few people outside of Washington, D.C., and call themselves national. You have these self-proclaimed national organizations not necessarily connected to things on the ground and not accountable to people on the ground."[54]

Accountability is a huge question, one that applies to agencies across the board; it is particularly troubling for nonprofits with a national scope who claim to represent a broad-based constituency. Collins notes the potential effects of the relationship between nonprofits and the funders to whom they are accountable, pointing out that nonprofits without corporate funders may have fewer constraints on their activity: "The question of who you're accountable to—that's where the corporate money puts a damper on insurgency. People at ACT UP are not accountable to any corporation and yet the people who are here in Boston organizing the march are starting to sit in the room with people who raise their eyebrows."[55] Hence, mainstreaming can occur when organizations feel greater accountability to their institutional funders than to their membership. The acceptance of donations to large national gay and lesbian organizations by suspect corporations may meet with resistance by membership, but such resistance may not cause the organizations to turn the money away. As I recounted above, one of the unmet demands of the Coors Boycott Committee was that GLAAD return the donation from Coors. In another example, the National Gay and Lesbian Task Force received a grant of over $100,000 from Nike in 1997, which became an issue of contention among members of the Task Force. Later faced with public opposition to this course of action, Executive Director Kerry Lobel stated that it had been a mistake to accept the money. Even when an organization does take its accountability to its membership seriously, the leadership must make such decisions on its own. Large national gay and lesbian organizations became, in the 1990s, more attractive to corporate and foundation funders, which enabled them to pursue their very important civil rights and visibility objectives. But did this new stream of money hinder organizations' accountability to members as well as deflect funds from smaller or local groups with more radical agendas?

Another factor that keeps small fringe organizations from being viable grant recipients has to do with the way funders allocate their expenses. Foundations, in particular, like to fund special projects, identifiable and discreet programs within a nonprofit. For the most part, it is considered anything from unsexy to unsound to fund general operating expenses. Large organizations tend to be able to afford to break their budgets down into project areas, while smaller organizations spend a much greater proportion of their budgets on general expenses such as overhead. Gurzinsky reports that "foundations like to give grants for a specific focus, while . . . what most of the small, community-based organizations require is operating expenses, for which grants can be sparse."[56] This tendency is confirmed by a "creative grantmaking" award given by the Council on Foundations to Robert Crane of the Joyce Mertz-Gilmore Foundation in 1995. Crane's stance in favor of general support grants flew in the face of decades of foundation wisdom. The recent growth of capacity-building and capacity-enhancing grants likewise represents a historical shift in foundation practice.

For a combination of reasons, then, the structure of funding to nonprofits affects not only individual organizations, but the shape of the gay and lesbian movement as a whole. Gurzinsky's summation has multiple implications for this social movement: "fringe groups tend to fall short of funders' requirements for one of four reasons: unpopular recipients; unpopular activities; the 'double bind' of untried and unproven activities; and general support for building maintenance and the like."[57] Taken together, it is easy to see how politically off-center, small, locally based lesbian and gay organizations—many challenged for all four reasons— would have great difficulty raising funds. Meanwhile, the larger, more centrist or liberal, national organizations whose budgets can be broken down into various program areas would grow bigger and stronger. This is not merely theoretical speculation. In the 1990s the fastest growing institutions in the gay and lesbian advocacy movement were large, of national scope, and of a politically centrist stripe, most notably Human Rights Campaign (HRC).

In some ways, the relationship between the movement and the market is embodied in concrete moments of alliance, cooperation, and "partnership" between particular for-profit and nonprofit entities. But in another way, the ethos of partnership has begun to pervade everywhere, so that Human Rights Campaign's Executive Director Elizabeth Birch could instruct a reporter in 1998: "This is what you write. . . . In the 1990s, there had to be a meeting of minds between raw activist spirit and the communications and marketing techniques that define a new voice for gay America."[58] Perhaps an exaggerated sense of self derives from this refinement of the link between civil rights struggles and free agency in the market; perhaps a proprietary sense naturally arises out of the fusion of oppositional politics with marketing principles; or perhaps it is the particular personality in question that caused Birch to add, "It came together in the person of Elizabeth Birch."[59]

In the face of criticism of HRC, Birch defended herself by saying, "'Imagine what you would have done if three years ago you woke up and found that someone had handed you the movement. . . . I'll bet you would have made most of the decisions I've made.'"[60] The personal arrogance of this statement, while stunning, is perhaps less meaningful than the fact that HRC is perceived as having great influence over what kind of work gets funded by the large donors with whom HRC leadership is close. Both Jean Harris of Basic Rights Oregon and Jan Bianchi of Equality Washington/Hands Off Washington have complained that HRC influences both strategic decisions (beyond those of their own staff) and the flow of money, exercising a "gatekeeper" function for the movement.[61] Again, the question of accountability, and of the nature of the relationship between national organizations and local initiatives, is raised here, as it was with respect to the economic education campaign in Louisville (see Chapter 4). I would argue that a healthy movement not only needs its fringes, but it needs smaller organizations with real autonomy from larger ones. Just as the market imperatives that affect the editorial content of a lesbian and gay magazine can have implications for the representation of the gay and lesbian community as a whole, so can market imperatives that affect the decisions in a dominant movement agency affect the course of the whole movement.

MARCHING: OUT OF THE
CLOSET AND INTO THE BANK

Having dealt at length with the practical aspects of the relationship between movement organizations and their financial partners, I turn now to the financing of perhaps the most symbolically weighty kind of event that the lesbian and gay community has engaged in: the pride march. Changes in the financing of pride marches demonstrate beautifully some of the dynamics discussed thus far, situated as they are in both local and national contexts, and bridging, as they came to do in the 1990s, large financial institutions, large and small nonprofits on the right and left, and their constituencies on the ground. Some of the earliest public demonstrations of gay and lesbian social identification were the pride marches, initially conceived as events to commemorate the Stonewall Rebellion of 1969. As early as 1970, organizers won permission from their home cities to assemble and march in the streets. Whereas in the 1970s, gay pride marches "aimed to establish the presence of gay people, to try to overcome invisibility," gay pride events of the 1980s took on a different focus.[62] Observing a reduction of leather and drag and a proliferation of service organizations, sociologist Richard Herrell argues specifically that the parades of the 1980s moved away from combating the invisibility of gay men and lesbians and toward a demonstration of similarity between gays and straights. Linking an assimilationist message to the political strategy of the movement in the 1980s, and noting the dramatization of that message in the Chicago parade of 1987, Herrell writes, "Civil rights legislation is advocated so that 'we can be just like the rest of you because we are just like the rest of you.'"[63] Highlighting "community" institutions from family to church to sports leagues to professional associations, the parade showed gay life as compatible, even continuous, with hetero-normative life. In this way of thinking, the difference between gays and straights is reduced to sexual difference, a difference increasingly relegated in gay and lesbian life to the private sphere—namely, the bedrooms—of people who are otherwise indistinguishable.

If the Chicago gay pride parade did indeed shift (and if other "Pride" events around the country similarly changed) from sending a "confrontationist" signal to sending an "assimilationist" message, then the parades would seem to provide a forum for expressing larger cultural and political trends. Yet the gay community is far from unified (intentional demonstrations of unity notwithstanding), and so the parades act as a battleground of sorts for competing strategies. As Herrell puts it:

> What it is to be gay itself is being argued about—is contested—in the mix of ways and discourse about how the gay community defines itself in a Chicago parade. How the community should "index"—should create—itself is the controversy. Watchers and marchers alike do not agree about—indeed fight about—how to define the community in the parade. The two modalities I describe as assimilationist and confrontationist are both present and unresolved in the parade today.[64]

Interestingly, the first marches in New York City were conceived as demonstrations of the spontaneous nature of the movement. As such, they would never be planned by an organizing committee, nor owned by anyone. Over the years, the New York City march, like marches in other cities, came to be elaborately planned, demonstrating a shift in the way the gay and lesbian community imagines itself and its movement.

The changes observable in the 1987 parade in Chicago were repeated around the country. In the 1990s, as the parades grew in size, they were increasingly populated by campaigning politicians and sponsoring banks, while the exhibitions of sexuality decreased. Coverage of the 1997 gay pride event in the *Boston Globe* was accompanied by the photo of an eleven-year-old boy, whose mother and partner follow behind. Visible behind them are contingents of Digital Equipment Corporation employees and BankBoston employees. Tellingly, the *Globe* reported, "This year, Pride Day apparently passed without any men exposing themselves or topless women putting on public displays of affection. Last year, parade organizers apologized for some participants who offended other participants and onlookers with such nudity."[65] (In fact, the parade the previous year had produced a significant scandal, which became known in Boston as "Bedgate," that split, or perhaps merely revealed splits within, the gay and lesbian community along lines of gender and politics.)[66] Crucially, at the same time that Boston Pride cleaned up (or straightened up) its act, it also began to rethink its financial status. The Pride Committee had carried a debt of $30,000 from the good, clean 1997 Pride Day described above as it headed toward the rainy day in 1998 for which that year's Pride had been scheduled. Compounding the $30,000 debt from 1997, the committee had already racked up $30,000 of additional debt for the 1998 parade by June. Given this financial situation, the two options—to postpone Pride or to cancel it altogether—were both certain to compound the debt. Into this quandary came a *deus ex machina* in the form of Harry Collings, the Executive Secretary of Boston's Redevelopment Authority and a major fund-raiser for selected gay and lesbian causes in Boston. Collings offered to raise all the money necessary to get the committee out of debt if they would reschedule rather than cancel Pride. In a mere three weeks, Collings raised $42,500, "enlisting the help of local marketing and fundraising consultant Will Woodruff and other prominent gay businesspeople," as "all the movers and shakers in town lined up to write four- and five-figure checks to Boston Pride."[67] It was more than the committee had been able to raise in a year, and combined with the $10,000-$15,000 in anticipated sales of tee shirts, it would leave the committee in the clear.

As far as the future of Boston Pride was concerned, Collings's influence made itself felt in the transformation of Pride into a professional organization. Collings asked gay businesspeople and bar owners in the area to participate in the Pride Committee, "something they have shunned in recent years."[68] Collings and Woodruff supported the addition of paid positions to the committee (which had been run entirely by volunteer labor to that point), including an executive director whose year-round job would be to "write grant proposals and obtain corporate sponsorship."[69] According to Woodruff, "From a corporate standpoint, 200,000 people participate in this event. If a company's logo is out there, whether you are BankBoston or a liquor distributor or a newspaper, whatever, that is powerful—$25,000 to $50,000 is pretty cheap sponsorship for something like this." The Pride Committee denied that there were any plans to hire an executive director, but it did admit that changes had to be made.

As the Pride Committee plowed ahead, commentators on all sides described the situation in terms that resonate with the issues and rhetoric common to discussions of the gay and lesbian niche market in the 1990s. For example, in vain defense of the erstwhile values of the march, Co-chair Eric Pliner expressed the hope that "for every 'business-minded' person who joins the committee in the future, there will be another new person whose interests are 'primarily political or cultural.'"[70] Like others in opposition to conflating business and politics, Pliner posited an opposition between the two modes. Even the business types seemed to agree that it would be a mistake to sacrifice the traditionally grassroots nature of the event to financial stability, underscoring the assumption that grassroots activity was opposed to (if not a throwback to an era before) the organization of economic clout in the gay and lesbian community. These same folks asserted that corporate sponsorship would not come with strings attached, and that the business community would "make room for everybody."[71] Others feared the change.

Becoming reliant on corporate funding would not just solidify these changes for Pride, it would make Pride into another mechanism for confusing economic gains for some with political gains for all. The field director for the National Gay and Lesbian Task Force expected these changes for some time and imagined that a Pride event subsidized by corporate money would remain a day of visibility. But she was afraid that Pride would be consolidating a trend that it had been moving toward since the late 1980s: "It is not politically meaningful anymore. It is culturally expressive."[72] Of course, cultural expression is important—and is political—and for many Pride-goers, it may have been more important than an expressly confrontational event forcing sexual liberation down the throats of innocent spectators and newspaper readers. But for the progressive constituency, Pride had already lost its political edge. Or rather, Pride's politics came to look like the politics of *OUT* magazine, which reduces representation to mere visibility. Dena Lebowitz, the former Chair of the Lesbian and Gay Political Alliance of Massachusetts (a self-described progressive political action group), offered this warning: "When you have a marketing event, you are not fundamentally challenging society in any real way. . . . [P]eople should not confuse status in the marketplace with equality."[73]

The situation facing Boston Pride was not unique. Cities around the country moved in the same direction as Chicago and Boston, as pride events originally designed to commemorate Stonewall became commercialized. Around the country, "marches" became "parades" and "rallies" became "parties." Where participants gathered at the end of such parades, the opportunities for shopping at booths proliferated, while floats in the parade itself were increasingly the displays of banks and professional politicians.[74] Of course, politicians and banks did not, by themselves, wrest these changes. While their interests are served by the exposure that pride marches offer, for a great proportion of the gay and lesbian population, the changes detailed here herald liberation. But once again, I have to ask whether changes wrought by capitalization can bring about liberation, equality, or justice for gay men and lesbians who are *not* represented by market-based politics.

MARCHING INTO THE MILLENNIUM

Given the symbolic value of pride marches over the course of their history, it is no surprise that splits in the community deepened over the planning of a "Millennium March" to take place in Washington, D.C., in spring 2000. From its conception in 1997, the Millennium March on Washington (MMOW) was the occasion for conflicts between national and state organizations and objectives, as well as conflicts between progressive and conservative constituencies within the movement, regarding both the process of organizing the march and its platform. Not least, the pathways of money within the movement wore themselves into grooves around the Beltway, as people in all corners contemplated the economics of the event. As proponents and opponents of the march squared off, gay and lesbian community members took the opportunity to articulate and rearticulate their understandings of the state of the movement at the turn of the century. Some celebrated the prospect of being televised while others bemoaned the corporatization of the movement, but none could fail to notice that the core values of the movement were the fundamental subject of debate.

The march was to be the fourth in a series of marches on Washington; marches in 1979, 1987, and 1993 had also taken years of planning from conception to realization. Early critics of the MMOW objected to the process by which it had been called and organized. A dissenting Ad Hoc Committee for an Open Process issued a "Call For an Open Process," describing the planning of the three earlier marches as follows:

> Each march was different as were the times during which they were organized. However, each one was run democratically with mass, grassroots involvement, and each followed a similar organizing scenario. . . . [T]he primary decision whether to have the event was made first, followed by deliberation on the name of the event, the politics, structure, leadership, and the organizing strategy. Then, throughout the country, open, democratically run meetings selected delegates, with mandates to include women and people of color, to a national steering committee, the highest decision-making body.

By contrast, the idea for the MMOW was consolidated in private meetings between Robin Tyler (a prominent lesbian producer) and leadership in Human Rights Campaign and in the Metropolitan Community Church

(MCC, an international nondenominational Christian church that claims millions of gay and lesbian members in the United States). Tyler, HRC, and MCC contacted a number of other groups just before issuing a press release that announced the march; the press release named LLEGO and the National Black Lesbian and Gay Leadership Forum (NBLGLF) among the march's cosponsors. Already, the organizers had chosen a very different organizing model than the one that had informed the previous march in 1993, which included parity requirements designed to ensure fair representation along lines of geography, race, gender, and significantly, class.

The organizers of the 1993 march had devised a number of ways to compensate for the self-selection process that normally enables people with more money to participate in the planning process, and the march itself, more easily.[75] For example, six white men from a single region decided to split one vote among themselves; that way, they could all participate, but "Just because more of them could afford to come did not mean that they should have more power or more votes."[76] How different this was from the experience of members of the Ad Hoc Committee for an Open Process, who showed up (uninvited) to an MMOW meeting, pleading for broader inclusion in the planning process, in which they and others might participate. Asked to sit in chairs around the periphery of the room (and thus denied a literal place at the table) but otherwise tolerated during the morning session, the Ad Hoc Committee members present were offered the following deal in the afternoon: they could share one vote among the nine of them, but they could not participate further in the discussion.[77] Note that the problem with this voting procedure bears similarities to the problem of voting with your dollars. Just as consumers and corporations are unequally endowed with the economic franchise, so are gay and lesbian community members unequally endowed with the ability to participate in decision making in the movement. Laissez-faire gay and lesbian identity politics is bound to reproduce exactly the same disparity in representation visible in the niche marketplace. News reports of a march organized without equal representation at every stage of planning are likely to look just like the pages of *OUT* magazine, marchers on the mall likely to look like majority-group Americans.

The Ad Hoc Committee for an Open Process, a diverse group of several experienced activists, pressed for the MMOW to adopt more democratic procedures and pressured the cosponsoring organizations to withdraw support for the MMOW. The Ad Hoc Committee also wanted the MMOW to start over from square one, to consider whether there was a sound political purpose for the march in the first place. The Ad Hoc Committee had two central doubts about the political implications of the MMOW. First, they worried that the march would conflict with marches on state capitols being planned around the country for the year 2000. At the time the MMOW was announced, the National Gay and Lesbian Task Force had already begun organizing fifty separate but coordinated marches on state capitols, in an initiative called "Equality Begins at Home"; learning about this plan did not deter the MMOW planners. In this way, the MMOW planning reproduced a familiar conflict between local organizing and the large national organizations. (NGLTF is a relatively large national organization, but the Equality Begins at Home marches depended largely on state structures and local framing of issues of prime concern in each state.) The question of accountability recurs here too, for HRC and MCC acted through their leadership and not through their memberships, at this stage.

Second, the Ad Hoc Committee worried about the platform for the march. By some accounts, the theme for the march was "Faith and Family"; by other accounts, no theme or platform had been announced. Either way, it seemed to the Ad Hoc Committee that there was little political warrant for the march and that its potential conflict with the more local and more expressly political marches was cause for reconsidering the whole idea. Even if faith and family had never been the intended themes, the very name of the march caused some to look deeper into the MCC's leadership in the event: "Millennium," wrote Stephanie Poggi, referred to "a thousand years of 'Christ's' reign on earth in which holiness is to prevail. HRC and UFMCC are clearly not adverse to conjuring up this particular sense."[78] MCC's own literature did not reassure on this score; the Reverend Elder Troy Perry addressed MCC's General Council with this rationale for MCC's huge financial and logistical role in the march: "I honestly believe this march will help us fulfill . . . our founding purposes. . . . I believe with all my heart that people who need to hear our message of Christian salvation will have an opportunity to hear and embrace the Gospel of Jesus Christ through our participation."[79] MCC's explicit statement that people of all religions were welcome had an unwelcoming effect, of course, as it suggested that they saw themselves as gatekeepers. The dominance of an organization as large as MCC in the production of the march seriously reduced the credibility of claims to inclusive process, as would be expected in an identity regime (and the absence of an explicit political purpose left gay and lesbian identity as the only imaginable basis for the march). When gay men and lesbians count mainly *as gay,* other identity features are subordinated, and gay itself comes to stand for other dominant identities within the gay and lesbian population. With respect to the Christian hegemony of the march, MCC's dominance preempted the equal participation of Jews, Muslims, atheists, and other non-Christians.

Ultimately, the march would even provide an occasion for economic maneuvers cloaked in the guise of politics, and in this way, it was the very paradigm of intersection between the gay and lesbian niche market and the gay and lesbian political movement. The perfect figure for this intersection was the competition between two websites, each of which offered users march-related services. News, polling, message boards, chat rooms, travel information, housing and hotel information, ride-sharing, reservations, and tickets were all available through the web. Then producer of the MMOW, Robin Tyler asserted that the official website—the one launched by PlanetOut—would "bring democracy to the movement by conducting polls of what issues are important to the community." [80] The website offered "streaming audio and video" of events as they took place, and it also offered translation into several languages. Donna Red Wing, Co-chair of the MMOW and HRC representative, called the website "the most valuable thing" to come out of the march, although as of this writing the MMOW had not created "a protocol for who gets access to information gathered on the people who say they are willing to have it used for marketing purposes."[81] PlanetOut also offered to donate $250,000 in cash and $75,000 worth of in-kind services. Money left over after paying for the march would be donated to community organizations.

Meanwhile, competitor Gay.Com Network set up a march service website of its own, whose profits, it seemed, would be kept by the company. Angered by the appearance of a company that might complicate PlanetOut's plans, Tyler charged that for Gay.Com to set up a rival web service was for them "to rape the movement."[82] In response, the chairman and CEO of Online Partners (Gay.Com's parent company) pledged to donate profits if it would settle the controversy. Moreover, he truly believed, "We have a giant community of gays and lesbians all over the world . . . and what we are doing is organizing our group of people, and I would call on every web-site to do exactly the same thing, because if everyone does then the march will be more successful."[83]

Of course, the success of the march is strictly a function of the measures of success, and there can be no agreement on what those measures should be. Nevertheless, it is inarguable that the manipulation of money in the name of identity has deeply ambivalent effects. In particular, a competitive model of politics, so clearly at work in both the charges against and the defense of the rivalry between Gay.Com and PlanetOut, will certainly replicate the logic of survival of the fittest. This model is so saturated with economic thinking, it is economic. It is important to challenge the model, to consider what communities, which individuals, and whose values are eliminated through the mainstreaming effects of fundraising on the gay and lesbian movement.

6

STEAL THIS SHOW: AWAY FROM IDENTITY AND TOWARD ECONOMIC JUSTICE

I opened this book with the claim that identity politics and identity-based market activity are interdependent systems, having grown up with and reinforced each other, always enabling and constraining each other. I claimed, further, that these systems have worked together to mainstream social movements. I have investigated this claim with reference to gay and lesbian communities over the course of the twentieth century, concentrating on the last thirty years, and especially the 1990s, as an optimal moment for exploring these dynamics. While the interdependency of the gay and lesbian movement and gay and lesbian market activity is a complex set of phenomena, I have particularly focused on the ways in which the market constrains political activity. I chose this focus partly to complement the more common and more celebratory emphasis on the ways in which the market enables political movements, and partly to analyze the promises that seem to accompany the convergence of the market on the political arena. As earlier chapters have demonstrated, that convergence of politics and the market is at least as old as the first written codes of liberal democracy; the contemporary lesbian and gay rights movement enacts the age-old cooperation and conflict among the state, capital, and the causes of freedom, or equality. The late-twentieth-century version of this relationship involves a historically unique role for "identity," and its renegotiation in a postindustrial, mass-consumption, culturally pluralist society.

Hence, any summary of this state of affairs must return to the question of the political utility of identity. Of course, conceptions of identity implicitly, or explicitly, underlie a whole spectrum of opinions about how the lesbian and gay movement should proceed. The large and liberal mainstream of the gay and lesbian movement is focused on the expansion of individual rights, most notably the right to marriage, the right to be out in the military, and the right to protection from discrimination. For this mainstream group, well represented by the large national gay and lesbian organizations in the 1990s, identity politics have seemed the most sensible vehicle for advancing the cause of enfranchisement for gay men and lesbians. It is precisely within this group that identity politics is taken as an article of faith, and so it is precisely here that the effects of the links between identity politics and identity-based market activity are most difficult to see. If little critique of identity politics issues from these quarters, this is because the rhetoric of liberal rights both presumes and reproduces a commitment to identity. Left-leaning gay and lesbian activists within the movement do not necessarily reject identity as the basis for organizing; as scholars have pointed out, "More militant gay politics stresses difference over similarity, and assertion over assimilation, but still generally posits a fixed minority political constituency."[1]

An interesting critique of identity comes from some gay men and lesbians who share with liberals a healthy respect for individual rights and freedom of choice. I call these folks "gay libertarians" to indicate their staunch belief in individual rights and choice, while they take great pains to distinguish themselves, by dint of their contempt for identity, from more liberal commentators on gay and lesbian politics. Within gay and lesbian media, some of the most vociferous objections to identity politics are founded in a supreme belief in individualism. Citing as objectionable the demand for conformity in the "lesbian community," one writer deplores the way that labels reduce all homosexual women to "lesbians."[2] Yet she disavows any connection between her distaste for uniform lesbian identity and a pro-assimilationist stance: "Hetero-cloning is not my answer to the problems lesbians face, individualism is."[3] From this point of view, identity politics represents group think and thus threatens the value of individualism.

The libertarian politic places a high premium on individual choice—the right and ability to self-define, the right and ability to act freely in the market, and the right and ability to self-define through action in the market. Another gay libertarian believes that gay identity politics may win civil rights, but they can't make you happy.[4] Accordingly, the pursuit of happiness takes place in the private arena; the individual pursuer in question must be free from the fetters of government, but he must also be free from the demands of public identification with a social group. Thus the individual is free from the demands of establishing common interest with others on any consistent basis. The distance between rights and happiness is broached in a radically free market, thus distinguishing this position from a progressive critique of rights.

The premium on individuals free from the establishment of common and collective political interest is, not merely coincidentally, consistent with the de facto tendency of libertarians to function in the class interest of free marketeers. Some white male libertarians have expressed confusion about why they seem to be subject to criticism on the basis of their white male identities, when they have gone to lengths not to identify as such, or as anything, in fact. Of course, they are right; it is not their white maleness that makes them libertarians; but the very privilege of whiteness and maleness is that they seem not to be identities, because they are the very norms against which "identity" marks its difference. Thus it could be imagined that "Gay White Males" were "PC's Unseen Target."[5] Because identity is defined by difference from dominant cultural, political, and economic positions, only those with unmarked identities can imagine that they are not identifiable with, or by, any group interest. Hence the libertarians' declamations of infinite individual variation among them—no doubt true—and their equally adamant charges against "quotas" and against the dictates of conformity within the "community," dictates supported by the notion of "gay identity." What is "quota" to them is "redistributionist" to progressives. To the libertarians, redistributionist strategies appear, in this light, as a subordination of personal qualities to reified "identity" markers. To others, such strategies are merely remedial; if such remediation were ever fully effected, identity markers would necessarily undergo significant change.

Another critique of identity, this one from a progressive viewpoint, holds that "the production of a politics from a fixed identity position privileges those for whom that position is the primary or only marked identity. The result for lesbian and gay politics is a tendency to center prosperous white men as the representative homosexuals."[6] In other words, the social dominance of whiteness and maleness leaves the gay part of their identity as the salient one for gay white men. The trouble is that the structure and practice of gay and lesbian rights organizations bear out this theoretical problem. In fact, it is the class position of white men (as a group), relative to the class positions of women and people of color (as groups), that puts a disproportionate number of white men at boardroom tables of for-profit and nonprofit agencies, and on the pages of magazines offered to both straight and gay consumers.[7] The consequences of building a political platform on the foundation of that gay-identified constituency—that is, on the foundation of that sort of identity basis—are manifold and include the marginalization of people with more than one marked identification: gay men or lesbians who are also people of color and/or poor and/or sick. For example, identity politics presents immediate problems for lesbians, who theoretically have common but distinct cause with both gay men and women. Should lesbians organize around their sexuality with gay men, or around their gender with straight women?[8] This problem is compounded for many gay men and lesbians by their multiple identities.

The embracing of the designation "queer" in the 1990s was partly a response to this critique, designed to counter charges of exclusion by holding up a more inclusive banner. Under the queer rubric went gay and lesbian, but also transgender, bisexual, questioning, leather, s/m, and even pro-gay straight people. This inclusivity model invites more kinds of people, at least rhetorically, into the identity category. In other words, if gay and lesbian identity is too narrow a category, is it not possible to expand the category? Of course, the model, in turn, has two problems, both of which involve potential political vulnerability. One, that the credibility of the movement is threatened by the inclusion and heightened visibility of transgenders, bisexuals, and other sexual minorities (who are even more threatening to the heterosexual norm than plain old gay men and lesbians), and two, that any identity category that broad risks the loss of identity referent. The elaboration of "queer" functioned partly as a way of keeping both inclusivity and credibility—on both realpolitik and theoretical levels. More fundamental than adding bisexuals, transgender people, two-spirit people, and questioning people, queer identity and theory embraced allies of whatever identity who believed in sexual liberation—liberation from gender and orientation categories. In this way, "queer" was an attempt to disrupt the inexorable process by which "[e]very production of 'identity' creates exclusions that reappear at the margins like ghosts to haunt identity-based politics."[9] As both an identity label and a theory, "queer" has revealed significant divides in the lesbian and gay polity. And queer politics have indeed given the lie to the premise of identity politics, which is that "all members of the group have more in common than the members have with anyone outside the group, that they are oppressed in the same way, and therefore that they all belong on the same road to justice."[10]

HISTORY OF NON-UNITY

As long as there have been multiple gay and lesbian organizations, it has been clear that the gay and lesbian population is not politically unified. And yet, usually in order to shore up claims for the political clout of the community, claims have in turn been made about the political interest of gay men and lesbians as though they did indeed compose a single constituency. The history of the gay and lesbian press speaks to a history of political difference, and even conflict over the goals and strategies of the gay and lesbian movement going at least as far back as the mid-1950s. Throughout the 1960s, proponents of a style of activism often called "militant" or "confrontational" and associated with radical objectives differed in print and at meetings from proponents of a style sometimes called "accommodationist" and associated with more liberal objectives. The most common opposition has been between single-issue and multi-issue platforms, including but not limited to the question of whether feminism and antiracism are core values of the gay and lesbian movement. Other familiar issues include the interests of national organizing versus the interests of local organizing, the value of political work versus the value of cultural work (or the relation of political work to cultural work), and debate about political process and structure (such as consensus voting and nonhierarchical organizational management schemas).

At innumerable junctures, movement organizations and activities manifested these kinds of political differences among gay men and lesbians. At many of those points, disagreements about tactics, objectives, and principles caused splinter groups or other splits. But there was never a time during which all gay men and lesbians were of one mind, not even at moments legendary for concerted action. The Gay Liberation Front (GLF) established itself in New York in 1969, following the Stonewall riots, breaking with traditional modes of gay activism. The GLF was marked by its "unashamed assertiveness" and its "determination to make links with other movements for social revolution such as the Black Panthers and Women's Liberation."[11] Yet, "within months there had already been a split within the GLF ranks with gay (mostly male, mostly white) activists who liked the new style but did not see why they should spend their energies in collaboration with other movements. In New York, these people left to start the single-issue Gay Activists Alliance which, with its combination of in-your-face manner and acceptance of male-identified formal organizing, was soon far more visibly successful than GLF."[12]

This split was very similar to a split that took place on the West Coast seven years later. In 1976, a group adopting the name Gay Action split off from Bay Area Gay Liberation (BAGL) in order to focus on "democratic rights and a mass movement approach, making coalitions with other progressive peoples while still maintaining the independence of the gay liberation movement."[13] By contrast, BAGL continued to consider itself an "anti-imperialist" group whose guiding analysis posited "gay oppression" as "a tool to keep people fighting each other instead of the ruling class."[14] Whereas Gay Action sought to make connections with labor and other "radical and minority" groups and lobbied for gay-friendly legislation, BAGL worked on housing issues and forged ties with gay prisoners, Native American and Puerto Rican solidarity groups, and "radical lesbians," as well as sponsoring the Effeminate Caucus of gay men.[15] While the split between these two groups in some ways foreshadowed internal splits in movement organizations later on, both groups avowed "progressive" values and both featured coalition work as central to their purposes. Here, coalitional organizing brought identity groups together to work on issue-based objectives, a trend that continued in the gay and lesbian movement, but one that also met with resistance in some quarters of the gay and lesbian community in the following decades.

By 1977, while gay men and lesbians across the country were rallying around the struggle to defeat Anita Bryant's forces (see Chapter 4), gay people were perhaps more integrated into local politics in San Francisco than they were in any other city in the United States. Entitled "Point, Counterpoint: Gay Politics San Francisco Style," a review of the state of affairs in the *Advocate* led off with a sidebar announcing that "San Francisco may boast one of the largest and most visible homosexual populations in North America, yet gay San Franciscans have seldom even come close to forging a political consensus."[16] Differing over the value of district elections; the responsiveness of Mayor George Moscone; the possibility of gays voting as a bloc; the effects of gay appointees in city positions; and the political representation in the city of gay men and lesbians as compared with the representation of blacks, Chinese, and Latinos, organizations and individuals dramatized the fact that "to view San Francisco gay people as a political monolith is a mistake."[17] As Jo Daly, the first lesbian appointee to the city's Human Rights Commission, said, "one of our mistakes is to use the term 'gay community.' Everyone uses it, but many gay San Franciscans feel they're not part of it. Sex orientation alone is not enough of a cohesive factor. They feel that the 'gay community' is more radical than they are. No one seems to realize how many gay Republicans there are."[18] Twenty years later, it was much harder to avoid this realization.

Similarly, activist leader Eric Rofes remembers joining a gay movement in the 1970s that was "overwhelmingly white," a movement without a consciousness of people of color as part of the gay community. By 1985, he and the white activists he knew had worked to develop a "strong consciousness that there were lesbians and gays of color who were seeking and wanting and organizing involvement in the gay community."[19] Meanwhile, the rise of AIDS in the 1980s had changed many things about gay and lesbian organizing, not least of which was the common segregation of men and women. Lesbians responded to AIDS in huge numbers; the epidemic may have been the basis of the most co-ed organizing done by gay men and lesbians. Yet, as writer and activist Jewelle Gomez saw it, because AIDS activism, for lesbians, often meant "moving out into dealing with gay men, it was terrifying to see how the context of feminism dropped away. Raising the issue of racism, became, for many gay men, a trauma."[20] Gomez feels that discussions of race and class became less of a commitment in the 1980s because of this work.

In 1990, in San Francisco, a large and active ACT UP chapter debated whether to cosponsor a demonstration against the visiting President Bush. The request to cosponsor came from CISPES (Committee for International Solidarity with the People of El Salvador). Because ACT UP made decisions by consensus, and because the membership disagreed about whether to join the demonstration, the decision took a very long time. A single vote to block the proposal meant turning down the request from CISPES, but much of the membership could not live with this conclusion. Over this decision, this ACT UP chapter broke into two: ACT UP San Francisco and ACT UP Golden Gate. ACT UP Golden Gate was formed by those who felt that ACT UP should not defray its few resources for fighting AIDS by joining up with other causes. ACT UP San Francisco was committed to analyzing the AIDS crisis in terms of the wider political context and to making connections between the fight for funding for AIDS and other political struggles. The new Golden Gate chapter was overwhelmingly composed of white men, while the San Francisco chapter retained its original composition, which was more mixed along lines of race and gender. Again, nothing about whiteness or maleness determines that an individual with either or both of those features will favor single-issue gay politics over progressive coalition, but that is the way it broke down, empirically speaking, in San Francisco in 1990.

Direct-action politics often dramatized these tensions. At least one participant in Queer Nation was drawn to the group precisely because it was a direct-action "queer group" and therefore "could be the starting point for bringing together a lot of progressive issues—queer, people of color, women—I thought it might be the kind of rainbow group that would lead all other groups."[21] However, another participant found the meetings "very disappointing, because race and gender were really marginalized."[22] Rather than working on racism and sexism in the group as a whole, Queer Nation separated into different caucuses, such as United Colors and LABIA (a lesbian caucus). For this latter participant, "Part of what turned me off is that it felt like any discussion of racism or sexism was referred to these different groups."[23] The practice of queer politics, then, did not automatically prevent the subordination of issues of race and gender to issues of sexuality. In that way, the word "queer" and queer politics reproduced some of the habits of "gay" identity politics.[24]

THE ESPERANZA CENTER

Conflicts within the gay and lesbian population have taken many forms. If class differences, as well as race and gender differences, often translate into, or correspond with, differences in political opinion, this is because of the ways in which systems of race, class, and gender privilege—or oppression—are internalized as experiences of "identity." Obviously, this is not true up and down the line, but it is important to notice patterns where they do exist. A prime example of correspondence between identity and political opinion was dramatized in the conflict around the Esperanza Center in San Antonio in the late 1990s. Founded in 1987, the Esperanza Center serves a diverse clientele, including immigrants, people of color, women, low-income people, and gay men and lesbians through programming that includes a cooperative art studio, a women's economic development project, and a video production training project for teenagers, and through fiscal sponsorship of the San Antonio Lesbian and Gay Media Project. The Center has also supported VAN, which organizes a local gay and lesbian film series.[25]

By 1998, after years of fits and starts, a campaign to defund Esperanza had finally succeeded in pressuring the San Antonio City Council to cut the Center's funding completely. As reported in *Sojourner,* "The campaign against Esperanza was initiated by conservative gay men who found some of the group's projects 'anti-Anglo,' 'anti-male,' 'pornographic,' and 'obscene.' They argued that Esperanza had 'flaunted' both lesbian sexuality and its activism, thus making 'responsible tax-paying citizens who want no more than equal rights' look bad."[26] Note that the argument against Esperanza resonates with the libertarians' fear of looking bad—read: radical, sexual, gender-bending—by association. Also significant is the way that conservative gay San Antonians found common cause with Christian and right-wing detractors of the Esperanza Center. What happened with Esperanza is quite complicated and is not yet resolved. As of this writing, Esperanza is suing San Antonio for discrimination; it will be a long time before the legal battle is concluded. But what is so dramatically demonstrated by this incident is that there are very serious political conflicts among people who seem to share the otherwise common feature of organizing under a gay banner. In their letter to the Mayor and the City Council members commending them on the decision to defund Esperanza, the men (all affiliated with gay nonprofit or for-profit organizations) who were active in the campaign criticized Esperanza for "damaging the cause of equal rights for gays and lesbians in San Antonio."[27] Rejecting the Center's charge that homophobia cost them their funding, the signers of the letter also questioned Esperanza's status as a "gay and lesbian organization." Instead, invoking a rather dubious distinction, they said it was a "political organization." Since they were themselves gay people largely involved in political organizations, their logic appears faulty. What they really objected to was the substance of the politics to which, in their perception, Esperanza was committed; in their words, "Its only goal is promoting a radical, pro-Castro, liberationist political agenda."[28] The exact nature of the damage they assessed to the gay and lesbian community was "the divisiveness it creates within by repeatedly injecting issues of class, race, and gender for self-serving purposes."[29] There are two underlying assumptions here: (1) that issues of class, race, and gender need to be "injected," as though they did not already pervade every corner of life in the United States, let alone nonprofit agencies trying to serve diverse constituencies on inadequate funding; (2) that Esperanza's politics and strategies were divisive. As for the first charge, the history alluded to above shows that divisive issues hardly need injecting into a movement in which they have always been present. As for the second, a group of gay men forging an alliance with the religious right hardly need look abroad for divisive strategies.

All the most common political divisions among gay men and lesbians over the decades came into play in the Esperanza Center's defunding. The Esperanza Center example shows that disagreements over strategy are tantamount to substantive disagreements. When cultural work is devalued or, more specifically, criticized for having political value, there are obviously profoundly different ideas about what politics is, and what the proper sphere for political activity is. Those who imagine that cultural work of any kind could ever be free of political value tend to be the same people who think that the market is a perfectly good place to enact and resolve political conflict.[30] The general idea that political values become "injected" into cultural work, like the specific idea that class, race, and gender issues become "injected" into gay and lesbian organizations, goes hand in hand with the fantasy that the market is amoral.

Meanwhile, substantive disagreements turn on conflicts between large national organizations and smaller, local, and/or grassroots organizations. Signers of the letter to the San Antonio City Council were members of national gay organizations, notably the Log Cabin Republicans.[31] In this episode, too, the recurring conflict between single-issue organizing and multi-issue and multiconstituency organizing came up again. Part of the reason the conservative gay men opposed funding was because the Center did not focus exclusively on gay men and lesbians, that it unnecessarily associated radical politics with the otherwise liberal gay-rights movement; these are men who generously fund more expressly "undiluted" single-issue undertakings. These are not merely questions of strategy—they represent a divergence of values at the most profound level within the gay and lesbian movement. And the movement had been dealing with these issues for decades by the time the Esperanza Center was defunded.

The gay and lesbian movement, like other identity-based social movements, came of age in a changing economic field, against the historical backdrop of the whole twentieth century during which economic causes and effects in the United States included a mass-consumption boom, the Depression, wartime expansion and prosperity, crises of the manipulation of supply and demand, periods of union-busting, corporate welfare, niche marketing, and the explosion of global high-speed information exchange. Meanwhile, the ever-changing definition of citizenship has tended toward the displacement of political values such as democracy, participation, individualism, rights, privacy—as well as social values such as identity—onto the market. Thus identity is by definition lodged in the sense of self or personhood and, therefore, is elaborated in and through market address and consumption in a cultural context where political enfranchisement is manifest as marketplace autonomy. Similarly, identity movements have been shaped by the changing economic contexts in which they emerged.

Efforts to democratize the economy at the end of the nineteenth century, like the New Deal decades later, were products of political organizing, such as the emergence of a labor movement in the 1930s and broader social movements working for inclusion. Those factors, and fear of more radical reforms, caused Franklin Roosevelt to become the champion of some safety nets, such as social security, unemployment insurance, and the right to organize. In effect, over time, "the pendulum has swung between organized capital and organized everyone else, capital holding the upper hand most of the time."[32] In the 1950s and 1960s, corporations could afford to share more at home (while pillaging from everywhere else), but with the expansion of the global economy, with the repression of alternatives abroad and of an organized left domestically, with Reagan's attacks on labor and organizing, and with attacks on different identity groups in the dismantling of affirmative action, people have been forced into defensive and reactive positions, and they have organized to counter these moves. Identity politics in the latter years of the twentieth century were largely shaped by such offensive and defensive maneuvers.

ECONOMIC JUSTICE

To offer critiques of identity politics is neither to forget nor fail to honor the amazing work that has been done in the name of identity, nor is it to condemn that stratagem. It is merely to suggest that its moment of effectiveness may be waning, as every political strategy eventually must. As activist Urvashi Vaid has written, "Identity-based organizing was necessary and it has been beneficial."[33] Without it, the libertarians might not enjoy the freedom of speech they exercise in the publication of their opinions. Nor would I. For Chuck Collins, Cofounder of United for a Fair Economy (UFE), organizing for economic justice came out of different identity politics movements. "We wanted to move through the lessons of identity politics to find common ground. We felt like the common ground was class issues."[34] Collins observed that there was a "majoritarian opportunity" around class issues, partly because class concerns everyone across all identities, but also because economic inequality contributed to the backlash against different identity groups—low-income women, gay men and lesbians, immigrants, people of color. "That scapegoating climate was something that unified people," said Collins, "we were all being targeted."

In particular, Collins's colleagues came from movements addressing concerns of labor, women, gay men and lesbians, low-income people, and civil rights. "We noticed more and more single-issue organizing going on, but no galvanizing ideological frame being built. We were struck by the changing class structure of the last two decades and the rising inequality of wages, incomes, and wealth. Could this be a banner many of our fragmented movements could unite under without losing the key issues that drive our constituents?"[35] For gay men and lesbians, as for members of any identity group, the growing disparity between rich and poor in the United States has probably magnified political differences among people who share some identity feature, but who do not share vision or strategy. In addition to the widely popular goal of legal equality, economic equality becomes an ever greater need for ever more people in this context. Activist John Anner concurs: "In a political system based in principle on equal opportunity and equality before the law, lack of formal access to the system is a powerful organizing handle."[36]

While bringing identity-based organizations into coalition seemed to promise a large constituency, a broad base, Collins stresses that his organization wasn't "interested in a populist economic agenda that ignored race, sexual politics and the lessons of identity organizing."[37] UFE's prescription for growth places a great weight on unions; if unions will put more resources into field mobilization, they believe that a significant "base" could be built up. Through the union apparatus, Collins projects, a great number of sympathetic people could "line up and do stuff," which is to say, enter into a range of modes of political participation. The other key to growth lies in strengthening the connections between national formations (such as Washington-based organizations and "paper" coalitions) and that base. A premium on these connections is also evident in the critique of the movement as lacking an infrastructure. According to this critique, the major national gay organizations are disconnected from gay and lesbian people, having "no relationship" to their daily lives; there is a "lack of integration between the decentralized community and the centralized power structure."[38] Thus, the structure of a movement has everything to do with its political strategies and objectives.

While civil rights were hanging in the balance of the strategies of the mainstream gay and lesbian movement, many questions hung to the left of the radar screen, simply absent from debates about political objectives and tactics in the lesbian and gay movement: questions of access to health care, to adequate housing, and to education and job training; questions of procedural fairness in the Immigration and Naturalization Services, in the Child Protective Services or other Department of Social Services agencies, and in the criminal justice system; questions of barriers to participation in social decision making—from xenophobia to monolingualism. Meanwhile, the movement's objectives and tactics acceded to the recasting of civil rights as consumer rights. If the African American civil rights movement has met with a similar fate, Patricia Williams explains this with reference to the macro-economic changes of the 1980s and 1990s: "Scarcely thirty years after Martin Luther King's dream of a day when his children would be judged by the content of their character alone, the Reagan-Bush presidencies were able to reverse the metaphor of the Freedom Train into a commodity with a high-priced ticket whose fare must be earned in the marketplace."[39] For gay men and lesbians, too, a trickle-down economics compelled an erstwhile liberation movement to redirect its energies toward the market.[40] As a result, the gay and lesbian movement's successes can be measured by the number, visibility, and financial viability of out entrepreneurs.

By the same token, "diversity" has achieved the status of good business practice. Encouraged by the mentality of downsizing to pick fewer employees more carefully, managers have come to see that the success of their businesses depends on attracting the most talented people, and if the universe of candidates is restricted because of a discriminatory policy, the business suffers. With this ethos in place, some amount of access to the market is opened up for women, people of color, even gay men and lesbians. Or is it? These opportunities are available to very few people; therefore, while this new premium on diversity promotes some amount of mobility for some people by inviting them into the ranks of management, this is not a business strategy that benefits any social group as a whole. As Anner put it, "While American capitalism has made room for increasing numbers of women and people of color in the ranks of the well-to-do and politically powerful, the problems of poverty, segregation, violence, illness, and institutional racism worsen for those trapped at the bottom of an economy that no longer seems to need them."[41]

Again, identity politics may successfully advance the interests of some members of any given identity group, especially those who already enjoy some form of social or economic advantage. Historically, identity politics has certainly advanced the legal interests of whole identity groups, but legal solutions, while necessary and fair, only go so far toward changing conditions equally within identity groups. I think the popularity of identity politics is based in the wish that the kind of psychic and cultural safety often felt in a community of origin would equate to political solidarity. But it is not always so. People may subscribe to the superstitious belief that they share something with all other members of a particular social group to which they belong, something like the subjection to categorical ascriptions made by people both within and outside of the same group. They may even like to think they share something *more* than that subjection. They may harbor a chauvinism based in the idea that whatever is thus shared is truly and inherently superior in some way. But when it comes to choosing political allies, to committing material and psychic resources to a joint venture, it makes much more sense, when possible, to choose trustworthy partners, people who share a vision, whether that vision is political, aesthetic, ethical, and/or otherwise social.[42] It is also crucial to establish trustworthy techniques for coalition work, since trusting across identity proves so difficult. It would be foolhardy to ignore the role of identity, or to expect it to whither away, but it would be equally foolhardy to think identity politics can provide the basis for radical social transformation. As Anner writes, "A reinvigorated social justice Movement . . . will have to develop mechanisms of reconnecting identity politics with class issues."[43]

Designating single-issue organizing as "the first obstacle" to progressive possibilities for the gay and lesbian movement, Urvashi Vaid calls for augmenting this strategy with coalition, partly because progressive social change depends on making connections between the causes of and solutions for systematic disadvantage for people of various identities.[44] But Vaid also maintains a conviction that coalitions are the most effective tool available. This conviction is based on "the real political experience that coalitions succeed. Coalitions have been behind every legislative victory we have earned: from the Hate Crime Statistics Act, to the Ryan White AIDS Care Act, to the Americans With Disabilities Act, to the many Civil Rights Acts to the local laws gay activists have passed, to the referenda we have defeated."[45]

Coalitions, of course, are not easy and they present their own challenges to democratic process. One political scientist describes the unstable nature of coalitions: "groups seldom bring equal amounts of political clout or resources to the coalition-building process. Hence, there are few opportunities to equalize the weight of coalition members, thus creating the conditions for instability."[46] John Anner recommends principles of coalition activism that foreground mechanisms for working with people who are different. Anner's principles recognize the difficulty of such work, while also recognizing the importance of communication, common ground, and a commitment to interrupting—or better, preventing—the distortions of white "privilege and nationalism."[47] Because communication is particularly necessary at moments of crisis, coalitions must develop structures for ongoing coordination and communication. They must commit resources to these structures. "Accordingly," agrees the political scientist, "working relations require a strategy, a reward structure, and an organization to resolve disagreements. This coordinating organization exists solely to promote communication between groups and to provide a forum for debating topics of common interest."[48]

Coalition work may be made more difficult by the promise of assimilation into the dominant majority culture. Yet this promise also makes "cultural linkages" across identity lines crucial if "minorities" are to resist identifying with the majority culture: "Our political culture discourages ethnic solidarity among certain minority groups by offering the possibility of total assimilation if old cultural practices are discontinued."[49] Albeit in different ways, assimilation is as much a promise and a threat for gay men and lesbians as it is for racial and ethnic minorities. Though of course, as activist Carmen Vazquez wisely observes, "Assimilation into existing democratic structures and radical militancy are not a contradiction. They are two essential strategies in a very complex dialectic for social change."[50] Over the course of the last several decades, gay and lesbian institutions have largely served the interests of identity, at every turn demonstrating that political practice and market practice have cosponsored certain regular effects: the promotion of assimilation, skewed visual and political representation of the diversity of people who identify in any way as gay and/or lesbian, differential opportunity for differently positioned gay and/or lesbian people, and the commodification of "homosexuality."

REPRESENTATION AS CULTURAL COMMODITY

In her important work on the commodification of homosexuality, Sarah Schulman points to one of the core contradictions at work in the relationship between the gay movement and the gay market: "We live in a society deeply conflicted about homosexuality but no longer able to deny its existence. This combination makes gay people simultaneously an ideal group for niche marketing and for the containment inherent in commodification to straight consumers."[51] While gay people now appear as consumers, our coming-out stories now appear as plots, our styles as *the* styles, our stuff as *the* stuff to buy. Or rather, as Schulman also argues, the more commodified an image of a gay person is, the less likely it is to be a "self"-representation. In the commodified version, we have no politics. In fact, in a whole range of ways, these images are assimilationist. The AIDS niche is a good example.

Many goods and services targeted for the gay and lesbian niche market are mass-produced goods, identity-neutral services; niche marketing mainly refers to the creation of an identity-based (or affinity-based) group of consumers. But with the advent of the AIDS crisis, an AIDS-related line of goods and services began to appear in the gay market; not all identity groups were equally implicated in the production and marketing of those goods and services. First viatical companies (which offer cash for the life-insurance policies of people living with AIDS), then insurance companies surging to compete with them, then pharmaceutical companies have played to a gay niche. The viatical companies' exploitation of AIDS may be the most crassly parasitical, but the profit-seeking motive of the viatical companies, is, naturally, shared by other profit-seeking enterprises.[52]

AIDS-related industries are among the biggest advertisers in the gay press. So, once again, the gay and lesbian press provides a distribution channel for lesbian and gay images that works in two directions. The gay and lesbian press disseminates images of gay people, mostly among gay people, and the gay and lesbian press brings corporate advertising into the hands of gay and lesbian people. Schulman corroborates the role of the press in the marketing of gay imagery: "In general, the national glossy gay magazines feed directly into the commodification of homosexuality and the targeting of the gay consumer. In fact, it often feels as though bringing gay consumers to straight industry is the main reason that these magazines exist. As a result, there is an increasing similarity between the mainstream media and the national gay press's versions of gay life."[53] Viatical and pharmaceutical companies are good examples of what Schulman means by the "straight industry" into whose hands the gay press delivers gay consumers. At the same time, as I discussed in Chapter 2, "[a]s gay magazines have had to exclude sex ads that formerly funded the gay press in order to upscale and attract advertising from major corporations, they've lost the foundation of their funding. This has shifted the financial dependency of the gay press from phone sex, sex toys, pornography, masseurs, and escort service ads to viaticals."[54] In this way, too, the changing financial structure of the gay press has affected its contents.

Because of the close relationship between political representation and representation in the media, the representation of gay people by major corporate advertisers—even in the gay press—mirrors the representation of gay people in large, especially national, gay political formations. In effect, "the vast majority of gay and lesbian people end up with no representation of their lives in the media. Instead we are bombarded by the A-list, white, male, buff, and wealthy stereotype that becomes the image in the American mind, of the average gay person."[55] Representation is a route to market incorporation and citizenship simultaneously, so misrepresentation also has implications for the possibility of enfranchisement. Citizenship apparently awarded on an identity basis (as is self-evident with respect to women and African Americans) actually empowers gay men and lesbians according to their economic and social status, not their sexual orientation (or gender or race).[56]

As a singularly pervasive form of representation, advertising has been one of the most significant vehicles of assimilationist ideology, for immigrants historically and for gay men and lesbians, among other social groups, in the 1990s. But advertising is not the only source of images of gay and lesbian identity and experience. Art is another such source. Artists in the business of generating alternative images seem to feel an "apprehension about the banalizing impact of mainstreaming."[57] Echoing Schulman's assessment that the United States is a society with a double-sided attitude toward homosexuality is the critique of mainstream images of gay and lesbian identity, such as those in advertising, Hollywood movies, and television: "What passes for gay in the mainstream is a marriage of convenience between the liberal impulse and the deeper terrors that make real queerness unbearable to straight society."[58] For one artist, the apparent acceptance of gay imagery by the "mainstream" carries a sinister political threat with it. "I think of the rainbow flag as a trap," he says. "It puts everybody and everything under the same banner. It's all so American. I mean, even the gay body has become generic. There's a kind of fascism here."[59] Likewise experiencing the undercurrent of U.S. national identity in the proliferation of gay-identity imagery, another artist invokes "the totalizing tendency of the mainstream."[60] Whenever gay or lesbian images converge with images of U.S. nationality, assimilation seems to threaten—or promise—that gay identity could fade into the mainstream. Thus gay men and lesbians, or rather, anti-assimilationists, face a paradox articulated as a quandary about distinctively gay or lesbian identity: "It was formed by oppression, but it's so bad to think it will go away."[61] A particularly gloomy statement of the same case issues from a scholar who observes that "along with the proliferation of gay images has come a loss of . . . 'sites of resistance' and their inevitable connection with desire"—this scholar's ultimate complaint about gay identity: "the thrill is gone."[62]

STEALING THE SHOW

Identity groups have often seemed to face two choices in response to the hazards and allure of assimilation: nationalism and socialism. Activist and writer Mab Segrest argues that "we have opted for the wrong model. We don't need a queer nationalism—as powerful as the militancy and anti-assimilationist stances of Queer Nation have been. We need a queer socialism that is by necessity anti-racist, feminist and democratic; a politic that does not cut us off from other people, but that unites us with them in the broadest possible movement."[63] Indeed, it seems to me that democracy is exactly what is at stake. In fact, by socialism, Segrest means "a more genuine *democracy,* where the citizens of our country have more direct access to *all* the decisions that affect us."[64] By whatever name, a more just and equitable political and economic arrangement would unyoke rights from property, so that dollars are not a requirement for participation in the processes by which social decisions are made. Call it democracy, call it socialism, it depends on common commitment to feminist and antiracist principles and to democratic procedure in movement organizations no less than in state organizations.

How would a movement for economic justice address the specific needs of social groups, honoring the identity differences that appear superficial in the marketplace? First of all, by fighting to win back and maintain the right to organize, a right that was badly eroded in the latter half of the twentieth century, particularly from the 1970s to the 1990s. Second, by addressing identity-based needs and inequalities without being identity specific. For example, raising the minimum wage is not a gender-specific intervention but it overwhelmingly affects the lives of working women. For women too, the right to organize has gendered implications, since the AFL-CIO is the largest group of working women in the United States. To reduce wage inequality would benefit women disproportionately since women are disproportionately underpaid, but again, this reform is not based primarily on identity.

Would an economic justice movement serve the needs of gay men, lesbians, transgender, bisexual, two-spirited, questioning, and queer people, in particular? Yes, if we could reconceive "l/g/b/t/ts/q/q issues" in light of the incontrovertible fact that l/g/b/t/ts/q/q identities cross lines of race, gender, class. The gay and lesbian movement needs to learn the lessons of other identity movements, and it also needs to join with those movements. As Segrest declares, "The struggles for racial equality and women's rights in the United States have a long and proud history with much to teach us. We need to know those histories. We need to honor them. We need to participate in today's civil rights struggle for racial and gender equality, or else the queer struggle for civil rights will not be won."[65] Untold thousands of gay and lesbian activists have helped make the United States safer for gay men and lesbians, by struggling against homophobia in individuals and institutions. I join with Segrest in honoring those activists and their work. I also join with those who imagine the future of gay and lesbian politics as a post-identity politics, aware as I am of the divisive effects of identity.

The lessons of the women's movement are available if we will learn them. Labor activist Susan Moir reminded the assembled crowd in Pittsburgh at the meeting of the Ad Hoc Committee for an Open Process that the suffragists made a tactical as well as an ethical error when they sold out their friends in the abolitionist movement.[66] Not only did they destroy an alliance between black women and white women, it took them another several decades to get the vote for women. Segrest applies this lesson to gay and lesbian organizing when she writes, "racism shapes all political movements in the United States. . . . In the lesbian and gay movement, much of our analysis has flowed from an understanding of gender, leaving race and class at two removes from our analysis. But approaches to racism have shaped the debates within our own community on issues such as passing and assimilation, radical transformation versus reform, legal strategies versus empowerment of the grassroots."[67] In any case, civil rights are necessary but not sufficient to the causes of equality and freedom. As Barbara Smith wrote in a letter to the planners of the Millennium March on Washington, "We don't simply need gay rights. We need social, political, and economic justice."[68]

The myth that choices made in the arena of private consumption equal votes in a democratic arena clearly appeals to those people who experience some sense of choice. The belief that consumers enjoy free choice in the marketplace is intimately related to the beliefs that diversity resides in morally neutral social differences and that "respect" for those differences grants social equality. Given the simultaneity of cultural, political, and economic dominance on the parts of men, white people, and of course middle-class people, diversity as a social value—that is, diversity negotiated in the marketplace—tends to pull for assimilation.

However, it is certainly not possible for consumers, acting individually, to contravene market forces; therefore, the question is not one of consuming "correctly" or "incorrectly" at the individual level. Neither are gay businesses categorically "at fault"; in fact, they are no different from other kinds of businesses, as a rule. Mainstream and gay businesses alike generally make contributions to nonprofit organizations; mainstream and gay businesses alike engage in target marketing for the purpose of making a profit.[69] If identity politics promotes the assumption that predictable political positions adhere to identity, identity-based consumption does the same thing. Thus, for example, one tenet of gay-based socially responsible consuming would have consumers support businesses that offer domestic-partnership benefits to their employees. A non-identity-based version of this strategy would involve merely broadening the criteria, patronizing businesses whose upper-management roster boasts women and people of color *and* who offer domestic-partner benefits *and* who conform to standards for the fair treatment of children working in their foreign plants, for example. But even this strategy still leaves the burden on individual consumers, as though they had more than buying power, and as though all gay and lesbian people would profit equally from this strategy; in reality, the owners and stockholders will enjoy the profit. Furthermore, this strategy leaves in place the logic of correct consumption as new and improved political participation. While it may have some positive, if negligible, effect on corporate policy and/or practice, it still withholds the franchise from people who have little consuming power, people who have little or no discretionary income.

Two simultaneous strategies can enable diverse people to gain true cultural and economic equality. One, liberal identity-based social movements who fight the good and necessary fight for rights need to strengthen their coalitional activity, working more closely with other identity-based movements. Two, premiums on equal access to all social institutions and benefits and on equal opportunity must inform the progressive platform across lines of identity. In fact, an economic justice movement in this country already exists, and it is growing. With objectives such as reducing the wage gap between executives and the lowest-paid workers within corporations, limiting CEO salaries, and reforming the tax structure, organizations such as United for a Fair Economy and Citizens for Tax Justice represent just two examples of political strategy and praxis whose constituency exceeds identity categories. Queers for Economic Justice, and Jews for Racial and Economic Justice are two more groups organizing beyond identity. Their successes would benefit people of diverse races, genders, sexual orientations, and even classes. In old-fashioned terminology, this movement is liberal to the extent that it seeks reform rather than revolution; yet the proposed reforms strike at least some Republican lawmakers as "the politics of . . . class warfare."[70] These Republicans are right: the reforms proposed are indeed radical, addressing root causes of racial and gender inequality, and hence the oppression of so many lesbians and gay men.

Constituted by marketing, identified by and through participation in gay and lesbian for-profit and nonprofit institutions, gay men and lesbians have reason to appreciate both the movement and the market that produce and reproduce gay culture. Rights are absolutely necessary, and they are clearly won through identity-based practices. But identity-based movement and market activity—while indispensable and inevitable on both individual and group levels—ultimately promote sameness, leaving difference vulnerable to appropriation and leaving it in place as grounds for inequality. If liberal rights and the rights of the consumer are the best possible outcomes of the partnership between identity politics and identity-based consumption, that is because they leave the structures of capitalism untouched. Progressive coalitions that focus on economic injustice may address those structures. They serve a diverse constituency, including gay men and lesbians. They dislocate the myth that private consumption can ever do the work of progressive political action.

In April 1998, Mike Lapham of United for a Fair Economy and a colleague set out to confound a symbolic action that Representative Dick Armey was about to take. Armey had come to Boston to dump a progressive tax code in the harbor, as a dramatization of his objections to the code. What he didn't expect was two protesters from UFE who set out in a plastic dingy representing working families. When Armey dropped the tax code overboard, he inadvertently overturned the protest dingy, forcing the "working family" to swim to shore. The Associated Press, Reuters, and other news agencies were on hand to cover the spectacle, and according to Lapham, "We stole the show." Ironically, Armey was in the harbor to reenact the symbolic origin of American revolutionary rejection of imperial rule—of taxation without representation. The protestors were there to remind him of the working people across a range of identities whose well-being depends on adequate political representation and fair economic arrangements. Their symbolic displacement beautifully dramatized the consequences of laissez-faire politics.

APPENDIX: THE BOYCOTT LITERATURE

Aceituno, Jane. "Word Dispatch: American Airlines." Email to the author. 17 April 1997.

"ACLU Right." *Sentinel* [San Francisco] 2 June 1977: 7.

"After Dade County Turning Defeat into Victory." Pamphlet. *Blazing Star* [Chicago] 1977.

Akin, Scott. "Colorado Boycott Picks Up Speed." *Advocate* 12 Jan. 1993: 18–19.

Alfred, Randy. "Thank you Anita . . . for Saving our Human Rights, or, Why Re-hire the Losing Team." *Sentinel* [San Francisco] 11 Aug. 1977: 6.

———. "From the Left." *Sentinel* [San Francisco] 11 Aug. 1977: 6.

———. "Miami Miscellany." *Sentinel* [San Francisco] 2 June 1977: 3.

———. "The (Orange) Seeds of Its Own Destruction." *Sentinel* [San Francisco] 24 March 1977: 6.

"Anita Bryant Campaign." *Bay Area Reporter* 14 April 1977: 7.

"Anita Canned as Orange Bowl Host." *Sentinel* [San Francisco] 30 Dec. 1977: 2.

"Anita Feels the Squeeze." *Bay Area Reporter* 3 March 1977: 2.

"Anita v. AFTRA: Show Biz Union to Refuse Services." *Bay Area Reporter* 26 May 1977: 8.

"Anita Wants Prayers in Schoolrooms." *Sentinel* [San Francisco] 9 Feb. 1978: 2.

"Anita Where Are You?" *Lesbian Tide* 7.1 (July-Aug. 1977): 1, 5.

"Anita Wins . . . But Gays Fight Back." *Blazing Star* [Chicago] June 1977: 1–2.

Atchison, Sandra D. "Bashing Gays—and Business." *Business Week* 7 Dec. 1992: 42.

———. "Herbal Teas in Hot Water." *Business Week* 1 March 1993: 42–43.

Ayres, B. Drumm, Jr. "Miami Votes 2 to 1 to Repeal Law Barring Bias Against Homosexuals." *New York Times* 8 June 1977: A1+.

"BAGL Open House." *Bay Area Reporter* 9 June 1977: 12.

"Bahr's Finances: Community Voice." *Gay Community News* 23 July 1977: 2.

Baker, Joe. "Anita . . . with the Smiling Cheek." *Advocate* 20 April 1977: 6.

"Banned Bryant." *Gay Community News* 18 Nov. 1978: 2.

"Bars Ban O.J." *Sentinel* [San Francisco] 21 April 1977: 1.

Beardemphl, W. E. Editorial. *Sentinel* [San Francisco] 24 March 1977: 7.

———. Editorial. *Sentinel* [San Francisco] 24 Feb. 1977: 5.

Bennett, Paula. "Speaking Out." *Gay Community News* 28 May 1977: 5.

Berlo, Beth. "Activists Demanding that GLAAD Return Donation from Coors." *Bay Windows* [Boston] 12 Nov. 1998: 1+.

"Blowing NGTF's Whistle." Letter. *Sentinel* [San Francisco] 5 May 1977: 7.

"Boycotting Anita." *Bay Area Reporter* 17 Feb. 1977: 4.

Breen, T. H. "Narrative of Commercial Life: Consumption, Ideology, and Community on the Eve of the American Revolution." *William and Mary Quarterly* L.3 (1993): 471–501.

Brill, David. "Fun and Fund-Raising Mark Fenway Fair." *Gay Community News* 9 July 1977: 7.

"Bruce Voeller in S.F." *Bay Area Reporter* 28 April 1977: 10.

"Bryant Agent Quits." *Gay Community News* 16 July 1977: 2.

"Bryant Aide Details Gay Dade County 'Errors.'" *Gay Community News* 17 Sept. 1977: 3.

"Bryant Backs off on Anti-Gay Battle." *Sentinel* [San Francisco] 6 Oct. 1977: 21.

"Bryant in Hiding." *Bay Area Reporter* 17 Feb. 1977: 4.

"Bryant May Lose Citrus Job." *Sentinel* [San Francisco] 20 June 1977: 1.

"Bryant on Way Out as O.J. Spokesperson?" *Gay Community News* 21 July 1977: 3.

"Bryant Rants . . . No Sunshine for Gays." *Lesbian Tide* 6.6 (May-June 1977): 16

"California: Another Dade County." *Gay Community News* 20 Aug. 1977: 1.

Case, Tony. "Honoring a Boycott." *Editor & Publisher* 16 Jan. 1993: 10–11.

Caudron, Shari. "The Colorado Boycott." *Industry Week* 1 March 1993: 48–54.

"Celebrities to Exercise Human Rights." *Bay Area Reporter* 21 July 1977: 11.

"Christopher Street Demo Club Boycott." *Bay Area Reporter* 31 March 1977: 7.

"Citrus Commission Renews Bryant's Contract." *Gay Community News* 30 July 1977: 1.

"Citrus Growers Halt Limbaugh Ad." *New York Times* 23 July 1994: A9.

"The Coors Controversy." *Advocate* 16 Nov. 1977: 11–16.

"Coors in Second Place." *Gay Community News* 3 Sept. 1977: 2.

Coward, Cheryl. "After Intense Pressure, Bank America Releases Its Stand Against the Boy Scout Ban." *Advocate* 22 Sept. 1992: 21.

Curry, George E. "The Resurgence of Boycotts." *Emerge* Feb. 1991: 50–56.

"Dade County: Into Your Closet or Fight." *Lesbian News* no. 24 (July 1977): 1, 10.

Dahir, Mubarak S. "Coming Out at the Barrel." *Progressive* June 1992: 14.

Davis, Ricardo A. "Activists Attack Colorado Marketers." *Advertising Age* 8 Feb. 1993: 47.

"Demos Back Gaycott." *Bay Area Reporter* 12 May 1977: 7.

"Do Advertisers Face a Negro Boycott?" *Printers' Ink* 13 Sept. 1963: 7.

"Economic Pressure." *Gay Community News* 16 July 1977: 4.

"Editorial." *Bay Area Reporter* 17 Feb. 1977: 8.

Edwards, Thomas M. "On the Right Side." *Sentinel* [San Francisco] 21 April 1977: 5.

Emerson, Jim. "Are Boycotts Passé?" *Advocate* 1 Nov. 1994: 36.

"Equal Time vs. Anita." *Gay Community News* 2 July 1977: 2.

Etherington, Robert. "Speaking Out: Power to the People." *Gay Community News* 30 July 1977: 1.

"5,000 Angry Gays Rally and March." *Bay Area Reporter* 9 June 1977: 2.

"Floridanita." *Sentinel* [San Francisco] 24 March 1977: 3.

Friedman, Milton and Rose Friedman. *Free to Choose: A Personal Statement.* London: Secker and Warburg, 1980.

"Fuming on the Slopes." *Economist* 6 Feb. 1993: A30.

Gallagher, John. "Boycott Blues." *Advocate* 4 May 1993: 27.

———. "Friend of No One?" *Advocate* 30 Nov. 1993: 48–52.

———. "Picking Up the Pieces." *Advocate* 15 Dec. 1992: 20–21.

———. "San Franciscans Weigh Coors' Sponsorship of Softball Tourney." *Advocate* 23 April 1991: 34.

Galst, Liz. "Southern Activists Rise Up." *Advocate* 19 May 1992: 54–56.

Gay Guerillas. Letter. *Leaping Lesbians* Sept. 1977: 11.

"Gay Miami Squeezes Anita." *Bay Area Reporter* 17 Feb. 1977: 2.

"Gay Nite-Life Coupon Book Idea Launched." *Bay Area Reporter* 22 Dec. 1977: 16.

"Get It Together." *Sentinel* [San Francisco] 19 May 1977: 7.

"God, Country, and Anita." *Lesbian News* no. 22 (May 1977): 1, 10.

Gordon, Eric. "Ballad of Anita Bryant." *Gay Community News* 20 Aug.1977: 5.

"Grape Juice Offered for O.J. Substitute." *Sentinel* [San Francisco] 17 June 1977: 1.

Harding, Rick. "Nashville NAACP Head Stung by Backlash from Boycott Support." *Advocate* 16 July 1991: 27.

Hoffman, Frank. "Just in from Frisco." *Christopher Street* 2:1 (July 1977): 3–5.

Holland, Peter. "How Straight Is Madison Avenue?" *Christopher Street* Jan. 1977: 26–28.

"Hollywood Accord Near: Police Reveal Vice Policy." *L.A. Advocate* 24 April 1974: 2.

Holmes, Steven. "Boycotts Rarely Have Impact on Bottom Line, but Actions Serve as Rallying Points," *New York Times* 15 Nov. 1996: D4.

"Idaho Gives Bryant . . ." *Lesbian Tide* 7.2 (Sept.-Oct. 1977): 19.

"Kick 'Protects' Anita at Rally." *Gay Community News* 23 July 1977: 1

Koffer, Douglas Allen. "The Lonely Battle." *Sentinel* [San Francisco] 5 May 1977: 4.

Laurence, Leo E. "Glide Boycotts San Francisco Firms that Won't Hire Homosexuals." *Advocate* 3 Nov. 1967: 3.

Lee, Charles. "Local Leaders Blast N.G.T.F. Statement." *Sentinel* [San Francisco] 10 March 1977: 1–2.

Leo, John. "When in Doubt, Boycott." *US News and World Report* 21 Dec. 1992: 35.

"Letters to Our Staff." *Bay Area Reporter* 17 March 1977: 29.

Levy, Herbert S. "A Need for Co-operation." Letter. *Sentinel* [San Francisco] 23 Feb. 1978: 5.

"Liberation Party Condemns Bryant." *Gay Community News* 13 Aug. 1977: 3.

Lorch, Paul. "Gaycott Topples Coors." *Bay Area Reporter* 1 Sept. 1977: 4.

McKuen, Rod. "The Squeeze Goes On: A Report from the Battlefield." *Christopher Street* June 1977: 4.

McNaught, Brian. "When Anita Sings the Battle Hymn of the Republic." *Gay Community News* 18 June 1977: 12–14.

Mandell, Jonathan. "The Boom in Boycotts." *New York Newsday* 13 March 1991: 58.

"March and Be Proud." *Bay Area Reporter* 23 June 1977: 4.

Marko, Jim. "Controversial Coors: Nixon, Reagan, and Anita (?) Too . . ." *Gay Community News* 23 July 1977: 4.

———. "Miami Man Shot Outside Dance." *Gay Community News* 16 July 1977: 2.

———. "Midge Costanza: Gay Rights Proponent at the White House." *Gay Community News* 9 July 1977: 11.

———. "Surviving the Orange Juice Squeeze." *Gay Community News* 28 May 1977: 14.

Martin, Robert K. "Anita and Hester." *Christopher Street* Aug. 1977: 43–46.

Mathers, Jay. "At Coors, a Storm Brewing Over Gay Rights." *Washington Post* 16 Sept. 1995: A1.

Mathews, Tom, Tony Fuller, and Holly Camp. "Battle Over Gay Rights." *Newsweek* 6 June 1977: 16–26.

Maupin, Armistead. "Boycott Colorado." *New York Times* 21 Nov. 1992, Late East Coast Edition, A19.

"Maybe There's Something in the Juice." *Time* 28 Feb. 1994: 14.

Melgaard, Michael J. "The New Politics of Fear: The 1977 Dade County Gay Rights Referendum." Ph.D. diss., U of North Dakota, 1992.

Mendenhall, George. "Anita Bryant—Job Rights for All?" *Bay Area Reporter* 17 March 1977: 6.

———. "Anita Talks: Paranoia Stalks the Orange Juice Queen." *Bay Area Reporter* 9 June 1977: 38.

———. "The Coalition Effect: Campaign Manager Ethan Geto Tells the Full Story to *Bay Area Reporter* in this Exclusive Article." *Bay Area Reporter* 9 June 1977: 4.

———. "The Coors Empire and Gay Rights, Pt. 1: Did Anita Get Coors Money? Are Gays Welcome at Coors?" *Bay Area Reporter* 21 July 1977: 19.

———. "Coors: Thousands for Sales but Gaycott Continues." *Bay Area Reporter* 23 Nov. 1977: 13.

———. "How to Deal with a Hate-Monger." *Bay Area Reporter* 28 April 1977: 10.

———. "Miami Coalition Head Talks to *Bay Area Reporter:* Exclusive Interview." *Bay Area Reporter* 28 April 1977: 4.

———. "Thousands Flow to Help Squeeze Anita." *Bay Area Reporter* 28 April 1977: 2.

"Miami Radio Talk Show Host 'Comes Out' on the Air." *Bay Area Reporter* 20 Jan. 1977: 8.

"Miami Referendums Rated 'Toss Up.'" *Gay Community News* 4 June 1977: 1.

"Miami Repeal Thwarted." *Sentinel* [San Francisco] 21 April 1977: 1.

Michelson, Peter. "Coors Beer, the Union Buster." *Nation* 15 April 1978: 434–436.

Milk, Harvey. "The End of a Year: the Beginnings." *Bay Area Reporter* 22 Dec. 1977: 16.

———. "Leave Anita Alone?" *Bay Area Reporter* 3 March 1977: 4.

———. "The List." *Bay Area Reporter* 28 April 1977: 7.

———. "A Nation Finally Talks About . . . 'It.'" *Bay Area Reporter* 9 June 1977: 17.

———. "Pools Within Pools." *Bay Area Reporter* 31 March 1977: 8.

Miller, Neil. "Anita 'Sees the Light' (Maybe)." *Gay Community News* 30 July 1977: 4.

Monteagudo, Jesse. "Anita and I: An Activist's Memoir." *TWN* 29 Oct. 1997: 12–17.

"Moon Over Miami: When Credit Is Due." *Sentinel* [San Francisco] 19 May 1977: 7.

Morris, Charles Lee. "Anita Has the Right to Speak, However." Editorial. *Sentinel* [San Francisco] 5 May 1977: 7.

———. "Local Gay Heads Miami Battle." *Sentinel* [San Francisco] 5 May 1977: 1–14.

———. "Local Leaders Blast N.G.T.F. Statement." *Sentinel* [San Francisco] 10 March 1977: 1–2.

———. "Miami Rally Draws 300." *Sentinel* [San Francisco] 5 May 1977: 1.

Moscone, George R. "Moscone Salutes Miami." Letter. *Sentinel* [San Francisco] 21 April 1977: 7.

"Murdered Man's Mother Sues Bryant for $5M." *Gay Community News* 23 July 1977: 1–6.

Neier, Aryeh. Letter. *Sentinel* [San Francisco] 21 April 1977: 5.

"New York Activism." *Gay Community News* 9 July 1977: 2.

Noble, Barbara Presley. "Gay Group Asks Accord in Job Dispute." *New York Times* 25 Nov. 1992: C4.

"Noble Nixes Washington." *Bay Area Reporter* 26 May 1977: 9.

"Notes from the Publisher." *Christopher Street* 1.9 (March 1977): 62.

"OIL Can Harry's Will Continue to Fight Anita Bryant and her Bigoted Forces." *Bay Area Reporter* 9 June 1977: 22–23.

"Only Three Weeks Left to Register to Vote." *Bay Area Reporter* 9 June 1977: 8.

"Oranges Sour on Anita." *Lesbian Tide* 9.6 (May-June 1980): 21.

Ortleb, Charles. "Ethan Geto." *Christopher Street* 2.2 (Aug. 1977): 21–33.

"Outspoken: On Boycotts and Betrayal." Editorial. *Outweek* 22 Aug. 1990: 4.

"The Pink Triangle Ranch." *Lesbian Tide* 8.1 (July-Aug. 1978): 27.

Plaster, Gip. "Queer Beer?" *Between the Lines* [Detroit] 29 Oct.–11 Nov. 1998: 18.

Post, Theresa J. "Groups Cancel Colorado Bookings in Wake of Gay Legislation." *Travel Weekly* 14 Dec. 1992: 14.

Putnam, Todd. "Boycotts Are Busting Out All Over." *Business and Society Review* 1993: 47–51.

———. Letter to the author. Sept. 1997.

"Queen Anita Loses Parade." *Lesbian Tide* 7.4 (Jan.-Feb. 1978): 21.

"Radio Stations Drop O.J. Ads." *Sentinel* [San Francisco] 6 Oct. 1977: 3.

"Rally Draws Crowd." *Sentinel* [San Francisco] 5 May 1977: 4.

Rhoads, Heather. "Boycott Colorado." *Progressive* Jan. 1993: 13.

"Rising Above Anita and the Nazis." *Sentinel* [San Francisco] 21 April 1977: 6.

Rohter, Larry. "Limbaugh's Pitch for Juice Roils Critics." *New York Times* 18 Feb. 1994: A12.

Sahagun, Louis. "Gays Weigh Alternatives to Boycotts." *Los Angeles Times* 9 Oct. 1995: A14.

Savan, Leslie. "Where the Boycotts Are." *Village Voice* 6 June 1989: 47–48.

———/*Village Voice*. "Activism in the Checkout Line: The Rising Tide of Boycotts." *Utne Reader* Sept.-Oct. 1989: 87–89.

"Save Our Children Bankrupt?" *Lesbian Tide* 7.3 (Nov.-Dec. 1977): 22.

Schmitz, Dann. "Miller Boycott Pits Gay Union Activists vs. the Gay Right." *Gay Community News* 8 March 1992: 3.

Shiflett, Dave. "The Hate State." *American Spectator* July 1993: 50–53.

Signorile, Michelangelo. "Anatomy of a Boycott." *Advocate* 12 Jan. 1993: 17.

Silk, Leonard and David Vogel. *Ethics and Profits: The Crisis of Confidence in American Business*. New York: Simon and Schuster, 1976.

Smith, N. Craig. *Morality and the Market: Consumer Pressure for Corporate Accountability*. London: Routledge, 1990.

Snyder, Adam. "Do Boycotts Work?" *Adweek's Marketing Week* 8 April 1991: 16–18.

"S.O.H.R. News." *Bay Area Reporter* 21 July 1977: 11.

Sprague, Joan. "Coors and Boycott." *Lesbian News* 40 (Nov. 1978): 1–2.

"The Squeeze Goes On." *Christopher Street* June 1977: 3–5.

Stencel, Mark. "The Growing Influence of Boycotts." *Congressional Quarterly* 1 (1991).

Stewart, Nikita. "Groups Boycott Distributor Over Wife's Conservative Politics." *Courier-Journal* [Louisville] 26 Aug. 1995: 8A.

———. "Stop Bryant Now." *Lesbian Tide* 6.6 (May-June 1977): 24.

"Strictly Business: A Gay PR Firm Helps Break a Gay Boycott of United Airlines." <http://www.guidemag.com/newsslant/strictly-business.html> August 1998.

"Surviving the Orange Juice Squeeze." *Gay Community News* 28 May 1977: 14.

"Swedish Gays Join Boycott." *Bay Area Reporter* 21 July 1977: 11.

Taatgen, H. A. "The Boycott in the Irish Civilizing Process." *Anthropological Quarterly* 65.4 (1992): 163–176.

"Tavern Guild Gives Large Sum to Miami Coalition." *Bay Area Reporter* 31 March 1977: 7.

"Teachers Endorse a Boycott Over Juice Ads on Limbaugh." *New York Times* 5 July 1994: A10.

"Texaco Was Just the Beginning: Expect More Civil Rights Tangles with Corporate America." *Business Week* 16 Dec. 1996: 34–35.

Thompson, Dai. "Speaking Out." *Gay Community News* 28 May 1977: 5.

Tilchen, Maida. "650 Picket Anita in Indianapolis." *Gay Community News* 22 Oct. 1977: 3.

"Turning off Anita." *Gay Community News* 24 Sept. 1977: 2.

"Universal Fellowship of MCC." *Bay Area Reporter* 14 April 1977: 8.

"An Urgent Appeal to Lesbian/Gay/Bisexual/Transgender People Regarding the Coors Boycott." Solicitation. Coors Boycott Committee. Oct. 1998.

Vogel, David. *Lobbying the Corporation: Citizen Challenges to Business Authority.* New York: Basic Books, 1978.

"Why Doesn't Somebody . . . ; Out and Around." *Christopher Street* 17 Feb. 1977: 3.

"Why We Should Still Boycott Orange Juice." *Gay Community News* 29 Oct. 1977: 5.

Wockner, Rex. "Helms Targeted Through Miller Beer Boycott." *Outweek* 1 Aug. 1990: 20.

Wockner, Rex and Andrew Miller. "Miller Beer Boycott, Aimed at Helms, Goes National." *Outweek* 15 Aug. 1990: 12–14.

NOTES

PREFACE

1. An advertisement for New York Telephone ("Part of the nationwide Bell Telephone System") showing an African American man in business clothing approaching a phone booth appeared in 1963. In the same year, New York mayor Robert Wagner's Committee on Job Advancement issued a request to 500 advertisers and agencies to integrate their advertising. Similar requests were made by the Congress of Racial Equality and the National Association for the Advancement of Colored People. Marilyn Kern-Foxworth, *Aunt Jemima, Uncle Ben, and Rastus: Blacks in Advertising, Yesterday, Today, and Tomorrow* (Westport, CT: Greenwood P, 1994) 116–117.

2. This book has since been written. I recommend to interested readers Margaret Finnegan, *Selling Suffrage: Consumer Culture and Votes for Women* (New York: Columbia UP, 1999). Finnegan examines how discourses of enfranchisement and consumption intersected with each other before the passage of the Nineteenth Amendment.

3. This process is the subject of David T. Evans's *Sexual Citizenship: The Material Construction of Sexualities* (New York: Routledge, 1993).

4. Readers interested in the electoral political arena should consult Mark Hertzog, *The Lavender Vote: Lesbians, Gay Men, and Bisexuals in American Electoral Politics* (New York: New York UP, 1996), and Kenneth Sherrill, "The Political Power of Lesbians, Gays, and Bisexuals," *P.S.: Political Science & Politics* 29.3 (1996), 469–473. Urvashi Vaid's *Virtual Equality: The Mainstreaming of the Gay and Lesbian Liberation Movement* (New York: Anchor/Doubleday, 1995) also includes a great deal of

information about the relationship between the gay and lesbian movement and electoral politics.

5. In *The Rise and Fall of Gay Culture* (New York: Hyperion, 1997), Daniel Harris argues that changes in gay (men's) culture in the second half of the twentieth century can only be understood as a function of assimilation. However, Harris focuses on more properly cultural phenomena; he also attends to the question of porn, which I have left untreated here. For more work on the nexus of gay and lesbian politics and culture, see David Bell and Gill Valentine, eds., *Mapping Desire: Geographies of Sexualities* (New York: Routledge, 1995); Michael Bronski, *The Pleasure Principle: Sex, Backlash, and the Struggle for Gay Freedom* (New York: St. Martin's, 1988) and *Culture Clash: The Making of Gay Sensibility* (Boston: South End P, 1984); Ellen Lewin, ed., *Inventing Lesbian Cultures in America* (Boston: Beacon P, 1996); and Sarah Schulman, *Stagestruck: Theater, AIDS, and the Marketing of Gay America* (Durham: Duke UP, 1988); Richard Goldstein has also contributed to the exploration of gay culture and its relation to assimilation; see, in addition to contributions to the *Village Voice,* his *Reporting the Counterculture* (Boston: Unwyn Hyman, 1989).

6. This work too has been begun, notably by Lisa Peñaloza in "We're Here, We're Queer, and We're Going Shopping! A Critical Perspective on the Accommodation of Gays and Lesbians in the U.S. Marketplace," *Gays, Lesbians, and Consumer Behavior: Theory, Practice, and Research Issues in Marketing,* ed. Daniel Wardlow (New York: Haworth P, 1996) 9–38; by *Homo Economics: Capitalism, Community, and Lesbian and Gay Life,* eds. Amy Gluckman and Betsy Reed (New York: Routledge, 1997); and by Badgett, Gamson, Piore, and Strub in *A Queer World: The Center for Lesbian and Gay Studies Reader,* ed. Martin Duberman (New York: New York UP, 1997).

INTRODUCTION

1. David Evans, *Sexual Citizenship: The Material Construction of Sexualities* (London: Routledge, 1993) 25.
2. Quoted in "Gays: A Major Force in the Marketplace," *Business Week* 3 Sept. 1979, 118–120.
3. I do not mean to argue that liberal democracy and capitalism absolutely require each other; in other words, I do not think that each one could exist

only if the other were present; however, I do mean to argue that their operations have been bound up with each other inextricably in the modern West. Likewise, I do not put forth a deterministic argument, meaning the book will not make claims about "cause" (although there will be many arguments about effects). Finally, this book will note, again and again, that the relationship between liberalism and capitalism is systematized, and that the cooperation between these systems has become so naturalized as to be frequently invisible. This work seeks to make visible the effects of the relationship between advanced capitalism and liberal democratic principles and practices on the late-twentieth-century gay and lesbian political movement in the United States.

4. Kirstie M. McClure, *Judging Rights: Lockean Politics and the Limits of Consent* (Ithaca: Cornell UP, 1996) 21.

5. Ibid., 21.

6. John Locke, *Second Treatise of Government,* ed. C. B. Macpherson (Indianapolis: Hackett Publishing Co., 1980) 19.

7. C. B. Macpherson, *The Political Theory of Possessive Individualism: Hobbes to Locke* (Oxford: Oxford UP, 1962) 4.

8. Adam Smith, "Wealth of Nations," *The Essential Adam Smith,* ed. Robert K. Heilbroner (New York: W. W. Norton, 1986) 168.

9. Money is, of course, the substance that makes standard values and equations of value possible. This is true for Locke and Smith as it is for Karl Marx and Georg Simmel, all of whom offer delightful treatments of the role of money.

10. The Declaration of Independence, which borrows heavily from Locke's writings, adapts his litany of things a citizen should be free to enjoy. Locke's list: "life, liberty, and private property." The Declaration: "life, liberty, and the pursuit of happiness."

11. William Leiss, *C. B. Macpherson: Dilemmas of Liberalism and Socialism* (New York: St. Martin's P, 1988) 60. Enlightenment philosophers did not write "or her"; whether "she" is implied has been the subject of long and bloody debate. Here, Leiss generously adapts the original idea in light of subsequent law and usage.

12. Patricia Williams, *The Rooster's Egg: On the Persistence of Prejudice* (Cambridge: Harvard UP, 1995) 233.

13. Smith, 176.

14. Ibid., 294.

15. Ibid., 324.

16. Ibid., 297.

17. The late-nineteenth and twentieth centuries showed how great the distance was between the legal franchise and the ability to exercise it.

18. Evans, 2.

19. Williams, 18.

20. Evans, 5. For gay men and lesbians, even as civil rights were progressively (if haltingly and incompletely) won, the market increasingly took over certain discriminatory functions, making citizenship for gay men and lesbians a matter of economic privilege rather than a matter of legal recognition and protection. Privatization affects different identity groups differently; Patricia Williams makes this point in relation to the African American community:

> No longer are state troops used to block entry to schools and other public institutions—segregation's strong arm, states' rights, has found a new home in an economic gestalt that has simply privatized everything. Whites have moved to the suburbs and politicians have withdrawn funds from black to white areas in unsubtle redistricting plans. No longer is the law expressly discriminatory (as to race and ethnicity at any rate; this is not yet the case in terms of sexual orientation)—yet the phenomenon of laissez-faire exclusion has resulted in as complete a pattern of economic and residential segregation as has ever existed in this country. (Williams, 25)

21. The phrase "possessive individualism" was first coined by C. B. Macpherson in a 1954 article called "The Deceptive Task of Political Theory." I quote from Leiss's recapitulation of Macpherson's theory.

22. John D'Emilio, "Capitalism and Gay Identity," *Powers of Desire: The Politics of Sexuality,* eds. Ann Snitow, Christine Stansell, and Sharon Thompson (New York: Monthly Review P, 1983) 100–113.

23. D'Emilio, 105.

24. Eli Zaretsky, *Capitalism, the Family, and Personal Life* (New York: Harper and Row, 1976) 57.

25. Describing the medical pathologization of homosexuality (among other non-procreative sexual behaviors) and its effects on the constitution of a social identity, Foucault writes of the late nineteenth century that a "new persecution of the peripheral sexualities entailed an *incorporation of perversions* and a new *specification of individuals. . . ."* Whereas a sodomite might previously have been guilty of perpetrating forbidden acts, "the nineteenth-century homosexual became a personage. . . . Nothing that

went into his total composition was unaffected by his sexuality." In a way that conditioned twentieth-century understandings of social identity as a basis both for political claims and for individual consumption, a person's homosexuality became "consubstantial with him, less as a habitual sin than as a singular nature." In the most oft-quoted line of Foucault's on this development: "The sodomite had been a temporary aberration; the homosexual was now a species." Michel Foucault, *The History of Sexuality: Volume 1,* trans. Robert Hurley (New York: Vintage Books, 1980) 42–43.

26. Chauncey writes that around the turn of the century, "a highly visible, remarkably complex gay male world took shape in New York City. That world included several gay neighborhood enclaves, widely publicized dances and other social events, and a host of commercial establishments where gay men gathered, ranging from saloons, speakeasies, and bars to cheap cafeterias and elegant restaurants." George Chauncey, *Gay New York: Gender, Urban Culture, and the Making of the Gay Male World, 1890–1940* (New York: Basic Books, 1994) 1.

27. Debates have raged about which comes first, chicken or egg, production or consumption, sometimes defining the opposition between Marxist and liberal economic theories—liberals tend to believe that demand produces and prescribes supply, while Marxists tend to believe that production supplies, over and above commodities themselves, the ideology that creates a sense of desire for commodities on the part of consumers. Perhaps Marxists have overlooked a relatively subtle comment made by Marx on the circuitry that relates production and consumption. Characterizing the relation as one of unity, or identity, Marx wrote: "Production, then, is immediately consumption, consumption is also immediately production. Each is immediately its opposite. But at the same time a mediating movement takes place between the two. Production mediates consumption; it creates the latter's material; without it, consumption would lack an object. But consumption also mediates production, in that it alone creates for the products the subject for whom they are products." (In Robert Tucker, ed., *The Marx-Engels Reader,* Second Edition [New York: W. W. Norton, 1972] 229.) For Marx, consumption precedes production, both materially and theoretically, not in the way of creating a demand, as in the account of liberalism, but because production is incomplete, socially meaningless, or "purposeless" without consumption.

28. Richard Ohmann, *Selling Culture: Magazines, Markets, and Class at the Turn of the Century* (New York: Verso, 1996) 21.

29. Ibid., 31.

30. Stuart Ewen, *Captains of Consciousness: Advertising and the Social Roots of Consumer Culture* (New York: McGraw-Hill, 1976) 219.

31. Louis Althusser, "Ideology and Ideological State Apparatuses," *Lenin and Philosophy and Other Essays,* trans. Ben Brewster (New York: Monthly Review P, 1971) 175.

32. Ibid., 182.

33. Lisa Peñaloza, "We're Here, We're Queer, and We're Going Shopping! A Critical Perspective on the Accommodation of Gays and Lesbians in the U.S. Marketplace," *Gays, Lesbians, and Consumer Behavior: Theory, Practice, and Research Issues in Marketing,* ed. Daniel Wardlow (New York: Haworth P, 1996) 32.

34. Roland Marchand, *Advertising the American Dream: Making Way for Modernity, 1920–1940* (Berkeley: U of California P, 1985) xx.

35. Peñaloza, 33.

36. Seyla Benhabib, "Models of Public Space: Hannah Arendt, the Liberal Tradition, and Jurgen Habermas," *Habermas and the Public Sphere,* ed. Craig Calhoun (Cambridge: MIT P, 1992) 84.

37. In modern Western societies, identity tends to be attributed to individuals (at the same time that it defines groups) and often appears to inhere in their bodies—in this way, it tends to function as an analog to labor. Like labor, identity is the possession with which subjects appear to be endowed, and with which they may choose to go to market and to court. While the idea of identity may enable modern rights movements, its invention does not free us from our bodies nor expand the range of choices available to our bodies. Recalling the Foucauldian paradigm that bodies are sites of subjection in modern regimes no less than in premodern regimes of power, Patricia Williams remarks, "It is with caution that we must notice that . . . we presumed free agents are not less but increasingly defined as body-centered. We live more, not less, in relation to our body parts, the dispossession or employment of ourselves constrained by a complicated pattern of self-alienation" (Williams, 232). Sexuality, like certain other identity features such as gender and race, and like labor, is simultaneously a basis for rights claims and a basis for "dispossession" and "self-alienation."

38. While not exactly an activist in the gay and lesbian movement, Sullivan's exposure as a public intellectual gives him perhaps more authority as a spokesperson than is appropriate. His solution is this: "that all public (as

opposed to private) discrimination against homosexuals be ended and that every right and responsibility that heterosexuals enjoy as public citizens be extended to those who grow up and find themselves emotionally different. And that is all. No cures or re-educations, no wrenching private litigation, no political imposition of tolerance; merely a political attempt to enshrine formal public equality, whatever happens in the culture and society at large." Andrew Sullivan, *Virtually Normal: An Argument About Homosexuality* (New York: Alfred A. Knopf, 1995) 171.

39. Elizabeth Bounds, "Between the Devil and the Deep Blue Sea: Feminism, Family Values, and the Division Between Public and Private," *Journal of Feminist Studies in Religion* 12.2 (1996), 117.

40. Ibid., 117. For a beautiful theoretical treatment of the relationships between the liberal state, rights movements, identity claims, and gender and sex, see Wendy Brown, *States of Injury: Power and Freedom in Late Modernity* (Princeton: Princeton UP, 1995).

41. Jeffrey Weeks, *Against Nature: Essays on History, Sexuality, and Identity* (London: Rivers Oram P, 1969) 85.

42. Ibid., 75.

43. Ibid., 78.

44. Ibid., 78.

45. There is an odd resonance between this passage in Weeks and Andrew Sullivan's claim for American exceptionalism with regard to the political viability of "homosexual freedom." Sullivan: "And this growth of homosexual freedom has continually had its vanguard in the United States, despite its tradition of fundamentalist Christianity, despite its capitalist system, despite its allegedly oppressive influence in world culture. It is even possible that the creation of this homosexual space occurred—paradoxically—by a fruitful clash with a hostile, dominant culture, a class that was given oxygen by the space and the liberties and the excesses that the New World provided" (76). The underlying assumption here is not only that homosexual experience is better in the United States than anywhere else, but also that the United States leads the rest of the world on an inexorable march to liberation, while evidence indicates that homosexual experience takes very different forms in other countries, and that expressions of the desire and need for increased safety, freedom, and cultural, political, and economic resources differ accordingly. Not all such movements around the world aspire to function, or will eventually, inevitably function, like the gay and lesbian movement in the United States. But yes,

the creation of "homosexual space" here is indeed related to the specific concept of liberty that spirited European colonial settlers to acquire the "New World." The gay rights movement in this country comes directly out of the convergence of the features listed by Sullivan, not despite them.

46. Weeks, 78.

47. By using the term "nonidentified queers," I mean to refer to a huge group with great internal variety—people who have sex with people of the same sex, but who do not identify as gay or lesbian or even as homosexual. Inside and outside of the United States, this is quite common. Inside the United States, the literature is voluminous that suggests that people who face multiple sources of oppression do not think of homophobia as the primary source, and do not endorse ranking oppressions in the way articulated by Weeks. For just a few classic statements of this case, see Combahee River Collective's "A Black Feminist Statement" of April 1977, in Zillah R. Eisenstein, ed., *Capitalist Patriarchy and the Case for Socialist Feminism* (New York: Monthly Review P, 1979), 362–372; Cherríe Moraga, *Loving in the War Years* (Boston: South End P, 1983); and Barbara Smith, ed., *Home Girls: A Black Feminist Anthology* (New York: Kitchen Table: Women of Color P, 1983) and *The Truth That Never Hurts: Writings on Race, Gender, and Freedom* (New Brunswick: Rutgers UP, 1998); and Gloria T. Hull, Patricia Bell Scott, and Barbara Smith, eds., *All the Women are White, All the Blacks are Men, But Some of Us are Brave* (Old Westbury, NY: Feminist P, 1982). There are far too many other examples to list them here.

48. The fuller passage reads: "In this country, lesbianism is a poverty—as is being brown, as is being a woman, as is being just plain poor. The danger lies in ranking the oppressions. The danger lies in failing to acknowledge the specificity of the oppression" (Moraga, 52).

49. Peñaloza, 15.

50. Mary Poovey, "The Abortion Question and the Death of Man," *Feminists Theorize the Political,* eds. Judith Butler and Joan W. Scott (New York: Routledge, 1992) 250.

51. Peñaloza, 26–27.

52. Fugate quoted in Peñaloza, 22.

53. Indeed, Peñaloza goes on to point out that "This categorization reduces gay and lesbian culture to sexuality, even as it smoothes over existing variation in activities, interests, and opinions among gay men and lesbians" (Ibid., 22).

54. Anne Phillips, *Engendering Democracy* (University Park Place: Pennsylvania State UP, 1991) 5.

55. Joyce Appleby, *Liberalism and Republicanism in the Historical Imagination* (Cambridge: Harvard UP, 1992) 29.

56. Appleby points to a division of labor according to which

> Dependency, lack of ambition, attachment to place and person—these qualities were stripped from the masculine carrier of inalienable rights and conferred upon women. In this ideological division of labor women became the exemplifiers of the personal and intimate, maintainers of family cohesion, and repositories of romantic fantasies about the past. This allowed the unsentimental, self-improving restlessly ambitious, free and independent man to hold sway as a universal hero. Without women to accept what was denied in men, the assertion of a uniform human nature could not have been maintained. (Appleby, 29)

This division of labor echoes the division of labor described by D'Emilio when he notes that the modern investment in the family as the site of affective bonds produces the modern version of the demonization of homosexuals. Without gays to serve as a site of projection for the deterioration of the family, the assertion of the natural basis and universal character of the family could not be maintained.

57. Williams, 25.

58. Miranda Joseph, "The Performance of Production and Consumption," *Social Text* 54 (1998), 25–61.

59. Evans, 5.

CHAPTER 1

1. Grant Lukenbill, *Untold Millions: Positioning Your Business for the Gay and Lesbian Consumer Revolution* (New York: HarperCollins, 1995) 22.

2. Stuart Elliott, "A Market That's Educated, Affluent, and Homosexual," *New York Times* 27 Sept. 1992, D27.

3. Philip H. Dougherty, "Homosexual Magazines in Bids," *New York Times* 17 July 1976, 55.

4. Robert Strand, "S.F. Gays Carry Heavy Clout in Politics, Finance," *LA Times* 18 Dec. 1977, 3.

5. Ibid.

6. Ibid.

7. Paul Lorch, Editorial, *Bay Area Reporter* 17 Feb. 1977, 8.

8. Ibid.

9. Ibid.

10. Those resorts are in Massachusetts, Florida, northern California, and New York, respectively.

11. Diane Weathers et al., "Where the Boys Are," *Newsweek* 30 July 1979, 63.

12. In addition to the pieces mentioned, *Business Week* opened the subject of a gay and lesbian niche market in 1979 with "Gays: A Major Force in the Marketplace," *Business Week* 3 Sept. 1979: 118–120.

13. Karen Stabiner, "Tapping the Homosexual Market," *New York Times Magazine* 2 May 1982, 34+.

14. Brad Edmondson, "Gays Make Tracks," *American Demographics* Nov. 1987, 22.

15. Ibid.

16. Richard V. Weekes, "Gay Dollars," *American Demographics* Oct. 1989, 48.

17. Cyndee Miller, "Mainstream Marketers Decide the Time is Right to Target Gays," *Marketing News* 26 (1992), 8.

18. Joan E. Rigdon, "Overcoming a Deep-Rooted Reluctance, More Firms Advertise to Gay Community," *Wall Street Journal* 18 July 1991, B1-B2; Joe Schwartz, "Gay Consumers Come Out Spending," *American Demographics* April 1992, 10–11; "Special Report: Marketing to Gays and Lesbians," *Advertising Age* 18 Jan. 1993, 29–37; David J. Jefferson, "Businesses Offering Products for Gays Are Thriving: Rise in Activism and Public Acceptance of Lifestyles Increases Demand," *Wall Street Journal* 22 April 1993, B2; Tammerlin Drummond, "Not in Kansas Anymore: With Other Tourists Shying Away, Miami Beach Woos the Nation's $17 Billion Gay and Lesbian Travel Market," *Time* 25 Sept. 1995, 54–56.

19. "Special Report: Marketing to Gays and Lesbians," 29–37; Hazel Kahan and David Mulryan, "Out of the Closet," *American Demographics* May 1995, 40–46.

20. Daniel Wardlow, ed., *Gays, Lesbians, and Consumer Behavior: Theory, Practice, and Research Issues in Marketing* (New York: Haworth P, 1996). Two years later Steven M. Kates authored *Twenty Million New Consumers! Understanding Gay Men's Consumer Behavior* (New York: Haworth P, 1998). This book is largely relevant to the questions entertained here, though the book is about the situation in Canada.

21. Founded in 1990, the Greater Boston Business Council's mission was: "to foster and promote the vitality and productivity of the gay and lesbian business and professional community" and "to promote a positive image of the diversity of lesbian and gay citizens and to strengthen our position in society, by providing opportunities and an environment for the personal, professional and social growth of our members and by networking with other gay and lesbian professional organizations, both locally and nationally." (*GBBC Business Counselor* Nov. 1997, 31). The emergence of specialized gay professional groups is a function of the economic segmentation that allows for a gay and lesbian niche market in the first place; such groups simultaneously populate the niche and seek to profit from it. For example, the newsletter of an association of therapists ran an article called "Targeting a Neglected Group: How to Attract A Wealthy, Under-Served Pro-Therapy Market." (*What's Working,* quoted in "Queers: The New Therapy Market Niche?" *In the Family* April 1999, 5.) The article spoke of a "marketing opportunity" for therapists: "Name a group of prosperous, well-educated Americans who constitute 3% to 10% of the U.S. population and have an average income more than twice that of the average American . . . Asian Americans? Good guess, but no. The answer is the gay and lesbian communities . . . and they have plenty of therapeutic issues."

22. Some of these works have already been cited, but I list them again here for full effect: Jean D. Albright, "Gays, Lesbians and Consumer Behavior," *Clout! Business Report* Sept. 1996, 8. Ronald Aslop, "Cracking the Gay Market Code: How Marketers Plant Subtle Symbols in Ads," *Wall Street Journal* 29 June 1999, Eastern Edition: B1+. Bruce Bawer, "Truth in Advertising," *Advocate* 11 July 1995, 80. *CLAGS News: The Center for Lesbian and Gay Studies, The Graduate School and University Center of the City University of New York* 4.2 (1994). Riccardo Davis, "Sky's the Limit for Tour Operators," *Advertising Age* 18 Jan. 1993, 36–37. Tammerlin Drummond, "Not in Kansas Anymore: With Other Tourists Shying Away, Miami Beach Woos the Nation's $17 Billion Gay and Lesbian Travel Market," *Time* 25 Sept. 1995, 54–56. Georgia Dullea, "With Varying Degrees of Openness, More Companies Lure Gay Dollars," *New York Times* 2 March 1992, D9. David W. Dunlap, "Gay Parents Ease into Suburbia: For the First Generation, Car Pools and Soccer Games," *New York Times* 16 May 1996, C1+. Brad Edmondson, "Gays Make Tracks," *American Demographics* Nov. 1987, 22. Stuart Elliott, "Advertising: For Gay Consumers, Sales Pitches Are Getting More Personal," *New York Times*

24 June 1994, D18. Steve Friess, "Target Practice: Advertising to Gays and Lesbians," *Advocate* 16 April 1996, 32–35. John Gallagher, "Ikea's Gay Gamble: Why Did a National Home-Furnishings Chain Build a Television Ad Around a Gay Couple?" *Advocate* 3 May 1994, 24–27. "Gays Celebrate and Business Tunes In," *Fortune* 27 June 1994, 14. James Hannaham, "Feeding the Gay Market," *OUT* Nov. 1996, 117+. Robin Hardy, "Donald Moffett: Advertprop: Advertising for the Homo Life," *Advocate* 27 Feb. 1990, 50–51. Wayne Hoffman, "The 'Gay 90s': New Era or Passing Fad?" *Bay Windows* (Boston) 21 Sept. 1995, 3–4. Steven A. Holmes, "Sitting Pretty: Is This What Women Want?" *New York Times* 15 Dec. 1996, D1. David J. Jefferson, "Businesses Offering Products for Gays Are Thriving: Rise in Activism and Public Acceptance of Lifestyles Increases Demand," *Wall Street Journal* 22 April 1993, B2. Bradley Johnson, "The Gay Quandary: Advertising's Most Elusive, Yet Lucrative, Target Market Proves Difficult to Measure," *Advertising Age* 18 Jan. 1993, 29–35. Hazel Kahan and David Mulryan, "Out of the Closet," *American Demographics* May 1995, 40–46. Laura Mansnerus, "Under Many Banners: Varied Voices in Gay Life Not Always in Chorus," *New York Times* 26 June 1994, D7. Peg Masterson, "Agency Notes Rise of Singles Market," *Advertising Age* 9 Aug. 1993, 17. Edwin McDowell, "Gay Cruises Draw Hostility in the Caribbean," *New York Times* 10 May 1998, travel section, 3. Cyndee Miller, "Mainstream Marketers Decide the time is Right to Target Gays," *Marketing News* 26 (1992), 8, 15. Josh Oppenheimer, "Queer Conceptions: Class, Sexuality, and Activism," *Perspective* March 1996, 11–12. Lisa M. Pottie, "Cross-Border Shopping and Niche Marketing: Academic Economics and Gay Studies," *College Literature* 24.1 (1997), 183–193. Joan E. Rigdon, "Overcoming a Deep-Rooted Reluctance, More Firms Advertise to Gay Community," *Wall Street Journal* 18 July 1991, B1-B2. Trudy Ring, "Beer Companies Target Gay Market," *Clout! Business Report* June 1996, 6. Joe Schwartz, "Gay Consumers Come Out Spending," *American Demographics* April 1992, 10–11. Karen Schwartz, "In Fits and Starts, Travel Industry Wakes up to Big Gay Market," *Bay Windows* (Boston) 26 Feb.–4 March 1998, 1. Cathy Seabaugh, "Friendly Skies Open for United Gays, Lesbians," *Clout! Business Report* June 1996, 16–17. Katherine E. Sender, "Selling Sexual Subjectivities: Audience Responses to Gay Window Advertising," *Critical Studies in Mass Communication* 16 (1999), 172–196. Mark Thompson, "Small Business Owners Experiencing a Natural Progression of Liberated Consciousness," *Advocate* 16 June 1976, 12–13. "Two Companies Aim at the Gay Market," *New*

York Times 13 April 1995, D8. "We Don't Buy It," *Advocate* 9 Oct. 1990, 86. Nancy Coltun Webster, "Playing to Gay Segments Opens Doors to Markets," *Advertising Age* 30 April 1994, S-6. Richard V. Weekes, "Gay Dollars: Houston's Montrose District is an Affluent, Overlooked Market—Gay Men and Women," *American Demographics* Oct. 1989, 45–48. Bill Wyman, "Selling Out: Atlantic Records' New Target Market: Gay Music Fans," *Rolling Stone* 16 Nov. 1995, 40. "The Voice of the Gay and Lesbian Community: *Clout! Business Report,*" <http://www.suba.com/~outlines/clouttmp.html> 28 April 1997. Steve Heimoff, "Gay Wine Marketing Slowly Follows Beer and Spirits' Lead: In Two Years Since the *Monthly* First Explored the Issue, Targeting Wine-Drinking Gays Just Barely Begins to Take Off," *Wine Business Monthly* March 1996, <http://smartwine.com/wbm/1996/9603/bm039603.html>.

"Family value: $102K: Mulryan/ Nash Designs Advertising and Marketing Strategies Targeted to Gay and Lesbian Consumers," advertisement, *Advertising Age,* 30 May 1994, S-6.

23. *Quotient* 1.1 (Dec. 1994).
24. Per Larson, "Gay Money," *Victory!* 15 (Jan./Feb. 1996), 12–14.
25. *Clout! Business Report* was a Chicago-based publication "For Gay, Lesbian, and Supportive Business Owners, Senior Executives, Professionals & Entrepreneurs," published by Lambda Publications, publishers of *Outlines, Nightlines, OUT Resource Guide,* and *BLACKlines.* Another resource with an entrepreneurial angle is Sue Levin, *In the Pink: The Making of Successful Gay- and Lesbian-Owned Businesses* (New York: Haworth P, 1999).
26. These, and the following, figures and studies are presented and reviewed in Amy Gluckman and Betsy Reed, "Lost in the Gay Marketing Moment: Leaving Diversity in the Dust," *Dollars and Sense* Nov.-Dec. 1993, 16+. They are reviewed again by Lee Badgett in a report that offers more accurate demographic data: M. V. Lee Badgett, *Income Inflation: The Myth of Affluence Among Gay, Lesbian, and Bisexual Americans* (New York: NGLTF Policy Institute, 1998).
27. Gluckman and Reed.
28. Overlooked Opinions' official reaction to allegations that they had unwittingly helped the radical right's case was terse: "It's not our fault; it's poor planning on behalf of the gay and lesbian nonprofit groups that have let the radical right set the agenda" (Lukenbill, 67).
29. Sean Strub is a leading gay marketer who has publicized the inaccuracies and misleading implications of this market research. Grant Lukenbill and

Stuart Elliott have also publicly rejected these data in favor of those presented by the Yankelovich Partners study of 1993.

30. These data from the Yankelovich study are graphed in Badgett, 12–13. There has been a range of analyses of income figures relating to the disparity between straight and gay earnings. Relevant factors include the effects of employment discrimination and the degree to which certain occupations require heterosexuality or "passing" behavior.

31. Kahan and Mulryan, 40.

32. Ewen, *Captains of Consciousness,* 36.

33. Nicola Field, "Over the Rainbow: Money, Class, and Homophobia," *The Material Queer: A LesBiGay Cultural Studies Reader,* ed. Donald Morton (Boulder: Westview P, 1996) 348.

34. Ewen, 85.

35. "Gay Consumers Come Out Spending," 10.

36. Beth Daley, "Vendors Reach Out to Gay Customers," *Boston Globe* 24 Nov. 1997, B1. Overlooked Opinions was also cited in *Genre* magazine's website in 1997, along with claims that gay men "demonstrate a pronounced brand loyalty." <http://www.genremagazine.com/adinfo.htm.>

37. Critical approaches to the gay and lesbian niche market called its very existence into question, along with its political causes and effects: C. Bard Cole, "'Gay Market' A Scam, According to Essay by Former Editor of Failed National Magazine," *Riotboy* 30 May 1997; and Phil Gochenour, "Virtually Queer: The Politics of the Gay Market" <http://www.pugzine.com/editol/html> 31 March 1997.

38. Quoted in Elliott, "A Market That's Educated, Affluent and Homosexual."

39. Quoted in Miller, 8.

40. Lukenbill, 182.

41. Ibid.

42. Rigdon, B1-B2.

43. "Business Reports," *American Demographics* Nov. 1987.

44. Gay Biz, "Pride Directory Online, 1996." <http://www.gaybiz.com/pride/welcom.html.>

45. David J. Jefferson, "Businesses Offering Products for Gays Are Thriving: Rise in Activism and Public Acceptance of Lifestyles Increases Demand," *Wall Street Journal* 22 April 1993, B2.

46. Quoted in ibid.

47. Evans, 7.

48. Alison Wonderland, "Shocking Gray, Part 2," *Best Plus Rude Girl 1–14,* 16.

49. Ibid.

50. Stuart Elliott as quoted in Steve Freiss, "Target Practice: Advertising to Gays and Lesbians," *Advocate* 16 April 1996, 32–35.

51. "New Internet Study Offers Insights About Gay Community Beliefs and Habits," Press Release (Westport, CT: Greenfield Online, 14 Oct. 1998) 1.

52. Frank Rich, "The Gay Decades," *Esquire* Nov. 1987, 87–99, quoted in David Mendelsohn, "When Did Gays Get So Straight?: How Queer Culture Lost its Edge," *New York* 30 Sept. 1996, 26.

53. Mendelsohn, 27.

54. Ibid., 31.

55. Lukenbill, 37.

56. Kahan and Mulryan, 46.

57. Weekes, 46.

58. Kahan and Mulryan, 46.

59. Lukenbill, 83.

60. Mark Seltzer, *Bodies and Machines* (New York: Routledge, 1992) 49.

61. Lukenbill, 37.

62. Ibid., 21.

63. Diane Anderson, "Gay Market—Dyke Dollars," *Girlfriends* July/Aug. 1996, 24+.

64. North East Regional Pride Conference, hosted by Jersey Pride, Inc., Spring 1997.

65. Michael J. Smith, *Colorful People and Places: A Resource Guide for Third World Lesbians and Gay Men . . . and for White People Who Share Their Interests* (San Francisco: Quarterly P, 1983) 12–13.

66. Ibid., 12.

67. *This Bridge Called My Back; All the Women Are White, All the Blacks Are Men, But Some of Us Are Brave;* and *Home Girls,* as mentioned above, are just a few of the publications in which women of color explored issues of racism in the women's movement and the lesbian movement.

68. National Gay and Lesbian Task Force Policy Roundtable, 1998.

69. The full passage reads:

> Today in almost every Gay/Lesbian community in the United States there are public places where people of color routinely face discrimination when trying to enter. They may be denied admission outright without excuse; they may be asked to produce three or four (or seven or eight) pieces of identification ("carding"); they

may be told that they are dressed improperly; or they may be served watered liquor or not served at all. This behavior is the Gay/Lesbian community's best-kept—and most shameful—secret. Only in a very few instances has it been publicly challenged.

A relatively new wrinkle in this practice has been the attempt to skirt civil rights legislation by having a club "go private." Local laws are researched and racist bar owners construct a web of admission rules and "membership" so they may deny entry to people of color while remaining as public a facility as possible:

"In Charleston there's only one place you can go—the streetcar. There are two other discos, but they're 'private.' When I first came to town we called ahead and got our name on the guest list (like you're supposed to), but when we arrived and they got a look at us, they couldn't seem to find a 'record' of the reservation. I learned quickly that you're more admissible if you're accompanied by White people; or if you're dressed right; or if you come along and 'act right.'—Or if you know the right person on the inside. But if you show up with brothers (or sisters) forget it! I was finally able to get a membership card to one place (after paying a $15 fee and waiting two weeks while they 'checked' my application), but on my second night there, the manager called me over and told me that he'd 'watched' me the night before and that I hadn't spent enough money—and would I please return the card. (At least I got my $15 back.) Later, a White friend told me that Whites are never 'clocked' like that."—Freddie; Charleston, South Carolina; 1983. (Michael J. Smith, 12–13)

70. Ibid.
71. Field, 348.
72. Weekes, 45–48; Anderson, 24+. This latter article actually draws attention to the fact that "dyke dollars" are less valuable than their male counterparts, because lesbians have more in common with all women economically than they do with gay men. To the extent that the mention of "gay dollars" implies gay men and women, it erases the real economic disparity between men and women as social groups.
73. Here are two examples of this formula, both of which utilize language similar to that found in the gay and lesbian context: "we can rebuild the black community by recycling our precious black dollars" (National Buy

Black Campaign website <http://www.successmarketplace.com/shops/ nbbc/>); "In most communities the dollar turns over six to eight times. Unfortunately, one dollar turns over less than one time in the African community" (The Buy Black Network website <http://www.ibuyblack. com/buyblack.htm>).

74. A similar question arises in consideration of socially responsible investing. I look more closely at that in Chapter 4.

75. Segregated economies rely on local businesses and are therefore increasingly harder to sustain in the face of the growth of chain retailing. They are also hard to sustain in the face of integration. For an interesting discussion of the ways in which integration of the mainstream insurance industry hurt a historically African American town by putting local black-owned insurance companies out of business, see Russ Rymer's *American Beach: A Saga of Race, Wealth, and Memory* (New York: HarperCollins, 1998).

76. This is complicated. The idea of enterprise zones, for example, presumes that identity dollars do stay inside of those zones. The truth is that this is differently true in different situations. Money spent on services rendered by local small-scale vendors is much more likely to stay inside the zone than money spent on commodities of any kind, but particularly multinational-brand commodities. Enterprise zones were imagined, by folks like Jack Kemp, as a solution to the obviously systematic impoverishment of historically African American neighborhoods by underinvestment. But the same logic is at work in the injunction to "Buy Black," a strategy designed to pump money into the same neighborhoods. The trouble is that the growth of the African American middle class does not automatically redress the system that disadvantages African Americans economically. The same would be true of gay men and lesbians if that social group were subject to systematic economic disadvantage. Whether gay men and lesbians are systematically disadvantaged is a matter of debate, but even if homophobia constrains employment and advancement opportunities, I would argue that racism is the basis for more regular and much larger-scale economic effects. For treatments of the historical relationship between African American identity and economic practice, see John Sibley Butler, *Entrepreneurship and Self-Help Among Black Americans: A Reconsideration of Race and Economics* (Albany: State U of New York P, 1991); Abram Harris, *Race, Radicalism and Reform,* ed. William Darity, Jr. (New Brunswick: Transaction Publishers, 1989); Manning Marable, *How Capitalism Under-*

developed Black America: Problems in Race, Political Economy and Society (Boston: South End P, 1983); August Meier, *Negro Thought in America, 1880–1915* (Ann Arbor: U of Michigan P, 1966).

77. Eloise Salholz et al., "The Future of Gay America," *Newsweek* 12 March 1990, 24.

78. Thomas Frank, "Why Can't Johnny Dissent," *Commodify Your Dissent,* eds. Thomas Frank and Matt Weiland (New York: Norton, 1997) 34. I thank Jennifer McTiernan for drawing my attention to this paradox.

79. David Serlin quoted in "Culture Wars," *Gay Community News* Spring 1997, 5.

CHAPTER 2

1. Rodger Streitmatter, *Unspeakable: The Rise of the Gay and Lesbian Press in America* (Boston: Faber and Faber, 1995) 52.

2. Some of the first homosexually identified people to gather together for expressly social and political reasons called their organizations "homophile." This word stood as the word for what might now be called "gay" (literally, "gay-friendly") for decades—probably from the establishment of the Society for Human Rights in 1924 through the 1950s and even into the 1960s.

3. *ONE* and body-building publications (to be discussed below) alike had fought in court for the right to distribute through the U.S. mails. From 1954 to 1958, courts entertained this question; finally, on appeal to the Supreme Court, *ONE* magazine defeated an obscenity charge leveled by the U.S. Postal Service, a victory that opened the way for the use of the mail by gay publications. *ONE* published stories, poems, and essays about, and usually by, homosexual men.

4. There was of course, much medical literature and some legal literature about homosexuality from the end of the nineteenth century onward, but while such literature may have helped disseminate concepts and vocabulary that gay men and lesbians could use to identify themselves and each other—and therefore may have contributed affirmatively to the formation of early gay and lesbian communities—such material was of course written in the language, and in the interests, of homophobic people and heterosexist institutions. With few exceptions, most literature of a more "positive" sort was suppressed, as with Radclyffe Hall's *Well of Loneliness,* published in 1928.

5. Streitmatter, 24.

6. Ibid., xiii.

7. Even referring to the press in the singular is problematic, implying as it does both unity of production and unity of consumption. It would be more accurate to speak of "presses," but I use the singular purposely to refer to the dominant strain among gay and lesbian publications. Of course there are exceptions—publications that run on little money, publications that are not produced or read by a powerful, homogeneous racial group (here, white) or a powerful, homogeneous gender group (here, men)—and they are clearly marked as exceptional here. Likewise, I modify the word press with "gay" to highlight male domination in the field; where I refer to the plurality that includes both centralized and more marginal publications, I use "gay and lesbian."

8. Examples include *Venus* and *SBC* (the "Afrocentric Homosexual Publication"), which target the African American gay and lesbian community; *QV Magazine*, the Latino men's journal that describes itself as the "first national magazine to address the needs of English-speaking gay Latinos"; and *Trikone Magazine* for lesbian, gay, and bisexual South Asians, which is produced by the nonprofit organization Trikone.

9. Established in Sept. 1967 as a newspaper called the *Los Angeles Advocate,* the *Advocate* is the oldest continuing gay periodical. As of this writing, *OUT* magazine claims a larger readership than that of the *Advocate,* but because this is a recent shift, and because of the unique historical place of the *Advocate,* I consider the *Advocate* the more significant historical publication. In June 1999, *OUT* claimed a circulation of 118,000 nationally.

10. At the 1998 Outwrite conference, Marla Erlien of *Gay Community News* reported that Henry Scott of *OUT* had formed focus groups of readers in which questions of gender were explored. Testing a magazine with 40 percent lesbian content, Scott found that women in focus groups read both men's and women's material, but that men didn't remember any lesbian content, presumably because they either read and forgot it or didn't read it. When Sarah Pettit was appointed editor in chief of *OUT,* in 1994, it seemed that this might establish a balanced gender focus in the magazine, but it didn't. She left the magazine in 1997.

11. Accordingly, *GCN* has been subjected to derisive charges of "political correctness" even before that term had gained the currency it has had in the 1990s.

12. This claim is obviously very impressionistic, but it is based on years of reading such publications and noting that letters to the editors are practically

exclusively written by women. It is also based on the difficulty of finding a review by a man of any lesbian periodical.

13. Readers interested in a truly thorough and fascinating history of the gay and lesbian press are encouraged to look at Rodger Streitmatter's *Unspeakable: The Rise of the Gay and Lesbian Press in America*. Also interesting is Jim Kepner's *Rough News, Daring Views: 1950's Pioneer Gay Press Journalism* (New York: Haworth, 1998).

14. Neil Miller, *Out of the Past: Gay and Lesbian History from 1869 to Present* (New York: Random House, 1995).

15. Miller, 419; Miller doesn't mention *Vice Versa*. Also Streitmatter, 38.

16. Streitmatter, 38.

17. In fact, this was still an issue in the 1990s, although easier access to the AP wire changes the nature of the problem.

18. Robert C. Doty, "Growth of Overt Homosexuality in City Provokes Wide Concern," *New York Times* 17 Dec. 1963, City Edition: A1+.

19. Ibid., A1.

20. Ibid.

21. Miller, 419.

22. Streitmatter, 61.

23. Ibid., 60.

24. Doty, A1.

25. Carol A. B. Warren, *Identity and Community in the Gay World* (New York: John Wiley and Sons, 1974) 118–119. Warren makes reference to the work of Evelyn Hooker, whose 1960s sociological studies of the gay community influenced Warren's work in the 1970s. For relevant work by Hooker, see "Male Homosexuality," *Taboo Topics,* ed. Norman Farberow (New York: Atherton Press, 1963) 44–55; "Male Homosexuals and Their 'Worlds,'" *Sexual Inversion,* ed. Judd Marmor (New York: Basic Books, 1965) 83–105; "The Homosexual Community," *Sexual Deviance,* eds. John H. Gagnon and William Simon (New York: Harper and Row, 1967) 167–184. Gagnon and Simon's other work may also be of interest.

26. The national English fetish in this country is manifest today in numerous local battles over English as the official language, denigration of alternatives to Standard Received English in the private sphere, and countless other ways in which the English language is used to mark the difference of U.S. national identity from Other national identities, as well as its superiority.

27. Warren, 119. Stephen O. Murray uses the term "de-assimilation" in his *American Gay* (Chicago: U of Chicago P, 1996).

28. Warren, 119.
29. Streitmatter, 72. Interestingly, *Vector* was issued by an organization called the Society for Individual Rights, itself established in 1964, which was, as its name suggests, an early gay rights organization. I point this out to reinforce the point that the rise of the press, the growth of a gay market, and the development of a movement based not only on rights but specifically on the rights of the individual are intimately linked.
30. Michael Bronski, "How Sweet (and Sticky) It Was," *Flesh and the Word 2: An Anthology of Erotic Writing,* ed. John Preston (New York: Penguin, 1993) 83.
31. I have not been able to find much in the way of published histories of gay and women's bookstores, but this history, unpublished though it is, is of central relevance to understanding the relationship between a gay niche market and the gay and lesbian movement. Likewise, gay and lesbian book publishing is a relevant topic I have left largely untreated here.
32. *Lesbian Connection* April 1977, 4.
33. Louie Crew, "Protest and Community: Gay Male Journalism Now," *Margins* 20 (1975), 14.
34. Ibid., 15.
35. Ibid.
36. Miller, 419.
37. As quoted in Streitmatter, 257–258. For a more elaborate and more horrifying account of this episode, see Streitmatter, 251–259.
38. Ibid., 255–256.
39. Mark Thompson, "RFD: A Magazine from the Heartland," *Advocate* 7 Jan. 1982, 21.
40. Ibid., 23.
41. Ibid., 21
42. For an interesting and comprehensive analysis of this moment, see Jane Gallop's *Around Nineteen Eighty-One* (New York: Routledge, 1991). *This Bridge Called My Back,* edited by Cherríe Moraga and Gloria Anzaldúa, was originally published in 1981 by the now-defunct Persephone Press, and it has been reprinted by Kitchen Table: Women of Color Press.
43. For a full-scale presentation of his philosophy of outing, see Michelangelo Signorile's *Queer in America: Sex, the Media, and the Closets of Power* (New York: Random House, 1993).
44. *1998 Gay Press Report* (New York: Mulryan/Nash, 1998) 10. This and the following statistics come from the Mulryan/Nash report.

45. Ibid., 6.

46. The first known gay advocacy organization in the United States was the Society for Human Rights, founded in Chicago in 1924 by Henry Gerber. The nine members wrote a charter announcing their goal to protect the rights of homosexuals "as guaranteed them by the Declaration of Independence." The Society also published a journal called *Friendship and Freedom;* it lasted less than a year, disbanding under legal pressure.

47. For a treatment of the development of gay urban communities, see George Chauncey, *Gay New York* (New York: Basic Books, 1994) and Michael Bronski, *The Pleasure Principle: Sex, Backlash, and the Struggle for Gay Freedom* (New York: St. Martin's, 1998). Also very helpful in understanding the relationship between gay and lesbian life and social space is the work of Lawrence Knopp, as well as two anthologies: Gordon Brent Ingram, Anne-Marie Bouthillette, and Yolanda Retter, eds., *Queers in Space: Communities/Public Places/Sites of Resistance* (Seattle: Bay P, 1997) and David Bell and Gill Valentine, eds., *Mapping Desire: Geographies of Sexualities* (London: Routledge, 1995). The latter has a wonderfully rich and extensive bibliography.

48. Streitmatter, 65.

49. Ibid., 77.

50. Miller, 420.

51. Scott Anderson, "The Gay Press Proliferates—And So Do Its Problems," *The Advocate* 13 Dec. 1979, 19–20.

52. Ibid.

53. Ibid.

54. "Gay Press Looks to Madison Ave.," *New York Times* 17 Dec. 1990, D11.

55. Ibid.

56. Ibid.

57. Ibid.

58. Willard Spiegelman, "The Progress of a Genre: Gay Journalism and Its Audience," *Salmagundi* 58/59 (1982), 320.

59. Ibid.

60. Ibid., 323.

61. Miller, 420.

62. Ibid.

63. Paul Lorch, Editorial, *Bay Area Reporter* 17 Feb. 1977, 8.

64. Paul Lorch, Editorial, "Final Thoughts on the Gay Press," *Bay Area Reporter* 17 March 1977, 10.

65. Ibid.

66. Philip H. Dougherty, "Homosexual Magazines in Bids," *New York Times* 17 July 1976, 55.

67. Ibid.

68. Ibid.

69. Scott Anderson, "The Gay Press," 19–20.

70. Ibid., 20.

71. Ibid.

72. *HX for Her* was basically a bar guide that announced itself as "The Totally Biased Politically Incorrect Party Paper for Lesbians."

73. James Darsey, "From 'Gay is Good' to the Scourge of AIDS: The Evolution of Gay Liberation Rhetoric, 1977–1990," *Communication Studies* 42.1 (Spring 1991), 43–66.

74. Miller, 419; Miller does note *GCN* as the exception.

75. Rather than elaborate on this here, I point the reader to the chapter on boycotts, which details some evidence for the claim that women were excluded from gay political life, in the organizing around Anita Bryant. That chapter presents a small fraction of such evidence.

76. Streitmatter, 21.

77. Spiegelman, 308.

78. Karla Jay, "A Look at Lesbian Magazines," *Margins* 23 (1975), 19.

79. Ibid.

80. For a good account of this radical feminist group, active in the early 1970s, see Karla Jay, *Tales of the Lavender Menace: A Memoir of Liberation* (New York: Basic Books, 1999).

81. Jackie St. Joan, "A Survey of Lesbian Publications," *Our Right to Love: A Lesbian Resource Book,* ed. Ginny Vida (New York: Touchstone Books, 1978) 246.

82. Ibid., 247.

83. Ibid.

84. Ibid., 246.

85. Shane Allison, "More Diversity," Letter, *XY* Feb. 1995, 6.

86. Tracy D. Morgan, "Pages of Whiteness: Race, Physique Magazines, and the Emergence of Public Gay Culture," *Queer Studies: A Lesbian, Gay, Bisexual, and Transgender Anthology,* eds. Brett Beemyn and Mickey Eliason (New York: New York UP, 1996) 282–283.

87. Alasdair Foster, *Behold the Man* (Edinburgh: Stills Gallery, 1988) 28.

88. Streitmatter, xi.

89. Photographs in "Greek" magazines contained such props as columns, togas, and other paraphernalia associated with Classical Greece.

All-American magazines used contemporary U.S. body-building imagery and poses.

90. Morgan, 286.
91. Ibid., 290.
92. Ibid., 291.
93. Ibid., 288.
94. Ibid., 289.
95. For a study of the historical relationship between gender, race, and citizenship in the United States, see Dana D. Nelson, *National Manhood: Citizenship and the Imagined Fraternity of White Men* (Durham: Duke UP, 1998).
96. Streitmatter, 49–50.
97. Jill Johnston, *Lesbian Nation: The Feminist Solution* (New York: Simon and Schuster, 1973). Benedict Anderson, *Imagined Communities: Reflections on the Origin and Spread of Nationalism,* revised edition (London: Verso, 1991).
98. Benedict Anderson, 6.
99. "It is always a mistake to treat languages in the way that certain ideologues treat them—as emblems of nation-ness, like flags, costumes, folkdances, and the rest. Much the most important thing about language is its capacity for generating imagined communities, building in effect *particular solidarities*" (Ibid., 133).
100. Streitmatter, 7.
101. Benedict Anderson, 61.
102. Ibid., 62.
103. Ibid., 75.
104. Ibid., 76.
105. Ibid., 80–81.
106. Ibid., 7.
107. Ibid., 135.
108. In his study "From 'Gay is Good' to the Scourge of AIDS: The Evolution of Gay Liberation Rhetoric; 1977–1990," James Darsey finds "unity" to be the most commonly invoked value. Interestingly, his explanation for the frequency of the invocation of unity bears striking similarities to the argument offered here:

> [U]nity is as difficult for the gay rights movement as it is for any movement where the constituency is a national rather than a regional or local community. Issues that may be defined geographi-

cally, a local ordinance for instance, must be ideologically transformed into a common cause. It is a problem that has plagued social movements in America from the Revolution onward. Gay
liberation in the United States has an advantage here in that it historically has been the political facet of a subcultural milieu, and
that subculture has been defined nationally. It is a largely urban
subculture in which there are certain centers recognized as the
province of gay people wherever they live. Gays in Idaho and gays
in Kentucky may share, as a part of their common cultural currency, a knowledge of bars in Greenwich Village or a repertoire of
experiences from "the Castro." Newspapers in the gay community
encourage this identification. . . . Gay publications, though identified with their places of origin, often have a national circulation
and provide national and international coverage. This kind of trans-
geographical consciousness encourages references to the gay community as a national phenomenon and a corresponding mentality in
which any threat is a threat to the whole. (48)

109. Quoted in Spiegelman, 309.
110. Ibid.
111. John Quincy Adams, quoted in Spiegelman, 324.
112. Spiegelman, 312.
113. Harry Britt in *Gay Sunshine* 8 March 1978, quoted in Spiegelman, 312.
114. All quotations in this section come from the panel discussion "State of the
National Queer Press" at the Boston Outwrite Conference in 1998, taped
by Cambridge Transcriptions.
115. Neil Miller, 420.
116. Streitmatter interview with activist Franklin Kameny, 24 Jan. 1993,
quoted in Streitmatter, 79.
117. Sean Strub, "The Growth of the Gay and Lesbian Market," *A Queer
World: The Center for Lesbian and Gay Studies Reader,* ed. Martin Duberman (New York: New York UP, 1997) 516.
118. *OUT* readers sometimes complained about the magazine's implicit political values, and *OUT* printed such letters, but the magazine did not seem
to adjust its editorial practice in light of those comments. For example, in
March 1999, one reader criticized the "*OUT* 100" issue for picturing only
11 people of color in an issue honoring 115 gay men, lesbians, and
straight allies: "Why not discard the 11 people of color altogether? You'll
have a number close to 100 and can retitle the article 'The White Out

100'" (M. Wong, New York). Another letter criticized *OUT*'s coverage (Dec. 1998) of the hate crime against Regan Wolf for its utter lack of feminist consciousness and a slant that amounted to "blaming the victim": "If this is the kind of treatment *OUT* is going to give serious lesbian issues, I'd prefer your previous policy of omission" (Kathleen Hildenbrand, San Francisco).

119. "Maybe Something in . . . Green," *OUT* April 1999, 25.

CHAPTER 3

1. Grant Lukenbill, *Untold Millions: Positioning Your Business for the Gay and Lesbian Consumer Revolution* (New York: HarperCollins, 1995) 37.

2. Frank Presbrey, *The History and Development of Advertising* (Garden City, NJ: Doubleday, 1929) 564.

3. Ibid., 559.

4. Ibid., 560.

5. Stuart Ewen, *All Consuming Images: The Politics of Style in Contemporary Culture* (New York: Basic Books, 1988) 18.

6. Presbrey, 358.

7. Ibid., 598.

8. Ibid., 598ff.

9. E. S. Turner, *The Shocking History of Advertising* (New York: E. P. Dutton, 1953) 214.

10. Roland Marchand, *Advertising the American Dream: Making Way for Modernity, 1920–1940* (Berkeley: U of CA P, 1985). See Chapter 3, "Keeping the Audience in Focus."

11. Presbrey, 613.

12. Marchand, 193.

13. Ewen, 63.

14. Ibid.

15. The foreign-language press, constituted by publications by and for migrant and immigrant workers, arose in the middle of the nineteenth century, as radical, socialist, and utopian workers formed clubs for the purpose of publishing periodicals. At several points in the 1840s, especially when a new ethnic community was established, individual editors took up publishing in order to operate free of the biases of the bourgeois, or mainstream commercial, press. Hoping to make a living at this work,

these editors launched both a "membership" press related to ethnic organizations and a commercial press, both of which would last for over a hundred years. (Dirk Hoerder, ed. *The Immigrant Labor Press in North America, 1840s–1970s, vol. 1: Migrants from Northern Europe* [Westport: Greenwood, 1987] 23).

Opponents of the foreign-language press argued that it "retards assimilation. By its very nature it tends to preserve the foreign language and sustain those feelings which bind the immigrant to his home country; it keeps him in touch with the events at home and thus evokes nationalistic tendencies." (William Carlson Smith, *Americans in the Making* [New York: D. Appleton-Century, 1939] 188). Noting that immigrants enjoyed more newspapers in the States than they had at home, that they enjoyed being able to maintain contact with other nationals across the States, and that the exchange of newspapers replaced the exchange of what would have been "gossip of the day in his home village" (Smith, 189), proponents argued that appreciation of these pleasures would endear the United States to the immigrant readers. If this was one way in which the foreign-language press promoted assimilation, it also did so because sufficient numbers of editors were committed to orienting foreign-born readers to the United States. One defense of the press quoted by William Carlson Smith pointed to the example of the Yiddish press: "A consideration of the nature of the subjects which it treats editorially, as well as the attitudes and sentiments which it expresses, warrants the conclusion that the influence which the Yiddish press radiates through its editorial columns is wholesome civically, and that it is a vital factor in the Americanization of its immigrant readers" (Smith, 192). Various opinions, contemporary with this debate, especially regarding schools, libraries, labor unions, industry, and politics, can be found in Winthrop Talbot, ed., *Americanization: Handbook Series* (New York: H. W. Wilson, 1920).

16. Smith, 190.
17. E. T. Hiller et al. quoted in Smith, 190.
18. John D'Emilio, "Capitalism and Gay Identity," *Powers of Desire: The Politics of Sexuality,* eds. Ann Snitow, Christine Stansell, and Sharon Thompson (New York: Monthly Review P, 1983) 100–113.
19. Ewen, 90.
20. Ibid., 90.
21. BIRTH OF A NATIONALISM. The question of how assimilation and nationalism are related is one that resonates in African American history as

well. In the scholarly, trade, and popular discourses alike, ethnicity has seemed to offer a model for understanding gay group identity; nationalism has offered another interrelated model for gay collective behavior. Just as the ethnicity model applied to gay men and lesbians brings with it the traces of its origins in European-American immigration history, borrowing nationalism as a model for gay community relations brings with it the traces of the black nationalism that was so important to the black civil rights movement. Both borrowed models are applied to gay men and lesbians at the price of distortion. Another price of borrowing those models is that the act of borrowing is so often forgotten or unacknowledged—a dynamic that recapitulates a history of presumption of whiteness, white domination, and white appropriation of black cultural products. With respect to nationalism, as with ethnicity, to say that there is such a thing as gay nationalism and that its development bears some similarities to the development of black nationalism is not to say that racial and sexual identity are analogous. Any similarities between black nationalism and gay and lesbian "nationalism" show that the market, the state, and concepts of citizenship converge in systematic ways on social groups organized in the pursuit of civil and economic rights.

The gay and lesbian movement is hardly the first to employ nationalism as a paradigm for emancipation. As a self-conscious liberation strategy, black nationalism predates gay nationalism. Although the latter adapted a variety of political strategies from the former, "post-1950s Black nationalism becomes an essential, yet largely unacknowledged, model for later liberation movements which concern themselves with body politics" (Amy Abugo Ongiri, "We Are Family: Black Nationalism, Black Masculinity, and the Black Gay Cultural Imagination," *College Literature* 24.1 [1997]: 282). Like other socially subordinated groups whose subordination was legitimated by claims about the nature, or the bodies, of people in those groups, African Americans who sought liberation through nationalism often subscribed to separatism. The separatist approach involved "inscribing" the redeemed black body "with the investments of a nation" (Ongiri, 282). This means that social groups whose oppression has taken the form of bodily devaluation (which also means groups whose disenfranchisement has been licensed by sociobiological claims of their inferiority) can effect their own revaluation by forming an alternative "nation." Within that nation, group members are, theoretically, enfranchised. Gay men and lesbians have attempted to revalue their supposedly inferior bodies through the creation of alternative community structures, but the lesbian and gay movement's unacknowledged debt to black nationalism obscures the extent to which gay liberation, too, has inscribed a redeemed lesbian/gay body—individual and collective—with the "investments" of a "nation."

Borrowing a nationalist model has created some of the same problems for the gay and lesbian movement that nationalism has created for black liberation, with the added complication that the question of nationalism has not been discussed in the gay and lesbian community as it has been in the African American community, perhaps because its origins are, as Ongiri states, unacknowledged: "Black nationalism's longing for a masculine, whole subjectivity to compete with the physical and psychic threat of disintegration incited by acts of racist violence against the Black body." So too has gay liberation, in its nationalist aspect, longed for a masculine, whole subjectivity, and proclaimed its existence as a warrant for acceptance in straight culture. Where black nationalism has been threatened by "Black male passivity, effeminization, Bisexuality and Homosexuality" (Francis Cress Wesling, "The Cress Theory of Color-Confrontation and Racism [White Supremacy]: A Psychogenetic and World Outlook," *The Issis [Yssis] Papers* [Chicago: Third World, 1991] 1), the gay liberation movement's often-unconscious adoption of nationalism has translated into a devaluation of effeminacy, bisexuality, and even homosexuality. One of the most troubling elements of the gay and lesbian movement is its legacy of internalized homophobia; the history of the movement demonstrates a continuous (though not universal) disavowal of effeminacy. This disavowal, of course, hurts effeminate men and women as a whole.

In an explicit statement of the case, Dr. Wesling, echoing statements made by Eldridge Cleaver, wrote about black struggle that "The practice of homosexuality is an accelerating threat to our survival as a people and as a nation" (Quoted in Ongiri, 285). Of course, not all black nationalists have supported such statements. There are also examples of black nationalist solidarity with gay liberation, of which the classic document is Huey Newton's "A Letter from Huey to the Revolutionary Brothers and Sisters About the Women's Liberation and Gay Liberation Movements" (*We Are Everywhere: A Historical Sourcebook of Gay and Lesbian Politics,* eds. Mark Blasius and Shane Phelan [New York: Routledge, 1997] 404–406). If the gay and lesbian liberation movement seems to be less attached to identity and also less nationalistic than the black liberation movement, I believe this misleading appearance follows from the fact that gay nationalism is more easily grafted onto U.S. nationalism; this graft is, in fact, more eagerly sought by gay nationalists than black nationalists, who have explored in a more serious and sustained way the possibilities for autonomous statehood, geographical territory, and other features of separate political nationhood.

As problematic as the importation of sexism and homophobia from certain strains of black nationalism is the fact that the importation remains unacknowledged, amounting to an act of appropriation of black culture by the gay and lesbian movement. Such appropriation reproduces the relations of domination and subordination that have so often characterized the relations between white and black people in the United States. As one example, "Michael Warner's *Fear of a Queer Planet: Queer Politics and Social Theory* obviously appropriates its title and its radical implications from Dr. Frances Cress Wesling's concept that white fear of genetic annihilation, or 'fear of a black planet,' forms the psychological basis for racism and white supremacy" (Ongiri, 286). The title of Public Enemy's 1990 album, "Fear of a Black Planet," clearly cites Wesling's concept, and according to Onigiri, "Warner's text . . . fails to address or even acknowledge the concerns of the theory, its creator, its later permutations, or its radical implications" (Ongiri, 286).

22. Many gay men and lesbians have indeed wanted to claim that sexuality-based social identity is analogous to ethnicity-based social identity. The debate about whether or not gay men and lesbians constitute an ethnic group goes back at least three decades in the social sciences, and almost as long in the arena of political organizing among gay men and lesbians. I will not be weighing in on this debate, nor attempting to resolve the question of whether gay and/or lesbian identities manifest the definitive characteristics of ethnic identities. Rather, I would briefly detail the terms of the debate. This debate is a minefield partly because usage slips around madly—as just one example, some people use "race" and "ethnicity" interchangeably. The problem of how race and ethnicity relate to national origin complicates usage. As an instance of this, see "The Political Power of Lesbians, Gays, and Bisexuals," in which Kenneth Sherrill writes, "In the United States . . . lesbians, gay men, and bisexuals are outnumbered and despised. Unlike most other potentially political groups, gay people are further disempowered by virtue of being born into

a diaspora" (Kenneth Sherrill, "The Political Power of Lesbians, Gays, and Bisexuals," *P.S.: Political Science & Politics* 29.3 [1996], 469). The use of the word "diaspora" implies that gay people's experience can be described in the lexicon of ethnicity, given that "diaspora" evokes first blacks and Jews, among other identity groups whose "national" origin is racial or religious.

Scholars David A. J. Richards, Warren Blumenfeld, Steven Epstein, Stephen Murray, and Dennis Altman have more to say in favor of drawing analogies between sexuality and race or ethnicity (see Bibliography). Most often, those in favor of borrowing a model of ethnicity to talk about gay men and lesbians see a provisional political utility in it; civil rights arguments based in precedent turn out to be relatively effective in achieving legislative reform. Steven Epstein contends that "This 'ethnic' self-characterization by gays and lesbians has a clear political utility, for it has permitted a form of group organizing that is particularly suited to the American experience, with its history of civil-rights struggles and ethnic-based, interest-group competition" (Steven Epstein, "Gay Politics, Ethnic Identity: The Limits of Social Construction," *Socialist Review* 17.93–94 [1987], 20).

This minefield seems to have been elegantly navigated by feminist scholars Amy Robinson and Janet Halley, both of whom warn of the dangers of analogizing racial, sexual, religious, and ethnic identities (see Bibliography). They count among the most significant dangers of analogical models of identity ignoring internal ethnic differences among people of any given identity group, and fundamentally misunderstanding the character of sexual, racial, ethnic, religious, or linguistic difference, which is to say, fundamentally misunderstanding the peculiar and distinct operations of racism, sexism, xenophobia, and other forms of prejudice and discrimination. Clearly, the stakes are far-reaching and include implications for constitutional interpretation of "protected classes," "immutability," and other terms central to judicial and legislative debate. Over and above their ethical objections to arguing for rights by analogy, Halley and Robinson believe that such arguments ultimately have political liabilities.

23. Hazel Kahan and David Mulryan, "Out of the Closet," *American Demographics* May 1995, 40, 42.

24. In "Gay Politics, Ethnic Identity," Steven Epstein provides one of the most schematic treatments of gay identity as ethnic identity. Of particular interest here is Epstein's reference to the resurgence of white ethnic pride

in the 1970s and 1980s. This was expressed in a range of cultural movements, following which white ethnicity has had a more positive valence. To put this back in market terms, the resurgence of ethnicity serves, and is served by, the rise of niche marketing, within which ethnic affiliation is a potential ground for target marketing.

Analyzing this recuperation of ethnic identity, Mitch Berbrier observes that in popular discourse, "ethnicity" and "deviance" are distinct (Mitchell William Berbrier, "Ethnicity in the Making: Cultural Space and the Ethnic/Minority Claims of the Deaf, Gays, and White Supremacists." Ph.D. diss. Indiana U, 1996). Of the two terms, ethnicity is good—a matter for pride—while deviance is stigmatized. Claims of ethnicity are, then, claims for group distinction of a positive, nondeviant nature, and such claims are made, according to Berbrier, by gay and lesbian and deaf constituencies and by white supremacists, among other groups; people opposing these groups describe them as deviant, while group defense lies in the claim to ethnicity.

25. Perhaps the legacy of black nationalism is instructive for gay men and lesbians: black cultural nationalism degenerated in the late 1960s and early 1970s as its discourse and symbolism was increasingly coopted and commodified (Michael Omi and Howard Winant, *Racial Formations in the United States from the 1960s to the 1980s* [New York: Routledge and Kegan Paul, 1986] 44). Two decades later the erosion of an identity-based cultural movement by cooptation and commodification undermined gay and lesbian artists (Richard Goldstein, "Queering the Culture," *Village Voice* 30 June 1998, 39–52).

26. Kenneth Sherrill cites an American National Election Study (1984–1994) that revealed that "lesbians and gay men are the object of overwhelmingly cold feelings on the part of the American people. Only illegal aliens, who are neither citizens, nor voters, rival lesbians and gay men in this regard" (Sherrill, 470).

27. James C. Worthy, *Shaping an American Institution: Robert E. Wood and Sears, Roebuck* (Chicago: U of Chicago P, 1984) 20.

28. Ten thousand such trade cards can be found in the Historical Collections Department of the Baker Library at the Harvard Business School.

29. Cardpacks are collections of advertisements printed on cards a bit smaller than index cards, shrink wrapped, and sent by mail to households. As of 1999, Triangle Marketing and Our Tribe Marketing were among the leading distributors of cardpacks to gay and lesbian households. In the mid-

1990s, most cardpack companies sent ads aimed at lesbians in separate cardpacks from those aimed at gay men. They also began to separate out porn-related cards from nonporn ads, with the understanding that mainstream advertisers would only agree to include their ads in cardpacks free of sexually explicit material.

30. Stuart Elliott, "As the Gay and Lesbian Market Grows, a Boom in Catalogues That Are 'Out, Loud, and Proud'," *New York Times* 10 Sept. 1993, C17.

31. Made in America, Proud Enterprises, Tzabaco, Shocking Gray, and Zebra'z have been among the most widely circulating gay catalogues; International Male and M2M, like analogs of the old physique magazines, are aimed at a gay consumer base without being explicit about it.

32. For material on gay ghettos, see Chapter 2, note 47.

33. William M. O'Barr, *Culture and the Ad: Exploring Otherness in the World of Advertising* (Boulder: Westview P, 1994) 201: "Only concerns about invasion of privacy have limited the development of such personalized messages. Information technology has already developed to the point at which individually tailored advertising messages would be possible." Note too that non-gay-or-lesbian identity is also negotiated in the marketplace; most consumption takes place in spaces that enforce compulsory heterosexuality. (It is also possible to enter the market virtually, but since the internet is produced and distributed so radically differently from printed matter, I will not broach those effects here.)

34. There have been cottage industries around for a long time, small-scale businesses aimed at gay and lesbian consumers. I think particularly of lesbian-separatist artisanal production. These are important phenomena, but my emphasis here is on large-scale production, distribution, and consumption.

35. Elliott, C17.

36. For a readable discussion of the dynamics of compiling and selling lists, see Erik Larson, *The Naked Consumer: How Our Private Lives Became Public Commodities* (New York: Henry Holt, 1992).

37. For more information on this, see Michael J. Weiss, *The Clustering of America* (New York: Harper & Row, 1988). It is interesting to note that the mailing list is also used as a tool for fundraising by nonprofit organizations, expressly gay and otherwise.

38. Kahan and Mulryan, 42.

39. Alfred C. Kinsey, *Sexual Behavior in the Human Male* (Philadelphia: W. B. Saunders, 1948).

40. Anne Cronin, "Two Viewfinders, Two Pictures of Gay America," *New York Times* 27 June 1993, E16.

41. Ibid.

42. O'Barr, 201.

43. The harmful influence of their now discredited statistical claims about average gay-household income is discussed in Chapter 1.

44. Changes in racial classifications used in the U.S. census show that the census shares with advertising the function of interpellation, meaning that both the state and the market actively produce identifications as much as, or more than, they respond to organic developments in identity and identification. See Omi and Winant for a discussion of changes in racial classification in the U.S. census.

45. Phone numbers of people willing to call in might also have been valuable as prospects for telemarketing, the next frontier of niche marketing to the gay and lesbian community.

46. An email exchange that took place on the web in the winter of 1996 perfectly illustrates the range of viewpoints on Community Spirit's census/ad. I have condensed these comments.

   Kenneth Sherrill wrote: "An alleged "census" such as this seriously distorts the demographics of the LGB population in the direction of Internet and e-mail users: younger, better educated and more affluent people. These data are then used by the radical right in their campaigns against protection for LGB rights and as "evidence" in court that LGB people do not merit strict scrutiny by virtue of being better educated and more affluent. Discredit this fraudulent abuse of social research. Do not participate in a process that harms our community. I have spent way too many hours testifying in cases to debunk this crap and to undo the damage these well-intentioned people do to our community."

   Rick Hillegas wrote: "I called the census and was disturbed that it seemed like an ad for a phone company. . . . The point of most of these 'gay censuses' is to help advertisers define the next generation of queer-oriented product. People who feel they're not getting enough queer product should, by all means, give Madison Avenue an ear-full. I for one am tired of having my queer identity obscured by some entrepreneur's concept of me as a target market. So I'll ignore this 'census' like all the others."

   Mike Dushane wrote: "While this type of census is going to be, without a doubt, somewhat distorted, it is more important to show that we at least exist and are not afraid to make our voices heard than to worry about the exact demographic information collected. Our big problem is not being seen as young and affluent, it is being seen as either A) a small group of radicals, or B) a silent and weak group of people. Not participating in this census, especially now that it is already in progress, would only artificially decrease our numbers even further than they already are due to the closetness of so many queers. Also, this census has been widely advertised not just on the internet, but also in a lot of hard-copy publications. I have seen ads for it in the queer papers here in Michigan."

47. Benedict Anderson, 175.

48. Ibid., 185.

49. Of course, it is problematic to determine racial identity through photographs, or by any visual means. Self-identification is a much better measure of belonging in a racial category. Nevertheless, with respect to this cardpack, it was difficult not to be struck by the apparent racial homogeneity pictured.

50. O'Barr, 12.

51. Amy Rashap, "The American Dream for Sale: Ethnic Images in the Magazines," *Ethnic Images in Advertising,* catalogue of the exhibition held at the Balch Institute for Ethnic Studies (Philadelphia) with the Anti-Defamation League of B'nai B'rith (New York), 22 May–7 Sept., 1984.

52. Though the following passage interprets the Tzabaco catalogue as a carrier of retrogressive racial politics, I do not mean to condemn Tzabaco in a simple way. Like so many mechanisms of capital, this for-profit agency also contributed to social change initiatives. Tzabaco was, for one thing, the principal sponsor of the GLSTN (Gay, Lesbian, Straight Teachers Network; now the Gay, Lesbian, Straight Education Network) Back to School Campaign, which encouraged gay adults to go back to their own schools to try to change the school environment for current students. And in the fall of 1997, following the death of Jacob Orozco in Utah, Tzabaco established a memorial fund. Orozco was a high school student whose struggle to form a gay-straight student alliance had met with severe opprobrium locally and in the Utah State Legislature and had made national news, as well. Orozco's suicide underlined the difficulties faced by gay youth, and Tzabaco responded quickly and appropriately.

53. Morgan, 280–282.

54. Ibid., 280.

55. Lukenbill, 1.

56. Jonathan Katz, *Gay American History: Lesbians and Gay Men in the U.S.A.* (New York: Thomas Y. Crowell, 1976) 8.

57. Bradley Johnson, "Economics Holds Back Lesbian Ad Market," *Advertising Age* 10 Jan. 1993, 34.

58. Ibid., 34.

59. Ibid., 34, 37.

60. John Gallagher, "Ikea's Gay Gamble: Why Did a National Home-Furnishings Chain Build a Television Ad Around a Gay Couple?" *Advocate* 3 May 1994, 24.

61. Ibid., 25.

62. Ibid.

63. Elliott, C17.

64. Morgan, 282.

65. Jess Wells, "Bringing up Baby: Parenting in the Gay Baby Boom," *Pride 98: Official Magazine for San Francisco Pride* (New York: Profile Pursuit, 1998) 83.

66. Lukenbill, 173.

67. The ad appeared in 1995.

68. The phenomenon of gay window advertising is analyzed by Danae Clark in "Commodity Lesbianism," *The Lesbian and Gay Studies Reader,* eds. Henry Abelove, Michele Aina Barale, and David M. Halperin (New York: Routledge, 1993) 186–201.

69. For a wealth of information and an interesting analysis, see T. J. Jackson Lears, *Fables of Abundance: A Cultural History of Advertising in America* (New York: Basic Books, 1994). I owe a great deal of my thinking about the cultural location, meaning, and role of advertisements—as well as my approach to their interpretation—to Lears.

70. It should be noted that advertising in mainstream media has recurringly appeared as a stratagem of nonprofit work. In particular, educational spots supporting gay and lesbian causes, with a public service aspect, have been imagined as early as 1977 in *Christopher Street*'s, "Why Doesn't Somebody . . . Why Doesn't Somebody Launch a National Advertising Campaign to Push Gay Rights Legislation on a National Level?" ("Why Doesn't Somebody . . ." *Christopher Street* 17 Feb. 1977, 3); and in Kirk and Madsen's *After the Ball: How America Will Conquer Its Fear and Hatred of Gays in the '90s* (New York: Doubleday, 1989). PFLAG prepared for broadcast a spot on homophobia and gay bashing (which was suppressed) in 1995, and HRC actually succeeded in broadcasting a spot on employment discrimination against gay men and les-

bians during the "Ellen" coming-out episode in spring 1997. On the PFLAG spot, see David Dunlap, "Gay Advertising Campaign on TV Draws Wrath of Conservatives," *New York Times* 12 Nov. 1995, A34. In July 1998, an ad war was conducted in the *New York Times* by right-wing coalitions and gay and lesbian coalitions, on the subject of ex-gay ministries. The rhetoric and images on both sides have been much discussed in the gay media.

71. Lisa Peñaloza, "We're Here, We're Queer, and We're Going Shopping! A Critical Perspective on the Accommodation of Gays and Lesbians in the U.S. Marketplace," *Gays, Lesbians, and Consumer Behavior: Theory, Practice, and Research Issues in Marketing,* ed. Daniel Wardlow (New York: Haworth, 1996) 33.

CHAPTER 4

1. T. H. Breen, "Narrative of the Commercial Life: Consumption, Ideology, and Community on the Eve of the Revolution," *William and Mary Quarterly* L.3 (1993), 495.

2. Chapter 3 treats more extensively the ways in which advertising to gay men and lesbians frequently appeals to its target market by claiming that consumption of the goods or services advertised amounts to political activism and benefits the community.

3. There is extensive debate about the existence and characteristics of the gay and lesbian niche market, debate that appears in the pages of the gay press as well as advertising trade publications. Begging the question of whether there is a viable niche market (see Chapter 1), I will nevertheless say unequivocally that the idea of a gay and lesbian niche market has been articulated more often and in more venues in this decade than in previous decades, and that significant market activity—on the part of both gay and mainstream producers—has been based on this idea.

4. Todd Putnam, "Boycotts Are Busting Out All Over," *Business and Society Review* (1993), 47.

5. The boycott against Nestlé was motivated by the fact that Nestlé distributed infant formula to women who didn't necessarily need it, that the use of the formula required water (which often meant that women combined it with contaminated water, thus making their babies sick), and that the instructions that were distributed with the formula were not always translated into local languages.

6. A widely circulated pro-"Ellen" email advised viewers to contact advertisers and "ask them to maintain sponsorship of the program and support freedom of choice."

7. Leo E. Laurence, "Glide Boycotts San Francisco Firms That Won't Hire Homosexuals," *L.A. Advocate* 3 Nov. 1967, 2.

8. "Hollywood Accord Near: Police Reveal Vice Policy," *L.A. Advocate* 24 April 1974, 2.

9. Milton Friedman and Rose Friedman, *Free to Choose: A Personal Statement* (London: Secker and Warburg, 1980) 222–223.

10. The idea that demand creates supply is opposed, for example, to the Frankfurt School idea that corporations are in the business of supplying, in addition to goods and services, the sense of need on the part of consumers—that ideology is a by-product of the manufacture of goods.

11. N. Craig Smith, *Morality and the Market: Consumer Pressure for Corporate Accountability* (London: Routledge, 1990) 2.

12. Quoted in Leonard Silk and David Vogel, *Ethics and Profits: The Crisis of Confidence in American Business* (New York: Simon and Schuster, 1976) 91.

13. Smith, 99.

14. David Vogel, *Lobbying the Corporation: Citizen Challenges to Business Authority* (New York: Basic Books, 1978) 46.

15. Ludwig von Mises, *Human Action: A Treatise on Economics* (London: William Hodge, 1949) 271.

16. Belief in the mechanism of competition led the old left to fight monopolies: "when we no longer have a choice which company to buy from, we will cease to have economic power, or any power" (Todd Putnam, letter to the author, Sept. 1997).

17. Smith, 33.

18. The boycott of Dow Saran Wrap is a good example of one that was probably ineffective economically, but carried some symbolic value and possibly affected the company's public image, which would, theoretically, eventually have hurt Dow.

19. Smith, 222.

20. These examples courtesy of Jane Kamensky.

21. Adam Snyder, "Do Boycotts Work?" *Adweek* 8 April 1991, 17.

22. Frederick E. Webster Jr., *Social Aspects of Marketing* (Englewood Cliffs, NJ: Prentice-Hall, 1974) 107.

23. For example, see John Kenneth Galbraith, "On the Economic Image of Corporate Enterprise," and Robert Dahl, "Governing the Giant Corpora-

tion," *Corporate Power in America,* eds. Ralph Nader and Mark J. Green (New York: Grossman Publishers, 1973).

24. Quoted in Smith, 6.

25. Ibid., 3.

26. T. H. Breen, 472.

27. Ibid., 484.

28. Ibid., 496.

29. Benedict Anderson, 498.

30. Ibid., 498–499.

31. "Miami Referendums Rated 'Toss Up,'" *Gay Community News* (Boston) 4 June 1977, 1.

32. Dai Thompson, "Speaking Out," *Gay Community News* (Boston) 28 May 1977, 5.

33. W. E. Beardemphl, "Editorial Comments," *Sentinel* (San Francisco) 24 Feb. 1977, 5.

34. Harvey Milk, "Leave Anita Alone?" *Bay Area Reporter* 17 March 1977, 4.

35. Ibid.

36. Ibid.

37. Ibid.

38. The National Gay Task Force became the National Gay and Lesbian Task Force in 1986.

39. Aryeh Neier, letter, *Sentinel* (San Francisco) 21 April 1977, 5.

40. Ibid.

41. George Mendenhall, "How to Deal with a Hate-Monger" *Bay Area Reporter* 28 April 1977, 10.

42. Thomas M. Edwards, "On the Right Side," *Sentinel* (San Francisco) 21 April 1977, 5.

43. Naturally, the debate rested in part on the availability of an alternative for consumers, which was California oranges. This issue, although minor, was explicit in the debate and it recalls the premium on choice in the marketplace; consumer choice is critical to the idea of economic democracy. Another minor issue concerned the prospect that "unfairly" persecuting Bryant would make her a martyr for the moral majority. NGTF was the main proponent of this argument, which I don't treat here because the merits or demerits of "persecution" are not specific to boycotting as a tactic.

44. Rod McKuen, "The Squeeze Goes On: A Report from the Battlefield," *Christopher Street* June 1977, 4.

45. Ibid.

46. "Bars Ban O. J.," *Sentinel* (San Francisco) 21 April 1977, 1.

47. "Gay Miami Squeezes Anita: O.J. Queen Juices for Straight Press," *Bay Area Reporter* 17 Feb. 1977, 2.

48. "Demos Back Gaycott," *Bay Area Reporter* 12 May 1977, 7.

49. "Floridanita," *Sentinel* (San Francisco) 24 March 1977, 3.

50. "Swedish Gays Join Boycott," *Bay Area Reporter* 21 July 1977, 11.

51. "Anita v. AFTRA: Show Biz Union to Refuse Services," *Bay Area Reporter* 26 May 1977, 8.

52. Harvey Milk, "Milk Forum: Pools Within Pools," *Bay Area Reporter* 31 March 1977, 8.

53. Ibid.

54. Gay Guerillas, Letter, *Leaping Lesbians* Sept. 1977, 11.

55. Charles Lee, "Local Leaders Blast N.G.T.F. Statement," *Sentinel* (San Francisco) 10 March 1977, 2.

56. W. E. Beardemphl, Editorial, *Sentinel* (San Francisco) 24 March 1977, 7.

57. Charles Lee Morris, "Anita Has the Right to Speak, However," Editorial, *Sentinel* (San Francisco) 5 May 1977, 7.

58. Ibid.

59. Mitzel, Letter, *Sentinel* (San Francisco) 5 May 1977, 7.

60. Ibid.

61. Thompson, 5.

62. Ibid.

63. In lesbian-feminist periodicals, comments about boycotting mostly followed the 6 June Dade County vote.

64. "God, Country, and Anita," *Lesbian News* May 1977, 10. This phrase, expressing NGTF's opposition to the boycott, was also quoted in *Lesbian Tide* May/June 1977, 17.

65. "Stop Bryant Now," *Lesbian Tide* May/June 1977, 24. It should be said, however, that lesbian periodicals in most parts of the country were getting their news about Miami secondhand from coverage in the *Gay Community News,* the *L.A. Advocate,* and other publications, due to the extremely small budgets on which the lesbian periodicals were run; financially speaking, there was no possibility of firsthand coverage, nor were their producers on the telephone or otherwise in communication with Dade County organizers.

66. Harvey Milk, "Milk Forum: A Nation Finally Talks About 'It'," *Bay Area Reporter* 9 June 1977, 17.

67. Frank Hoffman, "Just in From Frisco," *Christopher Street* 2.1 (July 1977), 3–5.

68. "March and Be Proud," *Bay Area Reporter* 23 June 1977, 4.

69. Ibid.

70. *Bay Area Reporter* 7 July 1977, 22–23.

71. Michael J. Melgaard, "The New Politics of Fear: The 1977 Dade County Gay Rights Referendum," Ph.D. diss., U of North Dakota, 1992, 205.

72. Randy Alfred, "From the Left," *Sentinel* (San Francisco) 11 Aug. 1977, 6.

73. People who came in from out of town to assist with the campaign included Representative Elaine Noble from Boston, San Francisco's pro-gay sheriff Richard Hongisto, California State Representative Willie Brown, feminist Gloria Steinem, and poet Rod McKuen.

74. Jesse Monteagudo, "Anita and I: An Activist's Memoir," *TWN* 29 Oct. 1997, 12–17. Ethan Geto was brought in from his position as Special Assistant to the Bronx Borough President in New York to act as Campaign Director of the Dade County Coalition for the Humanistic Rights of Gays (DCCHR) in spring of 1977, as the battle with Bryant was heating up; Monteagudo's memoir reports that Geto "centralized the DCCHR, gave all power to a five-person steering committee and all emergency powers to Jack Campbell as President," and thus both "alienated many supporters and kept the DCCHR from acquiring a base within South Florida's lesbian and gay community—a community that Geto and the others could never understand" (Monteagudo, 14–15). For another perspective on gender relations in the gay movement of the time more generally, see Dorianne Beyer's interview with Gloria Steinem: "Gloria Steinem" *Christopher Street* 2.2 (Aug. 1977), 7–12. See too Rita Mae Brown and Torie Osborn's comments about their experiences in the gay movement of the 1970s in Jeanie Russell Kasindorf, "Lesbian Chic: The Bold, Brave New World of Gay Women," *New York* 10 May 1993, 35.

75. Monteagudo, 12–17. Early on, when meetings still took place in a private club for gay men in Coconut Grove, Monteagudo remembers that "In spite of the presence of a 'token' lesbian co-chair, Rev. Lisa Berry of the MCC, most of the participants were men, a state of affairs that would continue to hold true. . . . There were no blacks, and only a handful of Latinos" (Monteagudo, 12). Later on in the campaign, Monteagudo notes that "the lack of lesbian presence on the board remained largely unnoticed, except, of course, by the lesbian community, which was already alienated from the male-dominated DCCHR" (Monteagudo, 15). The *Latinos pro Derechos Humanos,* working within the DCCHR, proposed to canvass Miami's Hispanic population, but this proposal was rejected by DCCHR leadership: "Latinos, they decided, were hopelessly homophobic, so it

would be best to keep them ignorant of the issue and away from the polls" (Monteagudo, 14).

76. In protest against (then) Burroughs Wellcome and its price gouging with AZT, members of ACT UP staged a performance on the floor of the New York Stock Exchange in Sept. 1989. This intervention was certainly economic, and was specifically related to a (then) largely gay niche, but the political action involved neither contribution nor consumption. For a thorough account, see Bruce Nussbaum, *Good Intentions: How Big Business and the Medical Establishment Are Corrupting the Fight Against AIDS* (New York: Atlantic Monthly P, 1990).

77. "Outspoken: On Boycotts and Betrayal," Editorial, *Outweek* 22 Aug. 1990, 4.

78. Leslie Savan/*Village Voice,* "Activism in the Checkout Line: The Rising Tide of Boycotts," *Utne Reader* Sept./Oct. 1989, 87.

79. The boycott of Coors was a complicated affair, starting in the late 1970s, which I will not go into here. Labor groups, women's groups, and gay groups found independent grounds and common cause against Coors at various points over a course of almost twenty years. Even in the late 1990s, community opinion on Coors was split, although the company has gone to some lengths to publicize its gay-friendly policies; they have advertised extensively in gay and lesbian media and have participated in gay and lesbian business expos in recent years.

80. The Fairness Campaign is a volunteer organization with educational and political-electoral arms, seeking to work in coalition with other groups committed to a broad vision of social justice—"broader than just gay rights," as Wallace describes it. The Fairness Campaign builds relationships with other organizations based on their historical dedication to antiracist, feminist, and antihomophobic work. Fairness is also a member organization of the Consumer Coalition for Justice (Carla Wallace, telephone interview with the author, 18 Sept. 1997).

81. Kentucky struck down its sodomy laws in 1992, in the famous *Wasson* decision.

82. Wallace interview.

83. Ibid.

84. Ibid.

85. Letter, signed by David Mixner, Sandra Gillis, William Waybourn, David Clarenbach, and Mark Barnes, printed in the *Letter* (Louisville) Sept. 1995, 3.

86. Wallace interview.

87. Nikita Stewart, "Groups Boycott Distributor Over Wife's Conservative Politics," *Courier-Journal* (Louisville) 26 Aug. 1995, 8A.

88. Ibid.

89. Wallace interview.

90. Eleanor Self, letter to the author, Sept. 1998.

91. Ibid.

92. As of this writing, the consequences of the economic action in Louisville are being played out in court. Donna Shedd has sued ten progressive and/or gay organizations for damage to her husband's career and for "harassing communications" because they received a subscription at their home addressed to "Vulva Shedd." CCJ takes no responsibility for this. At the same time, the Shedds are suing Miller Brewing Company for wrongful termination with the claim that David was fired because of his political associations. Meanwhile, Miller has consistently said that David Shedd was dismissed because of problems with his performance—for the frequency of his golf games rather than his familial or political associations.

93. Usually, in partnering arrangements between for-profit and nonprofit concerns, contractual agreements make explicit the requirements on the nonprofit in exchange for a donation. But there are unstated requirements as well, for example, fluency in corporate culture (including "appropriate" behavior at public events). See Chapter 5 for an in-depth discussion of these dynamics.

94. "Outspoken," 4.

95. Ibid.

96. Thompson, 5.

97. Todd Putnam, letter to author, Sept. 1997.

CHAPTER 5

1. David Harvey, "Money, Time, Space, and the City," *The Urban Experience* (Baltimore: Johns Hopkins UP, 1989) 185.

2. Although I have been quite active in the movement in a number of capacities, I am not a professional fund-raiser and have little education in fund-raising. Yet my limited experience in and around fund-raising has raised questions for me that seemed worth posing, even though I have no

special expertise in this area. In this chapter I have depended heavily on the anecdotal observations of a few particular individuals within the movement. Nevertheless, except where quoted, the opinions here are strictly my own; they derive largely from my affiliation with the International Gay and Lesbian Human Rights Commission.

3. While government is often a source of funding for nonprofits of all kinds, including gay and lesbian nonprofits, government funding to gay and lesbian advocacy organizations is very rare. Therefore, because what I am calling "the movement" is represented here by advocacy organizations, this chapter does not consider the mechanisms through which the government funds gay and lesbian nonprofits.

4. Yoko Yoshikawa, "The Heat is On 'Miss Saigon' Coalition: Organizing Across Race and Sexuality," *The State of Asian America: Activism and Resistance in the 1990s,* ed. Karin Aguilar-San Juan (Boston: South End P, 1994) 276.

5. Ibid., 281.

6. Ibid., 286–287.

7. Ibid., 283.

8. Ibid., 288.

9. Ibid., 288.

10. Ibid., 276.

11. Ibid., 276.

12. Javid Syed, telephone interview with the author, 14 Oct. 1998.

13. Ibid.

14. Ibid.

15. Julie Dorf, telephone interview with the author, 30 Sept. 1998.

16. This example, and the following one, come from my personal experience fund-raising in my capacity as Co-chair of the Board of IGLHRC.

17. This identitarian commitment, which showed up in a certain philanthropic orientation, was debated in the gay and lesbian media. For example, in a column that began with a list of "add-ons to the gay liberation movement"—"transgender," "youth with gender identity issues," "bisexual," and even "lesbian"—Paul Varnell asked: "Are these people in any reasonable sense 'gay' or 'gay and lesbian'? Are their issues ours?" Paul Varnell, "Gay, Bi, Trans, Drag, etc." *Windy City Times* 28 July 1994, 14. For information on gay and lesbian philanthropy, see *Creating Communities: Giving and Volunteering by Gay, Lesbian, Bisexual, and Transgender People,* Working Group on Funding Lesbian and Gay Issues (Washington,

D.C.: Institute for Gay and Lesbian Strategic Studies, 1998), along with surveys commissioned by the Gill Foundation and others conducted by the Washington *Blade.* These surveys point to significant gender differences with relation to philanthropy. Organizations tracking and/or promoting progressive philanthropy more generally include the National Network of Grantmakers, the National Alliance for Choice in Giving, and the National Committee for Responsive Philanthropy.

18. Many nonprofits put wealthy people on boards, with a tacit or explicit expectation that board membership obligates the wealthy board member to contribute certain amounts of money to the organization. It is impossible to generalize about whether their presence on the board affects program direction because the role of the board differs from organization to organization. However, it is not uncommon for program to be entirely staff driven. Nor is it uncommon for boards to have fund-raising as their central function.

19. Dorf interview.

20. Ibid.

21. Vaid's account is quite elaborate and has many more examples than are given here. It is very informative reading. Her whole book is important, but in connection with fund-raising issues, I recommend in particular Chapter 8, "Money and the Movement, or Looking for Mr. Geffen," *Virtual Equality: The Mainstreaming of Gay Liberation* (New York: Anchor Books, 1995).

22. Vaid, *Virtual Equality.*

23. Beth Berlo, "Activists Demanding That GLAAD Return Donation from Coors," *Bay Windows* (Boston) 12–18 Nov. 1998, 23.

24. Ibid.

25. Coors Boycott Committee pamphlet, 1998.

26. Dale Kurschner, "The 100 Best Corporate Citizens," *Business Ethics* May/June 1996, 24–35. Kurschner explained the criteria for the rankings:

> In creating the Business Ethics 100, we looked at employee ownership, women and minorities on the board and in the ranks, the treatment of gay men and lesbians, the presence of an ethics code or credo, and other social factors, including environmental issues. Financial performance was measured by year-to-year earnings changes, as well as five-year average annual earnings growth rates. Companies that had the best ranks in both social responsibility and earnings improvement received the top overall ratings. (24)

Acknowledging Coors' history of being boycotted by the AFL-CIO and sued by the Equal Employment Opportunity Commission in the 1970s, *Business Ethics* noted that the boycott officially ended in 1987 and that the company received an Outstanding Social Responsibility award from the Council on Economic Priorities in 1989. According to Kurschner:

> As of December 31, 1995, Coors reports that 21 percent of its employees are women; 18 percent of its managers are women; and none are on its board. But 40 percent of its board are minorities. It has a corporate-wide ethics program and a code of conduct; it addresses sexual orientation in its anti-discrimination policy; and it offers benefits to same-sex partners of employees. Five percent of annual net operating goes to philanthropic causes, and the company spent $33.5 million on environmental causes in 1995. (26)

Another chart in the story indicates that "minorities account for 13 percent of management and 18 percent of employees." (27)

27. Chuck Collins of United for a Fair Economy comments on the ambivalent nature of this phenomenon: "So now Shell Oil is a green company. Monsanto—one of the most despicable companies—hires Paul Hawkens, Mr. Socially Responsible Business to be their advisor, to pick off the pieces, but in a way it's a sign of success" (personal interview with the author, 26 Oct. 1998). Collins is suggesting that if the profit motive induces companies to adopt desirable policies, that may constitute "success." I am a bit more circumspect.

28. The link between gay and lesbian issues and the National Endowment for the Arts was drawn, or rather publicized, by the infamous case of the NEA Four, the four performance artists who were defunded by the NEA in 1990 because of the sexually explicit and/or homosexual content of their work.

29. Anthony Ramirez, "Philip Morris to Increase AIDS Donations," *New York Times* 30 May 1991, C3.

30. Ibid.

31. Dorf interview.

32. Ibid.

33. Jaymes Trief, "Credit Where Credit Is Due," *Advocate* 18 April 1995, 30.

34. Ibid., 29.

35. On this point, Trief quotes Howard Strong, *Credit Card Secrets You Will Surely Profit From* (Beverly Hills: Boswell Institute, 1989).

36. Trief, 29.

37. Dan Pallotta, talk at the Harvard Business School, 25 Feb. 1998 (see note 39).

38. Michele Frost, interview with the author, 20 July 1998.

39. The five ride routes were: Boston to New York, Chicago to Minneapolis, Los Angeles to San Francisco, Houston to Dallas, and North Carolina to Washington, D.C. The rides continue as of this writing. This and all following information about work involving Pallotta Teamworks comes from a talk on "The Emergence of Cause-Related Marketing in the 90s," with Joanne Mazurki, Director of Global Cause-Related Marketing at Avon, and Dan Pallotta, President and CEO of Pallotta Teamworks, at Harvard Business School, 25 Feb. 1998. Pallotta Teamworks is a for-profit company.

40. Matthew Sinclair, "Postcards from the Edge: Fundraising on the Fringe," *NonProfit Times* Aug. 1997, 26.

41. Ibid.

42. Working Assets sends bills to its customers with a space for "rounding up," meaning that customers are encouraged to overpay, with the understanding that any amount overpaid will join the 1 percent revenue to be given away.

43. Working Assets guidelines. These priorities are, to some extent, shared by a range of corporate foundations. Of course, there are exceptions, often involving donations to local or state groups in the state where the company's headquarters are located. Philip Morris's "Corporate Contributions: Guidelines" state that relative to one of its three funding focus areas—the arts—"we cannot consider proposals from arts groups located in areas where there is little or no Philip Morris employee presence" (6). And, "As in all other areas of funding, preference will be given to those organizations operating in communities where Philip Morris has a major presence" (6). On the one hand, this can be seen as a corporation acting responsibly toward the local communities on which it has a significant economic impact, addressing the social and cultural needs of those communities. On the other hand, it is also true that the need for good public relations is greater in places where awareness of the specific practices and policies of the corporation is greater.

44. Syed interview.

45. Ibid.

46. Dorf interview.

47. Ibid.

48. Ibid.

49. Sean Strub, "The Growth of the Gay and Lesbian Market," *A Queer World,* ed. Duberman, 516.

50. Sinclair, 24–25.

51. Ibid.

52. Ibid.

53. Syed interview.

54. Collins interview.

55. Ibid.

56. Sinclair, 25.

57. Ibid., 24.

58. J. Jennings Moss, "Capitol Gains," *OUT* April 1998, 113–114.

59. Ibid., 114.

60. Ibid.

61. Ibid.

62. Richard K. Herrell, "The Symbolic Strategies of Chicago's Gay and Lesbian Pride Parade," *Gay Culture in America,* ed. Gilbert Herdt (Boston: Beacon P, 1992) 231.

63. Ibid.

64. Ibid., 232.

65. Ellen O'Brien, "100,000 March to Celebrate Hub's Gay Pride," *Boston Globe* 8 June 1997, B8.

66. In the famous Bedgate episode, the Lesbian Avengers brought a float into the 1996 Pride parade, right behind the mayor and the police honor guard. The float included a bed on which women were invited to simulate lesbian sex. The purpose of the float was to "create a blatant image of lesbian sexuality. . . . It [was] political because lesbians are invisible in the mainstream world where no one can figure out what lesbians do in bed" (Anoosh Jorjorian, "Solidarity or Segregation? The Politics of the Dyke March," *Sojourner* June 1997, 8). The Lesbian Avengers' invention of the Dyke March, as an event that is separate from but related to the Pride parade, was prompted in part by the perception that "Pride became more of a commercial venue than a political venue," according to activist Harneen Chernow. Furthermore, the perception among some Boston-based dykes was that "The Pride Committee chair was male, regarded as being rather sexist. . . . The parade itself reflected the committee. The focus was on creating a space for white men," in the words of activist Beth Hastie. Fourteen of the fifteen committee members that year were

men and most of them were white. "We wanted to draw attention to the fact that the committee was not representing the community," commented Sarah Shreeves. Whether the Dyke March has done a better job of representing the community is also a matter of debate: Donna Finn of the Dorchester Women's Committee asserted that the march does not address issues relevant to working-class people, while Risé Riyo of the Queer Asian Pacific Alliance found that the march attracted "a lot of white chicks" (Jorjorian, 9).

67. Neil Miller, "Rescue Mission," *Boston Phoenix* One in Ten section, July 1998, 6.

68. Ibid.

69. Ibid.

70. Ibid.

71. Ibid.

72. Ibid.

73. Ibid.

74. For example, the *Official Pride Guide* of the Washington, D.C., pride event in 1997 named as "Presenting Sponsors" the conservative corporation Bell Atlantic; One-in-Ten, a nonprofit organization that organizes cultural and educational programs for Washington's gay, lesbian, bisexual, and transgender community; and the Whitman-Walker Clinic, a local health center focusing on health care for gay men and lesbians. "Major Sponsors" listed in the *Guide* were AKVA, American Potomac Distributing Company/Budwesier, OraSure—Distributed by SmithKline Beecham Consumer Healthcare, Skyy (vodka), United Airlines, and Z104 (a local radio station). While local gay businesses made it onto the roster of "Participating Sponsors," it is clear from this list that national corporate sponsors were the most significant contributors to the event. "Vendors and Exhibitors" outnumbered official "Contingents" by almost three to one.

75. Hussain, "Class Action: Bringing Economic Diversity to the Gay and Lesbian Movement," Gluckman and Reed, 241–248. Most people involved acknowledged that such procedures could result in meetings that were "contentious and chaotic" ("Call For an Open Process"). Nevertheless, the commitment to inventing democratic means produced a march that was indeed fairly diverse and "in the end the decisions were accepted because the process was fair and inclusive" ("Call For an Open Process").

76. Hussain, 245.

77. Leslie Cagan, "Millennial Missteps: Eclipsing a Grassroots Movement," *Gay Community News* 4.1 (1998), 18–23.

78. Stephanie Poggi, "Onward Christian Soldiers?" *Sojourner* June 1998, 9.

79. Letter from the Reverend Troy Perry to the members of the Universal Federation of Metropolitan Community Church's General Council.

80. Laura Brown, "Millennium March Draws Sponsor, Competitor," *Southern Voice* 6 May 1999, 24.

81. Bob Roehr, "Millennium March Slogs On, Despite Two Board Resignations," *Bay Area Reporter* (San Francisco) 6 May 1999, 14+.

82. Brown, 24.

83. Ibid.

CHAPTER 6

1. Lisa Duggan and Nan D. Hunter, *Sex Wars: Sexual Dissent and Political Culture* (New York: Routledge, 1995) 183. I like Duggan and Hunter's solution, which includes "disestablishing" the "state religion" of "heteronormativity." Imagining as a movement objective the condition that "public policy and public institutions may not legitimately compel, promote, or prefer intergender relationships," Duggan and Hunter point out that working toward this objective would enable queers to escape declaring movement membership on the basis of identity (189). If separating the state from institutionalizing values were a central political objective, it would obviate arguments about morality without displacing civil rights strategies. It would also enable a progressive social movement to break away from an exclusive focus on rights, and it would shift the ground for thinking about discrimination.

2. Norah Vincent, "Beyond Lesbian," *Beyond Queer: Challenging Gay Left Orthodoxy,* ed. Bruce Bawer (New York: Free P, 1996) 183.

3. Ibid.

4. Daniel Mendelsohn, "Scenes from a Mall," *Beyond Queer: Challenging Gay Left Orthodoxy,* ed. Bruce Bawer (New York: Free P, 1996) 165–170.

5. Stephen H. Miller, "Gay White Males: PC's Unseen Target" in *Beyond Queer: Challenging Gay Left Orthodoxy,* ed. Bruce Bawer (New York: Free P, 1996) 24–37. This article is about the "attack" on gay white men by "radical lesbian feminists" and the alleged quota system that ensconces the latter in positions of power in the gay movement while systematically excluding the former.

6. Duggan and Hunter, 184.

7. In the words of John Anner, "It becomes harder to sustain the fiction that 'we all have the same problem' when some members of the group are clearly doing a lot better than others, and when political strategies being followed clearly benefit some members of the group more than others. The result in many identity movements is a tendency toward elitism and assimilation in practice, coupled with a feigned dedication to solidarity with all the oppressed. . . . [I]dentity movements can pretend that their current particularist campaigns will still raise living standards for all members of the group but the evidence is overwhelmingly to the contrary" (John Anner, ed., *Beyond Identity Politics: Emerging Social Justice Movements in Communities of Color* [Boston: South End P, 1996] 9).

8. Ibid., 8.

9. Duggan and Hunter, 184.

10. Anner, 9.

11. Lisa Power, *No Bath but Plenty of Bubbles: An Oral History of the Gay Liberation Front, 1970–73* (London: Cassell, 1995) 3.

12. Ibid.

13. Howard Wallace, quoted in Bill Sievert, "Point, Counterpoint: Gay Politics San Francisco Style," *Advocate* 13 July 1977, 12.

14. Rama Hinton, quoted in Bill Sievert, "Point, Counterpoint: Gay Politics San Francisco Style," *Advocate* 13 July 1977, 12.

15. Ibid.

16. Ibid., 10.

17. Ibid.

18. Ibid.

19. Andrea Lewis and Robin Stevens, "At the Crossroads: Race, Gender, and the Gay Rights Movement," *Third Force* March/April 1996, 25. Eric Rofes was the executive director of the Shanti Project (an AIDS service organization in San Francisco) and of the Los Angeles Gay and Lesbian Community Services Center at different points in the 1990s.

20. Ibid. Jewelle Gomez is the author of a number of books, including *The Gilda Stories*.

21. Ibid.

22. Ibid.

23. Ibid.

24. For a brilliant analysis of Queer Nation and its manipulations of commerce, citizenship, and sexual identification, see Lauren Berlant and Elizabeth Freeman, "Queer Nationality," *The Queen of America Goes to*

Washington City: Essays on Sex and Citizenship, Lauren Berlant (Durham: Duke UP, 1997), 145–173.

25. Much of the information here about the Esperanza Center comes from Genevieve Howe, "Art Attack, Part Two: San Antonio's Esperanza Sues for Funding Discrimination," *Sojourner* Nov. 1998, 9+.

26. Ted Switzer quoted in Ibid., 9.

27. Rob Blanchard, National Gay and Lesbian Journalists Association; Michael McGowan, President, Log Cabin Republicans; Glenn Stehle; Ted Switzer, Publisher, *San Antonio Marquise;* Bryon Trott, San Antonio Gay and Lesbian Community Center. The affiliations are, of course, listed "for identification purposes only; the views expressed are not necessarily those of the organizations listed." And yet, the presence of the affiliations not only has an intimidating effect, it reminds its readers that these men travel in certain circles, "have friends" in those circles, and are not afraid they will be ejected from those organizations for signing this letter.

28. Ibid.

29. Ibid.

30. At first glance, it is easy to see why libertarian solutions might appeal to gay men and lesbians, since such solutions utilize the existing market system and promise freedom from government interference in private matters. But as Surina Khan points out, "Gay conservatives do not see the limits and, indeed, the dangers of identity-based politics centered only around gay rights" (Surina Khan, "Gay Conservatives: Pulling the Movement to the Right," *The Public Eye: A Publication of Political Research Associates* X.1 [1996] 10). In her analysis of gay and lesbian movement politics, Khan goes on to ask, "[W]hat impact will gay conservatives have on the gay movement? By abandoning coalition with other oppressed groups and choosing allies based primarily on shared economic philosophies, are they obstructing a movement toward human rights and dignity?" (Khan, 3). In other words, single-issue identity-based organizing and conservative economic strategies go hand in hand in the gay and lesbian movement.

31. One irony here involves the role of the Log Cabin Republicans, or rather its organizational identity. On its website, the Log Cabin Republicans sport three pictures of Abraham Lincoln. Certainly, the association between Abraham Lincoln and log cabins is well cemented in the public mind. Illinois, the state where Lincoln first held office (although not the state in which he was born and raised in a log cabin, which was Ken-

tucky!) bears the moniker of "log cabin state." Lincoln logs are a classic among children's toys. But there is a piece of missing history behind the log cabin. Lincoln did not make the log cabin an icon of populist politics. It was William Henry Harrison who did that (Sean Wilentz, "Property and Power: Suffrage Reform in the United States, 1787–1860," *Voting and the Spirit of American Democracy,* ed. D. W. Rogers [Chicago: U of Illinois P, 1992] 31–41). In his presidential campaign of 1840, Harrison first used the log cabin imagery on ribbons and other paraphernalia. Harrison's platform included a plank of universal white manhood suffrage, and this imagery was designed to appeal to the growing ranks of men eligible to vote, as property requirements for voting were gradually, and state by state, eroded over the course of the early nineteenth century.

Universal white manhood suffrage then is the ghostly plank that haunts the Log Cabin Republicans. And this trace carries the same ironies that are so common in the trajectory of liberal democracy. Universal white manhood suffrage was a progressive movement in its time, based in the principle that the right to vote should not be restricted to men with property. And yet, it hardly needs saying, this platform took for granted that race and gender were appropriate determinants of the right to vote. In various colonies and states at various points, Jews and Catholics had been explicitly excluded from voting, as had Native Americans; women and slaves could not vote in the nineteenth century; people below legal age and prisoners have never been allowed to vote. It was the recently emerged non-landholding producer class whose members exerted pressure to expand the suffrage to all free adult white men.

Soon after various reforms fell into place, some Americans questioned whether the widening of suffrage actually affected the structure of power. Workingmen radicals of the 1830s and 1840s raised the matter most insistently, claiming that merely abolishing property restrictions would rid the country of those monied men whom they called the "mushroom aristocracy." It seemed, as one newspaper reported, that the political elites had "disarmed the poorer classes by taking them into the body politic" (Wilentz, 38). In any case, the democratization effort was not based on the ethical ideal of free and equal participation in the political arena. "Southern reform spokesmen made no bones about their claims that democratization was a means to ensure greater unity among whites (and hence greater security for the institution of slavery) to be gained at the expense of that section's free black population" (Wilentz, 38).

According to historian Sean Wilentz,

> Connections between the market revolution and democratization
> can be discovered at several levels. The emergence of new local
> elites who came from outside the established gentry—urban and
> country merchants, manufacturers, lawyers, newspaper editors, and
> other professionals—clearly increased the pressure for change.
> Throughout the country, in various walks of life, there arose an ar-
> ticulate stratum of ambitious men who owed little or nothing to the
> old ideal of a landed freeholder citizenry and a benign, virtuous pa-
> trician leadership. In state after state, these new men of the market
> revolution played critical roles, either in mobilizing support for re-
> forms or in helping broker these reforms in state legislatures and
> constitutional conventions. (Wilentz, 35–36)

Compared with the gay and lesbian movement of the late twentieth century, there are interesting analogs here. New elites, ambitious men owing
little to the heterosexism of the social structures that spawned them, are
in a position to exert pressure for reform. The kind of reform that they
have played critical roles brokering in various legislatures is analogous to
universal white gay manhood suffrage. The Log Cabin Republicans reinforce this analogy with the trace, in their very name, of the universal white
manhood suffrage platform of William Henry Harrison.

Appended to a sympathetic piece on the invisibility of Republicans
within the gay community, the *Advocate* printed a special insert on lesbian Republicans, who suffer a double invisibility. Carol Newman, President of the Los Angeles chapter of Log Cabin, says there are more
Republican lesbians than are represented in her organization: "There's a
perception that Log Cabin has some attitudes that are old-fashioned,"
Newman says, adding that she has heard sexist remarks coming from
some of her Log Cabin brothers (J. Jennings Moss, "Coming Out of the
Republican Closet—One Lesbian at a Time," *Advocate* 29 Oct. 1996, 27).
As of spring 1996, all of Log Cabin's nineteen board members were men,
and the staff was dominated by men; both board and staff were overwhelmingly white. In other words, Log Cabin was not particularly concerned with racial or gender diversity or parity in its organization.

32. Chuck Collins, personal interview with the author, 26 Oct. 1998.
33. Urvashi Vaid, "Coalition as Goal Not Process," *Gay Community News*
Spring 1997, 7.

34. Collins interview.

35. Designing different curricula about economic inequality for Jewish, Protestant, and Catholic groups, for example, allowed UFE to tailor similar content to each constituency. "Taking the same story about the economy, but framing it in a way that connects with the concerns of whatever audience," Collins found that different action scenarios came out of each group. Furthermore, groups could then work together on economic issues. Certainly interfaith coalitions have been among the most successful, on this and other social issues.

36. Anner, 9.

37. Collins interview. UFE's leading campaigns center on tax fairness, closing the wage gap, corporate welfare, and new ownership models, and their strategies are research, education, and action. According to Collins, there are several components of the economic justice movement, including the labor movement (which, as of 1999, counts 13 million members); national research institutes like the Economic Policy Institute, which documents changes in the economy and makes policy proposals; other more formal coalitions like ACORN and third-party organizing efforts working on the electoral political plane, such as the Labor Party and the New Party; and local and regional groups that work on issues like wages and taxation. United for a Fair Economy sees itself as a hybrid, a movement-support organization trying to provide tools for organizing, research, and popular education.

38. Vaid, *Virtual Equality,* 224.

39. Patricia Williams, "Pansy Quits," *The Rooster's Egg* (Cambridge, MA: Harvard UP, 1995) 16.

40. Observing the political context of the United States in the 1990s in terms that resonate with those of Patricia Williams, Carmen Vazquez doubts the viability of any resistance movement that is not coalitional:

> From my perspective, then, it is not possible to secure passage of a lesbian/gay civil rights bill in a country that denies women the right to choose what we will do with our bodies. The values that celebrate burying Iraqi soldiers alive are the same ones that celebrate gay bashing; the values that support S&L bailouts above national health care are the same that support the quarantine of people with HIV. The value system and the people who think that women invite their own rape haven't any use for us. A country that thinks twelve-

year-old black children are expendable fodder for the War on Drugs doesn't give a damn about queer anybody. It never has and it never will—unless we and all the people this country thinks are expendable work together to change it. (Carmen Vazquez, "The Land That Never Has Been Yet: Dreams of a Gay Latina in the United States," *The 3rd Pink Book: A Global View of Lesbian and Gay Oppression,* eds. Aart Hendriks, Rob Tielman, and Evert van der Veen [Buffalo: Prometheus Books, 1993] 220).

41. Anner, 9–10.
42. The African American community has historically faced this conflict with respect to strategies for enfranchisement. It is described here by August Meier, with respect to the late nineteenth century:

> Philosophies of economic chauvinism and separate institutions were part of a larger complex of ideas involving self-help, race pride, and group solidarity, though it must be emphasized that such ideas were usually regarded as being a tactic in the struggle for ultimate citizenship.
>
> . . . A few individuals recognized a common interest across race lines, based in opposition to "wage slavery," but W.E.B. DuBois was unique as an intellectual and political leader who espoused socialism and identified the political interests shared by black and white workers. (August Meier, *Negro Thought in America 1880–1915: Racial Ideologies in the Age of Booker T. Washington* [Ann Arbor: U Michigan P, 1963] 50, 46–47)

For a latter-day manifesto of coalition politics, see Bernice Johnson Reagon, "Coalition Politics: Turning the Century," *Home Girls: A Black Feminist Anthology,* ed. Barbara Smith (New York: Kitchen Table: Women of Color P, 1983) 356–368.

43. Anner, 11.
44. Vaid, "Coalition as Goal," 8.
45. Ibid., 7.
46. Wilbur C. Rich, ed., *The Politics of Minority Coalitions: Race, Ethnicity, and Shared Uncertainties* (Westport, CT: Praeger, 1996) 7.
47. Anner, 155–156. Anner's principles are:

- Building personal relationships between members from different backgrounds;

- Actively engaging in solidarity campaigns, actions, and activities with social justice organizations in other communities;
- Challenging bigoted statements and attitudes when they arise;
- Holding regular discussions, forums, "educationals," and other workshops to enhance people's understandings of other communities and individuals;
- Developing issues, tactics, and campaigns that are relevant to different communities and that reveal fundamental areas of common interest;
- Examining and changing the organization's practices in order to hire, promote, and develop people of color;
- Confronting white privilege and nationalism;
- Hiring, recruiting, and training more people of color for leadership positions.

48. Rich, 6.
49. Ibid., 7.
50. Vazquez, 223.
51. Sarah Schulman, *Stagestruck: Theater, AIDS, and the Marketing of Gay America* (Durham: Duke UP, 1998) 107.
52. Schulman's work in this area exposes the practices of the viatical companies and analyzes the ethical issues they provoke. Here, I will borrow just one example; Schulman quotes a press release issued by one viatical company, Dignity Partners, in the face of new developments in AIDS medical treatment: "If treatments are effective in the long term, the company's results will be adversely affected" (Schulman, 141).
53. Ibid., 130–131.
54. Ibid., 139–140.
55. Ibid., 133.
56. In her trenchant critique of representations of people with AIDS, niche marketing to PWAs (people living with AIDS), and especially the ads of pharmaceutical and viatical companies, Schulman writes, "What these advertisements hide is the fact that most people use their settlements to pay medical bills and buy food," not to take a tropical vacation, as the ads seem to suggest (Schulman, 134 ff.).
57. Richard Goldstein, "Queering the Culture," *Village Voice* 30 June 1998, 44.
58. This is exactly what Sarah Schulman says in *Stagestruck* about what accounts for the popularity of the musical *Rent* as opposed to the novel she wrote from which, she alleges, it is lifted ("*Rent:* The Dirt," 5–38).

59. Richard Lukacs quoted in Goldstein, 49.

60. Science fiction writer Samuel Delaney quoted in ibid.

61. Musician Alicia Svigals quoted in ibid.

62. Wayne Koestenbaum (quoting Michel Foucault) quoted in ibid., 52.

63. Mab Segrest, *Memoir of a Race Traitor* (Boston: South End P, 1994) 241.

64. Ibid., 242.

65. Ibid., 222.

66. For material on some of the many points of intersection between the labor movement and the gay and lesbian community, see the June 1998 issue of *Resist*. Especially regarding coalition between the lesbian and gay movement and labor, see Susan Moir and Carol Schachet, "Gay and Lesbian Labor Gains a Voice," *Resist* June 1998, 1–3. In this connection, also see "An Interview with Susan Moir," in Gluckman and Reed, 229–240.

67. Segrest, 240.

68. Barbara Smith, "Where's the Revolution, Part II," *The Truth That Never Hurts: Writings on Race, Gender, and Freedom* (New Brunswick: Rutgers UP, 1998) 186.

69. Of course, some businesses contribute to nonprofits and some don't, but the identities of the owners, shareholders, and consumers do not determine whether businesses make such contributions or not.

70. Leo Rennert, "Tax Us More, Wealthy Protesters Say in D.C.," *San Francisco Examiner* 1 April 1998, A1+.

BIBLIOGRAPHY

Abelove, Henry. "From Thoreau to Queer Politics." *Yale Journal of Criticism* 6 (1993): 17–27.

———. "The Queering of Lesbian/Gay History." *Radical History Review* 62 (1995): 24–42.

Abelove, Henry, Michele Aina Barale, and David M. Halperin, eds. *The Lesbian and Gay Studies Reader.* New York: Routledge, 1993.

Abelson, Reed. "'Gay-Friendly' Fund Has Blue-Chip Focus." *New York Times* 1 Sept. 1996: section 3, 7.

"Advertising to Gay America: The Not-So-Subliminal Seduction." *Times Talks* Speaker Series Panel: Stuart Elliott, Stephanie K. Blackwood, Howard Buford, Jim Consolantis, Todd Evans, Mark Malinowski. New York. 8 April 1999.

Albright, D. Jean. "Gays, Lesbians and Consumer Behavior." *Clout! Business Report* Sept. 1996: 8.

Allison, Shane. "More Diversity." Letter. *XY* Feb. 1995: 6.

Alsop, Ronald. "Cracking the Gay Market Code: How Marketers Plant Subtle Symbols in Ads." *Wall Street Journal* 29 June 1999: B1+.

Althusser, Louis. "Ideology and Ideological State Apparatuses." *Lenin and Philosophy and Other Essays.* Trans. Ben Brewster. New York: Monthly Review P, 1971.

Altman, Dennis. *The Homosexualization of America, the Americanization of the Homosexual.* New York: St. Martin's P, 1982.

"A Market That's Educated, Affluent and Homosexual." *New York Times* 23 Sept. 1992: D27.

Anderson, Benedict. *Imagined Communities: Reflections on the Origin and Spread of Nationalism.* London: Verso, 1991.

Anderson, Diane. "Gay Market—Dyke Dollars." *Girlfriends* July/Aug. 1996: 24+.

Anderson, Scott. "The Gay Press Proliferates—and So Do Its Problems." *Advocate* 13 Dec. 1979: 19–20.

Anner, John, ed. *Beyond Identity Politics: Emerging Social Justice Movements in Communities of Color.* Boston: South End P, 1996.

Anzaldúa, Gloria and Cherríe Moraga, eds. *This Bridge Called My Back.* New York: Kitchen Table: Women of Color P, 1981.

Appleby, Joyce. *Liberalism and Republicanism in the Historical Imagination.* Cambridge: Harvard UP, 1992.

Aronowitz, Stanley. *Politics of Identity: Class, Culture, Social Movements.* New York: Routledge, 1992.

Arrington, Karen McGill and William L. Taylor, eds. *Voting Rights in America: Continuing the Quest for Full Participation.* Washington, D.C.: Leadership Conference Educational Fund, Joint Center for Political and Economic Studies, 1992.

Aunkst, Lisa R. "Fashion Clash: The Ways We Look in Contemporary Lesbian Culture." Paper. Boston College, 1998.

Badgett, M. V. Lee. *Income Inflation: The Myth of Affluence Among Gay, Lesbian, and Bisexual Americans.* New York: NGLTF Policy Institute, 1998.

———. "Thinking Homo/Economically." *A Queer World.* Ed. Martin Duberman. New York: New York UP, 1997: 467–476.

———and Nancy Cunningham. "Expanding the Resource Base for Community Organizations: Giving and Volunteering by Gay, Lesbian, Bisexual, and Transgender People." *Angles* 3.1 (May 1998).

Bawer, Bruce. "Truth in Advertising." *Advocate* 11 July 1995: 80.

———, ed. *Beyond Queer: Challenging Gay Left Orthodoxy.* New York: Free P, 1996.

Bayard, Marc, Chuck Collins, and Felice Yeskel. "Organizing Around the New Class Divide." *The Ark* Summer 1997: 33–39.

Beemyn, Brett and Mickey Eliason, eds. *Queer Studies: A Lesbian, Gay, Bisexual, and Transgender Anthology.* New York: New York UP, 1996.

Bell, David and Gill Valentine, eds. *Mapping Desire: Geographies of Sexualities.* London: Routledge, 1993.

Ben-Habib, Seyla. "Models of Public Space: Hannah Arendt, the Liberal Tradition, and Jurgen Habermas." *Habermas and the Public Sphere.* Ed. Craig Calhoun. Cambridge: MIT P, 1992. 73–98.

Beran, Nancy J., Connie Claybaker, Cory Dillon, and Robert J. Haverkamp. "Attitudes Toward Minorities: A Comparison of Homosexuals and the General Population." *Journal of Homosexuality* 23.3 (1992): 65–83.

Berbrier, Mitchell William. "Ethnicity in the Making: Cultural Space and the Ethnic/Minority Claims of the Deaf, Gays, and White Supremacists." Ph.D. diss. Indiana U, 1996.

Berlant, Lauren. "National Brands/National Body: Imitation of Life." *Comparative American Identities: Race, Sex, and Nationality in the Modern Text.* Ed. Hortense J. Spillers. New York: Routledge, 1991. 110–140.

———. *The Queen of America Goes to Washington City: Essays on Sex and Citizenship.* Durham: Duke UP, 1997.

Berlo, Beth. "Activists Demanding that GLAAD Return Donation from Coors." *Bay Windows* [Boston] 12–18 Nov. 1998: 23.

Bersani, Leo. *Homos.* Cambridge: Harvard UP, 1995.

Berubé, Allan and Jeffrey Escoffier. "Queer/Nation." *Out/Look: National Gay/Lesbian Quarterly* 11 (Winter 1991): 12–13.

Beyer, Dorianne. "Gloria Steinem." Interview. *Christopher Street* 2.2 (Aug. 1977): 7–12.

Blasius, Mark and Shane Phelan, eds. *We Are Everywhere: A Historical Sourcebook of Gay and Lesbian Politics.* New York: Routledge, 1997.

Blumenfeld, Warren J. "Gays as an ethnic group." Email to the author. 25 Dec. 1996.

Bond, Justin. "Queer." *Out/Look: National Gay/Lesbian Quarterly* 11 (Winter 1991): 14, 16–18, 20–23.

Bounds, Elizabeth. "Between the Devil and the Deep Blue Sea: Feminism, Family Values, and the Division Between Public and Private." *Journal of Feminist Studies in Religion* 12.2 (1996): 111–126.

Boyd, Nan Alamilla. "Shopping for Rights: Gays, Lesbians, and Visibility Politics." *Denver University Law Review* 75.4 (1998): 1361–1373.

Boykin, Keith. *One More River to Cross: Black and Gay in America.* New York: Doubleday, 1996.

Bram, Christopher. "Selling Homosexuality." *Christopher Street* 134 (Aug. 1989): 43–45.

Breen, T. H. "Ideology and Nationalism on the Eve of the American Revolution: Revisions Once in Need of Revising." *Journal of American History* 84.1 (1997): 13–39.

———. "Narrative of a Commercial Life: Consumption, Ideology, and Community on the Eve of the Revolution." *William and Mary Quarterly* L.3 (1993): 471–501.

Bronski, Michael. *Culture Clash: The Making of Gay Sensibility.* Boston: South End P, 1984.

————. "How Sweet (and Sticky) It Was." *Flesh and the Word 2: An Anthology of Erotic Writing*. Ed. John Preston. New York: Penguin P, 1993. 73–84.

————. *The Pleasure Principle: Sex, Backlash, and the Struggle for Gay Freedom*. New York: St. Martin's P, 1998.

Brown, Laura. "Millennium March Draws Sponsor, Competitor." *Southern Voice* 6 May 1999: 5+.

Brown, Wendy. *States of Injury: Power and Freedom in Late Modernity*. Princeton: Princeton UP, 1995.

Burton, Philip Ward and Robert J. Miller. *Advertising Fundamentals*. Second Edition. Columbus: Grid, 1976.

Butler, John Sibley. *Entrepreneurship and Self-Help Among Black Americans: A Reconsideration of Race and Economics*. Albany: State U of New York P, 1991.

Butler, Judith. "Merely Cultural." *Social Text* 15.3–4 (1997): 265–277.

Buy Black Network website <http://www.ibuyblack.com/buyblack.htm>

Cagan, Leslie. "Millennial Missteps: Eclipsing a Grassroots Movement." *Gay Community News* 4.1 (1998): 18–23.

Califia, Pat. "Like Cats and Dogs." *OUT* Aug. 1998: 44–49.

Carrier, James G. *Meanings of the Market: The Free Market in Western Culture*. Oxford: Berg, 1997.

Carter, Erica, James Donald, and Judith Squires, eds. *Space & Place: Theories of Identity and Location*. London: Lawrence & Wishart, 1993.

Chan, Sucheng, ed. *Social and Gender Boundaries in the United States*. Lewiston, NY: Edwin Mellen P, 1989.

Chauncey, George. *Gay New York: Gender, Urban Culture, and the Making of the Gay Male World, 1890–1940*. New York: Basic Books, 1994.

Chee, Alexander S. "Queer Nationalism." *Out/Look: National Gay/Lesbian Quarterly* 11 (Winter 1991): 14–19.

Chibbaro, Lou. "Budgets Up, Donors Down." *Washington Blade* 11 June 1999: 1+.

CLAGS News: The Center for Lesbian and Gay Studies, the Graduate School and University Center of the City University of New York 4.2 (1994).

Clark, Danae. "Commodity Lesbianism." *Gender, Race and Class in Media*. Eds. Gail Dines and Jean M. Humez. Thousand Oaks: Sage Publications, 1995. 142–151.

Clarke, Cheryl. "The Failure to Transform: Homophobia in the Black Community." *Home Girls: A Black Feminist Anthology*. Ed. Barbara Smith. New York: Kitchen Table: Women of Color P, 1983. 197–208.

Cole, C. Bard. "'Gay Market' A Scam, According to Essay by Former Editor of Failed National Magazine." *Riotboy* 30 May 1997: n.p.

Combahee River Collective. "A Black Feminist Statement" (April 1977). *Capitalist Partiarchy and the Case for Socialist Feminism.* Ed. Zillah R. Eisenstein. New York: Monthly Review P, 1979: 362–372.

Cooper, Michael. "Killing Shakes Complacency of Gay Rights Movement." *New York Times* 21 Oct. 1998: A1+.

"Creating Communities: Giving and Volunteering by Gay, Lesbian, Bisexual, and Transgender People." Research Project. Institute for Gay and Lesbian Studies/Working Group on Funding Lesbian and Gay Issues. Feb. 1998.

Crew, Louie. "Protest and Community: Gay Male Journalism Now." *Margins* 20 (1975): 14–21.

Cronin, Anne. "Two Viewfinders, Two Pictures of Gay America." *New York Times* 27 June 1993: E16.

"Culture Wars." *Gay Community News* Spring 1997: 4–5.

Cummons, John R. *Races and Immigrants in America.* New York: MacMillan, 1930.

Cunningham, Michael. "If You're Queer and You're Not Angry in 1992, You're Not Paying Attention." *Mother Jones* May/June 1992: 60–68.

Dahl, Robert. "Governing the Giant Corporation." *Corporate Power in America.* Eds. Ralph Nader and Mark. J. Green. New York: Grossman Publishers, 1973. 10–24.

Daley, Beth. "Vendors Reach Out to Gay Customers." *Boston Globe* 24 Nov. 1997: B1.

Dao, James. "Democrats Try to Talk Gay Group Out of Endorsing D'Amato." *New York Times* 11 Oct. 1998: A37+.

Darsey, James. "From 'Gay is Good' to the Scourge of AIDS: The Evolution of Gay Liberation Rhetoric: 1977–1990." *Communication Studies* 42.1 (1991): 43–66.

Davis, Madeline and Elizabeth Lapovsky Kennedy. *Boots of Leather, Slippers of Gold: The History of a Lesbian Community.* New York: Routledge, 1993.

———. "Oral History and the Study of Sexuality in the Lesbian Community: Buffalo, New York, 1940–1960." *Hidden from History: Reclaiming the Gay and Lesbian Past.* Eds. M. B. Duberman, M. Vicinus, & G. Chauncey, Jr. New York: New American Library, 1989. 426–441.

Davis, Philip, ed. *Immigrants and Americanization.* Boston: Ginn, 1920.

Davis, Riccardo. "Sky's the Limit for Tour Operators." *Advertising Age* 18 Jan. 1993: 36–37.

Dawson, Jeff. *Gay and Lesbian Online.* Los Angeles: Alyson Books, 1998.

de Grazia, Victoria, ed. *The Sex of Things: Gender and Consumption in Historical Perspective.* Berkeley: U of California P, 1996.

D'Emilio, John. "Capitalism and Gay Identity." *Powers of Desire: The Politics of Sexuality.* Eds. Ann Snitow, Christine Stansell, and Sharon Thompson. New York: Monthly Review P, 1983. 100–113.

———. *Sexual Politics, Sexual Communities: The Making of a Homosexual Minority in the United States, 1940–1976.* Chicago: U of Chicago P, 1983.

D'Emilio, John and Estelle B. Freedman. *Intimate Matters: A History of Sexuality in America.* New York: Harper and Row, 1988.

Dinkin, Robert J. *Voting Rights in America: A Study of Elections in the Original Thirteen States, 1776–1789.* Westport: Greenwood P, 1982.

Doty, Robert C. "Growth of Overt Homosexuality in City Provokes Wide Concern." *New York Times* 17 Dec. 1963, City Edition: A1+.

Dougherty, Philip H. "Homosexual Magazines in Bids." *New York Times* 17 July 1976: 55.

Douglas, Mary and Baron Isherwood. *The World of Goods.* New York: Basic Books, 1979.

Drummond, Tammerlin. "Not in Kansas Anymore: With Other Tourists Shying Away, Miami Beach Woos the Nation's $17 Billion Gay and Lesbian Travel Market." *Time* 25 Sept. 1995: 54–56.

Duberman, Martin, ed. *A Queer World: Center for Lesbian and Gay Studies Reader.* New York: New York UP, 1997.

———. *Stonewall.* New York: Dutton, 1993.

Duggan, Lisa and Nan D. Hunter. *Sex Wars: Sexual Dissent and Political Culture.* New York: Routledge, 1995.

Dullea, Georgia. "With Varying Degrees of Openness, More Companies Lure Gay Dollars." *New York Times* 2 March 1992: D9.

Dunkin, Amy. "Want to Put Your Money Where Your Conscience Is?" *Business Week* 8 Sept. 1997: 134.

Dunlap, David W. "Gay Advertising Campaign on TV Draws Wrath of Conservatives." *New York Times* 12 Nov. 1995: A34.

———. "Gay Parents Ease Into Suburbia: For the First Generation, Car Pools and Soccer Games." *New York Times* 16 May 1996: C1+.

———. "Gay Politicians and Issues Win Major Victories." *New York Times* 12 Nov. 1995: 34.

Edmondson, Brad. "Gays Make Tracks." *American Demographics* Nov. 1987: 22.

Elliott, Stuart. "Advertising: As the Gay and Lesbian Market Grows, a Boom in Catalogues That Are 'Out, Loud, and Proud.'" *New York Times* 10 Sept. 1993: C17.

———. "Advertising: For Gay Consumers, Sales Pitches Are Getting More Personal." *New York Times* 24 June 1994: D18.

———. "A Market That's Educated, Affluent, and Homosexual." *New York Times* 27 Sept. 1992: D27.

———. "A Sharper View of Gay Consumers." *New York Times* 9 June 1994: D1+.

Epperly, Jeff. "Corporate America on the Dole." *Bay Windows* [Boston] 1 June 1995: 6.

Epstein, Steven. "Gay Politics, Ethnic Identity: The Limits of Social Construction." *Socialist Review* 17.93–94 (1987): 9–54.

Evans, David T. *Sexual Citizenship: The Material Construction of Sexualities.* London: Routledge, 1993.

Ewen, Stuart. *All Consuming Images: The Politics of Style in Contemporary Culture.* New York: Basic Books, 1988.

———. *Captains of Consciousness: Advertising and the Social Roots of Consumer Culture.* New York: McGraw-Hill, 1976.

"Family Value: $102K: Mulryan/ Nash Designs Advertising and Marketing Strategies Targeted to Gay and Lesbian Consumers." Advertisement. *Advertising Age* 30 May 1994: 5–6.

Farberow, Norman, ed. *Taboo Topics.* New York: Atherton P, 1963.

Fernández, Charles. "Undocumented Aliens in the Queer Nation." *Out/Look: National Gay/Lesbian Quarterly* 12 (Spring 1991): 20–23.

Fineman, Howard. "Marching to the Mainstream: Gay Power Is Making Gains the Old-Fashioned Way—With Money and Insider Clout." *Newsweek* 3 May 1993: 42–44.

Finnegan, Margaret. *Selling Suffrage: Consumer Culture and Votes for Women.* New York: Columbia UP, 1999.

Foster, Alasdair. *Behold the Man.* Edinburgh: Stills Gallery, 1988.

Foucault, Michel. *The History of Sexuality: Volume 1.* Trans. Robert Hurley. New York: Vintage Books, 1980.

Fox-Kernworth, Marilyn. *Aunt Jemima, Uncle Ben, and Rastus: Blacks in Advertising, Yesterday, Today, and Tomorrow.* Westport, CT: Greenwood P, 1994.

Frank, Dana. *Purchasing Power: Consumer Organizing, Gender, and the Seattle Labor Movement, 1919–1929.* Cambridge: Cambridge UP, 1994.

320 | SELLING OUT

Frank, Thomas. *The Conquest of Cool: Business Culture, Counterculture, and the Rise of Hip Consumerism.* Chicago: U of Chicago P, 1997.

———. "Why Johnny Can't Dissent." *Commodify Your Dissent.* Eds. Thomas Frank and Matt Weiland. New York: W. W. Norton, 1997.

Freeman, Elizabeth. "Queer Bonds." Annual Convention of the American Studies Association. Pittsburgh, 1995.

Freiberg, Peter. "Gay Budgets Near $100 Million." *Washington Blade* 16 July 1999: 1+.

———. "Gay Donors Take Broad View." *New York Blade News* 27 March 1998: 10.

Friedman, Milton and Rose Friedman. *Free to Choose: A Personal Statement.* New York: Harcourt, Brace, Jovanovich, 1980.

Friess, Steve. "Target Practice: Advertising to Gays and Lesbians." *Advocate* 16 April 1996: 32–35.

Frisch, Peter G. "Opening Space." Editorial. *Advocate* 15 Oct. 1981: 6.

Fuss, Diana. *Essentially Speaking: Feminism, Nature and Difference.* New York: Routledge, 1989.

Gagnon, John H. and William Simon, eds. *Sexual Deviance.* New York: Harper and Row, 1967.

Galbraith, John Kenneth. *Economics and the Public Purpose.* Boston: Houghton Mifflin, 1973.

———. "On the Economic Image of Corporate Enterprise." *Corporate Power in America.* Eds. Ralph Nader and Mark. J. Green. New York: Grossman Publishers, 1973. 3–9.

Gallagher, John. "Cincinnati, Here They Come: The Log Cabin Club Selects a Boycott Target for Its Convention but Nobody Cares." *Advocate* 7 March 1995: 22.

———. "Dollars and Political Sense." *Advocate* 29 April 1997: 41–42.

———. "Ikea's Gay Gamble: Why Did a National Home-Furnishings Chain Build a Television Ad Around a Gay Couple?" *Advocate* 3 May 1994: 24–27.

———. "Million Dollar Mess." *Advocate* 4 Oct. 1994: 24–26.

Gallop, Jane. *Around Nineteen Eighty-One.* New York: Routledge, 1991.

Gamson, Joshua. "The Organizational Shaping of Collective Identity: The Case of Lesbian and Gay Film Festivals in New York." *A Queer World.* Ed. Martin Duberman. New York: New York UP, 1997. 526–542.

Garry, Joan M. "Ads Violate Civil Rights of Gays and Lesbians." Letter. *USA Today* 6 Aug. 1998: 12A.

"Gay and Lesbian Day at Walt Disney World." Webpage. <http://www.gayday. com/DisneyWorld/97> 28 April 1997.

Gay Biz, "Pride Directory Online, 1996." <http://www.gaybiz.com/pride/welcom.html> 28 April 1997.

"Gay Clout: The New Power Brokers: Thirty Men and Women—From Politicians to Artists—Who Have Emerged as Influential Advocates of Gay and Lesbian Causes." *Newsweek* 3 May 1993: 45.

"Gay Consumers Come Out Spending." *American Demographics* April 1992: 10–11.

"Gay Press Looks to Madison Avenue." *New York Times* 17 Dec. 1990: D11.

"Gays: A Major Force in the Marketplace." *Business Week* 3 Sept. 1979: 118–120.

"Gays at a glance; *The Northern Star,* April 27 1993." Webpage. "Polls & Surveys," <http://nz.qrd.org/qrd/www/misc/polls/stats–930427.html> 28 April 1997.

"Gays Celebrate and Business Tunes In." *Fortune* 27 June 1994: 14.

GBBC Business Counselor. A Publication of the Greater Boston Business Council. Nov. 1997: 31.

"'Genre': Advertising Information." Webpage. <http://www.genremagazine. com/adinfo.htm> 28 April 1997.

Glass, Sandra A., ed. *The Changing World of Foundation Fundraising: New Challenges and Opportunities.* New Directions for Philanthropic Fundraising 23 (Spring 1999).

Glass, Stephen. "Pat Speaks." *New Republic* 18 March 1996: 17.

Gluckman, Amy and Betsy Reed. "Lost in the Gay Marketing Moment: Leaving Diversity in the Dust." *Dollars and Sense* Nov./Dec. 1993: 16+.

Gluckman, Amy and Betsy Reed, eds. *Homo Economics: Capitalism, Community, and Lesbian and Gay Life.* New York: Routledge, 1997.

Gochenour, Phil. "Virtually Queer: The Politics of the Gay Market" <http:// www.pugzine.com/editol/html> 31 March 1997.

Goldstein, Richard. "Out of the Closet and Into the Lincoln Bedroom: Gay Money Makes Its Mark on Politics." *Village Voice* 25 Nov. 1997: 37+.

———. "Queering the Culture." *Village Voice* 30 June 1998: 39–52.

———. *Reporting the Counterculture.* Boston: Unwyn Hyman, 1989.

The Growing Divide: Inequality and the Roots of Economic Insecurity. Boston: United for a Fair Economy, 1998.

Hall, David D. *Cultures of Print: Essays in the History of the Book.* Amherst: U of Massachusetts P, 1996.

Halley, Janet. "Gay Rights and Identity Imitation: Issues in the Ethics of Representation." *The Politics of Law: A Progressive Critique.* Third Edition. Ed. David Kairys. New York: Basic Books, 1998. 115–146.

Hannaham, James. "Feeding the Gay Market." *OUT* Nov. 1996: 117+.

Hardy, Robin. "Donald Moffett: Advert Prop: Advertising for the Homosexual Life." *Advocate* 27 Feb. 1990: 50–51.

Harrigan, John J. *Empty Dreams, Empty Pockets: Class and Bias in American Politics.* New York: Macmillan, 1993.

Harris, Abram. *Race, Radicalism and Reform.* Ed. William Darity Jr. New Brunswick: Transaction Publishers, 1989.

Harris, Daniel. *The Rise and Fall of Gay Culture.* New York: Hyperion, 1997.

Harvey, David. *The Urban Experience.* Baltimore: Johns Hopkins UP, 1989. 185.

Heilbroner, Robert L., ed. with Laurence J. Malone. *The Essential Adam Smith.* New York: W. W. Norton, 1986.

Heimoff, Steve. "Gay Wine Marketing Slowly Follows Beer and Spirits' Lead: In Two Years Since 'The Monthly' First Explored the Issue, Targeting Wine-Drinking Gays Just Barely Begins to Take Off." Webpage. <http://smartwine.com/wbm/1996/9603/bm039603.htm> 28 April 1997.

Henry III, William A. "Not Marching Together: David Mixner Worked with Bill Clinton in Antiwar Days and Raised $3.5 Million from Gays for His Campaign—Now He Wonders if He's Still an F.O.B." *Time* 3 May 1993: 50–51.

Herdt, Gilbert, ed. *Gay Culture in America.* Boston: Beacon P, 1992.

"Here It Comes: Gay Day at Disney World for 1995." *Bay Windows* [Boston] 3 June 1995: 3.

Herrell, Richard K. "The Symbolic Strategies of Chicago's Gay and Lesbian Pride Day Parade." *Gay Culture in America.* Ed. Gilbert Herdt. Boston: Beacon P, 1992.

Hertzog, Mark. *The Lavender Vote: Lesbians, Gay Men, and Bisexuals in American Electoral Politics.* New York: New York UP, 1996.

Hetter, Katia. "God and Gays in the Republican Party: Is There a Place in the GOP for Homosexuals?" *US News & World Report* 29 May 1995: 38.

Hewitt, Christopher. "The Socioeconomic Position of Gay Men: A Review of the Evidence." *American Journal of Economics and Sociology* 54.4 (1995): 461–479.

Hoerder, Dirk, ed. *The Immigrant Labor Press in North America, 1840s–1970s, vol. 1; Migrants from Northern Europe.* Westport: Greenwood P, 1987.

Hoffman, Wayne. "The 'Gay 90s': New Era or Passing Fad?" *Bay Windows* [Boston] 21 Sept. 1995: 3–4.

Holmes, Steven A. "Sitting Pretty: Is This What Women Want?" *New York Times* 15 Dec. 1996: D1.

"Homosexuals and Politics: To the Tolerant, the Money." *Economist* 3 Oct. 1992: 29–30.

"Homosexuals: Impossible to Define?" *Economist* 27 May 1995: 27–28.

Howe, Genvieve. "Art Attack, Part Two: San Antonio's Esperanza Sues for Funding Discrimination." *Sojourner* Nov. 1998: 9+.

Hull, Gloria T., Patricia Bell Scott, and Barbara Smith, eds. *All the Women Are White, All the Blacks Are Men, But Some of Us Are Brave.* Old Westbury, NY: Feminist P, 1982.

Ingram, Gordon Brent, Anne-Marie Bouthillette, and Yolanda Retter, eds. *Queers in Space: Communities/Public Spaces/Sites of Resistance.* Seattle: Bay P, 1997.

Isaac, Katherine. *Ralph Nader Presents Practicing Democracy: A Guide to Student Activism.* New York: St. Martin's P, 1995.

Jay, Karla. "A Look at Lesbian Magazines." *Margins* 23 (1975): 19–23.

———. *Tales of the Lavender Menace: A Memoir of Liberation.* New York: Basic Books, 1999.

Jefferson, David J. "Businesses Offering Products for Gays Are Thriving." *Wall Street Journal* 22 April 1993: B2.

Johnson, Bradley. "Economics Hold Back Lesbian Ad Market." *Advertising Age* 18 Jan. 1993: 34, 37.

———. "The Gay Quandary: Advertising's Most Elusive, yet Lucrative, Target Market Proves Difficult to Measure." *Advertising Age* 18 Jan. 1993: 29, 35.

Johnston, Jill. *Lesbian Nation: The Feminist Solution.* New York: Simon and Schuster, 1973.

Johnston, Jo-Ann. "Putting Beliefs in Investments: New Wave of 'Socially Responsible' Funds Lets People Invest with Their Consciences." *Boston Globe* 19 May 1997: A8+.

Jones, Edgar R., *Those Were the Good Old Days.* New York: Simon and Schuster, 1959.

Jorjorian, Anoosh. "Solidarity or Segregation? The Politics of the Dyke March." *Sojourner* June 1997: 8–9.

Joseph, Miranda. "The Performance of Productivity and Consumption." *Social Text* 54 (1998): 25–61.

Kahan, Hazel and David Mulryan. "Out of the Closet." *American Demographics* May 1995: 40–46.

Kasindorf, Jeanie Russell. "Lesbian Chic: The Bold, Brave New World of Gay Women." *New York* 10 May 1993: 31–37.

Kates, Steven M. *Twenty Million New Consumers! Understanding Gay Men's Consumer Behavior.* New York: Haworth P, 1998.

Katz, Jonathan. *Gay American History: Lesbians and Gay Men in the U.S.A.* New York: Thomas Y. Crowell, 1976.

Katz, Jonathan Ned. *The Invention of Heterosexuality.* New York: Penguin Books, 1995.

Kellor, Frances. *Immigration and the Future.* New York: George H. Doran, 1920.

———. *Straight America: A Call to National Service.* New York: Macmillan, 1916.

Kepner, Jim. *Rough News, Daring Views: 1950s Pioneer Gay Press Journalism.* New York: Haworth P, 1998.

Khan, Surina. "Tracking Gay Conservatives." *Gay Community News* Summer 1996: 7, 26–28.

———. "Gay Conservatives: Pulling the Movement to the Right." *The Public Eye: A Publication of Political Research Associates* Spring 1996: 3–10.

Kifner, John. "Protestors Say the Police Created 'Havoc' at Rally." *New York Times* 21 Oct. 1998: B5.

Kinsey, Alfred C. *Sexual Behavior in the Human Male.* Philadelphia: W. B. Saunders, 1948.

Kirk, Marshall and Hunter Madsen. *After the Ball: How America Will Conquer Its Fear and Hatred of Gays in the '90s.* New York: Doubleday, 1989.

Kleppner, Paul. "Defining Citizenship: Immigration and the Struggle for Voting Rights in Antebellum America." *Voting and the Spirit of American Democracy.* Ed. Donald W. Rogers. Chicago: U of Illinois P, 1992. 43–53.

Kriesi, Hanspeter, et al. *New Social Movements in Western Europe: A Comparative Analysis.* Social Movements, Protest, and Contention 5. Minneapolis: U of Minnesota P, 1995.

Kurschner, Dale. "The 100 Best Corporate Citizens," *Business Ethics* May/June 1996: 24–35.

Larson, Erik. *The Naked Consumer: How Our Private Lives Become Public Commodities.* New York: Henry Holt, 1992.

Larson, Per. "Gay Money." *Victory!* Jan./Feb. 1996: 12–14.

Lash, Scott and John Urry. *Economies of Signs and Space.* London: Sage Publications, 1994.

Lears, T. J. Jackson. *Fables of Abundance: A Cultural History of Advertising in America.* New York: Basic Books, 1994.

Lebergott, Stanley. *Consumer Expenditures: New Measures & Old Motives.* Princeton: Princeton UP, 1996.

———. *Pursuing Happiness: American Consumers in the Twentieth Century.* Princeton: Princeton UP, 1993.

Lee, John Alan. "The Gay Connection." *Urban Life* 8.2 (1979): 175–198.

Leiss, William. *C. B. Macpherson: Dilemmas of Liberalism and Socialism.* New York: St. Martin's P, 1988.

Levin, Sue. *In the Pink: The Making of Successful Gay- and Lesbian-Owned Businesses.* New York: Haworth P, 1999.

Levine, Martin P. "Gay Ghetto." *Gay Men: The Sociology of Male Homosexuality.* Ed. Martin P. Levine. New York: Harper & Row, 1979. 182–204.

Levine, M. P. "Employment Discrimination Against Gay Men." *Homosexuality in International Perspective.* Eds. Joseph Harry and Man Singh Das. New Delhi: Vikas, 1980.

Lewin, Ellen, ed. *Inventing Lesbian Cultures in America.* Boston: Beacon P, 1996.

Lewis, Andrea and Robert Stevens. "At the Crossroads: Race, Gender, and the Gay Rights Movement." *Third Force* March/April 1996: 22–26.

Locke, John. *Second Treatise of Government.* Ed. C. B. Macpherson. Indianapolis: Hackett Publishing, 1980.

Lorch, Paul. Editorial. *Bay Area Reporter.* 17 Feb. 1977: 8.

———. Editorial. "Final Thoughts on the Gay Press." *Bay Area Reporter* 17 March 1977: 10.

Lovelock, Christopher H. and Charles B. Weinberg. *Public and Non-Profit Marketing.* Palo Alto: Scientific P, 1977.

Lubow, Arthur. "This Vodka Has Legs." *New Yorker* 12 Sept. 1994: 62–83.

Lukenbill, Grant. *Untold Millions: Positioning Your Business for the Gay and Lesbian Consumer Revolution.* New York: HarperCollins Publishers, 1995.

McClure, Kirstie M. *Judging Rights: Lockean Politics and the Limits of Consent.* Ithaca: Cornell UP, 1996.

McDowell, Edwin. "Gay Cruises Draw Hostility in the Caribbean." *New York Times* 10 May 1998: travel section, 3.

Macpherson, C. B. *The Political Theory of Possessive Individualism: Hobbes to Locke.* Oxford: Oxford UP, 1962.

McTiernan. Jennifer A. "The Limits of Individualistic Feminism in Late Capitalist America." Paper. Yale U, 1999.

Maggenti, Maria. "Women as Queer Nationals." *Out/Look: National Gay/Lesbian Quarterly* 11 (Winter 1991): 20–23.

Mansnerus, Laura. "Under Many Banners: Varied Voices in Gay Life Not Always in Chorus." *New York Times* 26 June 1994: D7.

Marable, Manning. *How Capitalism Underdeveloped Black America: Problems in Race, Political Economy and Society.* Boston: South End P, 1983.

Marchand, Roland. *Advertising the American Dream: Making Way for Modernity, 1920–1940.* Berkeley: U of California P, 1985.

Maree, Margaret. "Lesbians Discover Key West: 'Womenfest' Draws Highest Numbers in Years." *Bay Windows* [Boston] 28 Sept. 1995: 3, 10.

Marmor, Judd, ed. *Sexual Inversion.* New York: Basic Books, 1965.

Masterson, Peg. "Agency Notes Rise of Singles Market." *Advertising Age* 9 Aug. 1993: 17.

"Maybe Something in . . . Green." *OUT* April 1999: 25.

Meier, August. *Negro Thought in America, 1880–1915.* Ann Arbor: U of Michigan P, 1966.

Mendelsohn, David. "When Did Gays Get So Straight?: How Queer Culture Lost Its Edge." *New York* 30 Sept. 1996: 25–31.

Mercer, Kobena and Issac Julien. "Race, Sexual Politics and Black Masculinity: A Dossier." *Male Order: Unwrapping Masculinity.* Eds. Rowena Chapman and Jonathan Rutherford. London: Lawrence and Wishart, 1988.

Miller, Cyndee. "Mainstream Marketers Decide the Time Is Right to Target Gays." *Marketing News* 26 (1992): 8, 15.

Miller, Neil. *Out of the Past: Gay and Lesbian History from 1869 to the Present.* New York: Random House, 1995.

———. "Rescue Mission: Boston's Gay Business Community Bails Out Pride and Positions Itself to Take Over the Annual Parade." *Boston Phoenix* July 1998: One in Ten section: 6.

Miller, Stephen. "Who Stole the Gay Movement?" *Christopher Street* Oct. 1994: 16–19.

Mises, Ludwig von. *Human Action: A Treatise on Economics.* London: William Hodge, 1949.

Mohr, Richard D. *A More Perfect Union: Why Straight America Must Stand Up for Gay Rights.* Boston: Beacon P, 1994.

Moir, Susan and Carol Schachet. "Gay and Lesbian Labor Gains a Voice" *Resist.* June 1998:1–3.

Moraga, Cherríe. *Loving in the War Years: Lo que nunca pasó por sus labios.* Boston: South End P, 1983.

Morales, Edward S. "Ethnic Minority Families and Minority Gays and Lesbians." *Marriage and Family Review* 14.3–4 (1989): 217–239.

Morgan, Tracy D. "Pages of Whiteness: Race, Physique Magazines, and the Emergence of Public Gay Culture." *Queer Studies: A Lesbian, Gay, Bisexual, and Transgender Anthology.* Eds. Brett Beemyn and Mickey Eliason. New York: New York UP, 1996. 283–291.

Moritz, Marguerite J. "The Gay Agenda: Marketing Hate Speech to Mainstream Media." *Hate Speech.* Eds. Rita Kirk Whillock and David Slayden. Thousand Oaks, CA: Sage, 1995. 55–79.

Morton, Donald, ed. *The Material Queer: A LesBiGay Cultural Studies Reader.* Boulder: Westview P, 1996.

Moss, J. Jennings. "Capitol Gains." *OUT* April 1998: 112+.

———. "Coming Out of the Republican Closet—One Lesbian at a Time." *Advocate* 29 Oct. 1996: 27.

———. "The Outsiders." *Advocate* 29 Oct. 1996: 22–31.

Murray, Stephen O. *American Gay.* Chicago: U of Chicago P, 1996.

Nader, Ralph and Mark J. Green, eds. *Corporate Power in America.* New York: Grossman Publishers, 1973.

Nash, Edward L. *Direct Marketing: Strategy, Planning, and Execution.* New York: McGraw-Hill, 1995.

National Buy Black Campaign website <http://www.successmarketplace.com/shops/nbbc/>

Nelson, Dana D. *National Manhood: Citizenship and the Imagined Fraternity of White Men.* Durham, NC: Duke UP, 1998.

"New Internet Study Offers Insights About Gay Community Beliefs and Habits." Press Release. Westport, CT: Greenfield Online, 14 Oct. 1998.

Newman, Bruce I. and Jagdish N. Sheth. *A Theory of Political Choice Behavior.* New York: Preager, 1987.

Newton, Esther. *Cherry Grove, Fire Island: Sixty Years in America's First Gay and Lesbian Town.* Boston: Beacon P, 1993.

1998 Gay Press Report. New York: Mulryan/Nash, 1998.

Noble, Barbara Presley. "The Unfolding of Gay Culture." *New York Times* 27 June 1993: F23.

Nussbaum, Bruce. *Good Intentions: How Big Business and the Medical Establishment Are Corrupting the Fight Against AIDS.* New York: Atlantic Monthly P, 1990.

O'Barr, William M. *Culture and the Ad: Exploring Otherness in the World of Advertising.* Boulder: Westview P, 1994.

O'Brien, Ellen. "100,000 March to Celebrate Hub's Gay Pride." *Boston Globe* 8 June 1997: B1, B8.

"Official Pride Guide of the Capital Pride Festival" [San Francisco] 1–8 June 1997.

Ohmann, Richard. *Selling Culture: Magazines, Markets, and Class at the Turn of the Century.* New York: Verso, 1996.

Olasky, Marvin. *Patterns of Corporate Philanthropy: The Progressive Deception.* Studies in Philanthropy 12. Washington, D.C.: Capital Research Center, 1992.

Omi, Michael and Howard Winant. *Racial Formations in the United States from the 1960s to the 1980s.* New York: Routledge and Kegan Paul, 1986.

Ongiri, Amy Abugo. "We Are Family: Black Nationalism, Black Masculinity, and the Black Gay Cultural Imagination." *College Literature* 24.1 (1997): 280–294.

"Opening Space." *Advocate* 20 April 1977: 6.

Oppenheimer, Josh. "Queer Conceptions: Class, Sexuality, and Activism." *Perspective* March 1996: 11–12.

Ordover, Nancy. "Visibility, Alliance, and the Practice of Memory." *Socialist Review* Winter 1995: 121–134.

Osborn, Torie. "Is a Unified 'Queer Nation' Possible?" *Advocate* 9 April 1991: 90.

"Outgiving: Conference for Philanthropists Who Support Gay and Lesbian Organizations." Brochure. Washington, D.C.: Gill Foundation, Sept. 1997.

"Outspoken: On Boycotts and Betrayal." Editorial. *Outweek* 22 Aug. 1990: 4.

Park, Kyeyoung. "The Morality of a Commodity: A Case Study of 'Rebuilding L.A. without Liquor Stores.'" *Amerasia Journal* 21.3 (1995/1996): 1–24.

Parker, Andrew, Mary Russo, Doris Sommer, and Patricia Yaeger, eds. *Nationalisms and Sexualities.* New York: Routledge, 1992.

Peñaloza, Lisa. "We're Here, We're Queer, and We're Going Shopping! A Critical Perspective on the Accommodation of Gays and Lesbians in the U.S. Marketplace." *Gays, Lesbians, and Consumer Behavior: Theory, Practice, and Research Issues in Marketing.* Ed. Daniel L. Wardlow. New York: Haworth, 1996. 9–38.

Penn, Donna. "Queer: Theorizing Politics and History." *Radical History Review* 62 (1995): 24–42.

Phelan, Shane. "(Be)Coming Out: Lesbian Identity and Politics." *Signs: Journal of Women in Culture and Society* 18.4 (1993): 765–788.

Philip Morris. "Corporate Contributions: Guidelines."

Phillips, Anne. *Engendering Democracy.* University Park Place: Pennsylvania State UP, 1991.

Piore, Michael. "Economic Identity/Sexual Identity." *A Queer World.* Ed. Martin Duberman. New York: New York UP, 1997. 502–507.

Plummer, Ken. *Telling Sexual Stories: Power, Change and Social Worlds.* London: Routledge, 1995.

Poggi, Stephanie. "Onward Christian Soldiers?" *Sojourner* June 1998: 9+.

Poovey, Mary. "The Abortion Question and the Death of Man." *Feminists Theorize the Political.* Eds. Judith Butler and Joan W. Scott. New York: Routledge, 1992.

Pottie, Lisa M. "Cross-Border Shopping and Niche Marketing: Academic Economics and Gay Studies." *College Literature* 24.1 (1997): 183–193.

Power, Lisa. *No Bath but Plenty of Bubbles: An Oral History of the Gay Libertaion Front, 1970–1973.* London: Cassell, 1995.

Presbrey, Frank. *The History and Development of Advertising.* Garden City, NJ: Doubleday, 1929.

Pride, Armistead S. and Clint C. Wilson II. *A History of the Black Press.* Washington, D.C.: Howard UP, 1997.

Putnam, Todd. "Boycotts Are Busting Out All Over." *Business and Society Review* 85 (1993): 47.

"Queers: The New Therapy Market Niche?" *In the Family* April 1999: 5.

Radin, Margaret Jane. *Contested Commodities.* Cambridge: Harvard UP, 1996.

Ramirez, Anthony. "Philip Morris to Increase AIDS Donations." *New York Times* 30 May 1991: C3.

Rashap, Amy. "The American Dream for Sale." *Ethnic Images in the Magazines.* Catalogue. The Balch Institute for Ethnic Study, Philadelphia. 22 May–7 Sept. 1984.

Reagon, Bernice Johnson. "Coalition Politics: Turning the Century." *Home Girls: A Black Feminist Anthology.* Ed. Barbara Smith. New York: Kitchen Table: Women of Color P, 1983. 356–368.

Reich, Robert B. *The Work of Nations.* New York: Vintage Books, 1991.

Rennert, Leo. "Tax Us More, Wealthy Protesters Say in D.C." *San Francisco Examiner* 1 April 1998: A1+.

Rich, Frank. "The Gay Decades: Out of the Closet and into the Living Room: Nine Episodes in the Most Dramatic Cultural Assimilation of Our Time." *Esquire* 108.5 (Nov. 1987): 87–99.

Rich, Wilbur C., ed. *The Politics of Minority Coalitions: Race, Ethnicity, and Shared Uncertainties.* Westport: Praeger, 1996.

Richards, David A. J. "Identity and the Case for Gay Rights: Race, Gender, Religion as Analogies." Ph.D. diss. New York University, 1998.

Rigdon, Joan E. "Overcoming a Deep-Rooted Reluctance, More Firms Advertise to Gay Community." *Wall Street Journal* 18 July 1991: B1-B2.

Riggle, Ellen D. and Alan L. Ellis. "Political Tolerance of Homosexuals: The Role of Group Attitudes and Legal Principles." *Journal of Homosexuality* 26.4 (1994): 135–147.

Ring, Trudy. "Beer Companies Target Gay Market." *Clout! Buisness Report* June 1996: 6.

Robinson, Amy. *Ethics, in an age of disappointment.* New York: New York UP, forthcoming.

Roehr, Bob. "Millennium March Slogs On, Despite Two Board Resignations." *Bay Area Reporter* 6 May 1999: 14+.

Rogers, Donald W., ed. *Voting and the Spirit of American Democracy.* Chicago: U of Illinois P, 1992.

Rohrer, Judy. "Is It Right to Focus on 'Rights'?" *The Harvard Gay & Lesbian Review* 3.1 (1996): 56–58.

Rotello, Gabriel. "Transgendered Like Me." *Advocate* 10 Dec. 1996.

Rymer, Russ. *American Beach: A Sage of Race, Wealth, and Memory.* New York: HarperCollins, 1998.

Sailer, Steve. "Why Lesbians Aren't Gay." *National Review* 30 May 1994: 42–45.

St. Joan, Jackie. "A Survey of Lesbian Publications." *Our Right to Love: A Lesbian Resource Book.* Ed. Ginny Vida. New York: Touchledge Books, 1978. 246–249.

Salholz, Eloise, et al. "The Future of Gay America." *Newsweek* 12 March 1990: 20–26.

"San Francisco." *Christopher Street* 2.2 (Aug. 1977): 14.

Satuloff, Bob. "Gaylienation." *Christopher Street* 172 (13 Feb. 1992): 2–3.

Scafide, Kyle. "Celebrating 20 Years." *Impact* 9–24 May 1997.

Scanlon, Jennifer. *Inarticulate Longings: The Ladies' Home Journal, Gender, and the Promises of Consumer Culture.* New York: Routledge, 1995.

Schoofs, Mark. "Straight to Hell." *Village Voice* 11 Aug. 1998: 56–58.

Schudson, Michael. *Advertising, the Uneasy Persuasion: Its Dubious Impact on American Society.* New York: Basic Books, 1984.

Schulman, Sarah. "The Making of a Market Niche." *Harvard Gay and Lesbian Review* Winter 1998: 17–20.

———. *Stagestruck: Theater, AIDS, and the Marketing of Gay America.* Durham, NC: Duke UP, 1998.

Schur, Edwin M. "Homosexuals: A Minority Group?" *Crimes Without Victims: Deviant Behavior and Public Policy: Abortion, Homosexuality, Drug Addiction.* Englewood Cliffs, NJ: Prentice-Hall, 1965: 95–96.

Schwartz, Joe. "Gay Consumers Come Out Spending." *American Demographics* April 1992: 10–11.

Schwartz, Karen. "In Fits and Starts, Travel Industry Wakes up to Big Gay Market." *Bay Windows* [Boston] 26 Feb.–4 March 1998: 1.

Scot, Donald Cameron. *Something in Orange.* San Francisco: Camdon Minibooks, 1978.

Seabaugh, Cathy. "Friendly Skies Open for United Gays, Lesbians." *Clout! Business Report* June 1996: 16–17.

Segrest, Mab. *Memoir of a Race Traitor.* Boston: South End P, 1994.

Seltzer, Mark. *Bodies and Machines.* New York: Routledge, 1992.

Sender, Katherine E. "Selling Sexual Subjectivities: Audience Respond to Gay Window Advertising." *Critical Studies in Mass Communication* 16 (1999): 172–196.

Sennett, Richard. *The Fall of Public Man.* New York: Alfred A. Knopf, 1977.

Sherrill, Kenneth. "The Political Power of Lesbians, Gays, and Bisexuals." *P.S.: Political Science & Politics* 29.3 (1996): 469–473.

Sievert, Bill. "Point, Counterpoint: Gay Politics San Francisco Style." *Advocate* 13 July 1977: 10–12.

Signorile, Michelangelo. *Queer in America: Sex, the Media, and the Closets of Power.* New York: Doubleday, 1993.

Silk, Leonard and David Vogel. *Ethics and Profits: The Crisis of Confidence in American Business.* New York: Simon and Schuster, 1976.

Sinclair, Matthew. "Postcards from the Edge: Fundraising on the Fringe." *Non-Profit Times* Aug. 1997: 23–26.

Singer, Bennett L. and David Deschamps, eds. *Gay & Lesbian Stats: A Pocket Guide of Facts and Figures.* New York: New P, 1994.

Slagle, Anthony. "In Defense of Queer Nation: From Identity Politics to a Politics of Difference." *Western Journal of Communications* 59 (1995): 85–102.

Smith, Adam. "Wealth of Nations." *The Essential Adam Smith.* Ed. Robert C. Heilbroner. New York: W.W. Norton, 1986.

Smith, Anna Marie. "Resisting the Erasure of Lesbian Sexuality." *Modern Homosexualities: Fragments of Lesbian and Gay Experience.* Ed. Ken Plummer. New York: Routledge, 1992. 200–213.

Smith, Barbara. "Where's the Revolution?" *Nation* 5 July 1993: 12–16.

——. "Where's the Revolution: Part II." *The Truth That Never Hurts: Writings on Race, Gender, and Freedom.* New Brunswick: Rutgers UP, 1998.

Smith, Barbara, ed. *Home Girls: A Black Feminist Anthology.* New York: Kitchen Table: Women of Color P, 1983.

Smith, Michael J. *Colorful People and Places: A Resource Guide for Third World Lesbians and Gay Men . . . and for White People Who Share Their Interests.* San Francisco: Quarterly P, 1983.

Smith, N. Craig. *Morality and the Market: Consumer Pressure for Corporate Accountability.* London: Routledge, 1990.

Smith, William Carlson. *Americans in the Making.* New York: D. Appleton-Century, 1939.

"Special Report: Marketing to Gays and Lesbians." *Advertising Age* 18 Jan. 1993: 29–37.

Spiegelman, Willard. "The Progress of a Genre: Gay Journalism and Its Audience." *Salmagundi* 58–59 (1982): 308–325.

Stabiner, Karen. "Tapping the Homosexual Market." *New York Times Magazine* 2 May 1982: 34+.

Still, Richard R. and Edward W. Cundiff. *Essentials of Marketing.* Englewood Cliffs, NJ: Prentice-Hall, 1966.

Strand, Robert. "S.F. Gays Carry Heavy Clout in Politics, Finance." *Los Angeles Times* 18 Dec. 1977: 3, 36–37.

Strasser, Susan. *Satisfaction Guaranteed: The Making of an American Mass Market.* New York: Pantheon Books, 1989.

Streitmatter, Rodger. *Unspeakable: The Rise of the Gay and Lesbian Press in America.* Boston: Faber and Faber, 1995.

Strong, Howard, ed. *Credit Card Secrets You Will Surely Profit From.* Beverly Hills: Boswell Institute, 1989.

Strub, Sean. "The Growth of the Gay and Lesbian Market." *A Queer World.* Ed. Martin Duberman. New York: New York UP, 1997. 514–518.

"Studies of the Gay Population in the U.S." Webpage. <http://www.nyu.edu/pages/sls/gaywork/gypopula.html> 28 April 1997.

Sullivan, Andrew. *Virtually Normal: An Argument About Homosexuality.* New York: Alfred A. Knopf, 1995.

Sunstein, Cass R. *Free Markets and Social Justice.* New York: Oxford UP, 1997.

Summer, Bob. "A Niche Market Comes of Age." *Publishers Weekly* 29 June 1992: 36–41.

Talbot, Winthrop, ed. *Americanization.* The Handbook Series. New York: H. W. Wilson, 1920.

Teal, Donn. *The Gay Militants.* New York: St. Martin's P, 1995.

Thomas, R. E. "Marketing a New Capitalism." *CBI Review* 4.14 (1974): 23–28.

Thompson, Mark. "RFD: A Magazine from the Heartland." *Advocate* 7 Jan. 1982: 21+.

Thompson, Mark. "Small Business Owners Experiencing a Natural Progression of Liberated Consciousness." *Advocate* 16 June 1976: 12–13.

Torres, Vicki. "The Pride Fund: Pride and Making Money Need Not Be Mutually Exclusive." *The Lesbian News* March 1997: 40.

Trief, Jaymes. "Credit Is Where Credit Is Due: Gay Credit Cards Seem to Offer an Effortless Way to Support Gay Causes—But Nothing Is as Simple as It Seems." *Advocate* 18 April 1995: 29–31.

Tucker, Robert C., ed. *The Marx-Engels Reader.* Second Edition. New York: W. W. Norton, 1978.

Turner, E. S. *The Shocking History of Advertising.* New York: E. P. Dutton, 1953.

"Two Companies Aim at the Gay Market." *New York Times* 13 April 1995: D8.

"Two Viewfinders, Two Pictures of Gay America." *New York Times* 27 June 1993: E16.

"U.S. Census Bureau: The Official Statistics." Webpage. <http://www.census.gov/cgi-bin.> 1 Jan. 1997.

United States Department of Justice/ Immigration and Naturalization Services. *Our Immigration: A Brief Account of Immigration to the United States.* Government Document. 3 June 1980.

Vaid, Urvashi. "Coalition as Goal Not Process." *Gay Community News* 22.4 (Spring 1997): 6–9.

———. "Thoughts on the Movement's Style." *Gay Community News* 23.2–3 (Fall-Winter 1997–98): 8–11.

———. *Virtual Equality: The Mainstreaming of Gay & Lesbian Liberation.* New York: Doubleday, 1995.

Varnell, Paul. "Gay, Bi, Trans, Drag, etc." *Windy City Times* 28 July 1994: 14.

Vazquez, Carmen. "The Land That Never Has Been Yet: Dreams of a Gay Latina in the United States." *The 3rd Pink Book: A Global View of Lesbian and Gay Oppression.* Eds. Aart Hendriks, Rob Tielman, and Evert van der Veen. Buffalo: Prometheus Books, 1993. 229–240.

Vezeris, Steve. "History of the Rainbow Flag." *Out in All Directions: The Almanac of Gay and Lesbian America.* Eds. Lynn Witt, Sherry Thomas, and Eric Marcus. New York: Warner Books, 1995.

Vogel, David. *Lobbying the Corporation: Citizen Challenges to Business Authority.* New York: Basic Books, 1978.

"The Voice of the Gay and Lesbian Community: 'Clout! Business Report.'" Webpage. <http://www.suba.com/~outlines/clouttmp.html> 28 April 1997.

Walton, Jean. "Introduction: Racialized Lesbian Desire on the Transnational Scene." *College Literature* 24.1 (1997): 78–82.

Wardlow, Daniel L., ed. *Gays, Lesbians, and Consumer Behavior: Theory, Practice, and Research Issues in Marketing.* New York: Hayworth P, 1996.

Warner, Michael, ed. *Fear of a Queer Planet: Queer Politics and Social Theory.* Minneapolis: U of Minnesota P, 1993.

Warren, Carol A. B. *Identity and Community in the Gay World.* New York: John Wiley and Sons, 1974.

Warren, Steve. "Gay Day at Disney with Nary a Hitch: Miami Man Is Bashed During Annual Outing at Magic Kingdom." *Bay Windows* [Boston] 15 June 1995: 3.

Weathers, Diane et al. "Where the Boys Are." *Newsweek* 30 July 1979: 62–65.

Webster Jr., Frederick E. *Social Aspects of Marketing.* Englewood Cliffs, NJ: Prentice-Hall, 1974.

Webster, Nancy Coltun. "Playing to Gay Segments Opens Doors to Markets." *Advertising Age* 30 April 1994: 5–6.

"We Don't Buy It." *Advocate* 9 Oct. 1990: 86.

Weekes, Richard V. "Gay Dollars: Houston's Montrose District Is an Affluent, Overlooked Market—Gay Men and Women." *American Demographics* Oct. 1989: 45–48.

Weeks, Jeffrey. *Against Nature: Essays on History, Sexuality, and Identity.* London: Rivers Oram P, 1991.

Weightman, Barbara A. "Commentary: Towards a Geography of the Gay Community." *Journal of Cultural Geography* 2.2 (1981): 106–112.

Weiss, Michael J. *The Clustering of America.* New York: Harper and Row, 1988.

Wells, Jess. "Bringing up Baby: Parenting in the Gay Baby Boom." *Pride 98: Official Magazine for San Francisco Gay Pride.* New York: Profile Pursuit, 1998: 80–84.

Weltge, Ralph W., ed. *The Same Sex: An Appraisal of Homosexuality.* Philadelphia: Pilgrim P, 1969.

Wesling, Francis Cress. "The Cress Theory of Color-Confrontation and Racism (White Supremacy): A Psychogenetic and World Outlook." *The Issis (Yssis) Papers.* Chicago: Third World P, 1991. 1–15.

"Why Doesn't Somebody . . . ." *Christopher Street* 17 Feb. 1977: 3.

Wideman, John Edgar. Introduction. *The Souls of Black Folks.* By W. E. B. Du Bois. New York: Vintage Books, 1990.

Wilentz, Sean. "Property and Power: Suffrage Reform in the United States, 1787–1860." *Voting and the Spirit of American Democracy.* Ed. Donald W. Rogers. Chicago: U of Illinois P, 1992. 31–41.

Williams, Patricia. *The Alchemy of Race and Rights.* Cambridge: Harvard UP, 1991.

———. *The Rooster's Egg: On the Persistence of Prejudice.* Cambridge: Harvard UP, 1995.

Williams, Raymond. *Problems in Materialism and Culture.* London: NLB, 1980.

Williamson, Judith. *Decoding Advertising: Ideology and Meaning in Advertising.* London: Boyars, 1978.

Wolfe, Maxine. "Invisible Women in Invisible Places: Lesbians, Lesbian Bars, and the Social Production of People/Environment Relationships." *Architecture & Comportment/Architecture & Behavior* 8.2 (1992): 137–158.

Wonderland, Alison. "Shocking Gray, Pt. 2." *Best Plus Rude Girl 1–14:* 16.

"Working Assets 1996 Donations Report: Simple Acts, Real Progress: How Our Nonprofit Groups Are Changing the World." Brochure. San Francisco: Working Assets, 1997.

Worthy, James C. *Shaping an American Institution: Robert E. Wood and Sears, Roebuck.* Chicago: U of Chicago P, 1984.

Wright, Lawrence. "One Drop of Blood." *New Yorker* 25 July 1994: 46–55.

Wyman, Bill. "Selling Out: Atlantic Records' New Target Market: Gay Music Fans." *Rolling Stone* 16 Nov. 1995: 40.

Yoshikawa, Yoko. "The Heat Is on 'Miss Saigon' Coalition." *The State of Asian America: Activism and Resistance in the 1990s.* Ed. Karin Aguilar-San Juan. Boston: South End P, 1994. 275–294.

Young, Lauren. "New Fund Aims at Gay Market." *San Francisco Examiner* 24 June 1996: B1+.

Zarembka, Arlene. "Flaunting Community's 'Wealth' Can Be Costly." *Washington Blade* 24 Nov. 1995: 33.

Zaretsky, Eli. *Capitalism, the Family, and Personal Life.* New York: Harper and Row, Publishers, 1976.

INTERVIEWS

Collins, Chuck. Personal interview. 26 Oct. 1998.

Dorf, Julie. Telephone interview. 30 Sept. 1998.

Frost, Michele. Personal interview. 20 July 1998.

Horowitz, Susan. Telephone interview. 16 July 1998.

Syed, Javid. Telephone interview. 18 Sept. 1998.

———. Telephone interview. 14 Oct. 1998.

Wallace, Carla. Telephone interview. 14 July 1998.

———. Telephone interview. 18 Sept. 1998.

CORRESPONDENCE

Putnam, Todd. Letter to the author. Sept. 1997 (n.d.).

Self, Eleanor. Letter to the author. 11 Sept. 1998.

Strub, Sean. Email to the author. June 17, 22, 29; July 13, 1998.

INDEX